Adam, Eve, and the Devil

Hebrew Bible Monographs, 65

Series Editors
David J.A. Clines, J. Cheryl Exum

Editorial Board
A. Graeme Auld, Marc Brettler, David M. Carr, Paul M. Joyce,
Francis Landy, Lena-Sofia Tiemeyer, Stuart D.E. Weeks

ADAM, EVE, AND THE DEVIL

A NEW BEGINNING

Second Enlarged Edition

Marjo C.A. Korpel & Johannes C. de Moor

SHEFFIELD PHOENIX PRESS
2015

This work is dedicated to Othmar and Hildi Keel
for their groundbreaking work on iconography and the Bible

Published by Sheffield Phoenix Press
Department of Biblical Studies, University of Sheffield
45 Victoria Street, Sheffield S3 7QB England

www.sheffieldphoenix.com

A CIP catalogue record for this book
is available from the British Library

Typeset by Johannes C. de Moor
Printed by Lightning Source

ISBN 978-1-909697-89-8 (paperback)
ISSN 1747-9614

Contents

Preface 1 and 2 ix

Abbreviations xi

1. Introduction 1

2. The Adamic Myth in the Eastern Mediterranean 5

    2.1 Concepts of Creation in Ugarit 5

    2.2 KTU 1.107 and KTU 1.100 15

    2.3 The Death of Adammu 24

    2.4 The Scene of Action 29

    2.5 Immortality by Procreation 44

    2.6 What's in a Name? 53

    2.7 'Adam' and 'Eve' as Divine Beings 57

    2.8 Iconographic Representations 59

    2.9 Ḥôrānu's Turnabout (KTU 1.100:61-69) 74

    2.10 The Invincible Evil 78

    2.11 Conclusions 82

3. Similar Motifs in the Ancient World 89

    3.1 Introduction 89

    3.2 Egyptian Myths 89

    3.3 Mesopotamian Myths and Epics 93

    3.4 Iranian Religions 106

    3.5 Greek Myths 108

    3.6 Conclusions 111

4. THE RECEPTION IN THE HEBREW BIBLE 115
4.1 Preliminary Remarks 115
4.2 Genesis 1 116
4.3 Genesis 2–4 123
4.4 Genesis 5–9 145
4.5 Isaiah 14 151
4.6 Ezekiel 28 163
4.7 Ezekiel 29–32 171
4.8 The Serpent Tamed 172
4.9 Conclusions 177

5. THE RECEPTION IN PARABIBLICAL LITERATURE 181
5.1 Introduction 181
5.2 The Book of the Luminaries 181
5.3 The Book of the Watchers 182
5.4 Jubilees 186
5.5 The Wisdom of Ben Sira 187
5.6 The Animal Apocalypse 190
5.7 The Similitudes 191
5.8 Testaments of the Twelve Patriarchs 192
5.9 Qumran 192
5.10 2 Enoch 195
5.11 The Wisdom of Solomon 198
5.12 The Apocalypse of Abraham 199
5.13 The Ladder of Jacob 203
5.14 The Life of Adam and Eve 204
5.15 The Apocalypse of Moses 205
5.16 The Apocalypse of Baruch 207
5.17 The Apocalypse of Adam 208

5.18 The Primordial History in Islam 209
5.19 Conclusions on Parabiblical Literature 211

6. The Reception in the New Testament 215
6.1 Preliminary Remarks 215
6.2 The Gospel According to Matthew 215
6.3 The Gospel According to Mark 218
6.4 The Gospel According to Luke 219
6.5 The Gospel According to John 223
6.6 The Book of Acts 226
6.7 The Letter of Paul to the Romans 228
6.8 The Letters of Paul to the Corinthians 230
6.9 The Letter to the Hebrews 237
6.10 The First Letter to Timothy 238
6.11 The First Letter of John 240
6.12 The Book of Revelation 241
6.13 Conclusions on New Testament 249

7. General Conclusions 253
7.1 Introduction 253
7.2 Summary of the Results 254
7.3 Epilogue 260

Appendix 1: KTU 1.107 265
Appendix 2: KTU 1.100 275

Bibliography 283

Index of Subjects 317

Index of Texts 352

Preface to the First Edition

In the past decennia a wealth of new texts from the ancient Near East has become available. Many of them deal with the creation of the world and the primordial history of humankind and are unknown to the general public. Their relevance to the interpretation of the first chapters of the Bible has been recognized by quite a number of fine scholars, but very often they had to conclude that crucial evidence from the Canaanite sources they suspected to have existed behind the biblical accounts was still missing. In this book we will present a theory filling that gap. It is based mainly on a fresh interpretation of Ugaritic and other textual data from the ancient Near East. We hope it will contribute significantly to the study of the Bible and parabiblical literature such as the Dead Sea scrolls and pseudepigrapha. Ultimately we think that also theologians will have to rethink the far-reaching consequences they have drawn from the first chapters of the Bible. Because we believe to have identified iconographical evidence supporting our theory, including the oldest pictures of Adam, Eve and the Devil ever identified, we dedicate this book to Othmar and Hildi Keel. They and their extremely successful 'Nachwuchs' have revolutionized biblical scholarship by demonstrating that systematic study of ancient artefacts elucidates the Bible in many ways.

It is a welcome development that nowadays the trustees of many museums and libraries are permitting the use of photographs of their treasures for scholarly purposes. Nevertheless we have obtained express permission for the illustrations in this book whenever this was still possible.

Several colleagues were kind enough to read the manuscript (or parts of it) in a preliminary state. Special thanks are due to Christoph Uehlinger who saved us from many an error. We profited from his judicious criticism and valuable suggestions. Among those who were willing to discuss our unseasoned ideas orally with us were Bob Becking, Pierre Bordreuil, Manfried Dietrich, Meindert Dijkstra, Valérie Matoïan, Tryggve Mettinger and Klaas Spronk. We are grateful to the Editors of the series Hebrew Bible Monographs for having accepted our manuscript for publication and the

Publisher for having produced the printed edition in record time. Ailsa Parkin of the Press pointed out a number of inconsistencies in our manuscript which we were able to correct in time thanks to her keen eye.

We are indebted to the Department of Philosophy and Religious Studies of the Faculty of Humanities, Utrecht University, the Netherlands, for their willingness to participate in the production costs of this book.

The personnel of the libraries of Leiden University, Utrecht University, Netherlands Institute for the Near East Leiden, Theological University of the Reformed Churches Kampen, Protestant Theological University Amsterdam and Groningen have been most helpful. We thank especially the librarian of the latter institution, Wiljan Puttenstein, for his excellent services.

We thank Herma and Emiel Hulsebos for having borne the brunt of the care for Marjo's parents in the years we were working on this study.

Finally we thank Janny de Moor for her cheerful support. She drew our attention to the spectacular Armenian dish 'Ararat Pilav'. In a time when she herself was extremely busy completing two voluminous manuscripts, she was kind enough to read our entire manuscript with a critical eye. Her comments and corrections were very valuable to us.

The Authors

Preface to the Second Edition

The first edition got a lot of publicity which helped us to improve and expand the book in many respects. Special thanks are due to John Day, Manfried Dietrich, Meindert Dijkstra, Dineke Houtman, Chris Jeynes, Magnar Kartveit, Antti Laato, Eric Peels, Jacques van Ruiten, Paul Sanders and Günther Stemberger who commented on parts of our presentations at various conferences and/or wrote constructive reviews of the book. Hans Renkema helped enormously by installing TeXShop and converting Semitic Postscript fonts to the format required by this program.

The Authors

ABBREVIATIONS

All abbreviations of series, handbooks and journals in this book are according to: Redaktion der RGG^{4}, *Abkürzungen Theologie und Religionswissenschaft nach RGG*^{4} (UTB, 2868), Tübingen 2007. For texts from Antiquity abbreviations current in English are used, mostly following D.J.A. Clines, *The Sheffield Manual for Authors and Editors in Biblical Studies*, Sheffield 1997. In addition the following abbreviations occur.

CHANE	Culture and History of the Ancient Near East (Leiden).
DCH	D.J.A. Clines (ed.), *The Dictionary of Classical Hebrew*, 8 vols., Sheffield 1993–2011.
ETCSL	The Electronic Text Corpus of Sumerian Literature: http://etcsl.orinst.ox.ac.uk/.
Fs.	*Festschrift*.
GM	Göttinger Miszellen: Beiträge zur ägyptologischen Diskussion, Göttingen.
HAHAT	H. Donner *et al.* (eds.), *Wilhem Gesenius Hebräisches und Aramäisches Handwörterbuch über das Alte Testament*, Lief. 1–2, Heidelberg ^{18}1987–1995.
HCOT	The Historical Commentary on the Old Testament (Kampen / FLeuven).
KTU	M. Dietrich, O. Loretz & J. Sanmartín, *Die keilalphabetischen Texte aus Ugarit, Ras Ibn Hani und anderen Orten* Dritte, erweiterte Auflage, Münster 2013.
Lane	E.W. Lane, *An Arabic-English Lexicon*, 8 Parts, London 1863-1885.
NIDOTTE	W.A. van Gemeren (ed.), *New International Dictionary of the Old Testament Theology and Exegesis*, 5 vols, Carlisle 1996.
SAA	State Archives of Assyria (Helsinki).
SAAS	State Archives of Assyria Studies (Helsinki).
SBL.WAW	Society of Biblical Literature: Writings from the Ancient World (Atlanta).
StEL	*Studi Epigrafici e Linguistici sul Vicino Oriente antico* (Verona).

1
Introduction

The biblical story of Eden has fired the imagination of countless painters, sculptors, writers and scholars. The tragic loss of eternal life close to God in paradise, the deceitful speaking serpent, the obvious links with sexuality, the curse of having to toil and labor all your life and finally the inevitable death – all this was irresistible stuff for fantasies as well as countless articles and books reflecting on life and death, sin and salvation, reality and illusion.[1]

In this book we will present fresh evidence from the ancient Canaanite city of Ugarit that hitherto has not been taken into account in studies on the biblical traditions about the primordial history of humankind. Since 1928 many tablets written in one of the oldest alphabetic scripts in the world have been excavated in the ancient kingdom that bore the name of its capital, Ugarit.[2] The tablets all date from the thirteenth century BCE but certain traditions incorporated in the literary texts may be much older. The Ugaritic language is a dialect of the family of languages that are commonly called 'Canaanite'.[3] These languages are related to the Hebrew language and because the Bible contains only a late selection from a Hebrew literary tradition that must have been much richer, the texts from Ugarit have helped scholars to better understand many words, expressions and ideas in the Bible.

This is also the case with regard to religion. In this study we intend to show that Ugarit throws light on the primeval history as it is told in the Bible and in parabiblical pseudepigraphic works. Of course ancient Oriental and Greek stories about cosmogony and the creation of humankind have been compared with biblical accounts many times before, lately in excellent studies by Othmar Keel and Silvia Schroer, André LaCocque, Tryggve Mettinger,

---

[1] To mention only three totally different recent works of this nature, Gadjimuradov & Schmoeckl 2007; Elior 2010; Hendel 2013.

[2] Modern Ras Shamra on the Syrian coast, almost opposite the eastward pointing 'finger' of Cyprus.

[3] All aspects of the civilization of Ugarit have been treated in depth in Watson & Wyatt 1999. Overviews are found in Young 1981; Loretz 1990; Cornelius & Niehr 2004; Yon 2006; Lawson Younger 2007.

Helge Kvanvig, Bernard Batto, John Day and Christopher Hays.[4] It is not necessary to repeat this exercise here. We will confine ourselves to a first, rather superficial review of similarities and differences between a number of biblical texts dealing with primordial times and the Ugaritic material we will present in Chapter 2. In Chapter 3 we will briefly discuss a number of comparable ancient Near Eastern texts. Chapter 4 will be devoted to a comparison of this material with the well-known stories in the Hebrew Bible. It will appear that Ugaritic/Canaanite traditions about the origin of humankind have been incorporated in Hebrew sources of totally different origin and date. In Chapter 5 we hope to demonstrate that this is also the case with passages about Adam, Eve and the Devil in pseudepigraphic works some of which are contemporaneous with the latest books of the Hebrew Bible. In Chapter 6 some passages in the New Testament will be discussed.

The fresh findings will necessitate a reconsideration of arguments with regard to the origin and meaning of these biblical and parabiblical sources, but obviously we must confine ourselves to a first, preliminary inventarisation which we hope will be elaborated by others more qualified than we are.

Is this merely an exercise in the history of religions then? Of no value to the theology of the Old Testament? Obviously it is impossible to give a full exposition of our stance in these matters here. With scholars like Tryggve Mettinger,[5] Werner Schmidt,[6] Otto Kaiser,[7] James Barr,[8] – to mention only a few who certainly do not agree in every respect! – we are of the opinion that it it is wrong to make a sharp distinction between the religion of Israel and biblical theology.[9] Recently we wrote,

---

[4] Keel & Schroer 2002; LaCocque 2006; Mettinger 2007; Kvanvig 2011; Batto 2013; Day 2013; Hays 2014.

[5] Especially Mettinger 1987.

[6] Especially Schmidt 1968, 10th expanded edition of 2007.

[7] Especially Kaiser 1993-2003.

[8] Especially Barr 1999.

[9] The situation is summarized succinctly by Graham Davies, 'What is common to these (and other) writers is the determination to give value to those elements of the Old Testament which were not entirely "distinctive" to Israel (the watchword of an earlier generation) but were shared, to a greater or lesser degree, with neighbouring civilisations. This is a step of major *theological* significance.' (Davies 2006, 175). Note that Davies does

> In our opinion previous generations of scholars made a big mistake when they tried to safeguard the Bible from the despicable pagan world by placing it in a watertight compartment. Just as we ourselves are children of our time and are constantly confronted with the harsh reality of a world of non-believers and adherents of different religions, reacting to it by apologetics or adaptive strategies, so it was in the circles in which the Bible originated. More and more parallels between ancient Israel and its Near Eastern neighbours are being discovered. This should not alarm us. God has chosen to reveal himself in a specific historical situation, just as we live in such a situation. Recognizing this basic datum helps us to appreciate the courage, open-mindedness and mental power of those who mediated the word of God in biblical times. At the same time it becomes absolutely clear that no theology can simply transpose concepts meant for a totally different situation to our present world. Isolating the Bible from its world ultimately leads inevitably to an unworldly, fundamentalistic type of faith.[10]

So we will attempt to present both differences and similarities between the biblical narratives and the myths circulating in the world of the Bible, hoping to get a clearer sight of what may yet be regarded as the distinctive ideas of both.[11] Because meanwhile so many other religions and nations are indebted to the Hebrew Bible it is often glossed over that it is a *Hebrew* Bible. God, humans and the serpent in paradise all spoke Hebrew according to Genesis.[12] This alone should be a warning not to dismiss distinctiveness too lightly.

In order to avoid the risk of circular reasoning (cf. Miller 2003, 304) we have decided not to work with our own definition of 'primal' or 'primeval' humanity, but to let the documents from Antiquity speak for themselves.

---

not deny the value of the differences.

[10] Korpel & De Moor 2013, 174-175.

[11] This is the current trend in responsible comparative research that seeks to avoid parallelomania, cf. Hays 2014, 32-37.

[12] On Jewish speculations about the Adamic language and their different views on the value of translations of the Bible, see Smelik 2013.

2
The Adamic Myth in the Eastern Mediterranean

2.1 *Concepts of Creation in Ugarit*

Ugarit was a metropolis on the Syrian coast towards the end of the thirteenth century BCE. It had contacts all over the eastern part of the Mediterranean, trading from its ideally situated port Maʾḫadu[1] with Egypt, Cyprus, Crete, the Aegean Islands and Anatolia. Its extensive production of purple and wine made Ugarit a sought-after trading partner. Caravans connected the kingdom with Phoenicia and Palestine to the south, with Mesopotamia in the east, and with Anatolia in the north. Some of the scribes of Ugarit were trained in Babylonia. Although the Canaanite dialect of Ugarit was the main language spoken, Egyptian, Akkadian, Hurrian and Hittite were some of the other languages spoken and written in this kingdom (Bordreuil 2014).

In such an internationally oriented state several religions were operative, so religious and cultural exchange were fairly intensive. The polytheistic religion of Ugarit itself made it possible to adopt foreign deities in the pantheon whenever it seemed expedient. However, to maintain its identity as a state it was necessary to assign the highest rank to the deities Ugaritians, or rather the ruling elite, regarded as indigenous.[2]

In a recent study Jan Lisman summarizes his opinion about the theme of 'beginnings' in Ugarit as follows,

> My summarizing conclusion is that at this moment there exist no Ugaritic texts about 'Beginnings' comparable with the Sumerian or Akkadian ones as discussed in this study (Lisman 2013, 218).

This is certainly true, but his verdict is based on an *argumentum e silentio*. In reality there exists sufficient evidence to assume that one or more myths about primordeal times must have existed in Ugarit.

---

[1] Present-day Minet el-Beida.
[2] See e.g. L'Heureux 1979; Handy 1994; Cho 2007.

One way of establishing rank in the divine world was drawing up lists in which the most important deities occupied the highest positions. In many god lists of Ugarit *ʾilʾib*, 'Ilu-the-Father',[3] is followed immediately by *ʾil* 'Ilu (God)'.[4] Other lists, however, are headed by *ʾil* 'Ilu', followed by *ʾilh* 'Ilāhu',[5] or are headed by *ʾilh* followed by *ʾilhm* 'Ilāhūma'.[6] In the list KTU 1.148:23-34 *ʾilʾib* is followed by *ʾarṣ wšmm* 'Earth-and-Heaven' and *ʾil* 'Ilu'. The latter sequence corresponds to a succession found with Philo of Byblos: Ouranos (Heaven) – Earth – Elos (Kronos).[7] In KTU 1.109:15-18 *ʾilʾib* is followed by *bʿl ʾugrt* 'Baʿlu-of-Ugarit', *bʿl ḫlb* 'Baʿlu-of-Ḫalab [Aleppo]'. KTU 1.109:19-23 has the sequence *ʾilʾib*, *bʿl*, *dgn* 'Daganu', *ʿnt ḥlš* 'ʿAnatu of *Ḥlš*'. In KTU 1.123:1 *ʾab wʾilm* 'the Father and the gods', is followed by *ʾil šr* 'Ilu (and) Šarru',[8] Daganu and Baʿlu. Baʿlu and his father Daganu were clearly rising in rank. Finally KTU 1.65:1-11 offers *ʾil* 'Ilu', *bn ʾil* 'the children of Ilu', *dr bn ʾil* 'the families of the children of Ilu', *mpḫrt bn ʾil* 'the assembly of the children of Ilu'.

These observations suggest that *ʾilʾib* 'Ilu -the-Father', *ʾil* 'Ilu' and *ʾilh* 'Ilāhu' all designate more or less the same supreme deity.[9] Ilāhū is a broken plural expressing the majesty and multiplicity in the highest divine being.[10] Ilāhūma, however, is a genuine plural[11] comprising all deities who were seen as Ilu's offspring,[12] including

---

[3] For this rendering, De Moor 1980 and 1997, 330-332; cf. Lambert 1981.

[4] KTU 1.47:2-3; 1.109:12-13; 1.118:1-2; 1.148:10; 1.162:6-7.

[5] E.g. KTU 1.39:2-4; 1.109:24-28.

[6] E.g. KTU 1.39:5-8; 1.41:11-13, 14-17, 30-32.

[7] Attridge & Oden 1981, 46-49. The pair Heaven and Earth is ubiquitous in ancient religions, e.g. the Egyptian pair Geb and Nut (Earth and Heaven) and the Babylonian pair AN/*šamû* 'Heaven' and KI/*erṣetu* or Uraš, 'Earth' (cf. Lambert 2013, 311-315, 407-408, 334-335, 352-353).

[8] With pairs of deities the *w* was sometimes omitted. In this case *ʾil wšr* is attested in KTU 1.107:37'. See our explanation of *šr* in Section 2.6.

[9] Also in other religions of the ancient Near East great gods could be identified with their fathers, See e.g. Lambert 2013, 303. It is no valid objection to this thesis that *ʾilʾib(m)* occurs as 'father god(s), ancestral god(s)' in KTU 1.17:I.26 par. After their death kings and great heroes were thought to be united with Ilu, cf. footnote 12.

[10] De Moor 1997, 179, n. 382, despite Pardee 1999, 286; 2000, 35-39.

[11] Actually a double plural, like *bhtm*.

[12] So with Pardee 1999, 286; 2000, 38. It is likely that this is also a designation of the royal ancestors of Ugarit who were united with Ilu after their

his son-in-law Baʿlu for whom this title was an honorific. This collective designation tallies with the plurals that are found in KTU 1.65:1-3.

However, it is likely that the (partial?) equation of Il'ibu with Ilu is a later development. The list in which *ʾilʾib* is followed immediately by *ʾarṣ wšmm* 'Earth and Heaven' which in turn is followed by *ʾil* 'Ilu' (KTU 1.148:23-25; *Ugaritica V*, 321, no. 170:13-15)[13] suggests that it was actually 'Il'ibu 'Ilu the Father' who created first of all heaven and earth which provided the basic conditions for all the rest.[14] Apparently this father creator role was transferred to Ilu, the head of the Ugaritic pantheon. Thus far the widely attested Canaanite deity *ʾl qn(y/h) šm(y)m wʾrṣ* 'El the Creator of Heaven and Earth'[15] is not attested in any published Ugaritic alphabetic text, but it is highly likely that this is purely accidental. He occurs in Hurrian religious texts as El-Kunirsa, 'El the Creator of the Earth'.[16] According to a Canaanite myth preserved in Hittite Elkunirsa was married to Ašertu, clearly the same goddess as the Ugaritic Aṯiratu,[17] the wife of Ilu. He dwelt in a 'tent' at the headwaters of the Euphrates river.[18] A Hurrian incantation from Ugarit invokes him as 'Ilu who creates (all) the living' and equates him with the Hurrian/Hittite god Kumarbi (Dietrich & Mayer 1997). In a Phoenician text from Karatepe he is called *ʾl qn ʾrṣ* 'El the Creator of the Earth' (KAI 26:A.III.18). In another text from Karatepe *ʾl wʿlyn* 'El-and-Elyon" immediately precedes *šmyn wʾrq* 'Heaven and Earth' (KAI 222:A.11). All this agrees with the theogony as described by Hurrians and by Philo of Byblos (De Moor 1980, 185). In Palmyra both the shortened form

---

death. Cf. Del Olmo Lete 1987, 42-43, 64-65; De Moor 1997, 330-331. Also Philo of Byblos reports that the Phoenicians regarded Ἐλωεὶμ as a plural designating the allies of El (Attridge & Oden 1981, 50-51).

[13] Cf. De Moor 1970a, 199.

[14] Also Curtis 2012 concluded that *ʾilʾib* probably preceded Ilu but he did not take into account all relevant data.

[15] Also the reversed order occurs: *ʾil qn(h) ʾrṣ wšmm* 'El the Creator of Earth and Heaven'.

[16] Haas 1994, 172-173; Röllig 1999; Dijkstra 2013. On the grammatical construction of the name in non-Semitic sources we prefer the opinion of Weippert 2014 over that of McAffee 2013.

[17] The Ugaritic *ṯ* equals Hebrew *š*.

[18] Hoffner 1990, 69-70. See also Section 2.4 below.

ʾlqwnʿrʾ 'El the Creator of the Earth' and the fuller form *ʾl qwnʾ ʾrʿʾ wšmyʾ* 'El the Creator of Earth and Heaven' are preserved (Milik 1972, 182-183). In Gen. 14 we find the following sequence: אֵל עֶלְיוֹן 'El-Elyon' (v. 18, also in v. 20), אֵל עֶלְיוֹן קֹנֵה שָׁמַיִם וָאָרֶץ 'El-Elyon, the Creator of Heaven and Earth' (v. 19), a title claimed for the God of Abraham in v. 22: יְהוָה אֵל עֶלְיוֹן קֹנֵה שָׁמַיִם וָאָרֶץ 'YHWH-El-Elyon, the Creator of Heaven and Earth'.[19] On an ostracon found in Jerusalem, dated in the late eighth or early seventh century BCE, *ʾl qn ʾrṣ* 'El the Creator of Earth' is attested.[20] As late as the second century CE (*ʾdn*) *ʾl qn ʾrṣʾ*, '(the Lord) El, the Creator of the Earth', was still venerated according to a Neo-Punic inscription (KAI 129:1). Probably the names connecting El with the creation of the earth alone are merely shortened forms of the fuller name.

So we get the following correspondences of the primordial creator gods,

UGARIT	HURRIANS	CANAANITES	PHILO BYBLIUS
ʾilʾib	*Alalu*	אל (עליון) קנ(ה)	Ἐλιοῦν καλούμενος Ὕψιστος
ʾarṣ wšmm	*Anu*	ארץ ושמם	Οὐρανὸς καὶ Γῆ
ʾil	*Kumarbi*[21]	אל	Ἦλος ὁ καὶ Κρόνος

Both the Hurrian *Song of Kumarbi* and Philo Byblius in his *Phoenician History* relate that the succession of these primordial gods was accompanied by extreme violence, including the castration of Anu/Ouranos.[22] Nothing of the kind is found in the extant Ugaritic tablets and if we are right that Ilʾibu and Ilu were in the process of merging it is not to be expected that they fought for the position of highest god.

In KTU 1.179:9' and KTU 1.100:1 the pair of deities *šmm wthm* 'Heaven and Flood' occurs among other primordial deities.[23] This suggests that just as in other creation myths of the ancient Near

[19] This would seem to fit into the pattern of claiming El's prerogatives for YHWH. Cf. Ps. 115:15; 121:2; 124:8; 134:3; 146:5-6. However, an early association of YHWH and El is not impossible, cf. De Moor 1997, 332-335.

[20] See lately Bornstein 2013.

[21] In Ugarit also *ʾil kmrb*, KTU 1.42:6-8.

[22] Hoffner 1990, 40-43; Attridge & Oden 1981, 46-55.

[23] See Section 2.6 below.

East the earth was created by raising it up from the primordial ocean.[24]

Among these most ancient gods are also *ṯkmn wšnm* who in Ugarit are often mentioned directly before or after Ilu or Ilāhūma, or the assembly of the gods.[25] Apparently they were strong enough to carry the highest god Ilu home when he is dead drunk – a duty of sons.[26] In our opinion *ṯkmn* is the Atlas of Ugarit who carries the pillar supporting heaven on his shoulder. According to Philo of Byblos Atlas was a brother of Kronos (El), so he belonged to the primordial deities (Attridge & Oden 1981, 46-49). Ultimately this tradition goes back to the Hittite myth of the titan Upelluri who supports the cosmos with the basalt column Ullikummi on his shoulder.[27] Ullikummi was the fruit of intercourse between Kumarbi, 'the Father of All Gods', and a huge rock laying in a cold spring.[28] This background suggests an explanation for the names of *ṯkmn wšnm*: the first element derives from *ṯkm* 'shoulder', with the characteristic *-n* to be discussed further on (Section 2.6), whereas the second element may be related to Arabic *sanām* 'bump' (on a camel's back), but also a designation of an elevation in the middle of the earth.[29] Ilu seems to have used *ṯkmn wšnm* to support the firmament like a tent over the earth.[30] As we shall see (Section 2.4), it is significant that Ullikummi consisted of basalt, a volcanic rock.

So Ilu seems to have been the deity who separated heaven and

---

[24] Cf. Allen 1997, 5-6, 11-15; Lambert 1988, 126. For the Hebrew tradition see Section 4.2.

[25] KTU 1.39:3; 1.40:34; 1.65:4(!); 1.141:31.

[26] KTU 1.114:18. Cf. KTU 1.17:I.30-31 par.; Gen. 9:21-23.

[27] Hoffner 1990, 55-59; Haas 1982, 137, 152, 159-160; 1994, 89, 94-95. More remotely comparable are the Egyptian primordial pairs Shu and Tefnut as members of the Heliopolitan Ennead, and Laḫmu and Laḫamu in Babylonian cosmology, cf. Lambert 1985a; 1985b, 447-448; 2013, 417.

[28] Hoffner 1990, 52. Compare the Ugaritic primordial pair of deities *ʿn* 'Source' (more or less feminine) and *ʾabn* 'Stone' (more or less masculine), cf. Section 2.6 below.

[29] Kazimirski 1860, t. 1, 1153. It is still uncertain whether *šnm* in the frequent expression *ʾab šnm* is this god ('the Father of Šanāmu') or that the title should rather be rendered 'the Father of Years", in accordance with other Ugaritic texts indicating Ilu's hoary age. See the discussion in Smith 1994, 185-186; Pardee 2000, 39-41; Bembry 2011.

[30] Cf. Isa. 40:22; Ps. 19:4.

earth in the beginning, like the Sumerian god Enlil,[31] the Babylonian god Marduk,[32] the Hittite/Hurrian Kumarbi (Hoffner 1990, 52-61) and YHWH/El/Elohim, the God of Israel.[33] The Canaanites distinguished an Upper Flood above the firmament and a Lower Flood below the earth. Ilu dwelt at the confluence of the two (see below Section 2.4). According to the Ugaritians he was the Creator of the cosmos. In accordance with the Northwest Semitic glorification of cattle breeding he was still depicted as a tent-dweller, even though his 'camp' had all the characteristics of a luxurious palace,

KTU 1.3:V.5-11

ʾidk[.]l[*ttn.p*]n*m*	Then she headed straight
(6) [ʿ*m.*ʾ*il*].*mbk nh*r[*m.*]	for Ilu at the fountain-head of the two Rivers,
[*qr*]*b.*ʾa[*p*]q (7) [*thm*]*tm.*	in the middle of the streambed of the two Floods.
tgl.ḏd ʾ*il*[.]	She appeared in the encampment of Ilu
w*tb*ʾu(8) [*qr*]*š.m*[*l*]*k.*ʾab [*.šnm.*]	and entered the camp of the King, the Father of Years(?),
m*ṣr* (9) [*t*]bʾ*u.*	she entered the stronghold,
*ḏ*d*m.*q*ny*[*.w*] ʾ*ad*n.[ʾ*i*]*l*m	the encampment of the Creator and Lord of the deities.[34]
(10) q*lh.yš*mʿ.*ṯr.*[ʾ*i*]*l.*ʾ*abh.*	The Bull Ilu her father heard her voice.
y[ʿ*n.*ʾ*i*]l (11) *bšb*ʿ*t.ḥ*[*d*]*rm*	From the seven chambers[35] Ilu answered ...

Also the passage KTU 1.3:V.19-21 indicates that Ilu's 'encampment' equaled a 'palace' (*bhtm* ‖ *hkl*). Moreover, this passage reveals that Ilu was not only the Creator of the cosmos, but also the Father and Lord of all the other deities.

KTU 1.3:V.19-21

(19) *wt*ʿ*n.btlt.*ʿ*n*[*t.*]	And the Virgin ʿAnatu answered:
[*bnm.*]bh*t* (20) *k.y* ʾ*ilm.*	'Let not the sons of your mansion, O Ilu,
bnt[.]bh[*t*]k.ʾ*a*[*l.tš*]*mḫ*	let not the daughters of your mansion rejoice,

[31] Cf. Section 3.3.1.

[32] En. el. IV.135ff. Cf. Lambert 2013, 169-171.

[33] Cf. Gen. 1:6-7; 2 Sam. 22:16; Ps. 36:7; Job 28:11; 38:16; Prov. 3:19f.

[34] The Ugaritic term for Lord is ʾ*adn*, related to Hebrew אָדוֹן and אֲדֹנָי 'Lord'.

[35] Cf. KTU 1.3:V.26-27. For the chambers and lockable rooms of El, cf. Job 37:9.

(21) *ʾal.tšmḫ.b*nm[.*h*]k*l*[*k*] let not the children of your palace rejoice![36]

As in other creation myths of the ancient Near East, creation and procreation were not sharply distinguished in Ugarit. Ilu in his role of the potent Father of all other deities is often called *ṯr*, 'Bull' and once *ʾal* 'Ram'.[37] In KTU 1.23 Ilu has intercourse with two women (*ʾaṯtm*) at the same occasion. These women are characterized as *mštʿltm* 'two women willing to let themselves be mounted' (Tropper 1990, 78). They are probably humans.[38] Ilu's penis grows 'as long as the ocean' and the women give birth to Šaḥaru (sunrise red) and Šalimu (sunset red). These two creatures appear to be enormously hungry and open their mouths from earth to heaven to swallow the birds of heaven and the fish from the sea (KTU 1.23:61-63). Apparently they were giants. The same terminology is used to describe the enormous mouth of Môtu, the god of death.[39]

In the polygynous society of Ugarit a man had one main wife and as many concubines as he could afford.[40] The same was true in the world of the deities. Ilu's main wife was Aṯiratu who corresponds to Ashera in the Bible. She is called *qnyt ʾilm* 'creatress of the gods'.[41] Ilu and Aṯiratu did not need physical contact to create. In the incantation KTU 1.169 a young man who is possessed by demons is touched with a statuette of Ilu,

---

36 Not only declared enemies of Baʿlu like Yammu and Môtu, but also other members of Ilu's family used to rejoice in the misfortunes of their brother-in-law. Cf. KTU 1.6:I.39ff.

37 Cf. De Moor 1997, 48-49, 71-72; 2008, 181, n. 16. Also the Hurrian *Song of Ullikummi* ascribes extraordinary sexual potency to Kumarbi who, as indicated above, was equated with Ilu. Cf. Hoffner 1990, 52.

38 Hendel 2004, 24, rejects this possibility on the ground that they may just as well be the goddesses Aṯiratu and *Rḥm(y)* who are mentioned in KTU 1.23:13, 16, 24, 28. However, he overlooks the possibility that the women were thought to impersonate the goddesses. Moreover, the circumstance that the women are offered the option to refuse sexual intercourse by calling Ilu 'my father' instead of 'my husband' (KTU 1.23:40, 43, 46) argues in favor of human partners. In the divine world incest was no problem. Moreover, Hendel himself admits that in other mythologies of the ancient world sexual encounters between deities and humans were common topics (Hendel 2004, 27-34).

39 KTU 1.5:II.2-3.

40 Marsman 2003, 370-377, 681-682.

41 Del Olmo Lete & Sanmartín 2003, 706.

KTU 1.169:12-15

lbš (13) *ʾil.yštk.*	May the robe of Ilu make you –
ʿrm.ʾil.yštk	may the nakedness of Ilu make you
(14) *lʾadm.wd.ḫ̮ṭm.lʾarṣ.*	a human, yes, someone who is awake on the earth,
zrm (15) *lbn.ʾadm.*	(may they make) the strange one a son of humans!
bʾanšt.np<š> ẓl	When the fury of the soul of the shade starts,
(16) h*n.bnpš.ʾaṯrt.rbt.*	look! in the soul of Lady Aṯiratu,
bl(17) *[b.yṣ]rk.lṯtm.*	in the he[art of your Po]tter,[42] may you be molded!

The Potter is Ilu, as in KTU 1.16:V.26-30 where he shapes a winged healing spirit from clay. Like Creator deities in Egyptian and Mesopotamian religious texts[43] Ilu is able to create human beings from clay or soil. The expression 'son of humankind' apparently means a normal healthy person here. What is striking is the high level of abstraction. Even though the verb *lwṯ* 'to mold' as well as the epithet 'Potter' evoke a rather realistic image of two deities busy modelling clay, the real creative act is described as an interior psychological process. A shared thought of the Creators is enough. Creation by word alone is attested in KTU 1.12:I.14-33 where Ilu ignores the advances of two minor goddesses and simply orders them to bear carnivorous monsters. Even though the god Baʿlu was the son of Daganu, Ilu could yet be described as his Creator,

KTU 1.3:V.35-36 par.

(35) *ʾany.l yṣḥ.ṯr ʾil.ʾabh.*	The Bull Ilu, his father, groaned (and) cried out,
ʾil (36) *mlk.dyknnh.*	Ilu, the King who had established his existence,[44]

It has long been observed that this resembles Deut. 32:6 fairly closely,[45]

הֲלוֹא־הוּא אָבִיךָ קָּנֶךָ	Is not he your Father, your Creator?

---

[42] The Editors of KTU^3, 162, read: bʿr*k* here, but this must be an error as inspection of Pardee's excellent copy as well as the photograph on disk in Bordreuil & Pardee 2004 show. נפש and לב are a frequent pair in the Hebrew Bible.

[43] And God in the Bible, cf. Gen. 2:7; Isa. 64:7; Job 10:9, also Isa. 27:11; 43:1; 44:2, 24; 45:9, 11; Jer. 10:16; 51:19.

[44] Here the verb for 'to establish existence' is *kwn* L-stem, Del Olmo Lete & Sanmartín 2003, 448.

[45] E.g. Sanders 1996, 150-151.

הוּא עָשְׂךָ וַיְכֹנְנֶךָ	He your Maker who established your existence?[46]

Because this is said to the people of Israel, the sense is clearly metaphorical here too. As in Egypt and Mesopotamia the act of creation can be described as 'building, constructing'. Ilu is called *bny bnwt*, 'Builder of things built',[47] he is the Creator *par excellence.* The circumstance that he also creates when the inhabited world is long there demonstrates that the Ugaritians believed in *creatio continua.*

So Ilu/El was the almighty Creator of everything. Even the mere invocation of his name was thought to have creative force. When Dani'ilu calls up the spirits of dead heroes in the hope that he will be able to kiss the lips of his murdered son Aqhâtu once more, the appearance of the spirits is described as follows,

KTU 1.22:I (IV?): 4-7

ṯm [5] *ṯkm.bmṯkm.'aḫm.*	There, shoulder to shoulder, were the brothers,
qym.'il [6] *blsmt.*	whom Ilu caused to rise in a hurry.
ṯm.yṯbš.šm.'il.mtm	There the name of Ilu brought the dead into being,[48]

---

[46] Here too the second verb is *kwn* L-stem.

[47] Del Olmo Lete & Sanmartín 2003, 233-234. Cf. Becking & Korpel 2010.

[48] The reading *yṯbš* is disputed. Virolleaud 1941, 16, 19 read *yšbś* (at that time Virolleaud still transcribed *ṯ* as *š*, and *š* as *ś*). Herdner 1963, t. 1, 96 and t. 2, Fig. 66, followed him. Pitard 1992 was the first to dispute this reading. Pardee 2011, 32 expresses himself more cautiously: it might be a *ṯ*, but more likely an ', but finally he opts decidedly for *y'bš* (52). This was followed by KTU[3], 65.
It is certain that the scribe overwrote a vertical wedge with an ', but whether he wanted to correct the wedge or wanted to change it into a *ṯ* is impossible to decide. We believe that KTU 7.163:4 might be adduced in support of the reading *yṯbš* (see Appendix 1). In that case the scribe wanted to make a wordplay with *y'bš* in the next line. In any case the parallel *y'bš* in line 7 should be seen as related to Akkadian *epēšu* 'to make, create' and Arabic *'bš* IV 'to arrange, make better, do good' (Kazimirski 1860, t. 2, 156). See Korpel 1996, 100, 3; exchange of *b* and *p* is not uncommon in Ugaritic, cf. Tropper 2012, § 33.112–33.112.36.
In the bilingual Sumerian-Akkadian composition *The Founding of Eridu* (Lambert 2013, 366-375) many different verbs for creating are used, e.g. *epēšu* 'to make', *banû* 'to build', *šakānu* 'to establish', *ramû* 'to throw down, found'. However, also *šubšû* 'to bring into being' occurs (line 33). So we may regard *epēšu* and *šubšû* in this text as a case of distant parallelism.

(7) *yʿbš.brkn.šm.ʾil.ġzrm*	the blessing of the name of Ilu (re)created the heroes.

Yet some other Ugaritic deities are also able to create, be it on a far more modest scale. Baʿlu recreates birds that he himself had slaughtered at the instigation of king Dānîʾilu.[49] He aspires to become the successor of Ilu, also as an at least as potent procreator,

KTU 1.10:III.4-11

(4) *wyʿny.ʾalʾiyn*[*.bʿl*]	And [Baʿʿlu] the Almighty answered:
(5) *lm.*k*qnyn.*ʿlt[*k*]	'Surely I can mount [you] like our Creator,[50]
(6) *kdrd<r>.dyknn*[*n*]	like the old generation that created [us]!'
(7) *bʿl.yṣġd.mlʾ*i[*.yd*]	Baʿlu strode forward with a filled ['hand'],[51]
(8) *ʾil* h*d.mlʾa.ʾu*ṣ[*bʿh*]	the god Haddu filled [his] 'fin[ger]'.[52]
(9) *btlt.p btlt.*ʿn[*t*]	The orifice of the Virgin ʿAna[tu] was deflowered,[53]
(10) *wp.nʿmt* ʾa*ḫt.*b[*ʿl*]	yes, the orifice of the most graceful of Baʿlu's sisters.

In the work of the scribe Ilimilku of Ugarit a gradual rise to power of the young, vigorous rain god Baʿlu at the expense of the ageing Ilu is discernable and finally this even included control of the *thmtm*, 'Two Floods', previously the exclusive domain of Ilu.[54] However, the Ugaritic myths still reflect a stage in the development of the Ugaritic religion in which Baʿlu has not yet succeeded in replacing his father-in-law as the supreme creator (De Moor 1997, 71-110). This is one of our main reasons to doubt that the Ugaritic *Myth of Baʿlu* may be adduced as a prime example of Hermann Gunkel's scheme 'chaos (combat) followed by creation'.[55]

---

[49] KTU 1.19:III.12, 26, the verb is *bny* 'to build', as in Ilu's epithet. The circumstance that this is a reversable miracle is proof of Baʿlu's considerable powers, comparable to Marduk's proof of superiority over all other deities, Section 3.3.5.

[50] The Bull Ilu, the procreator of the gods. In several other passages Baʿlu transforms himself into a young bull to mount a cow: KTU 1.11:3 (reading *y*n*bd<l>*); 1.5:V.18-21. This motif was also adopted in Egypt (Stadelmann 1967, 132-133).

[51] 'Hand' is a euphemism for the penis.

[52] Euphemism, as in Middle Hebrew.

[53] The verb is *btl*, explaining ʿAnatu's epithet *btlt* 'Virgin, Young Woman'.

[54] KTU 1.19:I.45. Cf. Korpel 1990, 561-562; Korpel 1998, 105-111. In the first millennium Baal Shamem, 'the Baal of Heaven', becomes the *qnh dy (ʾ)rʿh*, 'Creator of the Earth' (KAI 244:3).

Possibly also the sun goddess became a creatress in Ugarit.[56] Since the sinister god Ḥôrānu[57] too has *bnwt*, 'things built, offspring' (KTU 1.100:62) and even the god of death Môtu had at least one child,[58] creative powers were not totally confined to the highest god Ilu, the Creator of 'All'.

2.2 *KTU 1.107 and KTU 1.100*

Two Ugaritic tablets are of prime importance to this investigation: KTU 1.107 (RS 24.251+) and KTU 1.100 (RS 24.244).[59] They were reedited in a most admirable way by Dennis Pardee.[60] The great number of improvements over Virolleaud's *editio princeps* (Virolleaud 1968, 564-580) has rendered much previous work on these tablets obsolete, including some early studies by one of us (De Moor 1977; 1988b). Nevertheless even the best-preserved tablet KTU 1.100 poses many problems, as correctly observed by David Clemens,[61] Manfried Dietrich and Oswald Loretz.[62] The two tablets were found at approximately the same location,[63] were written by the same scribe[64] and belong to one and the same mythological composition, with KTU 1.107 preceding KTU 1.100. The latter is one of the best-preserved tablets from Ugarit, but unfortunately the former is very badly damaged, making its interpretation extremely hazardous. Its abrupt start renders it likely that a third tablet preceded KTU 1.107, but as we will see later, some of this preceding narrative can be reconstructed from other

---

55 For a reappraisal of Gunkel's hypothesis see Scurlock & Beal 2013.

56 Again the verb is *bny* 'to build', see Section 2.2 below.

57 The vocalization of the name will be explained below, Section 2.6

58 *Qẓb* 'the Sting', cf. 'the first-born of Death', Job 18:13. See Appendix 1.

59 In the Appendices 1 and 2 we give our reading and philological interpretation of the two tablets.

60 Pardee 1988, 193-256. See now also Del Olmo Lete 2014, Figs. IV-VII, Plates V-VIII.

61 Clemens 2001, *passim*.

62 Dietrich & Loretz 2009b. As will become clear, we disagree with Pardee's interpretation of KTU 1.100 (Pardee 1997; Bordreuil & Pardee 2004, 36-44).

63 Bordreuil & Pardee 1989, 299-300; Pardee 2000, 193, 228-229.

64 Pardee 2000, 228: 'A vrai dire, nous ne voyons pas de critère qui empêcherait d'attribuer les tablettes 7 et 8 à la même main.' (Eng. transl.: Frankly, we do not see any criterium which would prevent us from attributing the tablets 7 [= KTU 1.100] and 8 [= KTU 1.107] to the same hand).

sources which seem to suggest that the missing tablet contained some kind of creation story ending in a rebellion of one of the gods which disturbed the cosmic order. In the preceding section we have shown that it is a reasonable assumption that Ilu (El) was the main character of this Ugaritic creation story and that it was he who fashioned the first human being (Section 2.1).

KTU 1.100 and 1.107 are often regarded as incantations with magic rituals to cure a person bitten by a snake.[65] Although the main part of the text is formulated as a description of mythological events in the *past*, its use as an incantation against snakebite is not impossible, because there exists a Sumerian parallel for this (Römer 2007).

However, the mythological narrative and especially the cosmic consequences of the poisoning (e.g. fog obscuring the sunlight) are difficult to reconcile with the genre of an incantation. In their discussion of KTU 1.100 Manfried Dietrich and Oswald Loretz have therefore correctly observed that this text cannot simply be characterized as an incantation against snakebite.[66] Meanwhile a genuine Ugaritic snake charm has been published by Pierre Bordreuil and Dennis Pardee and this text is completely different.[67]

Throughout the two tablets the sun goddess Šapšu plays an important role which is understandable because she is able to address deities in all parts of the cosmos during her daily journey through heaven and underworld. In this case the fact that her rays are obscured by fog may be seen as an extra reason for herself to intervene. In KTU 1.107:13 the primordial deity Adammu calls her his 'creatress',[68] which explains her concern for his fate.

According to KTU 1.100 eleven great deities of the Ugaritic

---

[65] Lately Del Olmo Lete 2013; 2014, with ample discussion of earlier interpretations. Unfortunately the advocates of this interpretation treated the two tablets separately because they overlooked Pardee's statements quoted above.

[66] Dietrich & Loretz 2008, 137 [reprint of a 2003 article].

[67] Bordreuil & Pardee 2004, 69-70, Text 18 (= KTU 1.178). See also Hawley 2004; Dietrich and Loretz 2009a; Del Olmo Lete 2012b; Del Olmo Lete 2014, 173-187 with Fig. IX, Plate X.

[68] Appendix 1. This way of addressing Šapšu need not mean that she was Adammu's real creatress or mother because 'creator' or 'creatress' could be used as an honorific title, see e.g. Hornung 1971, 142-143; *CAD* (B), 87a-89a.

pantheon, including its head Ilu, are invoked with a plea to neutralize the deadly poison of a snake, but apparently none of them is able to do anything against it.[69] Finally Ḥôrānu[70] is invoked. He is a sinister god who is the father/creator[71] of all serpents embodying demonic powers.[72] It seems likely that as their father also Ḥôrānu himself could take on the shape of a monstrous serpent.[73]

Ḥôrānu owned at least a fortress or house in the Netherworld, possibly he even ruled over a complete city situated at the exit of the Netherworld in the east.[74] but in contrast to the god of death Môtu he was apparently allowed to leave the realm of Death temporarily because he returns there after a leave of absence.[75] Since he is also invoked to execute a curse on earth (see below) it is clear that he sometimes visited the world of the living.

In the extant part of KTU 1.107 Ḥôrānu has no longer a place among the celestials (cf. Section 2.6). Like the god of death Môtu, he does not receive sacrifices in Ugarit.[76] Probably he was banned from heaven (cf. Section 2.6). His revenge seems to have been that he made the Tree of Life in 'the vineyard of the great gods' inaccessable to the hitherto immortal gods by taking on the shape of a huge serpent that poured its poison on the tree.[77] As a result the living world was endangered, necessitating an appeal to the

---

[69] The fragmentary state of KTU 1.107 renders it impossible to establish the number of deities invoked on that tablet.

[70] This vocalization instead of the customary Ḥoron(u) will be explained below.

[71] This follows from KTU 1.100:62 where the serpents are called *bnwth* 'his creatures/posterity'.

[72] Their demonic nature is evident in KTU 1.82:13, 27, 41, cf. 6, 32, 35; RS 92.2014 (= KTU 1.178 (cf. Bordreuil & Pardee 2001).

[73] In KTU 1.100:74 Ḥôrānu seems to be called 'the Dragon-serpent'.

[74] KTU 1.100:58, 67-68; KTU 1.179:29, 33. Cf. De Moor 1987, 175-181; Del Olmo Lete 2011. For the city see KTU 1.100:62 *ykr ʿr dqdm* 'he left the city of the east'.

[75] KTU 1.179:33, cf. De Moor 2008.

[76] In marked contrast to the god of plagues Rašpu and to Yammu, the god of the unruly sea, who are the recipients of all kinds of sacrifices. For other sinister deities excluded from the sacrificial cult see De Moor 1970a, 222; Gurney 1977, 42, n. 1. In KTU 1.106:30 *ʾišm ʾar* [...] should *not* be emended, cf. Pardee 2000, 590, 599.

[77] As a result of Ḥorranu's act the Tree of Life became unattainable for good, like the plant that could have granted Gilgameš immortality. Cf. Section 3.3.2.

whole pantheon to provide a cure against the poison.[78] As an example we quote one of these passages,

KTU 1.107:44'-45'

ʾ*isp*.špš *lhrm.ġrpl.*	Collect, (Oh) Šapšu, the fog from the mountains,
ʿ*l* ʾ*arṣ* (45′) [*š*]pt.*ḥmt.*	on the earth the poison-lips,
lp[*.n*]*ṯk.*ʾ*abd.*	from the mouth of the Biter the destruction,
*lp.*ʾ*akl.ṯm d*l	from the mouth of the Devourer the paralysis of the lame one.[79]

Two other Ugaritic passages may provide a clue to the nature of the offense that had resulted in Ḥôrānu's banishment. The first lines of KTU 1.2:I are unfortunately damaged, but the sea god Yammu seems to blame Baʿlu for having risen in revolt to the authority of Yammu's father Ilu, who was the nominal head of the pantheon (KTU 1.2:I.2 ʾ*at tb*ʿ[t] 'you have risen';[80] 1.2:I.3 ʾ*at.yp*ʿ*t.b* 'you stood up against').[81] The rest of the quarrel can be reconstructed with more confidence,

KTU 1.2:I.3-9

[*wy*ʿ*n*] (4) ʾ*al*ʾ*iyn.b*ʿ*l*	[And] almighty Baʿlu [answered],
[ʾ*agršk.lks*ʾ*i. mlkk*]	[I will chase you from your royal chair,]
[*lnḥt.lkḥṯ*] (5) *drk*{.}*tk.*	[from the seat of the throne] of your dominion,
*mš*ṣ[ṣk.kʿṣr.ʾudnk]	making you fly [up from your aerie like a bird!][82]
[*ylm.ygrš.bktpk*]	[Yagruš will hit you on your shoulder]
(6) *br*ʾ*išk.*ʾ*aymr* [.]	Ayyamur (will hit) you on your head![83]
[*wy*ʿ*n.zbl.ym.*]	[And his Highness Yammu answered,]

[78] Ilu makes a similar appeal to all other deities in the *Legend of Kirtu* (KTU 1.16:V.9-28).

[79] For philological comments, see Appendix 1.

[80] In KTU 1.14:I.14 the same verb describes the rebellion of one of Kirtu's wives against her husband. Such an offense could entail her execution (cf. Marsman 2003, 663-671).

[81] An Egyptian stele from the Baal-temple in Ugarit equates Seth with Baal Zaphon (Caquot & Sznycer 1980, 24 and Fig. XII). Both gods were rebels (cf. Te Velde 1984).

[82] For the restorations see KTU 1.1:IV.24-25; 1.2:IV.12–13; 1.3:IV.1-3; 1.22:II.18.

[83] Yagrush and Ayyamur are the names of the magic weapons fashioned by the technician among the gods, Koṯaru. Eventually Baʿlu will use these weapons to defeat Yammu (KTU 1.2:IV).

[yṯb] (7) *ṯpṭ.nhr.*	Judge Naharu [replied],
yṯb[r. dhrn ybʿl.]	O Baʿlu, may Ḥôrānu smash -,
[yṯbr.ḥrn] (8) *rʾišk.*	may Ḥôrānu [smash] your head,
ʿṯtrt.[šm bʿl.qdqdk.]	ʿAṯtartu, consort of Baʿlu, your skull.
[trd] (9) *[m]mt.mṭ.*	[May you go] down [to the p]lace of death below,[84]
tpln.bg[bl.šntk.]	may you fall down at the summit of your years,
[bḥpnk.wtʿn.]	in your full bloom,[85] and yet be humbled!

A similar passage is found at the end of the *Legend of Kirtu* where Kirtu's eldest son Yaṣṣibu challenges his father to abdicate,

KTU 1.16:VI.40-58

yʾu gh (41) *wyṣḥ.*	He raised his voice and cried,
šmʿ mʿ.l krt (42) *ṯʿ*	Now listen, O Kirtu, nobleman,
ʾištmʿ.tqġ ʾudn	listen well, let your ear be attentive!
(43) *k ġz.ġzm.tdbr*	Ah! The most generous man you drive away[86]
(44) *wġrm.ṯṯwy.*	but the usurer you allow to stay.
šqlt (45) *bġlt.ydk.*	You have let fall your hand down in slackness,!
l tdn (46) *dn.ʾalmnt.*	You do not judge the case of the widow,
l ṯṯpṭ (47) *ṯpṭ qṣr.npš.*	you do not try the case of the impatiently waiting,
l tdy (48) *ṯšm ʿl.dl.*	you do not drive robbers away from the poor.
lpnk (49) *l tšlḥm.ytm.*	Before your (eyes) you do not let the orphan eat
bʿd (50) *kslk.ʾalmnt.*	(nor) behind your back the widow.
km (51) *ʾaḫt ʿrš.mdw.*	Ah! You are a brother of the bed of sickness,
ʾanšt (52) *ʿrš zbln.*	you are a companion of the bed of illness.
rd.lmlk (53) *ʾamlk.*	Abdicate the kingship, let me be king!
ldrktk.ʾaṯb (54) *ʾan.*	(abdicate) your dominion, let me throne!
wyʿny.krt ṯʿ.	But Kirtu, the nobleman, answered,
yṯbr (55) *ḥrn.y bn.*	Oh son, may Ḥôrānu smash -,
yṯbr.ḥrn (56) *rʾišk.*	may Ḥôrānu smash your head,
ʿṯtrt.šm.bʿl (57) *qdqdk*[!].	ʿAṯtartu, consort of Baʿlu, your skull!
tqln.bgbl (58) *šntk.*	May you fall down at the summit of your years,

[84] Cf. Deut. 28:43; Prov. 15:24. On *mmt* as a designation of the realm of death see Job 33:22 and De Moor 1971, 186.

[85] The expression *bḥpnk* is difficult, cf. Smith 1994, 280-281; Del Olmo Lete & Sanmartín 2003, 366. All cognates mean 'handful, fist', here probably used in a metaphorical sense.

[86] Root *ġzz* 'to be generous, munificent'. The parallelism is antithetical.

bḥpnk.wtʿn	in your full bloom, and yet be humbled!

Significantly, in both passages a younger personage rebels against an old ruler. The circumstance that the feared god Ḥôrānu is asked to smash the head of the offender might point to the fact that Ḥorrānu himself had once rebelled in a similar way against the head of the pantheon and was thrown from heaven for this offense, even though he repented later on.[87] Not only the Netherworld was open to him, but also the air. The *Legend of Aqhâtu* betrays how the Ugaritians may have imagined Ḥôrānu's execution of such rebels. Aqhâtu who insulted the goddess ʿAnatu was killed by a hired assassin in the shape of a bird of prey that pierced his temple, but the falconer who launched him was ʿAnatu herself (KTU 1.18:IV.17-26 par.), also in the shape of a raptor. In a subtle way the Ugaritic narrator indicates later on that the slayer of Aqhâtu was actually the goddess ʿAnatu-ʿAṯtartu.[88]

When Aqhâtu's sister Puġatu goes out to kill the assassin of her brother she disguises herself as ʿAnatu, even wearing the same kind of falconer's glove (*tʿrt*) that ʿAnatu herself had used.[89] The assassin forces her to give him wine to drink and when he has emptied the goblet she has put in his right hand, he brags,

KTU 1.19:IV.57

byn.yšt.ʾilʾa.	Through wine, Oh Lady, I become strong!
*ʾilš*nn[.] [58]ʾil dyqn*y.ḏdm*	I can scol[d] (even) Ilu, the creator of the encampments!
yd.*mḫṣt.ʾaq*[*h*]*t ġ*[59]*zr.*	The hand that slew the hero Aqhâtu
*tmḫṣ.ʾalpm.ʾi*b.*št*	will slay two thousand foes of the Lady!

Drunken drivel[90] by which he compares himself to the highest god Ilu who was scolded by his scorpion-guard for his drunkenness.[91] The implication is that Yaṭṭipānu can hold his liquor better than

[87] See Section 2.9 below. Apparently Ḥôrānu became a kind of 'licensed' executioner. According to Stokes 2014 'Satan' would not mean 'accuser' but 'executioner'.

[88] De Moor 1997, 98, n.321; 257, n. 218.

[89] KTU 1.18:IV.18 par.; 1.19:IV.45.

[90] We now derive the name of the assassin, *Yṭpn*, 'Yaṭṭipānu', from the root *nṭp* 'to utter drunken drivel', cf. Mic. 2:6, 11.

[91] Cf. KTU 1.114:20.

the head of the pantheon. Evidently this was blasphemy comparable to the insurrection of Ḥôrānu which we assume to have been narrated in the tablet that probably preceded KTU 1.107. Like Ḥôrānu, Yaṭṭipānu is depicted as a raptor, diving to kill his victim by pecking his temple (KTU 1.18:IV.30-37; 1.19:II.38 with Judg. 5:26.). The circumstance that he operates next to ʿAnatu in avenging Aqhâtu's insolence suggests that he was a manifestation of the avenger Ḥôrānu.[92] Seth, with whom Ḥôrānu was equated in Ugarit (Sections 2.6 and 2.9), was known as a notorious drunkard.[93]

Also in Egypt the Canaanite god Ḥaurōn/Ḥoron was represented as a falcon (images on the next pages). It is difficult to say whether this should be attributed to Canaanite influence in Egypt or from the falcon shape of Horus, with whom Ḥaurōn/Ḥoron was identified during the New Kingdom. In the curse referred to above Ḥôrānu and ʿAṯtartu are paired, just as ʿAnat and Ḥaurōn are paired in a curse preserved in the magical Egyptian papyrus Harris 501, 'Ḥaurôn makes thy fangs impotent, thy foreleg is cut off by Arasphes, after ʿAnat has cut thee down' (I.7).[94]

The Ugaritians may have borrowed this falcon imagery, although it is uncertain that a falcon standard from Ugarit represented Ḥôrānu.[95] The Ancients were often unable to determine the species of high-flying raptors which explains why they used designations like 'vulture', 'black kite', 'falcon' and 'eagle' indiscriminately. In any case Ḥôrānu and ʿAnatu/ʿAṯtartu were apparently seen as a pair of raptors who could be invoked to mete out capital punishment.[96]

---

[92] See further below. In Arabic *nṯf* may designate dripping of venom, but also 'to accuse someone of a crime' (Freytag, vol. 4, 295-296; Kazimirski 1860, t. 2, 1285) which brings to mind the commonly assumed meaning of 'Satan'.

[93] Te Velde 1977, 7.

[94] Translation Albright 1937, 3 (Arasphes is Reshef). Cf. Tazawa 2009, 71, Doc. 35. This parallel demonstrates that the invocation of ʿAṯtartu is by no means misplaced in a curse against Baʿlu (contra Smith 1994, 281).

[95] Usually the falcon is identified as the Egyptian god Horus, but the problem is that Horus, Ḥawrān, Baʿal and Seth were all more or less equated during the New Kingdom. Cf. Te Velde 1997, 63-73. Seth too is often depicted with wings, Te Velde 1977, Fig. 8 and Pl. IX; Cornelius 1994, *passim*, under his designation 'Baal-Seth'.

[96] Also the magical weapon Ayyamur which strikes the sea god Yammu on

Fig. 1: The falcon representing Ḥaurōn as the protector of the young Pharao Ramses II *in situ* at Tanis (after Montet 1935, Pl. XI)

We have chosen this photograph[97] because it shows the difference in proportions between normal human beings and the young pharaoh with his protector.

his skull is compared to an eagle (*nšr*), KTU 1.2:IV.19-22. We deem it not impossible that the falcon on a staff found at Ugarit was used to kill criminals instantly by a blow on the temple.

[97] Montet 1935, 12, 14, Pl. X-XI; Tazawa 2009, 62-63, Doc. 6, Doc. 7; 67-68, Doc. 20; 119, B; Gräbner 2011.

Fig. 2: The falcon's head found at the same site. It appeared to be a perfect fit (after Montet 1935, Pl. X)

Meindert Dijkstra pointed out to us that the restored image can be inspected in the Cairo Museum (JE 64735). On its base pharaoh Ramses II is described as *mery-n-Huran*, 'Beloved of Huran/Hawran/Hôran'.

Fig. 3: Falcon standard from Ugarit (Musée du Louvre, AO 11599)

The banishment of Ḥôrānu from the realm of the celestials has an obvious parallel in Isaiah 14:9-21 which, though ostensibly predicting the fall of the Babylonian king, reflects a myth about the fall of

Hēlēl, 'the Morning Star, son of Dawn',[98] who was thrown down into the realm of Death because he wanted to place his throne above the stars of God to become God's equal (Isa. 14:13-15; cf. Gen. 3:5).[99] It is important to note that Hēlēl's rebellion takes place in heaven, not on earth. This as well as the occurrence of a deity *hll* in Ugarit (cf. Section 2.5) makes it difficult to accept that in Isaiah 14:12 הֵילֵל is *not* the name of a god (so Spronk 1998, 726), although its author was evidently mocking about the divine status many oriental kings aspired to (see also Ezek. 28:6, 9, 16). According to KTU 1.107 and 1.100 this was precisely what threatened life in heaven and on earth, and seems to have been caused by Ḥôrānu before he repented (Section 2.9).

So Ilu, the highest creator of everything, had an adversary in primordial times who tried to depose him: Ḥôrānu. Eventually this evil opponent repented and took the side of Ilu. This will appear to be of great significance to the debate about the emergence of Satan and other demoniacal powers in the Bible and para-biblical literature. Although we cannot subscribe to the interpretation Gregorio del Olmo Lete gave of the two Ugaritic tablets which are the main basis for this study, he definitely was on the right track when he wrote,

> Therefore, *ḥrn* represents a primordial situation, parallel to the one that *ʾil* governs and commands. Consequently, we are invited to interpret KTU 1.100 in a mythical setting ... and to take it not merely as an incantation against empirical snake bites but rather as a canonical mythical text (Del Olmo Lete 2014, 206).

2.3 *The Death of Adammu*

KTU 1.107 seems to allow for the hypothesis that the gods eventually decided to send one of their own ranks to the earth with the instruction to recover the Tree of Life,[100]

---

[98] For a fuller treatment of this passage see Section 4.5 below.

[99] E.g. Spronk 1986, 139-227; Barr 1992, 48. Ezek. 28 is based on a similar tradition. Hilāl was a god in pre-islamic religion, cf. Van den Branden 1950, 11, 135, 357; Ryckmans 1951, 8.

[100] See Appendix 1 for textual and philogical notes.

[(1)]	[ ]
[m]*n.b*['arṣ].*hl*[k.ln]	['Whoever is] go[ing] on [the earth for us?]
(2) [b(?)]krm 'il*m.rbm*.	[into(?)] the vineyard of the great gods?'
nʿ*l*[*y.g*]m*r*	The champion was exalted,
(3) [yt]n [.'a]r*ṣ.bdh.*	[they gave the e]arth in his hand.
*yd*r*m*[.]p'*it*[.]'*adm*	The brow of Adammu flowed,
(4) [nḥ]š '*iṯ*[l].*yšql.yṯk*[*h*]	[the serpent] let fall spitt[le], it bit [him]!
h*n p bl.*	Look! The devouring mouth!
hn (5) [šnt(?)] q*ṯ*b*t.*	Look! The stinging [fangs]!
pẓr.pẓr [.]	Frantically he tried to loosen (it),
w*.p nḥš* (6) ['aḫd(?)]	but the mouth of the serpent [stuck(?)]
[*yṯ*]q.nṯ*k.l ydʿ.*	He did not know how to bind the Biter,
l bn.lpq ḥmt	nor did he understand how to conquer the poison.
(7)[tml]'u*nh.ḥmt.*	The poison [filled(?)] him,
wtʿbtnh.'abdy	yea, the Destroyer made him twist.
(8)[tpl.bš]r*.šrǵzz.*	The flesh of Šarruǵāzizu [fell].
ybky.km nʿr	He wept like a boy,
(9) [*wydmʿ.*] k*m.ṣǵr.*	[and shed tears] like a little one.
*š*pš*.bšmm tqr'u*	Šapšu called from heaven,
[(10) *hn.mdʿ.*]*nplt.yṯ*[b]y	['Look! Why] did it fall, Oh my fr[iend?]
mdʿ.nplt.bšr (11) [š]rǵzz.	Why did the flesh of [Š]arruǵāzizu fall?
w*tpky.*k[*m.*]nʿr.	And (why) do you weep like a boy,
tdmʿ.km (12) [ṣ]ǵ*r.*	do you shed tears like a little one?'
bkm.yʿny[*.šrǵzz.*]	Thereupon [Šarruǵāzizu] answered,
[yṯb.lh]*wth*	[he came back to her w]ords,
(13) [*t*]ʿ*nn.bnty š*[*pš*].	'Please answer me, my creatress Šapšu:
[lm.'an.lmt.] h*lk*	[Why am I] on my way [to death?]'
[(14)ṯ]*b.kmm.lk*l[.]msp[*r*]	Return ditto to the whole recitation.

So Adammu's death was decided by the great gods, probably with the consent of his creator Ilu and the latter's wife Aṯiratu. Being the highest god Ilu could allow himself such duplicity.[101] Ilu's opponent was '*abdy*, 'the Destroyer', like אֲבַדּוֹן in later Hebrew.

[101] In KTU 1.1:IV Ilu decides to replace Baʿlu as his viceroy by Yammu at the urging of Aṯiratu. In KTU 1.2:I.36-38 he executes this decision to the detriment of his totally unsuspecting son-in-law Baʿlu. In KTU 1.5:VI.11-26 Ilu feigns to be mourning over Baʿlu's death.

The remnants of the damaged last lines of the Obverse of KTU 1.107 seem to indicate that Šapšu mourned over the death of Adammu. Unlike Heracles/Hercules who defeated the serpent,[102]

Fig. 4: Hercules defeats the serpent in the Tree of Life (terracotta plate, second to third century CE; Staatliche Antikensammlungen, Munich, Room 2, Accession Number SL 89, Loeb Collection)

Adammu failed to carry out his assignment to remove the serpent from the Tree of Life. According to the Ugaritic myth, the first humanlike being was a total failure. As a result, humankind would die out. Of all creatures humans were closest to the gods. After all, they descended from a god.

In several places the Hebrew Bible indicates that of all God's creatures humankind is closest to himself, both physically and psychologically (Gen. 1:26-28; 2:7; 3:5; 5:1-2; 9:6; Ps. 8:5-9).[103]

---

[102] See Fig. 4. A never investigated possible explanation of the name of Heracles is 'the One called Erra (Ḥarra)' which would be in accordance with the fact that Ḥôrānu partially restored the tree which had withered under the influence of the poison. On the equation of Ḥôrānu with the Babylonian god Erra see Section 3.3.8 below.

[103] Hurowitz 2009, 263-265, with some earlier literature. There are even traces of the androgynous nature of the earliest humanoids in the Bible. Cf. Section 4.2 and also Sections 3.3.1; 5.4; 5.12; 5.17.

This differs markedly from most Mesopotamian myths about the creation of humans.[104] Although the Bible and these myths agree in attributing to humankind, especially to the king, the power to rule over other creatures,[105] they remain inferior to the highest gods and have to serve them. In this connection it is interesting that KTU 1.107 attributes considerable power to Adammu,

nʿ*l*[*y.g*]m*r*	The champion was exalted,
(3) [yt]n [.ʾa]rṣ.*bdh*.	[they gave the e]arth in his hand.

This high position did not mean that humankind became almighty. As Victor Hurowitz has shown, one Mesopotamian tradition states '[when] the great gods assigned the "spirit" of mankind to the rank of the highest gods, and firmly established their *k.* [*kataduggû*] in order to direct them'.[106] This text seems to imply that the human spirit belongs (or once belonged) to the rank of the highest deities but that the latter used the *kataduggû* to control humankind. According to Hurowitz the Sumerian loanword *kataduggû* 'combines the human and the divine because, although the audible utterance is made by the person, its content and efficacy are determined ultimately by the gods.' (Hurowitz 2009, 271). '*Kataduggû* is given to humankind so that the gods can guide them, but it is humankind itself that does the speaking. The gods may ultimately be the bosses, dictating to the spirit what is said, but humans are their own task masters actually pronouncing the orders.'[107]

Unfortunately the extant text of KTU 1.107 does not indicate if the divine being Adammu actually died, but since it would be useless to invoke the help of so many deities if no cure was expected, it seems likely that the ancestor of humanity lived on somehow, be it not as an immortal celestial anymore.[108] It is the

The objections raised by Noort 2000 are not convincing. Of course זָכָר וּנְקֵבָה means 'male and female' *after* the splitting of the primal human, but P had to resolve the problem of Adam's initially undifferentiated state.

[104] See e.g. Dietrich 2001, 293-301; Hurowitz 2009, 265-268. In both *Atraḫasīs* and *Enūma ēliš* a god is slaughtered whose blood is mingled with clay to produce the first intelligent human being (see Sections 3.3.1; 3.3.5 and 3.3.6). As far as we can see, no such ploy was thought up in Ugarit.

[105] E.g. Gen. 1:26, 28; Ps. 8.

[106] Translation *CAD* (K), 297b.

[107] Hurowitz 2009, 272-273. Cf. Korpel & De Moor 2012, 139-229; 279-304.

[108] Philo of Byblos writes about the gods of the Phoenicians, 'for them some

sun goddess Šapšu who plays a crucial role in this conflict between Ḥôrānu and Adammu.[109]

On the basis of KTU 1.179:8'-9' it may be assumed that Adammu's wife was the goddess Kubaba,[110] but in the preserved portions of KTU 1.107 she is not mentioned. However, in view of the fragmentary state of the tablet this may well be accidental. Line 27' seems to refer to her, although at that moment she too may have been demoted to the human condition already,

(27') [ʾ*at̲t.*]*ṭbt*.n*p*š [ ] a good-natured w[oman.] [ ]

The reading is practically certain.[111] Even if the conjecture [ʾ*at̲t*] is rejected, it is certain that a woman is meant (feminine *ṭbt*) and she can hardly be anybody else than Adammu's partner. Of course one is reminded of Gen. 2:18 'It is not good that the human should be alone; I will make him a helper as his counterpart.' Some scholars have speculated that behind the various strands in the Yahwistic account of Genesis 2–3 an older narrative can be discerned in which only *one* person (Adam) played a role.[112] The Ugaritic story as interpreted here renders this hypothesis unlikely.

The 'good-natured [woman]' appears only just before a big lacuna. There is no indication of any 'original sin' committed by the pair and it is even unlikely that something of this kind happened in between because in the Obverse of tablet KTU 1.107 the poisoning of the whole world has already started. If the 'good-natured woman' was the first truly human female, it is interesting that some Jewish sources differentiate between a first Eve who became the feared female demon Lilith after a row with Adam about their relative positions during sexual intercourse, and a second, truly human Eve who was Adam's faithful partner.[113]

---

gods were mortal and some immortal' (Attridge & Oden 1981, 33.

109 Just as she intervenes in the struggle between the god of death Môtu and the god of life Baʿlu in favor of the latter (KTU 1.6:VI.22-29).

110 See De Moor 2008, 181, 186, and Sections 2.5 and 2.7 below.

111 See our comments KTU 1.107:27' in Appendix 1.

112 See e.g. Westermann 1974, 265-266.

113 Hutter 1999, 521; Teugels 2000, 113-116.

2.4 *The Scene of Action*

The belief that once upon a time a 'paradise' existed, or still exists somewhere, is widespread.[114] For a long time it was thought that certain Sumerian texts pointed to Dilmun in the Persian Gulf as the place where Mesopotamian people thought that paradise had been located. However, this proved to be a misconception.[115] This study will give some fresh indications about its location.

Ḥôrānu dwelt in 'the city of the east' which he left, presumably in a westward direction, to enter the 'vineyard of the great gods', the Canaanite version of Eden where he seems to have turned the Tree of Life into a Tree of Death (KTU 1.100:62). The Arašīḫ mentioned in KTU 1.100: 63-64 is the Hurrian name of the Tigris. Here two major tributaries must have been meant, probably the Great Zab (Akkad. *Zaban elû* 'Upper Zaban'; Arab. Zab al-Kabir) and the Small Zab (Akkad. *Zaban šaplû* 'Lower Zaban'; Arab. Zab al-Saghir), across from the city of Assur on the Tigris.[116]

The location of Ilu's abode is described in the texts of Ugarit as *mbk nhrm* || *qrb ʾapq thmtm*, 'the fountain-head of the two Rivers, || in the middle of the streambed of the two Floods', KTU 1.4:IV.21-22 par.[117] We believe that these two rivers are the Euphrates and the Tigris which both originate in the mountainous region of east Turkey.[118] The two Floods (*thmtm*) are the Upper and the Lower Flood as inexhaustible sources of water (rain and springs) feeding the two great rivers of Mesopotamia.[119] Like the

---

[114] Hartenstein 2009, 36-37. The word 'paradise' is derived from Median **paridaeza* meaning 'enclosure'. Cf. Bremmer 1999, 1-5; Hartenstein 2009, 36; Becking 2011, 4. Since it also became a designation of a vineyard of the gods it is admissable to use it in this context.

[115] Noort 1999, 32-33; Katz 2007; Day 2013, 28. Contrast Hartenstein 2009, 40-41.

[116] Del Monte & Tischler 1978, 524-525; Astour 1987, 18-19, 21.

[117] For a fine discussion of earlier proposals to locate the abode of Ilu see Smith 1994, 225-234. The texts of Ugarit create the impression that Ilu lived far away at the horizon of the habitable cosmos (Korpel 1990, 464), but evidently great distance was defined by the limited perspective of the Ancients.

[118] This idea was mentioned in passing by Day 1994, 38 and Dijkstra 2013, 83.

[119] Compare the description of the headwaters of the river Jordan in Ps. 42:7-8 and see also *CAD* (T), 156.

Tigris, the Euphrates has two major tributaries, Kara Su (Western Euphrates) and Murat Su (Eastern Euphrates). So the two great rivers of Mesopotamia originated in four tributary streams which all descended from the massif of Mt Ararat.[120] Several Mesopotamian iconographic representations show an elderly deity sitting on a mountain from which four streams gush out.[121]

The quest for the location of Eden seems endless.[122] Of course it was thought early on that it must have been located fairly close to the point where the ark of Noah stranded. According to the *Epic of Gilgamesh* the ark grounded on Mt Niṣir or, as others read the name, Mt Nimuš. It should be noted that the Hebrew text of Gen. 8:4 has a plural (or dual),[123] so that any mountains or pair of mountains in Urarṭu qualifies, also Pir Omar Gudrun (2588 m) which some Assyriologists now favor.[124] Possibly the Assyrians moved the name of the Ark-mountain southwards to the more unassailable-looking Pir Omar Gudrun[125]

However, it would seem that the first top to rise up from the waters of the Deluge was more likely the highest peak in the region. Moreover, in some brilliant studies John Day has demonstrated that both the Priestly writer and Berossos must have known certain Babylonian traditions which differed from the ones on which Lambert based his identification with Pir Omar Gudrun and both locate the landing place of the ark in Armenia (Day 2000, 29-32; 2011). One Old Babylonian personal name from Larsa in south Babylonia is hardly sufficient to postulate the existence of a deity Nimuš and the reading Niṣir in the Gilgameš Epic might well rest on folk etymology.[126] According to Gilg. Ep. IX.42 scorpion-men

[120] For later iconographic representations of the four streams see Stone 2008b.

[121] See e.g. Keel 1972, 39, Fig. 42; 40, Fig. 43; 103, Fig. 153; 104, Fig. 153a; 122, Fig. 185.

[122] See e.g. Albright 1922; Scafi 2006. We disagree with Westermann 1974, 294 and Mettinger 2007, 67 who state that it is spurious to ask for a definite location of the garden of Eden.

[123] In Biblical Hebrew dual and plural construct have the same form.

[124] Lambert 1986; Dalley 1991, 133, n. 135; George 2003, 516; Finkel 2014, 281-290.

[125] Finkel 2014, 294. This may have happened under the rule of Ashur-naṣir-apli II (883-859 BCE) who boasted to have conquered Mt Niṣir, cf. Grayson 1976, No. 556 (pp. 128-129).

[126] This is proposed by Streck 1998-2001. The sign MUŠ can also be read ṢIR.

were guarding (*i-na-aṣ-ṣa-ru*) the gate into Mt Māšu. According to IX.45 they guard (*i-na-aṣ-ṣa-ru*) the sun at both sunrise and sunset.[127] This must have been a very ancient Mesopotamian tradition because it is already attested in the Akkad period (2350-2150 BCE).[128] So Niṣir might be still another (Assyrian) name of Māšu, meaning something like 'the Guarded One'.[129] In KTU 1.114:10-11 a 'gatekeeper of the house of Ilu' occurs who in line 20 is described as *ḥby* 'the crawler',[130] and *bʿl qrnm wḏnb*, 'he who possesses horns and a tail', so apparently a scorpion(-man).[131] He prevents the dead-drunk Ilu from sliding down into the earth while ʿAnatu and ʿAṯtartu go out to collect herbs that will help the inebriated god to regain consciousness (KTU 1.114:21-22). In KTU 1.3:V.11-12 the dwelling of Ilu is described as containing 'seven chambers' || 'the entrances of eight lockable rooms' which would seem to indicate that Ilu lived in seclusion.[132]

It is interesting to note that according to some Jewish Hekhalot traditions God resided not in heaven, but was sitting on a cherub under the Tree of Life in the terrestial garden of Eden after the expulsion of Adam and Eve.[133] Actually the two traditions need not be in conflict because the original Canaanite traditions about Ilu's abode situate it on a high mountain at the edge of the world where heaven and earth meet (see Section 2.1). A similar location is attributed to the Elysean Fields where privileged dead were thought to stay (Homer, *Odyssey* IV.561-569).

The mountains of Ararat are situated in East Turkey (earlier West Armenia) in the region that was once called Urarṭu, and

---

127 On an Assyrian seal the scorpion-men are depicted to the left and right of the gate to the Netherworld from which the sun rises. See Keel 1972, 24, Fig. 24; Keel & Schroer 2002, 206, Fig. 155.

128 Cf. Keel & Schroer 2002, 78, Fig. 50. The two gatekeepers are horned, but lack tails here.

129 Assyrian *niṣirtu* '(guarded) treasure', *ašar niṣirti* 'hidden place, secluded place', cf. Sargon 8, 220 (Mayer 2013, 118-119).

130 Cf. Standard Arabic, Palestinian Arabic, Amharic, Mehri, Soqoṭri, Jibbāli.

131 For 'horns' as a term for the pincers of a scorpion see *CAD* (Q), 137. For its tail, *CAD* (Z), 101a. Nys 2013 offers excellent Assyrian glyptic representations of these benevolent hybrids.

132 According to Philo of Byblos Kronos (= El) would have surrounded his own dwelling with a wall (Attridge & Oden 1981, 50-51).

133 Gruenwald 2014, 89-90, 237.

this is most likely the region where Ilu dwelt on a mountain range (Ugaritic *ḫršn*, a Babylonian loanword).[134] This location of the garden of Eden was suspected by several scholars.[135]

Mt Ararat is a dormant, snow-capped volcanic dome that is the highest peak in Turkey (5.137 m).[136] Nowadays Mt Ararat is called Agrĭ Dağı 'Heavy Mountain' in Ottoman Turkish. In Armenian it is *Masis*. Next to the main mountain there rises another volcanic peak, Turkish Küçük Ağrı Dağı, 'Little Ararat' (3.925 m).[137] Actually the two mountains are part of a long chain of volcanoes many of which bear names which testify to their once fiery nature, e.g. Tendürük Daği 'Brazier Mountain', which also has two main craters: Cehennem Tepe (3.542 m)[138] and Tendürük Gölü 'Brazier Lake' (3.301 m).[139] The main tributary of the Euphrates, the river Murat Su, rises in this region.

The mountain was visible from the western part of Assyria. In Akkadian the corresponding name of these twin mountains is *māšu* 'twin' and there is a corresponding pair of mountains in the east where the sun rises.[140] It is significant that in Hittite mythology the giant Upelluri was described as 'the dreaming god', an apt description of a dormant volcano. He shares this epithet with Elkunirsa, 'El the Creator of the Earth'.[141] This epithet also fits Ilu, the

---

[134] KTU 1.1:II.23; III.11-12. Cf. Lipiński 1971, 41-58; Del Olmo Lete & Sanmartín 2003, 408; Singer 2007. The God of Israel is often called אֵל שַׁדַּי 'El the Mountain dweller', cf. Day 2000, 32-34 (with earlier literature) and *CAD* (Š) 1, 43. He seems to occur in the heavily damaged Ugaritic text KTU 1.108:12 which might perhaps be read [*wyšt.ym. m*]*dd.*ʾ*il.šdy ṣd mlk* [13][ʾ*ab.šnm*] '[And may drink Yammu, the belo]ved of Ilu Šadday, the hunter of [the Father of Šanāmu (or: of Years)']. Yammu is a recipient of sacrifices in KTU 1.39:13 and 1.46:6 (par.).

[135] E.g. Wenham 1987, 66; Noort 1999, 30-31; Day 2000, 29-32; 2011.

[136] The height stated in the sources we consulted varies a little. It is located at 39° 42.113'N 44°, 17.899'E. See Mittmann & Schmitt 2001, Map A.I.1.

[137] The two volcanoes are easy to find on the Internet. For an 1862 CE painting of the two cones see Wartke 1993, Fig. 11.

[138] In Turkish Cehennem is also the name of the Valley of Hinnom near Jerusalem, the fiery Gehenna.

[139] Blumenthal & Van der Kaaden 1964, 10-13. The water of the crater lake is still lukewarm.
See the surprisingly accurate descriptions of the volcanic areas in which God as well as the Devil were supposed to dwell in 1 En. 22:2-4 (Section 5.3 below) and *Apocalypse of Abraham* 15:5-7 (Section 5.12 below).

[140] Cf. George 2003, 864-865; Ravn 1960, 25, Fig. 19; Keel 1972, 18, Fig. 9.

highest god of the Ugaritic pantheon, a dreamer too (KTU 1.6:III). The circumstance that Ullikummi with whom Upelluri supported the firmament was a basalt column confirms the volcanic nature of Upelluri, Ullikummi, Elkunirsa and eventually Ilu.

In Ugarit the mountain of Ilu was also called *ǵr ks* (KTU 1.1:III. 12).[142] With regard to this designation Ugaritologists have thought up many different but philologically unconvincing solutions,[143] but the obvious rendering is: 'the mountain of the Cup', the 'Cup' being a metaphor for a crater.[144]

Fig. 5: Aerial photograph of Mt Ararat (the mountain of Ilu) and to the right of it Little Ararat as seen from the Turkish side (photograph Vardart78.deviantart.com).

141 Dijkstra 2013. On the divine prerogative of undisturbed sleep see also Batto 2013, 139-157. However, deities were able to remain awake while sleeping. Philo of Byblos tells us this of Kronos (= Ilu/El). Cf. Attridge & Oden 1981, 58-59 as well as Korpel & De Moor 2012, 258-261.

142 Another name of Ilu's mountain was *ǵr ll*, 'Mountain of the Night'. For a lucid treatment of this name see Lipiński 1971, certainly to be preferred over Niehr's speculative argument (Niehr 2001).

143 See Del Olmo Lete & Sanmartín 2003, 408.

144 The Greek word κρατήρ designates both 'a bowl in which wine was mixed with water' and the 'mouth of a volcanoe' (Liddell & Scott 1968, 991).

Fig. 6: Gold-plated statuette of Ilu from Ugarit. He raises his right hand in blessing. According to textual and other iconographic evidence his left hand must have grasped a beaker (Damascus Museum, Inv. 3573).

In Ugarit Mt Ararat was apparently identified with the white-haired god Ilu,[145] and it is understandable that the steep crater of Little Ararat was seen as a gigantic cup in Ilu's hand, the latter also of divine proportions. In several iconographic representations Ilu is depicted with his right hand raised in blessing and a cup of wine in his left hand[146] and KTU 1.15:II.16-21 confirms this.

---

[145] Just as Enlil is already called 'the Great Mountain' in many Sumerian compositions and as Mt Zaphon was identified with its owner Baʿlu, De Moor 1987, 234, n. 203. See for another beautiful 3D picture of the complex: http://commons.wikimedia.org/wiki/File:Ararat_3D_version_2.gif.

[146] See e.g. Keel 1972, 186-187; Cornelius & Niehr 2004, 44-45. Sometimes two streams (Euphrates and Tigris?) flow from this vessel and two bands of swirling water suggest a connection with the Upper and Lower Floods. Cf.

The two mountains are depicted on some ancient Near Eastern cylinder seals as the place where the sun rises or goes down (Fig. 7).

Fig. 7: Cylinder seal (British Museum), Old Akkadian period (*c.* 2300-2200 BCE). The sun god is rising from the twin mountains in the east, brandishing the saw he uses to open the earth. Two attendants hold open the doors for him. (cf. Collon 1982, 172, Pl. XXV).

Possibly the Ancients attributed the melting of rocks around the craters to the great heat of the sun.[147]

Usually the sun god on the next seal (Fig. 8) is also interpreted as rising from the twin mountains, but in our opinion it is just as well possible that here he is going down into the earth. The god putting his foot on the mountain is the wise creator-god Enki/Ea. Two streams full of fish flow from his shoulders. The winged goddess on the other mound is Inanna/Ishtar, goddess of love and war. A tree grows from her mound and she reaches a bunch of dates down to the sun god before he goes on his way.

Uehlinger 1992, esp. Fig. 2-5. Obviously, in Mesopotamia the enthroned god must have been the creator god Enki/Ea or his son Marduk who became the creator of the cosmos.

[147] In this connection an inscription from Kuntillet ʿAjrud is interesting, *bzrḥ* ... *ʾl wymsn hrm* 'when El shines forth ..., the mountains melt' (Renz 1995, 59, 62, 64). El is represented here as the rising sun (Gen. 32:22; Exod. 22:2; Judg. 9:33, etc.). See also Deut. 33:2; Ps. 68:8-9; Mic. 1:3-4; Hab. 3:8. Also the Sinai/Horeb traditions in the Bible connect the theophany with volcanic phenomena. This is possible because the eastern mountain chain bordering the Great Rift Valley continues through Edom and beyond along the Gulf of Aqaba. There are still several volcanic vents in the area formerly called Edom, some of them more than 1500 m high (Baly 1974, 235). The volcanic nature of the Yahwistic theophany descriptions has been recognized by many scholars, lately by Dunn 2014. However, Dunn's geological information is defective, as a phrase like this demonstrates, 'Canaan–almost completely devoid of volcanic mountains' (424).

Fig. 8: Cylinder seal (British Museum), Old Akkadian period (*c.* 2300-2200 BCE. The sun god seems to descend between the twin mountains in the west.

These very old seals demonstrate that the concept of the twin mountains and the rising/descending sun[148] must have originated very early. It seems that the light beams issuing from the shoulders of the sun god are fading while he is descending into the earth for his nightly journey.

Fig. 9: The two cones of Mt Ararat as seen from Armenia, with the vineyards of the Khor Virap Monastery in the foreground.
Grayscale reproduction of the color photograph by © Niko Lipsanen 2009.
License under Creative Commons CC BY 4.0.

[148] As in the rest of Mesopotamia the sun is male on these seals, whereas in Anatolia and Ugarit the sun was female.

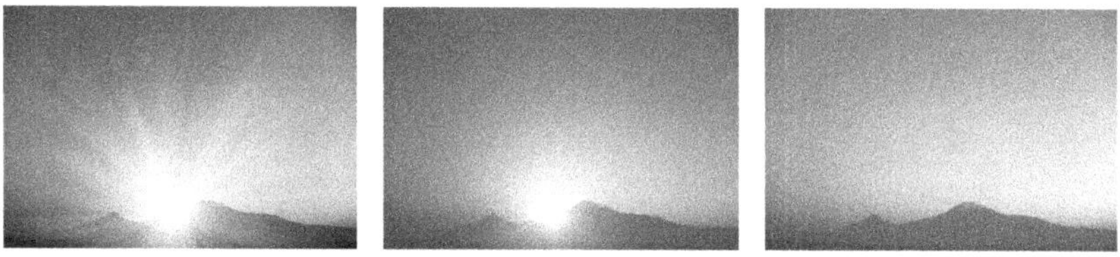

Fig. 10: Sunset between the twin mountains in the west, seen from Armenia (from color photographs by Mr Arakelian/Shutterstock.com).

One can imagine that this impressive sight gave rise to the assumption that the hot sun disappeared in the earth between these two high mountains.

The two volcanic cones may be dormant nowadays, but the Armenians know full well that they once spitted fire. One of their most popular festive dishes is the *Ararat Pilaf*, two mounds of rice or bulgur (burghul),[149] surrounded by fruits. The apples are hollowed out, the hollows lined with aluminium foil and filled with warmed brandy. 'On a large oval serving platter mound the hot pilaf in two separate peaks, one large, placed on the right, and one small, placed on the left, to resemble Mount Ararat.' Then the brandy is ignited to imitate a volcanic eruption (Uvezian 1974, 223-224). On the dust cover of the book by Sonia Uvezian a fine color photograph of this spectacular dish is found (Fig. 11).[150] A stele from Ugarit shows Ilu enthroned and raising his left hand to a god or king standing before him, not in blessing as some have proposed, but beckoning, welcoming him (Fig. 12).[151] In his right hand Ilu has a bowl with a peculiar triangular shape on or in it, with a lower triangle partly obscuring a higher one.[152] The vessel in Ilu's hand is hardly a drinking bowl. So the two triangles pointing upward from it must be food. Could this be an early example of the Ararat Pilaf? It may seem an outrageous suggestion, but then few traditions are as tenacious as cooking lore. For El acting as a gracious host, see KTU 1.5:IV (De Moor 1987, 76) as well as Isa. 25:6; 55:1-3; Ps. 23:5.

---

[149] Cereal based foods similar to bulgur (burghul) did exist already in Antiquity, cf. Curtis 2001,196, with further references.

[150] Uvezian 1974. Here we reproduce it in grayscale. We owe this valuable information to Janny de Moor, culinary writer.

[151] The fingers are bent inwards, the thumb outwards (cf. Caquot & Sznycer 1980, 23). Other statuettes depict Ilu blessing with his right hand.

[152] Keel 1972, 186, Fig. 283; Cornelius & Niehr 2004, 45, Fig. 68.

Fig. 11: Ararat Pilaf flambé
(grayscale reproduction from the dust cover of Uvezian 1974).

Fig. 12: Stele from Ugarit depicting Ilu enthroned (after Keel 1972, 186, Fig. 283). The god is beckoning someone standing before him to come closer. He is offering him a bowl of food (Ararat Pilaf?).

Usually scholars assumed the figure standing before Ilu to be a human king, because he is standing whereas Ilu is enthroned, he is also depicted smaller than Ilu and comes with an offering of a liquid (wine?) in his left hand. However, he has a serpent-scepter in his right hand,[153] and therefore he might well be Ḥôrānu, the master of snakes, coming to offer his subjection to Ilu (see Section 2.9 below). Ilu magnanimously offers him food in return, a covenantal gesture.[154] So if the figure standing before Ilu is indeed Ḥôrānu, Ilu shows himself a compassionate and merciful god who forgives a repentant rebel.[155]

So the the entrance to the Netherworld was located between the two mountains where the sun went down. In KTU 1.4:VII.49

[153] This was cleverly observed by Dijkstra 2006, 31 on the basis of many other such staffs in Antiquity. Note that the material of the stele is serpentine, the snakeskin stone.
[154] Cf. e.g. Viberg 1992, 70-76.
[155] Cf. Korpel 1990, 165-166.

this entrance is described as the *npš* || *gngn* ('throat' || 'gullet') of the god of Death Môtu.[156] The most elaborate description of this entrance in the west is found in KTU 1.4:VIII.1-9,

[1] ʾid*k.*ʾal.*ttn.pnm*	Then you must head straight
[2] *ʿm.ġr.trġzz*	for the mountain *Trġzz*,
[3] *ʿm.ġr.ṯrmg*	for the mountain *Ṯrmg*,[157]
[4] *ʿm.tlm.ġṣr.ʾarṣ*	for the two mounds at the edge of the earth.
[5] *šʾa.ġr.ʿl.ydm*	Lift up a mountain with your hands,[158]
[6] *ḫlb.lẓr.rḥtm*	a forested hill with your palms
[7] *wrd.bt ḫpṯt* [8] *ʾarṣ.*	and descend into the House of Freedom[159] of the earth,
tspr.by[9] r*dm.ʾarṣ*	be counted among those who went down into the earth.[160]

The standard version of the Babylonian *Epic of Gilgameš* describes the hero's arrival at the twin mountain Māšu,[161]

> Gilgameš Epic IX.37-41
> The name of the mountain is Māšu. When he arrived at the mountain Māšu which daily guards sunr[ise and sundown],[162] whose tops support the firmament of heaven, whose flanks reach down into the Netherworld ...[163]

Gilg. Ep. IX.170 and X.79-86 suggest that the fearless hero Gilgameš traveled through the dark Netherworld from west to east, keeping well ahead from the burning sun. After a long journey

---

156 In KTU 1.5:V.13 the pair is *npš* || *knkn*. Actually the word for 'gullet' signifies a pipe or tunnel.

157 The vocalisation of these non-Semitic names is unknown. For various proposals see Smith & Pitard 2009, 711-712, and p. 42 below.

158 Divine strength!

159 Euphemism for the Netherworld which in reality was a 'land of no return' (cf. 2 Sam. 22:5f.; Ps. 116:3; Job 10:21; 16:22 and for more parallels De Moor 1971, 185-186; Smith & Pitard 2009, 714-716). In 2 Kgs 15:5 'house of freedom' is a euphemism for a place of total confinement, a leper house. In Ps. 88:6 we read 'among the dead I am 'free' '.

160 Cf. Ps. 88:5.

161 Akkadian *māšu* means 'twin' and was also used as a designation of the sun god, cf. *CAD* (M) 1, 401-403.

162 Here we follow Parpola 1997, 101, whose restoration is supported by line 45.

163 Our rendering.

through the Netherworld he arrives at a beautiful garden where 'the trees of the gods' grow, laden with bunches of grapes and other fruit, but all made of precious stones. Among them is a carob tree (Gilg. Ep. IX.172-193). The description of the enormous size of Mt Māšu suggests that it is Mt Ararat and so the garden must have been located in the *west* as seen from Mesopotamia. Possibly the scribe confused the eastern and western entrances of the Nether World (so Tigay 1982, 35). In any case the phrase 'which daily guards sunr[ise and sundown]' fits Mt Ararat well. It depends on one's point of view whether one sees the sun go down between the twin mountains (from Armenia) or go up (from Turkey).[164]

Finally Gilgameš arrives at the place where Ūta-napišti lives, the hero who survived the Deluge in the ark and was awarded eternal life by the gods (Gilg. Ep. X-XI). It is logical to assume that also Ūta-napišti stranded close to the Ararat. Thc Babylonian story of the Deluge resembles the biblical narrative in so many respects that it must be assumed that the biblical account is dependent on the much older Mesopotamian traditions. This is so well known that it is not necessary to spell it out yet another time here. Gilgameš asks Ūta-napišti to share the secret of eternal life with him, but being totally exhausted, Gilgameš fails to pass the test Ūta-napišti proposes: he is unable to stay awake for a whole week (Gilg. Ep. XI.207-241). As a consolation prize Ūta-napišti discloses to Gilgameš that he might collect a rejuvenating plant at the bottom of a fountain in a sea.[165] Of course the hero succeeds in obtaining this thorny plant, but on the way back to the inhabited world a snake steals it from him and sloughs its skin, proof of the renewal of its life.[166] It is, therefore, not without significance

---

[164] For the latter see the following description of a mountaineer climbing the mountain from Doğubayazit in Turkey:
'So what is it that wakes me at 5.30 when all still is dark and cold? The skies clear, coffee in hand I ride east towards sunrise, towards the Iranian border. Soon the first rays touch the snowy tops of Ararat. Then 6.09 or a bit later the orange ball goes up to the right of Lesser Ararat, Ararats shorter brother.'
(http://www.thisfabtrek.com/journey/asia/turkey/20091017-van.php).

[165] Possibly 'the Sea of Nairi', Lake Urmia (see below).

[166] Gilg. Ep. XI.278-309. Also Philo Byblius knew a tradition that in this way snakes rejuvenated themselves infinitely. Cf. Attridge & Oden 1981, 64-65.

that in the Ugaritic myth about the death of Adammu this motif reappears.[167]

In Armenia the name of Mt Ararat is Masis which would seem to be directly derived from the Akkadian *māšu*. The description in the Gilgameš Epic matches the account Shalmaneser III (859-824 BCE) gives of his campaigns to Urarṭu. He visited 'the Sea of Nairi', also called 'the Sea of the Setting Sun' (Lake Urmia) several times (Yamada 2000, 275-281, 373) and explored the sources of Euphrates and Tigris (Yamada 2000, 281-284). Sargon II's description of Mt Simirria during his campaign in Urarṭu (714 BCE) seems to be inspired by Shalmaneser's account,

> Sargon 8, lines 18-22 (Mayer 2013, 98-99)
> Mt Simirria, an enormous peak which rose like a sharpened lance head[168] and whose summit was higher than (other) mountains, the abode of Bēlet-Ilī,[169] whose two tops support the heaven, whose foundation reaches down into the Netherworld, on which as on the back of a fish there is no passageway and the climb of which is extremely difficult, into whose flanks deep gulleys are cut and which is terrible to behold, which is not good to ascend with chariots (and) onrushing horses, very difficult to traverse even by foot soldiers ...[170]

Could Mt Simirria be the Ugaritic mountain *Ṯrmg*, one of the mountains at the entrance of the Netherworld? Mangling of foreign names is a universal phenomenon. However that may be, we seriously doubt that either Gilgameš or Sargon II ever climbed the Twin Mountains.[171] By claiming this exploit they became unassailable heroes, close to divine status. Nevertheless other elements in Sargon's account[172] of his eighth campaign seem fairly reliable,

[167] Cf. Section 2.5. In our opinion Lambert 1985b, 440, over-emphasizes the difference between a rejuvenating plant and a rejuvenating tree.

[168] Apparently a traditonal exaggeration derived from Ashur-anṣir-apli II's account of his conquest of Mt Niṣir, cf. Grayson 1976, No. 557 (p. 129).

[169] 'Mistress of the gods', in this connection possibly ʿAnatu who dwelt on Mt Inbabe, the 'mountain of the deities'.

[170] Our rendering.

[171] In any case the mural showing Sargon's ascent on horseback (Wartke 1993, Fig. 57; Mayer 2013, 63, Fig. 1) as well as his own account (Mayer 2013, lines 18-28) can hardly be trusted. The similar description of the mountain Uauš in line 96-102 shows that Sargon's scribe used standard phrases.

for example, his narrative about the extremely fertile valleys at the feet of the Urarṭaean mountains.[173]

Obviously taking the mythological descriptions of Ilu's abode on the twin mountains seriously is as spurious as looking for traces of the ark on Mt Ararat. Just as the magnificent 'palace' of the Ugaritic weather god Baʿlu on Mt Ṣapānu in reality was nothing but a gold-edged mass of clouds (Korpel 1990, 82-83), Ilu's dwelling was a figment of imagination. In view of the gigantic size of its inhabitants (Section 2.8) the Canaanite version of 'paradise' may well have been imagined as covering the entire upper reaches of the Euphrates and Tigris. It may certainly be assumed that the garden of Eden was patterned after a spacious temple garden[174] or a palace garden[175] but its enormous mythical proportions should be taken into account.

The designation 'vineyard of the great gods' implies viticulture. The earliest evidence of viticulture is found in the northern Zagros range of western Iran (Transcaucasia), fairly close to Mt Ararat. It is generally assumed that the consumption of 'wine', a very ancient 'Kulturwort', spread from there over the entire ancient world.[176] So there is a grain of truth in both the Ugaritic tradition about 'the vineyard of the great gods' (*krm ʾilm rbm*, KTU 1.107:2) and the Hebrew story about Noah's vineyard (Gen. 9:20-21). Was Ilu regarded as the inventor of wine?

Unfortunately, the extant texts of KTU 1.100 and 1.107 do not indicate whether there was, or had been, a Tree of Life in 'the vineyard of the great gods', but it seems likely that as a result of the snake's poison the Tree of Life in the Ugaritic version of Eden had become a 'Tree of Death', *ʿṣ.mt*.[177] The Tree of Death was a

---

172 Even though there is no consensus with regard to the route Sargon took, cf. e.g. Rigg 1942; Muscarella 1986; Zimansky 1990; Jakubiak 2004; Mayer 2013, 60-73.

173 Full granaries (lines 219, 262, 274, 295), hidden wine cellars (line 220), splendid orchards and vineyards (lines 223, 225, 265, 276, 296, 303, 327), tall trees (lines 226, 227, 266-267, 276, 303, 327, 329). He also captured much gold in Urarṭu (lines 352, 356, 358, 369-378, 380-381, 386, 406). Armenia and Kurdistan do have significant deposits of copper and gold.

174 Dietrich 2001; Keel & Schroer 2002, 88-91; Klopper 2006.

175 Cf. Gordon 2013, 18-19 with bibliography.

176 Unwin 1996, 80; Curtis 2001, 186-187; McGovern 2007; Barnard 2010.

177 KTU 1.100:65 and Gen. 2:17; 3:3-4, 19.

hybrid, partly a juniper, partly a vine,[178] partly a date palm.[179] The juniper is an evergreen tree or shrub which cannot grow in the desert (Jer. 48:6). So the tree which Ḥôrānu uprooted and trimmed according to KTU 1.100:64-67 was still partly recognizable as the former Tree of Life.[180]

It is more difficult to identify the eastern twin mountains where the sun was supposed to rise. Ḥôrānu dwelt in 'the city of the east' (KTU 1.100:62). Since the twin mountains in the west were volcanoes the craters of which were thought to give access to the subterranean route of the sun from west to east and taking into account Ḥôrānu's fiery nature (cf. Section 2.6) it stands to reason that the eastern entrance to the Netherworld has to be sought in a volcanic region in Syria. The obvious candidate then is the Ğebel el-Drūz. The highest cone there is Tell Qeni (1.803 m)[181] and possibly Tell Qlēb[182] (1.608 m) as its twin. Also the Syrian volcanoes are all extinct, are much lower than the Ararat and are located on the fringe of the great Syrian desert. So it may be surmised that Ilu banished Ḥôrānu from his lofty mountain and threw him down into this desolate place. In KTU 1.107:28'-31' the sun goddess Šapšu sends a good genius to this eastern entrance of the Netherworld to convince Ḥôrānu to bind the serpent (as manifestation of himself) and remove its poison that is paralyzing life on earth, thus clearing the way for a recreated humanity.

2.5 *Immortality by Procreation*

At the end of KTU 1.100 there is a section which describes a wedding ritual. Bride, groom and an officiant (cantor) take turns in reciting a few phrases from love poems. The speakers remain unidentified, as was the custom in ancient Near Eastern love poetry.[183]

---

[178] Like the tree of *mt wšr*, 'Death-and-the-Prince (Ḥôrānu)' described in KTU 1.23:8-11.

[179] On many ancient oriental seals the Tree of Life is depicted as a date palm. For the various shapes chosen by the artists see Merrillees 2005, 135-136.

[180] Cf. Appendix 2.

[181] Kimberly 2010, 447. According to Doergers 1860, 408: Tell el-Gene.

[182] Also spelt Qleib.

[183] Meier 1992, 38 on Song of Songs: 'Since there is no stage external to the actors' words, the reader relies entirely upon the dialogue itself to indi-

(Ritual:)

(Groom:)

(70) *bʿdh.bhtm.mnt.*	‘‘Behind her the mansion’ is my incantation.’[184]

(Officiant:)

bʿdh.bhtm.sgrt	‘Behind her the mansion she closed,
(71) *bʿdh.ʿdbt.ṯlṯ.*	behind her she let down the bronze (bolt).’[185]

(Groom:)

ptḥ.bt.mnt	‘‘Open up the house’ is my incantation.’

(Officiant:)

(72) *ptḥ.bt. wʾubʾa(!).*	‘Open up the house, that I may enter,[186]
hkl.wʾištql	the palace that I may come in.’

(Bride:)

(73) *tn.km.<mhry.> nḥšm.*	‘Give a serpent as <my bridal gift.>,[187]
yḥr.tn.km (74) *mhry.*	give a lizard as my bridal gift,[188]

---

cate change of speakers and individuals spoken to.’; Korpel 2003, 90: ‘A striking resemblance between all these ancient love lyrics is the lack of any introduction of the direct speech of the lovers so that it is often hard to identify who is who.’

There is no reason at all to surmise that Ḥôrānu wedded the ‘Mare’ *pḥlt*, as Pardee 1997 conjectures. Whereas he admits that the previous instances of *mnt* must be interpreted as ‘my incantation’ (cf. *mnty* in line 9), here the pronominal suffix would suddenly be absent.

184 The groom quotes the first few words of the songs he wants the officiant to recite on his behalf.

185 Hardly the complete song. Probably it was the beginning of a song about the well-known theme of the locked-out lover. See e.g. Kitchen 1999, 339; Sefati 1998, 291:11; Foster 2005, 945; Song of Songs 2:9b; 5:2-6.

186 The eroticism of the metaphor is evident.

187 The connection between snake charming and the solemnization of marriage has a very interesting parallel in Egypt, cf. Drioton 1957, 60-61. In Babylonia pregnant women used to wear amulets of the demon Pazuzu to protect them against the child-robbing demon Lamaštu. The penis of Pazazu is a serpent. He is often depicted next to the sacred date palm. Cf. Heeßel 2004, Abb. 2, 21, 30. Of course the snake is understood as a phallic symbol in many other cultures, but in this particular context a Sumerian parallel furnishes conclusive evidence: ‘he lifted his penis, brought the bridal gift’, cf. Kramer 1969, 53; Vanstiphout 1997, 120-121; Lisman 2013, 159.

188 The solution proposed by Dietrich and Loretz 2009b, 80-82, involves one redundant word and two omissions which seems a bit too much. What clinches the matter is the circumstance that the Arabic cognate *waḫr* or

wbn.bṯn.ʾitnny	yes, a son of the Dragon as a present for my love.'[189]

(Groom:)

(75) *ytt.nḥšm.mhrk.*	'I give a serpent as your bridal gift,
bn bṯn (76) *ʾitnnk*	a son of the Dragon as a present for your love.'

A golden pendant from Ugarit shows the goddess of love (ʿAnatu or ʿAṯtartu) with serpents issuing from her flimsy waistcloth (Fig. 13 on next page). The liturgical passage quoted renders it likely that the real purpose of KTU 1.107 and 1.100 was to provide the mythological background of a marriage ceremony. The serpent is a phallic symbol expressing the double nature of the procreation process: dangerous to the woman who in Antiquity often died in pregnancy or childbirth (Stol 2000, 27-48), but at the same time indispensable to the survival of the human race. Throughout the ancient Near East this was one of the most pressing concerns of humanity.[190]

This passage provides us with a clue to KTU 1.100:1 *ʾum.pḥl.pḥlt* 'The Mother of the male breeding animal (and) the female breeding animal'. Like Akkadian *puḫālu*, Ugaritic *pḥl* designates any kind of breeding animal, also a ram.[191] Manfried Dietrich and Oswald Loretz were absolutely right when they observed that the circumstance that Ugaritic *pḥl* in the texts published thus far mostly designates a he-ass does not imply that it is always that kind of species. Initially they opted for the translation 'männliches Zuchttier'.[192]

---

waḥrah is a *venomous* reptile (Kazimirski 1860, t. 2, 1499). Snakes and lizards were regarded as animals belonging to the same class, cf. Buchholz 2000, Abb. 18c; Pientka-Hinz 2009, 206-207.

189 The Dragon is probably a designation of Ḥôrānu here. Cf. אֶתְנַן as a present for love, Deut. 23:19; Hos. 2:14; Mic. 1:7.

190 See e.g, Beckman 1983. Interestingly, Tobias' prayer before the consummation of his marriage with Sarah in the Book of Tobit 8:6 starts with a reference to the creation of Adam and Eve.

191 *CAD* (P), 479b-480b.

192 Dietrich 2004, 19; Dietrich & Loretz 2008, 128-129. Unfortunately they returned to stallion ('Hengst') and mare ('Stute') later on (Dietrich & Loretz 2009b, 91; Loretz 2011, 61-63). The insertion of the copula '(und)' in their rendering of *ʾum pḥl pḥlt* "'Mutter' / 'Herrin' von Hengst (und) Stute' is justified with pairs of deities.

Fig. 13: Golden pendant from Ugarit (Musée du Louvre, AO 14714)
(For a color picture see Cornelius & Niehr 2004, 2).

It has gone unnoticed that also in KTU 1.107 the bride seems to be exhorted to accept intercourse,

(46′) [tqb(?)]*l.bl tbḥ*[*l*]l	[May you be recepti]ve, may you arouse the male,
tzd.ʿrq.dm	may you be hot, exude blood!
(47′) [ ]	[ ]
ʿ*r*q[. n]*pš*	exude life![193]

When the Sumerian creator Enki was aroused on seeing the rivers Euphrates and Tigris he was compared to an impatient bull who lifted his penis, his bridal gift.[194] In one of the texts describing the erotic encounters between Inanna and Dumuzi the latter is compared to a he-goat covering the female (Bottéro & Kramer 2011, 105). The imagery of the man as a lusty animal balances the representation of the woman as a female animal in heat.[195]

[193] See for philological comments Appendix 1.
[194] Cf. Section 2.5.

In Arabic *faḥl* can even designate a husband.[196] This is another argument against an exclusively animalistic interpretation.

Fig. 14 Renewal of life by sexual intercourse. Cylinder seal from Cyprus, *ca.* 1500 BCE (after Keel & Schroer 2002, 95, Fig. 77). In our opinion the big scorpion under the bed symbolizes the threat of death to life on earth.

In view of the high rank of Kubaba and Adammu in the list of deities KTU 1.179:9' where just as the two breeding animals in KTU 1.100:1 they precede even *šmm wthm* 'Heaven and Flood' it is possible that *pḥlt* || *pḥl* equals the pair Kubaba || Adammu. If so, the original pair of humanoids is presented here as a primeval example to bride and groom.

The vital role of women in the eternal line of sexual reproduction explains the numerous images of goddesses subduing snakes, also in Ugarit itself.[197] In the serpent spells of the Pyramid Texts the serpent Rīr-Rīr is called *im ḥw*. Steiner interprets this as 'Mother of the Serpents', but Becking proposes 'Mother of life/ Mother of the living' (Becking 2012, 216) which comes fairly close to Gen. 3:20: 'The man called his wife's name Eve (*Ḥawwāh*), because she was the mother of all living.' The idea that women defeated Death by bearing children is also attested in Sumer (Bottéro & Kramer 2011, 53). And of course, the subduing of the serpent

[195] See for this imagery e.g. Jer. 5:8; Ezek. 23:20; Song 1:9.
[196] Fagnan 1923, 130.
[197] See e.g. Buchholz 2000, Abb, 2a, 2b, 3a, 13a, c, d, 15a, b, 22; Yon 2006, Pl. 16, 58a.

is a condition to fertility and child-bearing according to Gen. 3:15 (see also Gen. 1:28).

In view of the role of Šapšu as the life-preserving goddess in KTU 1.107 and 1.100[198] it seems admissable to see her as the speaker of KTU 1.107:19ff. As in line 9, her direct speech is introduced by almost the same formula as the one used to introduce her intervention in favor of the god of life Baʿlu in KTU 1.6:VI.22-23. The circumstance that she is shrieking this time indicates that she is mourning over his impending death. She seems to promise help in KTU 1.107:19-23 and to mourn about Adammu's impending death.

After a long lacuna it seems that in KTU 1.107:27' Adammu gets a wife. Subsequently the protective genius Šēdu is summoned to go to the Netherworld, apparently to convince Ḥôrānu to release his deadly grip on the cosmos (KTU 1.107:28'-31').[199]

It is likely that the Kôṯarātu, the Ugaritic goddesses overseeing conception and childbirth, were involved in the struggle against the primordial serpent endangering life on earth (Herrmann 1974). If Ḥôrānu is identical to Hēlēl who fell from heaven according to Isa. 14:12,[200] it may be significant that the Kôṯarātu are said to be the daughters of Hilālu.[201] Elsewhere in Ugarit they are described as *snnt* 'swallows'. The shape of these birds in flight resembles a crescent and the name of Hilālu actually means 'crescent' in Arabic (Kazimirski 1860, t. 2, 1435). They symbolise the temporary victory of life over death by the process of childbirth.

However, in KTU 1.24:42 *Hll* is called *bʿl gml* 'the lord of the crooked staff (= crescent moon)'.[202] This indicates that he himself is not the crescent moon, but controls it, so *hll* in the sense of 'crescent' is a case of metonomy, the part designating the whole. It is far more likely that *hll* is a blazing star, probably Aldebaran.[203]

---

[198] In a Ugaritic incantation we read *ql.špš.ḥw*, 'voice of Šapšu, bring to life!' (KTU 1.82:6).

[199] See below Section 2.9 on the relation between Ḥôrānu and Šēdu.

[200] For the connection between Satan and the moon during the fall of Adam see 3 Baruch 9:7. Cf, Section 5.16 below.

[201] KTU 1.24:40-42; 1.17:II.26-42; KTU 1.179.

[202] In Palestinian Arabic *hilāl* also designates a long, curved knife with which branches of palms are cut off (Denizeau 1960, 542).

[203] The brightest star of the Hyades, α of Taurus (Lane, 847). In several Semitic

Especially if such a blazing star seemed to stand 'in' the crescent moon this was seen as an important omen.[204] The circumstance that Aldebaran is sometimes visibly occulted may well have given rise to the myth that he 'fell from heaven'.

Fig. 15: The bright star Aldebaran reappearing after occultation by the moon (public domain).

When Aldebaran reappears after occultation by the crescent moon at dawn the well-known symbolism of the Ottoman-Turkish flag becomes visible. Thus the customary rendering of *hll*/הֵילֵל by 'Morning Star' may be maintained. Its identification with the planet Venus, however, must be abandoned as far as the Canaanite traditions are concerned.

We can only guess why Ḥôrānu/Hilālu fathered the Kôṯarātu-midwives, but it might be to ensure that procreation would never stop again.[205] In a later Phoenician inscription they have become seven concubines of Ḥaurān in an incantation that was still meant

---

languages the verb *hll* means 'to shine, blaze'. Cf. Job 31:26. In Thamudic inscriptions *hll* is the name of a god (see Section 2.2).
Shipp 2002, 77-79 and Van der Sluijs 2009 propose different astronomical solutions, but their arguments are rather speculative and do not take into account that only Aldebaran is occulted by the moon. On the speculative nature of Shipp's article see Clements 2007.

[204] *CAD* (Š) 3, 229a. The star in the crescent is a very ancient symbol, cf. Keel 1998, Figs. 14, 49a, 90. A very fine example of this astral symbolism has been found in Ugarit itself (Matoïan 2008, Pl. XVII.6).

[205] Cf. KTU 1.107:53' 'she will not die [.........] Kōtharātu'. De Moor 1987, 145, n. 37, has tried to explain their names. Only the last one eluded him at the time. However, now we propose to analyse *prbḫṯ* in KTU 1.24:49 as *pr* 'fruit' + *b* 'in' + *ḫṯ* 'dung' (Arab. *ḫitty*), *'inter faeces et urinam nascimur'* (Augustine of Hippo).

to facilitate conception and childbirth.[206] This would seem to support our identification of Ḥôrānu/Ḥaurānu and Hilālu.

Possibly KTU 1.107:52' also expresses the idea that humankind will live on by procreation,

[bn]*t.nš.bḥ*[y.tky(?).]*mt* [ ] by li[fe] [the daughte]rs of humankind will [defeat(?)] Death.[207]

In view of the preceding story it is likely that this promise was pronounced by Šapšu. If so, a seal impression from Tell Atchana/Alalakh in northern Syria becomes highly interesting. It was found in level VII of the tell and therefore can be dated between 1720-1650 BCE (Collon 1975, 143).

Fig. 16: Seal impression from Tell Atchana/Alalakh, Level VII (after Collon 1975, 53, No. 94).

The goddess in a flounced robe to the left might well be Šapšu. The three rays issuing from her shoulder may be compared to the three rays issuing from both shoulders of the Babylonian sun god Šamaš on the relief heading the well-known stele of Hammurabi.[208] The angle of her arm suggests that, as on other similar seals, her hands were turned open toward her breast. Her face is turned to the left. Dominique Collon has interpreted this as a gesture of greeting.[209] In our opinion greeting would require that the palms of the hand were turned outwards. Both hands turned inwards

[206] KAI No. 27:16-17, 22-27. Cf. Lipiński 1995, 363-366; Rüterswörden 1999, 426.

[207] See Appendix 1 for philological details.

[208] See e.g. Keel 1972, 267, Fig. 390.

[209] Collon 1975, Plate XVI, Nos. 219, 192, 217 and the discussion on pp. 181-182. Compare also Uehlinger 1992, 357, Fig. 1, with 344: 'mit offenbar nach innen (zu sich) gewendeter Handfläche grüßend(?)'.

are a universal gesture accompanying speech: reciting, arguing, pleading, supplicating, lamenting.[210] In KTU 1.107:15-24 the sun goddess Šapšu is lamenting when she learns that Adammu will die. On the seal two nude figures are standing behind her, a man without genitals is raising his hands in supplication, the woman with one hand cupping her invisible breast and the other raised to a star (Ḥôrānu?). The nude humans are smaller than the goddess, so they are not divine or their rank is lower. Still smaller are the two marching little males to the right. The mortal offspring of Kubaba and Adammu? A fish separates them from what seems a somewhat larger hairy head, possibly a deity living below the primordial Flood.

In the Ugaritic cult the renewal of life through procreation was celebrated during the New Year festival in autumn from which the Hebrew Feast of Booths became a demythologized version, though it remained connected with the fertility of women.[211]

One of the texts of this genre (KTU 1.23) is very interesting since it describes some ceremonies of the New Year festival that was celebrated in autumn when the eagerly awaited rains marked the end of the hot, dry summer which was the season attributed to Môt, the god of death. The first of the new wine was pressed during this feast and everybody was allowed to drink his fill from it. The New Year festival celebrated the renewal of life which was symbolized by a sacred marriage rite in which the king, the queen and a priestess seem to have participated.

In one of the Ugaritic rituals for the New Year festival Ḥôrānu's uprooting and trimming of the Tree of Death is re-enacted, but Ḥôrānu himself is identified with a vine.

KTU 1.23:8-11

[8] *mt.wšr.yṯb.*	Môtu-and-Sharru[212] is sitting,
bdh.ḫṭ.ṯkl.	with the staff of bereavement in one hand,
bdh [9] *ḫṭ.ʾulmn.*	the staff of widowerhood in the other.

[210] See e.g. Gruber 1980, 50-60; Dominicus 1994, 68, Fig. 16, 3.5; 75, Table 3.5; 78, Fig. 17; 90, Fig. 21.

[211] The main elements of this festival were already described in De Moor 1972, but see also De Moor 1987, 117-128; 187-190; De Moor 2014.

[212] The Ugaritians loved to pair deities, in this case Death and the Prince (Devil). See Section 2.6.

yzbrnn.zbrm.gpn	The pruners of the vine shall prune him,
[10] *yṣmdnn.ṣmdm.gpn.*	the binders of the vine shall bind him,
yšql.šdmth [11] *km gpn*	they shall let him fall on the terrace like a vine!

Death has been defeated and cycle of life can start again. The binding of the Devil (Prince) recalls Adammu's inability to bind the serpent that attacked him from the Tree of Life (KTU 1.107:6, Appendix 1). In many other extra-biblical texts the binding of the Devil and his demons survived (cf. Chapter 5 and Section 6.3).

2.6 *What's in a Name?*

One of the problems with ancient mythology is that deities bore many names, mostly standardized epithets. A well-known Ugaritic example is Baʿlu. It took Ugaritologists many years to discover that his 'real' name was Haddu (Dussaud 1936). This has to be kept in mind when we are going to delve deeper into the position of Ḥôrānu and Adammu in the Ugaritic pantheon.

At the head of several Ugaritic lists of deities we find *ʾilʾib*, Ilu in his role of the father god who begot all other deities (cf. Section 2.1). The lists of deities invoked in KTU 1.107:37'-44' and KTU 1.100:3-60 are practically the same, but in KTU 1.107 the pair of deities Ilu-and-Ḥôrānu heads the list whereas in KTU 1.100 Ilu is at the head and Ḥôrānu at the end which might be an indication of his demotion in the pantheon.

The circumstance that in Egypt, Anatolia[213] and Phoenicia the deity was called Ḥaurān or Ḥaurōn, as well as Ḥôrōn in Hebrew, has convinced us to abandon the etymology we proposed in the first edition of this book.[214] However, we still think that the name

[213] After our presentation of the main elements of our theory at the 75th anniversary of the Oudtestamentisch Werkgezelschap in Nederland and België (May 16, 2014) Meindert Dijkstra drew our attention to KUB 12, 61 (Bo 3064) + KBo 36,40 (Bo 4107) = Ms C column III. In this badly damaged Hurrian tablet the name of the deity is spelled ᵈ*Ḫu-ra-a-nu* as well as ᵈ*Ḫu-u-ra-nu*, pointing to a pronunciation then and there as *Ḥôrānu*. According to this Hurrian text he was the chief magician among the gods.

[214] Ḥorrānu, from the root *ḥrr* 'to be hot, be ablaze'. Cf. De Moor 1971, 179; Leslau 1991, 243; Bron *et al.* (eds), 2010, 929-930 (for other proposals see Rüterswörden 1999, 425).

was associated early on with the root *ḥrr*. Part of the region east of Damascus which is still called Ḥaurān bears the name Ḥarra.[215] In the Semitic languages roots *mediae geminatae* and *mediae waw* often change places.[216] In KTU 1.5:II.5 the verb *ḥrr* describes the heat caused by the god of death Môtu.[217]

As with the names of other Ugaritic deities, e.g. *ʾalʾiyn*, *ltn*, *rdmn*, *mntn*, the ending *-ānu* was appended to the noun **ḥawr*, making its meaning something like 'the Blazing One'.[218] Ḥôrānu is the Ugaritic 'Lucifer'. If the Ḥaurān was his homeland, it may be significant that this area is an impressive volcanic landscape.

In the pantheon of Ugarit Ilu and Ḥôrānu formed a merismatic pair, Ilu 'the Benevolent' (*lṭpn*) in opposition to Ḥôrānu 'the Blazing One', also called *šr* 'the (Evil) Prince'. In our opinion the pair *ʾil šr* which precedes the pair *dgn wbʿl* in KTU 1.123:3-4 equals the pair *ʾil wḥrn* which precedes the same pair *dgn wbʿl* in KTU 1.107:38'-39', thus confirming the identity of *šr* and *ḥrn*. In KTU 1.23:8 the pair *mt wšr* 'Death-and-the-Prince' confirms that *šr* is a Netherworld deity, associated but not identical with Môtu, the god of death.[219] Since Môtu is the Ugaritic equivalent of the Egyptian

---

215 Cf. Wetzstein 1860, 1-99; Baly 1974, 216-219. Moreover, Wetzstein 1860, 20-21, proposes a connection with Jer. 17:5-6. The region called Ḥaurān is attested in Ezek. 47:16, 18 and in several Assyrian inscriptions, cf. Tadmor 1958, 40.

216 Cf. e.g. Joüon & Muraoka 2006, §§ 80o, 82o. In this case a factor contributing to the contamination of the two roots may have been the existence of derivations of √*ḥwr* meaning 'blackness, fog' (Bron *et al.* 2010, 850-851, who consider a possible connection with a biconsonantal root *ḥr* from which also √*ḥrr* emerged. See for the general picture with regard to biconsonantal roots Del Olmo Lete 2008b, 53-86.

217 Cf. Arabic *ḥarūr* as a designation of the fire of Hell. See also *ḥrḥrt* in KTU 1.2:III.11 || *ʾišt* 'fire'.

218 Roberts 1971 assumes a slightly different meaning for the name of Erra: 'scorched earth', but does not exclude 'scorching one', cf. Roberts 1971, 13a. For the ending *-ānu* with personal names see Van Soldt 2010, esp. 317-322, who seems to have overlooked that the suffix also occurs after feminine names.

219 Just as the Babylonian god Nergal (= Erra) is not identical to Ereškigal, the real mistress of the Netherworld. Cf. Hutter 1985, 71. Even in a very late Armenian text Satan is described as the personified death (Stone 2008, 145).

We reject the proposal of Bordreuil & Pardee 2004, 183 ('homme et prince'). Pardee's abrasive review of Smith 2006 in Pardee 2007 does not

Netherworld deity Osiris (De Moor 1987, 87-90), it would seem that Šarru/Ḥôrānu corrresponds to the Egyptian god of rebellious disorder Seth. In KTU 1.123:13 the pair *ʿd wšr* is attested. Long ago De Moor has proposed to connect this combination with Arabic *ʾal-ʿaduww* 'the Enemy' and *ʾal-šarr* 'the Evil (One)', both designations of Iblīs, the Devil.[220] Actually Ugaritic *šr* equals Hebrew שַׂר, 'prince' and it is attested in this meaning in Ugaritic.[221] It was seen as a typical characteristic of princes and kings that they had their benevolent and malevolent traits.[222] In postexilic times the concept arose of a 'Prince of Accusation' (שׂר המשׂטמה) or an Angel of Accusation' (מלאך המשׂטמה) who ruled over the demons and was an ally of Belial.[223] It is generally assumed that המשׂטמה is related to Hebrew שָׂטָן 'Satan'.[224] The Ugaritic evidence shows that the concept of an evil divine or angelic prince is much older than previously thought.

In the Jerusalem Talmud (j. Sanh. 25d (VII.9) and in Aramaic incantation bowls the evil angel who turned around to become a guardian angel is still called *sr/śr* 'the Prince'.[225]

Of course it is a pity that the tablet which probably related the nature of Ḥôrānu's rebellion has not been preserved. However,

---

enhance his credibility.

220 De Moor 1970b, 314.This proposal was endorsed by Tsumura 1974.
The Crawford Syriac text of Revelation has an interesting variant in 9:11, 'And over them is an angel, the Angel of the Abyss, whose name is Abbadon in Hebrew, but in Aramaic his name is Šārā' (text Gwynn 1897, 12, translation De M.). If the original form of the name was *šarr*, the spelling Šārā is normal in Syriac. However, in this 12th century manuscript the variant might well be ascribed to Muslim influence.
The balsam-tree, Arabic *balasān*, from the same root as Iblīs, was allegedly 'beneficial in cases of barrenness, and counteracts poisons and the bite of vipers' (Lane, 248).

221 Del Olmo & Sanmartín 2003, 842 under *šr* III.

222 The Egyptian *Loyalist Teaching* (Brunner 1988, 178-184); Mic. 5:6-7; Prov. 16:14-15; 19:12; 20:2, cf. Wagenaar 2001, 301-303; Clines, *DCH*, vol. 8, 189.

223 CD 16:5; 1QS 3:23; 1QM 13:4, 11; 4Q225, Frag. 2, col. i:9; Frag. 2, col. ii:6, 7, 13-14, etc.; Mk 9:34 par.

224 See e.g. *HAHAT*, 1281, under שׂטם; Clines, *DCH*, vol. 8, 122, 697, both with further references. In our opinion it is possible that there is a connection with Hebrew and Aramaic שׂוט and Akkadian *šāṭu/šēṭu* 'to scorn, disdain', also used of rebellion against deities. The ending *-ān* is appended to the names of many powerful deities (see above).

225 See e.g. Rossell 1953, 142; Shaked *et al.* (eds) 2013, 331.

we think that Philo of Byblos whose reliability was boosted enormously by the discovery of the Ugaritic tablets has preserved a later Canaanite version of what may have happened beforehand. He relates that Ouranos (Heaven) who had been exiled by Kronos (El) secretly sent three of his daughters, Astarte, Rhea[226] and Dione,[227] to kill Kronos (Attridge & Oden 1981, 50-51). It seems reasonable to suppose that behind these three the Ugaritic trio ʿAṯtartu, Aṯiratu and ʿAnatu is hiding. We have seen already that these goddesses were seen as avenging angels perfectly capable of killing.[228] ʿAnatu even threatens to kill her own father Ilu if he does not let her have her way (KTU 1.3:V.22-25). Philo goes on to relate that Kronos discovered the complot and made the three lasses his wives. When Ouranos found out, he sent Destiny, Ὥραν, and other allies into battle against Kronos. However, Kronos won these over too and kept them at his side (Attridge & Oden 1981, 52-53). We think that we may identify Destiny with the Ugaritic goddess Manātu (Fate) who like Ḥôrānu was allowed to travel freely through the air and through the Netherworld, and was even able to thwart Ḥôrānu (De Moor 2008). This emboldens us to propose that Ὥραν (Hôran) is not 'Period, Season', as one might think on the basis of Greek, but none other than Ḥôrān(u).[229] If so, the latter's rebellion consisted in an attempt to depose Ilu/El who, however, succeeded in forcing him to repent. This would explain the presence of the merismatic pair *ʾil wḥrn* in the Ugaritic pantheon. However, Ḥôrān(u) hardly kept his position as a celestial. The star which according to Philo had fallen from heaven and which Astarte had found and had consecrated in Tyre (Attridge & Oden 1981, 54-55) might well be the star of Ὥραν.

---

[226] Mother of all deities, cf. Hesiod, *Theogony*, 453-491.

[227] According to Pseudo-Apollodorus of Alexandria (second century CE) she was a daughter not of Kronos, but of Ouranos (Heaven) and Ge (Earth) (*Library*, 1.1.3).

[228] Section 2.2. Aṯiratu threatened to kill Kirtu, a 'son of Ilu'. Cf. De Moor 1997, 91-95.

[229] In later Canaanite dialects the case ending *-u* was dropped.

2.7 *'Adam' and 'Eve' as Divine Beings*

KTU 1.100 starts with a list of very ancient deities. After Šapšu follows a remarkable sequence of dyads in KTU 1.100:1-2 which seems to presuppose the following cosmology,[230]

šmm wthm
Heaven (± masculine) and Flood (± feminine)

ʿn (w) *ʾabn*
Source (± feminine) (and) Stone (± masculine)

pḥl (*w*) *pḥlt*
Male breeding animal (and) Female breeding animal.

The earliest divine beings seem to have been assumed to be androgynous, sometimes slightly more the one, then the other.[231] As in several other creation myths of the ancient Near East heaven and the primordial flood are the first elements to be intermingled.[232]

Source and Stone are the next pair, but they are still not warm-blooded beings. Philo Byblius speaks of τινα ζῷα οὐκ ἔχοντα αἴσθησιν, 'some living creatures without sensation' very early in his cosmogony.[233] Only with the last pair of deities living beings are introduced in the form of creatures able to reproduce by sexual intercourse.

Thus far the only time that the pair *šmm wthm* reappears in a Ugaritic text is in the tablet KTU 1.179:9'. There they are preceded by the pair [*kbb*]*wʾadm* '[Kubaba] and Adammu' (cf. De Moor 2008, 181, 186). Kubaba and Adammu/Adamma /Adamu (spellings and gender vary) are attested in Ebla, Mari, Anatolia, Ugarit, Assyria and Egypt, etc.[234] In Ebla Adammu was venerated

[230] The deities are cited in reverse order of ancestry.

[231] Cf. Van Dijk 1964; Clifford 1994, 18-21; Jüngling 1994; De Moor 1998a; Lapinkivi 2004, 155-166; LaCocque 2006, 117-130. See also the Janus-headed deities in Uehlinger 1992, 358, Fig. 2, 37, 8, who sees them as functional, not androgynic.

[232] E.g. Allen 1997, 10; Dijkstra 2011, 56. In the Babylonian creation myth *Enūma eliš* the fresh water flood Apsû and the salt water flood Tiāmat are the first to be mingled. Cf. En. el. I.1-5.

[233] Attridge & Oden 1981, 36-37.

[234] Gröndahl 1967, 278; Laroche 1968, 499, 503; Roberts 1972, 14; Schoors 1972, 28; Haas 1982, 96-99; 1994, 406-409; Hawkins 1981; Singer 1992; Hess

'in the garden' (*gú-núm*, Mander 2008, 42). In Ugarit they are ancient deities who have long been relegated to the Netherworld. It is generally admitted that the most likely etymology for Adammu is Northwest Semitic 'the red one' and it is logical to suppose that the ancestor of all humanity was deified, like so many other famous personalities in the ancient Near East. If so, Adam was originally a very early Semitic deity who became the eponym of humankind. In this connection it is remarkable that according to Gen. 2:7 – and in contrast to Gen. 1:26-28 – the first human being was created *before* all other living creatures (Gen. 2:19).

It has long been suspected that Eve too was a once powerful mother goddess (so e.g. Wyatt 1999) who in the Hebrew canonical tradition was demoted to the status of the female human being to whom the first sin was attributed. Shawna Dolansky, for example, writes,

> The story of the Garden of Eden suggests that earlier mythologies existed in which a goddess figure was likely involved in creation; such a story, however, has been lost to us, and we are left with the version that inverts her role and marginalizes the goddess to such an extent that she is no longer directly present in any myths (Dolansky 2007, 21).

In this contribution we hope to have demonstrated that this is a too pessimistic evaluation of the actual situation. Ilu's wife Aṯiratu was involved in the creation of deities and human beings (Section 2.1). Moreover, in Neo-Punic inscriptions a goddess *Ḥwt* occurs. Once she is invoked as *rbt ḥwt ʾlt* 'Lady Ḥawwat, goddess!'.[235]

Some scholars have proposed to connect Eve with the Hittite and Syrian goddess Ḫebat, consort of the weather god Teššub.[236] Kubaba is occasionally grouped with the deities around Ḫebat. Initially both Adammu and Kubaba were androgynous deities.[237]

1993, 14-19; Lipiński 1995, 316-8; Van Gessel 1998, 55-6; Mander 2008, 15, 41-2; Durand 2008, 256. In Hurrian god lists they are often preceded by the twin deity Nubadig, also a very ancient pair which is also attested in Ugarit, cf. Van Gessel 1998, 341-345; Del Olmo Lete & Sanmartín 2003, 229.

[235] Donner and Röllig, *KAI*, No. 89:1. This is still the most convincing interpretation, but different interpretations of these inscriptions have been proposed, cf. Lipiński 1995, 412-416.

[236] References with Haas 1994, 384, n. 19.

Kubaba is also attested as Adamtu, the femine form of Adammu.

At the head of the list of deities in KTU 1.179:8'-12', immediately preceding the pair Kubaba and Adammu, is a deity called *ʾal* (KTU 1.179:8'). The word *ʾal* is attested elsewhere in Ugaritic and designates 'a ram (of exceptional quality)'.[238] Here it is an epithet of the highest god Ilu whose name was derived from the same root *ʾwl* 'to be strong'. Apparently he is heading the list here in his capacity of *ʾilʾib* 'Father god' and as such he is also the *ʾab ʾadm*, 'Father of humankind' or 'Father of Adammu' (cf. Section 2.1). The epithet 'Ram' highlights his potency, just like his more frequent epithet 'Bull'. Both epithets were also used for the Egyptian supreme creator Amun-Re[239] and perhaps originally also for the Hebrew El.[240]

2.8 *Iconographic Representations*

The serpent threatening the entire cosmos according to KTU 1.100 is a serpent that has sloughed its skin and when this happens in spring the snake is at its most venomous (Bordreuil 1985). It seems likely that the snake was guarding the Tree of Life for Ḥôrānu, like the snake(s) guarding the tree with the golden apples in the garden of the gods according to Greek mythology.[241] It is certainly significant that according to Hesiod (eighth century BCE) and Pseudo-Apollodoros of Alexandria (second century CE) this was an immortal dragon with a hundred heads which spoke 'with many and diverse sorts of voices'.[242] A Greek vase identifies the serpent guarding the Tree of Life[243] in the garden of the deities

---

[237] Haas 1994, 406-407, 556.

[238] Cf. De Moor & Spronk 1984, 241; Del Olmo Lete & Sanmartín 2003, 47-48. In texts from Mari and Boghazköy *alu* – in our opinion *ālu* – 'refers exclusively to the few choice males of a flock used for breeding purposes.' (*CAD* (A) 1, 375a).

[239] Cf. Assmann 1983, 199; Sadek 1987, 14; Korpel 1990, 311; De Moor 1997, 48-49.

[240] Gen. 22:13-14; 49:24 and the original text of Hos. 8:6.

[241] Buchholz 2000, 121-127, 166. See also Charlesworth 2010, 58-124.

[242] Hesiod, *Theogony*, 820-868; Pseudo-Apollodoros, *Library*, 2.5.

[243] Cf. for this aspect Buchholz 2000, 122-125.

Fig. 17: The snake Ladon encircling the apple tree of the Hesperides. Okeanos (ocean) and Strymon (a river) are sitting left and right of the tree. The names of Ladon, Okeanos and Strymon have been written on the vase itself. The vase is dated *ca.* 475 BCE (after Buchholz 2000, 166, Abb. 23).

as Ladon (Fig. 17 on the previous page). This brings to mind the name of the Ugaritic sea serpent Lôtānu who was associated with evil.[244] To the Greeks a name ending in *-ōn* must have sounded more familiar than a name ending in *-ān*. Mangling of foreign names is a common phenomenon.

According to Job 41:11-13[19-21] flames and steam come forth from the mouth of the Leviathan.[245] His heat causes the sea to boil (Job 41:23[31]). Rev. 12:15-16 relates that the serpent poured water from its mouth (cf. KTU 1.166:28 *mm.bbṯn* 'water from the Dragon'). The Egyptian version of this serpent, Apophis, is sometimes said to be burning (Ritner 1997, 32, 4). Iconographic representations of the monster sometimes depict it as a flaming creature in a boiling sea (Keel 1972, 44-45).[246] Possibly the monster also occurs in KTU 1.107:17,

(17) [b]š*l* *ytk.b*lt[*n*(?)]   [boi]ling liquid pours forth from Lôt[ānu(?)]

The name of the Leviathan must be derived from the root *lwy* 'to follow, surround'. The great sea serpent encircling the cosmos has the form of a 'wreath' (Hebrew לִוְיָה and לֹיָה), so its tail is perpetually fleeing (*brḥ*) from its own biting mouth.[247]

The almost literal correspondence between Isa. 27:1 and KTU 1.5:I.1-3 proves that Israel must have been acquainted with the Canaanite tradition about the primordial serpent (see also Job 26:10, 13). The Ugaritic form *Ltn* may have been vocalized *Lîtānu* (so Emerton 1982), but the Greek Ladon suggests a dissimilated form of *Lôtān(u)*. The Ugaritic personal name Lôdānu may be derived from the name of the monster.[248] It was not unusual to give infants names of terrifying animals, e.g. a-ab-ba-*ba-áš-ti* 'Tiāmat is my protecting angel' (Lambert 2013, 237) or נָחָשׁ, Nahash, 'Serpent'.

---

[244] KTU 1.5:I.1. Cf. Job 3:8; 40:25 [tr. 40:20]; Ps. 74:14; 104:26; Jes. 27:1 [2x].
[245] The forked tongue of the *Cerastes* vipers is a fiery red, suggesting flames when they project it rapidly.
[246] For later parallels see Angel 2006, 45. A giant serpent speaks Egyptian (Lichtheim 1997b). See also Section 3.5.1 on the garbled speech of Typhon.
[247] Stricker 1953; Keel 1972, 36, Figs. 38-39; 37, Fig. 40.; 38, Fig. 41; Lambert 2013, 238-240. For later representations, see Whitney 2006, 114-123.
[248] Bordreuil 2012, 53-54 writes Ludānu, but Ugaritic and Akkadian had no other way of expressing the vowel *ô*.

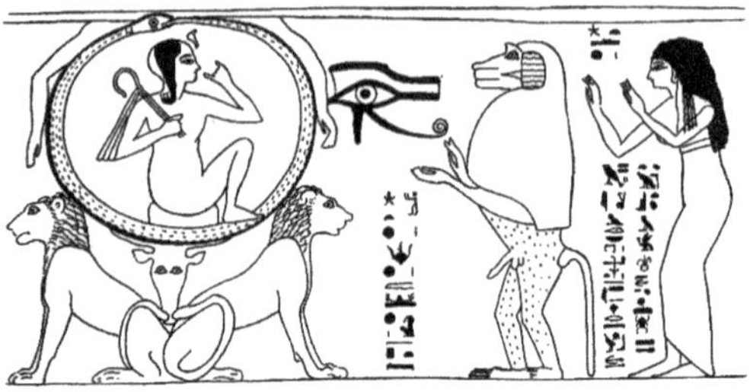

Fig. 18: The youthful sun god is still shut in by the primordial sea which is depicted as a circular serpent chasing after its own tail. However, he plants his foot already on the beast (after Stricker 1953, 11, Fig. a).

The name Lôtān(u) might be derived then from a shortened form *law > *lô (similar to קָו from קוה).

In our opinion a Cypriote cylinder seal from the Late Bronze period illustrates the scene described in KTU 1.107.[249] Textual, architectural and other physical evidence indicates a very close commercial, cultural and religious relationship between Cyprus, at that time called Alašia, and Ugarit which with its port Maʾḫadu (Minet el-Beida) was situated ideally vis-à-vis the island.

Fig. 19: Cylinder seal from Cyprus in Fribourg, Sammlungen BIBEL+ORIENT, VR 1992.21 (Datensatz 346), dated 1450-1150 BCE.

To the left of the man in the middle stands a date palm, the Tree of Life (cf. Kvanvig 2011, 143-145). From its roots two serpents

[249] See Fig. 19.The cylinder seal BM 89326 (No. 112 in Colon 1987, 37) which is sometimes described as the 'Adam-and-Eve-seal' is hardly comparable.

rise up,[250] one of which has a forked tongue, the other bites the man in his right arm. The unnatural bend of the arm suggests that he is suffering or is trying to shake off the serpent. With his left arm he tries to ward off a three-headed serpent. This monster has two fishtails or feet of a sea bird. A smaller fish is swimming next to it. The horned head of another emerging sea monster is depicted below it.[251]

The Akkadian *bašmu* is a mythological horned viper living in the sea and in swamps (Pientka-Hinz 2009, 205). Probably the genus *Cerastes* stood model for this creature, but the real habitat of these extremely venomous vipers is the desert or well vegetated oases,[252] so it may be a case of transference of characteristics.

Fig. 20: A horned viper (after Tristram 1875, 273, who calls it *Cerastes hasselquistii* and identifies it with שְׁפִיפֹן in Gen. 49:17).

Cerastes cerastes L. and the related genus *Cerastes gasperettii* are so-called 'sidewinders' which means that they move by a lateral,

[250] Snakes like to make their nests between the roots of trees. Cf. the Sumerian composition *Gilgameš, Enkidu and the Underworld*, lines 42, 85, 129, 140.

[251] For similar horned sea monsters see e.g. Keel 1972, 43-44, Fig. 47, 48, 49. This type of horned head is very common on Syrian and Cypriote seals, cf. Mazzoni 1986, Pl. 33-35.

[252] Wagner & Wilms 2010, 297, with the photographs of the horned head of *Cerastes cerastes* L. on page 301, No. 5. On its life-threatening venom, Warrell 2004. Jerome translates the second snake in Gen. 49:17 by *cerastes*.

undulating movement[253] which may have suggested that it had lived originally in the sea before it was confined to the desert. The snakes burrow in the sand to take their prey by surprise.

In its mythological form the *bašmu*'s length is sometimes described as sixty 'double miles', i.e. 600 kilometers. According to some sources it could have multiple heads and could be compared to a duck. It was probably related to the *ušumgallu*, *mušḫuššu* or *mušmaḫḫu*, great mythical dragons.[254]

Fig. 21: Photograph of the horned *Cerastes gasperettii* (after Stümpel & Joger 2009, 188, Fig. 8).

The horned head on Cypriote seals is usually interpreted as a bull's head. This is unlikely because usually bulls (and other animals) were depicted with complete bodies. We prefer to interpret it as a horned sea monster because of the marine creatures just above its head on the seal of Fig. 19.[255] The fact that *Cerastes* burrows in the sand so that only its camouflaged head is visible

[253] For an instructive BBC film see http://www.arkive.org/arabian-horned-viper/cerastes-gasperettii/video-ga00.html and video-ga08.html.

[254] Cf. *CAD* (B), 141-142; *CAD* (M) 2, 277b-278a; Wiggermann 1994, 166-169; 1997, 34-35; Pientka-Hinz 2009, 205. In our opinion the fabulous nature of these monsters allows us to take physiological details like the occasional presence of two or more legs with a grain of salt. See e.g. Collon 1987, No. 786.

[255] What has been interpreted as the ears of a bull are probably drillings portraying the puffed up cheeks of the horned sea viper. This is suggested by the seal 89477 in the British Museum depicting the victory of the weather god over the horned monster (cf. Collon 1987, No. 195).

explains the fact that its body is left out on these seals, but on several other iconographic representations the winding of the snake is imitated.[256] 'Winding' is exactly what the word *ʿqltn* describing Lôtānu/Liwyātān means in Ugaritic and Hebrew.[257]

The Akkadian *bašmu* corresponds to Ugaritic *bṯn*,[258] another name of the big sea monster. It is certain that Hebrew בָּשָׁן (Bashan) equals Ugaritic *bṯn* because in later times the Bashan area was called Batania which is the Aramaized form of the noun.[259] Hebrew פֶּתֶן, usually translated as 'viper' or 'asp', is another Aramaized form of the word (Kogan 2006, 295-296). In Ps. 91:13 פֶּתֶן is paired with the תַּנִּין, the feared 'tuna sea dragon'. In other words, Bashan can mean nothing but 'sea dragon' and it designates the long mountain range that runs through Transjordan. A gigantic serpent indeed.[260] In this connection the Ugaritic incantation KTU 1.83 is highly interesting,[261]

KTU 1.83:3-13

(3) [tb]*ʾun.bʾarṣ* (4) m*ḫ*n*m.*	you should go into the land of Mahanaim.[262]
ṯrp ym.(5) *lš*n*m.tlḥk.* (6) *šmm*	Freeze[263] Yammu (whose) forked tongue licks the sky,

[256] Keel 1972, 38, Fig. 41; 43, Figs 47-48; 44, Fig. 50; 47, Fig. 55.

[257] Del Olmo Lete & Sanmartín 2003, 177.

[258] For the exchange of *n* and *m* see e.g. Lipiński 1997, § 11.7.

[259] In Aramaic *t* is the normal replacement of *ṯ* in Ugaritic.

[260] Ps. 74:14, Ezek. 29:5 and Ezek. 32:3-6 preserve the memory of a big sea serpent that is thrown down into the desert. Cf. Miglio 2013, 34-35. In 1 En. 60:8-9; 4 Ezra 6:49-52 and 2 Apoc. Bar. 29:4 the Behemoth (originally dry land, but later also a sea-monster) and Leviathan have been conflated.

[261] In all essential readings we follow the excellent edition by Pitard 1998.

[262] Apparently Mahanayim in the Bashan area, *tell Ḥağğāğ*, cf. Mittmann & Schmitt 2001, Taf. B.IV.5.

[263] We take the verb *ṯrp* as a denominative of Akkadian *šurīpu* 'ice' and connect this with the legends about the solidifying of the sea like glass, Rev. 15:2, also Rev. 4:6, and Midrash Mekhilta Beshallaḥ 5 explaining Exod. 15:8 as follows: 'the sea solidified on both sides and became a sort of glass crystal'. Interestingly, the same passage offers an alternative explanation stating that the sea was turned into rocks. The verb קפא in Exod. 15:8 designates the solidifying of the תְהֹמֹת בְּלֶב־יָם, 'the solidifying of the *thmt* in the heart of the sea'. The תְהֹמֹת seem to be sea monsters here. See also Sir. 43:20-25 and the Ketiv in Zech. 14:6, the latter implying that on the day of the eschatological theophany no frost and solidifying of sea(monsters) will be necessary anymore. Also compare Greek πάγος 'crag, rock, frost' from πήγνῦμι 'to freeze into ice, solidify'.

ṯrp (7)*ym.ḏnbtm.*	you should freeze Yammu-of-the-forked-tail!
(8) *tn!n.lšbm* (9) *tšt.*	You should put Tunnanu[264] to the muzzle,
trks (10) *lmrym.lbnn*	you should bind him to the heights of the Lebanon.[265]
(11) *pl.tbṯn.y ymm*	Fall down![266] You will be ashamed,[267] Oh Yammu!
(12) *hmlt.ḫt.y* nh[*r*]	(your) roaring[268] is shattered, O Naharu!
(13) l *tph.mk*	You surely will see the Pit,[269]
tḥmr.[bḥmr]	you will be smeared with clay.[270]

Apparently the person who commissioned this little text hoped for a definitive removal of the threatening Sea who is clearly identified here with the serpentine monsters living in his watery body. Compare the following line at the end of the *Myth of Baʿlu*,

KTU 1.6:VI.51

bym.ʾarš.wtnn	In Yammu are Arišu and Tunnanu.[271]

The modern reader may find it difficult to imagine such identifications of what we see as completely different entities, but there are many examples of this way of thinking in the ancient Near East.

Since 'Bashan' means 'serpent dragon' and is a designation of Yammu's sea monster(s) in Ugarit (*bṯn*) the underlying myth might be that the dark and sometimes glassy looking volcanic rocks of Bashan (cf. Baly 1974, 213-9) consist of the petrified body of the sea monster.

264 Our word 'tuna', Hebrew תַּנִּין, a sea monster in the Bible too and not clearly differentiated from the Sea himself. Cf. Pitard 1998, 276; 2007. Differently Miglio 2013, 46-47 who does not take into account that metamorphosis was a common phenomenon with deities. For biblical and other parallels, cf. Korpel 1990, 553-9; De Moor 1987, 11.

265 The mountain range to the north of Bashan was variously called 'Hermon', 'Shiryon', 'Senir' and 'Anti-Lebanon'.

266 Imperative of *npl.* Cf. KTU 1.2:IV.25-26. 'Yammu' is the sea god.

267 The energic imperfect *tbṯn* from *bṯ* 'to be ashamed' creates a wordplay with *bṯn* 'dragon'.

268 The Ugaritic word *hmlt* is related to the Hebrew verb המה, 'to roar' and the noun הָמוֹן, 'roaring'. Cf. Isa. 17:12; 51:15; Jer. 6:23; 31:35; 50:42; 51:42; Ezek. 39:11; Ps. 65:7. 'Naharu' means 'river', 'sea current'.

269 The throne of Death.

270 Not 'foam', as some would have it, because that root is *ḫmr* in Ugaritic. The word *ḥmr* 'clay' is attested as an epithet of corpses in the muddy Netherworld. See KTU 1.5:I.14-22.

271 Arišu and Tunnanu were marine monsters. See also KTU 1.3:IV.3-4 'There are ma[ggots] crawling in Yammu, there are worms [in] Naharu!'.

Fig. 22: Volcanic glass (Obsidian) is mostly black, but sometimes it is transparant. This specimen exhibits wildly undulating patterns, giving rise to the idea that it once was liquid like the raging sea. (photograph J.C. de Moor)

Ugarit entertained close connections with the Bashan area. The Ugaritians were acquainted with the Bashan and the Ḥaurān as areas connected with the Canaanite cult of the dead.[272] We think that scholars in Antiquity have racked their brains about this very peculiar chain of mountains. They found a solution in assuming that it was the solidified body of a giant sea monster, the Leviathan.[273] Certain features of the volcanic landscape looked

[272] De Moor 1997, 103-207, with earlier literature.

[273] It is not easy to distinguish what real species may have stood model for this monster. We think it was a mythological magnification of a terrestial serpent (see the discussion above). However, a whale is another possibility. Eugen Wirth gives this graphical description of Hermon, Anti-Lebanon and Čebel Ansariye, 'Alle drei Gebirge erheben sich wie breite, gedrungene Walfischrücken über ihr Vorland.' (Wirth 1971, 47). If a modern observer can make such a comparison, the Ancients could do the same, the more so since the sperm whale (*Physeter macrocephalus*) did occur in the Mediterranean Sea and is mentioned in a Ugaritic text (KTU 1.5:I.15). Herman Melville's novel *Moby Dick* was definitely not the first to connect this giant sea creature with the Leviathan. Cf. Zwart 2000.

like the remnants of the scaly skin of an enormous reptile.

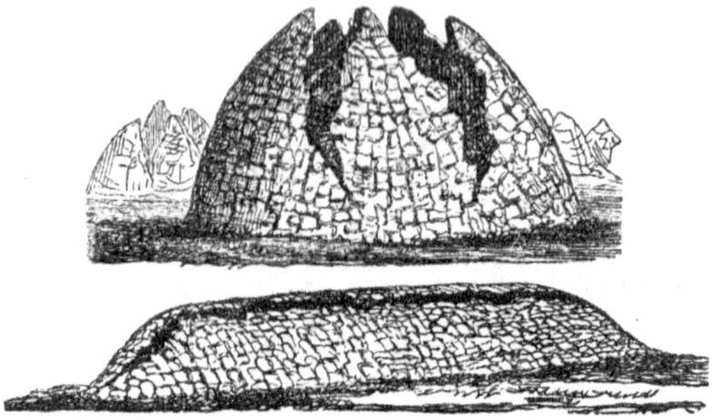

Fig. 23: Volcanic features in the Ḥaurān resembling the skin of a giant serpent (after Wetzstein 1860, 13, see also 19).

It is easy to follow their reasoning. Fossils of mollusks and fish are found in calcareous deposits on Mt Lebanon and Mt Hermon. The ancient lava flows of the Ḥaurān looked like a solidified sea, as the following description by George Smith indicates,

> On the east the Plain is framed by a long low line of blue. As you approach, the blue darkens, and stands out an irregular bank of shiny black rock, from thirty to forty feet high, split by narrow crevasses as the edge of a mud-heap is split on a frosty day. Climb it and you stand on the margin of a vast mass of congealed lava, three hundred and fifty square miles in extent, which has flowed out upon the Plain from some of the now extinct craters in the centre of it, and cooling, has broken up into innumerable cracks and fissures. Sometimes it looks like an ebony glacier with irregular crevasses. Elsewhere it 'has the appearance of the sea, when in motion beneath a dark, cloudy sky, and when the waves are of good size, but without any white crests of foam.'[274]

Mt Lebanon and Mt Hermon were seen as the 'horns' on the head of the gigantic Transjordanian 'dragon'. In Assyrian times the Ḥaurān was called Qarnīna and this name is preserved in the toponym of ʿAštarōt-Qarnayim, 'Astartes-of-the-two-Horns', where once upon a time Rephaim, 'giants' would have lived (Gen. 14:5). The placename *ʿAṯtarātu* occurs in the second tablet of the Ugaritic Adammu myth (KTU 1.100:41) as the cult center of the

[274] Smith 1898, 615-616, quoting Merrill 1881, 11.

god Māliku, a Netherworld deity (Spronk 1986, 187) who is one of the deities invoked in vain to neutralize the poison of the snake that bit Adammu.

In one of the oldest poems of the Bible, Psalm 68,[275] the singer asks contemptiously,

Psalm 68:16-17

הַר־אֱלֹהִים	Mountain of Elohim,
הַר־בָּשָׁן	Mount Bashan,
הַר גַּבְנֻנִּים	Mountain of the burial grounds,[276]
הַר־בָּשָׁן	Mount Bashan,
לָמָּה תְּרַצְּדוּן	why did you lay in wait,
הֶהָרִים גַּבְנֻנִּים	mountains of the burial grounds,
הָהָר חָמַד אֱלֹהִים לְשִׁבְתּוֹ	Oh mountain on which Elohim desired to stay,
אַף־יְהוָה יִשְׁכֹּן לָנֶצַח	yea, (where) YHWH (desired) to stay forever?

The verb רצד denotes the lurking of serpents (Lane, 1002-1003). Apparently the poet was still acquainted with the myth of the serpentine origin of the Bashan.

Also the poisonous 'fog' threatening the world[277] can be explained on the basis of this theory. In historic times none of the volcanoes of the Ḥaurān has erupted.[278] There are, however, still many places on the Golan, the Jebel el-Druz and Palmyra where hot sulfuric springs and vents emitting sulfuric gases testify to the volcanic activity of the region in times long past.[279] It is certainly possible that these vents emitting noxious gasses were much more active 3200 years ago than they are now so that they gave rise to the tales about a poisonous 'fog' on the mountains emitted by the giant Bashan serpent.

Although tiāmat in the Babylonian Creation Epic is clearly distinguished from her helpers, the giant serpents,[280] she herself

---

275 Cf. De Moor 1997, 171-191.

276 We now connect this word with Arab. *ǧabbānah* (Lane, 377) as a designation of the megalithic monuments on the Bashan (see Section 6.3).

277 KTU 1.107:32'-45', cf. Appendix 1.

278 There are reports about an eruption of eṣ-Ṣafâ as late as 1850 CE, cf. http://www.volcano.si.edu/volcano.cfm?vn=230050 but these rest on a misunderstanding of Wetzstein 1860, 9-10. Also other reports of recent volcanic activity in Syria are unreliable, cf. Neumannn van Padang 1963, XI-XII.

279 Wetzstein 1860, 23-24; Burdon *et al.* 1953, 381; Wolfart 1966, 13.

is also depicted as a huge horned dragon (*bašmu*).[281]

Fig. 24: Cylinder seal depicting Marduk's victory over Tiāmat. The skin of the horned monster is scaly, like the skin of the Leviathan according to Job 41:7-8[15-16] (British Museum, AN89589).

So the snake 'in the vineyard of the great gods' (KTU 1.107:2) was a giant serpent, a Leviathan, the primeval evil beast from the sea threatening to eradicate the divine ancestor of humankind. It is definitely remarkable that some late rabbinic sources identify the serpent in Eden with the Leviathan (Whitney 2006, 95-96). This observation enables us to explain the small enigmatic figure next to the right leg of the man on the cylinder seal from Cyprus (Fig. 19). On the basis of other iconographic material it may be assumed to be a tiny human being.

Fig. 25: Cylinder seal (British Museum), dated 1920-1740 BCE. Tiny human beings next to gods.

---

[280] Among them the Bašmu, En. el. I.134-144; II.19-30; III.27-34, 81-92.

[281] Note, however, the sceptical remarks of Lambert 2013, 232-236.

A similar difference in proportion is seen between the small king standing before the huge god Baʿlu on the well-known stele from Ugarit.[282] Also in Mesopotamia and Egypt artists used such differences in proportion to express the greatness of deities or kings as compared to normal human beings.[283] Famous kings and heroes became ancestral deities after their death and acquired corresponding tallness.[284] It must be kept in mind that Adammu was a god before he died. If the snake attacking him was the Leviathan, Adammu himself must have been a huge man too.

In the Mesopotamian and Ugaritic tradition he may have been identified with one of the antediluvian divine sages (*apkallū*).[285] Several scholars suspect that also the Babylonians believed that initially humans were immortal.[286] Philo of Byblos relates that the mortal children of Genos and Genea, the offspring of Aeon and Protogonos, were of very great size and stature (Attridge & Oden 1981, 40-41).

Although rabbinical tradition did not accept the divine status of Adam,[287] traces of his gigantic dimensions are still found in

---

282 For a fine description see Bordreuil 2013, 38-40, with Fig. 1. Cf. below Fig. 29.

283 Iversen & Shibata 1975; Robins 1990, 1994; Vittmann 1995.

284 Cf. De Moor 1976, as emended by Korpel 1996b, 100-102. See also Smith 1988. We maintain this interpretation which is not affected by the excellent epigraphic study of Pardee 2011. The tallness of their spirits is implied in KTU 1.22:IV.8: *ṯm ṯmq rpʾu bʿl* || *mhr bʿl wmhr ʿnt* 'There towered the Saviors of Baʿlu, the warriors of Baʿlu and the warriors of ʿAnatu'. We connect *ṯmq* with Arabic *samaq/ka* 'to be tall' (Lane, 1411). In Palestinian folklore the *mārid* 'Rebel' was a giant evil spirit whose head reached the clouds (Canaan 1929, 12).

285 For recent discussions of the Mesopotamian *apkallū*-tradition and its aftermath see Orlov 2005; Hendel 2004, 28-29; Kvanvig 2011, 107-158. Kvanvig does not discuss the Ugaritic evidence, but it is certain that the scholars of Ugarit were acquainted with the *apkallu*-tradition because according to KTU 1.41:50 the king had to sacrifice on the roof of the temple to 'Pirigallu of the Third Heaven' who corresponds to the Sumerian *apkallu* Piriggalnungal, cf. De Moor 1986, 258; 1987, 165, n. 58; Pardee 2000, 209. After the Flood the *apkallū* were relegated to the Netherworld (Kvanvig 2011, 161-162).

286 Oshima 2012, 423, with earlier literature.

287 According to Gen. R. VIII.10 the angels who wanted to worship Adam as a god were mistaken, but non-rabbinical texts make him divine (Van der Horst 1999).

Jewish[288] and Islamic traditions.[289] His shortening is hinted at in KTU 1.107:8-9, repeated in 1.107:10-12,

(8) [tpl.bš]r. *šrġzz.*	The flesh of Šarruġāzizu [fell].
ybky.km nʿr	He wept like a boy,
(9) [*wydmʿ.*] *km.ṣġr.*	[and shed tears] like a little one.

The little fellow next to the right leg of the figure on the Fribourg seal (Fig. 19) seems to be a human being whose height was reduced to normal proportions. He wears a sword which might symbolize the enmity between the serpent and humankind (cf. Genesis 3:15). There is only one tree to be seen on this seal which has some relevance to the long-standing debate about the question if there were only one tree in Eden or two. Since the tree is much taller than the gigantic Adammu it must have been a 'Weltbaum', a tree of enormous proportions.[290] This accords remarkably well with the opinion of Rabbi Meir who held that the tree in paradise was wheat. When they objected to him that an ear of grain cannot be described as a tree, he replied, 'It grew lofty like the cedars of the Lebanon' (Gen. R., XV.7).

So the Adammu seal from Cyprus may be regarded as a microscopic picture of a macrocosmic event that took place in the hoary past of the early history of the created world. The tale of Adammu who was bitten by a monstrous serpent seems to have been popular on Cyprus in the Late Bronze Age. We know of two seals (Fig. 26 and Fig. 27) that are similar to the one reproduced in Fig. 19, probably they were executed in the same workshop.

---

288 Midrash Gen. R. I.26 states that God created Adam as an unformed mass (*gōlem*) extending from one end of the earth to the other (Gen. R. VIII.1; cf. Lev. R. XIV.1). Also according to Lev. R. XX.2 Adam was a huge figure (Wazana 2008, 122). According to Gen. R. XII.6 the rabbis estimated Adam's height between one hundred and nine hundred cubits (a cubit was about 50 cm). See further b. Sanh., 38b, 100a; b. Ḥag., 12a.

289 The canonical Islamic tradition attributes a height of 60 cubits to Adam. According to some authors he was shortened *after* the Fall to this height (Schöck 1993, 69, 83-84, 111, 119). This may have been derived from b. Sanh., 38b where Adam's diminished height after the Fall is mentioned.

290 The excellent technical description of the seal in Keel-Leu & Teisier 2004, 325-326 might be slightly adapted in the light of the above observations.

Fig. 26: Cylinder seal from Cyprus
(British Museum, AN00087412_001),
dated 1450-1050 BCE.

On this seal too[291] serpents jump forward from the base of the date palm. The mouth of the serpent to the right side of Adammu opens wide to bite him in his right arm which is bent in the same unnatural way as on the seal of Fig. 19. Here too a three-headed sea-monster is attacking Adammu from his left side. It has a spiky tail for which the artisan sacrificed the fish on the other seal.[292] The small fellow at the right leg of the man is replaced by the shape of an oxhide ingot. The next seal will show that this was more or less a trademark of Cyprus, a large-scale producer of bronze at the time (see also Mazzoni 1986, Pl. 33). The three drillings above the tail of the sea-monster are probably a symbolic representation of a woman. The head is shaped in the same way as that of Adammu,[293] the two other circular drillings can represent hardly anything else but her breasts. Fine lines suggest her hands cupping the breasts.[294] The serpent to the right of the date palm opens its mouth to bite her too.[295]

[291] The seal is also reproduced and discussed in Kenna 1971, No. 98; Mazzoni 1986, 176, Pl. 33, III.37.

[292] We were unable to identify the vague shape between Adammu and the three-headed serpent. A jellyfish?

[293] And other humans on Syrian and Cypriote seals, cf. Mazzoni 1986, Pl. 32-35; Reyes 2001, 56-57, esp. Fig. 71.

[294] A widely attested gesture, cf. Keel & Uehlinger 1992, 39, Fig. 25b; 41, Fig. 27a, 27b; 63, Fig. 50; 111, Fig. 121b, 122a; 373, 321a-c; many illustrations in Keel & Schroer 2010.

[295] The longish shape above the head of the serpent is perhaps an unsuccessful attempt to draw a branch, because on all other seals the tree has an equal number of branches on both sides.

Fig. 27: Cylinder seal from Cyprus (British Museum), dated 1450-1050 BCE.

The third seal from Cyprus is less expressive because the artisan devoted a lot of space to oxhide ingots, two of them to the sides of the head of Adammu and one under what looks like a sun emblem,[296] but could just as well be a source since fish are swarming around it.[297] Or a navel?[298] To the left of Adammu the head of the sea-dragon is visible again (cf. Fig. 19) and from the other side he is attacked by a standing sea-monster. It is uncertain whether this creature has one or three heads.

It may be purely accidental, but on all three seals Adammu seems to have a long, vertical scar on his chest (cf. Gen. 2:21).[299]

2.9 *Ḥôrānu's Turnabout* (KTU 1.100:61-69)

Ḥôrānu belatedly showed regret and undid his evil deed because his own venomous offspring would die out too if he persisted. This turnabout made him a suitable avenger when someone committed the same crime for which he himself had been punished. KTU 1.100:61-69 relates his repentance,[300]

---

[296] Cf. the Egyptian sign N 5, *rʿ*. This seal is also reproduced and discussed as No. 114 in Kenna 1971, No. 114. Like the ingot, this symbol was popular on Cyprus, cf. Mazzoni 1986, Pl. 33-34.

[297] Cf. 1 En. 60:7 'the female monster whose name is Leviathan, to dwell in the depths of the ocean, above the fountains of the waters'.

[298] Cf. Keel & Schroer 2010, 88-91.

[299] See also Mazzoni 1986, Pl. 33, III.39. A10.

[300] For philological comments see Appendix 2.

(61) *bḫrn.pnm.trġnw.*	Ḥôrānu's face turned pale,
wtṯkl (62) *bnwth.*	since his creatures would remain childless.[301]
ykr.ʿr.dqdm	He left the city of the east.
(63) *ʾidk.pnm.lytn.*	Then he headed straight
tk ʾaršḫ.rbt	for Great Arashikh
(64) *w'aršḫ.ṯrrt.*	and for Little Arashikh.
ydy.bʿṣm.ʿrʿr	He removed the juniper from the trees,
(65) *wbšḫt.ʿṣ.mt.*	yes, the Tree of Death from the shrubs.
ʿrʿrm.ynʿrn(!)h	The juniper — he shook it out,
(66) *ssnm.ysynh.*	the date-cluster — he put it away,
ʿdtm.yʿdynh.	the scab[302] — he took it off,
yb(67) *ltm.yblnh.*	the wart — he carried it off.
mġy.ḥrn.lbth.	Ḥôrānu went to his house
w(68) *yštql.lḥẓrh.*	and proceeded to his residence.
tlʾu.ḥ<m>t.km.nḫl	The poison had become weak like a wadi,
(69) *tplg.km.plg*	it had flowed away like a ditch.

The Tree of Life seems to have become a contorted Tree of Death by the serpent's venom, but this Tree of Death was removed by the same god who was responsible for the loss of the Tree of Life. Immortality was lost to Adammu and his wife, but life on earth could continue through procreation.

In Egypt Ḥaurān > Ḥaurōn is evidently an imported Canaanite god.[303] He became associated with the great Sphinx of Gizeh[304] and as such he was the protector of several Pharaohs and was iden-

[301] If all the gods summoned would have turned against the snakes the offspring of Ḥôrānu would have been exterminated. Therefore Ḥôrānu relents. In KTU 1.169:9-10 the same god is invoked as a helper against flying demons. So he had considerable powers which in some cases he wielded in favor of human beings.

[302] A metaphor. Apparently the Tree of Life had become contorted by the poisonous spittle of the serpent, and its life-giving dates became uneatable (cf. 1 En. 24:4). As a result, it was not as pleasant to the eyes as the Tree of Life anymore (cf. Gen. 2:9; 3:6; Song of Songs 7:8-9). The Tree of Death now resembled the knotty stem of a vine. Ḥôrānu removes the most ugly bulges as well as its poisoned fruit.

[303] On a basalt statue of a sphinx he is described as 'Ḥaurōn of Lebanon' (Tazawa 2009, 70, Doc. 32).

[304] This may suggest a connection between Ḥôrānu and lions, but we are not as confident as Lipínski 1996, 260-262, in identifying any winged god standing on a lion as Horon/Ḥôrānu.

tified with Horus, the falcon god.[305] Like other Egyptian deities, Ḥaurōn was invoked to give 'life, prosperity and health' and as a savior from attacks of wolves.[306] He is often called 'lord of the sky',[307] which should be understood as 'ruler of clouds'.[308] Probably this is due to his association with Seth who was the Egyptian form of the Canaanite weather god Baal during the New Kingdom. Sometimes he is also associated with Shed, a good healer god who also occurs in KTU 1.107:28'.[309] An amulet depicts Ḥaurōn as a subduer of snakes.[310]

Fig. 28: The Canaanite gods Ḥaurōn and Shed depicted as subduers of snakes on an amulet from Deir el-Medina, 19th-20th dynasty. On the left Ḥaurōn is depicted as a falcon, on the right Shed in anthropomorphic form (after Tazawa 2009, Pl. X, 2.1.3 Doc. 21).

[305] Cf. Van Dijk 1989; Rüterswörden 1999; Tazawa 2009, 60-71. Cf. Fig. 1-2 above.

[306] Albright 1937; Gray 1949; Stadelmann 1967, 85; Helck 1971, 455; Rüterswörden 1999, 426; Tazawa 2009, 61, Doc. 3; 64, Doc. 11.

[307] Tazawa 2009, 60, Doc. 1; 62-63, Doc. 4, Doc. 5, Doc 8; 65, Doc. 12, Doc. 13.

[308] Tazawa 2009, 60, Doc. 1; 131-132.

[309] Lipínski 1995, 329-332; Tazawa 2009, 160-163.

[310] Tazawa 2009, 68, Doc. 21, Pl. X. See also many pictures of Seth as a subduer of snakes in Cornelius 1994.

So Ḥôrānu/Ḥaurōn seems to have had a sympathetic side too, like other Netherworld deities in the ancient Near East (De Moor 1990). This explains why Ḥôrānu could be invoked as a helper against the serpent-demons who were under his control: *ḥrn ḥbrm wġlm dʿtm* 'May Ḥôrānu be a comrade and the Youth a friend' (KTU 1.169:9-10).[311] After his turnabout the Ugaritic predecessor of the Devil became an ambiguous figure: a feared excutioner of rebels like himself, but also a formidable ally against evil powers. It may seem illogical that on New Year's Eve Ḥôrānu is prayed to be an ally of the good deities in the cosmic battle against his own offspring, but obviously people feared that he might revert to his former evil state. The Youth is probably the protective genius Šēdu who is paired with Ḥaurōn on the amulet Fig. 28 where he wears a parietal braid of hair as a symbol of his youth.[312]

The good side of Ḥôrānu is also expressed in the alternative name of the first humanlike being: Šarruġāzizu 'the Prince (Devil) is generous'. In the heavily damaged line KTU 1.107:30' Ḥôrānu seems to receive the epithet *ʾark ḥnt*, 'long of mercy'.[313]

As we have seen, also the highest god Ilu allowed himself such duplicity (Section 2.3). A similar ambiguous character was attributed to the Ugaritic goddess of love *and* war ʿAnatu. She dupes the young hero Aqhâtu with a fake promise of marriage and has him murdered during his wedding party, but afterwards laments loudly about his death (KTU 1.17:VI–1.19:I). The same unpredictable behavior was ascribed to other deities in the ancient Near East, e.g. the Babylonian god Erra (see Section 3.3.7) and the Egyptian rebel god Seth.[314] It seems possible that Ḥaurōn and Seth were identified at a very early date. According to our reconstruction of the Ugaritic myth the sun goddess Šapšu and the former rebel god Ḥôrānu were together responsible for the preservation of life on earth.

Perhaps this is depicted on a cylinder seal from Ugarit, dating from the first half of the second millennium BCE:

---

[311] Compare KTU 1.6:VI.49-50.

[312] Cf. Tazawa 2009, 68, Doc. 22.

[313] Also Philo of Byblos attributes a double character to the immortal snakes, the first of them 'a very beautiful serpent in the form of a hawk' (Attridge & Oden 1981, 64-69). For the epithet *šarru*, cf. Section 2.6.

[314] Cf. Te Velde 1977; Meurer 2005; Mathieu 2011 and Section 3.2.2.

Fig. 29: Cylinder seal RS 9.889 perhaps depicting Šapšu and Ḥôrānu as saviors of life (after Amiet 1992, No. 39).

On this seal a Seth-like god with a crooked staff or snake in his hand talks to a goddess in a long mantle over a stylized tree which has been identified as a date palm.[315] The mantle and headdress of the goddess resemble the well-known pictures of the sun god or sun goddess ascending between the two mountains at the edge of the cosmos.[316] Her inwards turned hands seem to indicate that she is arguing. The Egyptian *ankh*-sign indicates prolonged life. Seth reappears in partly theriomorphic form next to Enkidu (or a scorpion-man?) subduing a lion. The rolling wave patterns above and under these figures may represent the Upper and Lower Floods (Uehlinger 1992, esp. Fig. 2-5).

2.10 *The Invincible Evil*

Unfortunately Ḥôrānu, the master of serpents, was an unreliable ally. He may have repented, but his offspring continued to be a threat to the world. The Ugaritic incantations against demons in the form of monstrous snakes, including the Baṯnu (Bashan) and Lôtānu (Leviathan),[317] prove that the Ugaritians did not believe that their god of the life-bringing rains Baʿlu had defeated the powers of evil once and for all when he defeated the Sea god.[318]

A well-known stele from Ugarit celebrated Baʿlu's victory over

[315] Cf. Schaeffer *et al.* 1983, 35-39; Onnis 2012.
[316] See above Figs. 7 and 8.
[317] KTU 1.82:13, 27, 41, cf. 6, 32, 35; KTU 1.178, all discussed above.
[318] This section is based partly on De Moor 1997, 88–91.

Yammu. The great *Myth of Baʿlu* that formed the central piece of the religious traditions of Ugarit can hardly be called a joyful message of salvation to all humankind. On the contrary, this myth was never intended as testimony of any final victory over the forces of evil, and it was never understood as a closed chapter of primordial history. Surely Baʿlu did defeat Yammu, but in contrast to Marduk who annihilated Tiāmat once and for all, Baʿlu did *not* destroy the Sea (Yammu).

KTU 1.2:IV.27-31

(IV.27) *yqṯ bʿl. wyšt.ym.*	Baʿlu dragged and put down Yammu,[319]
ykly.ṯpṭ.nhr	he wanted to finish off Judge Naharu.
(28) *b.šm.tgʿrm.ʿṯtrt.*	ʿAṯtartu rebuked the Name,[320]
bṯ lʾalʾiyn.bʿl	'Be ashamed, Oh Baʿlu Almighty!
(29) *bṯ.lrkb.ʿrpt.*	Be ashamed, Oh Rider on the Clouds!
*k šbyn.z*b[*l.ym.*]	For his Highnesss Yammu is our captive,
[*k*] (30) *šbyn.ṯpṭ.nhr.*	[for] Judge Naharu is our captive!'[321]
wyṣʾa.b[*ph.rgm*]	And when the word had left her mouth,
ybṯ.nn.ʾaliyn.bʿl.	Baʿlu was ashamed for her.

So it is his own consort ʿAṯtartu who prevents Baʿlu from finishing off his monstrous opponent. Later on Ilu's wife Aṯiratu seems to fear that Yammu might escape again (KTU 1.4:III.1-6). In a still later episode Baʿlu himself refuses to let the divine artisan Kôṯaru put a window in his palace lest Yammu might insult his daughters again (KTU 1.4:VI.7-14), so Yammu is still alive. As a matter of fact, Baʿlu himself would not have been able to slay the sea-god.

---

319 We maintain this interpretation of De Moor 1971, 138 (with earlier literature); Del Olmo Lete & Sanmartín 2003, 721. Contrast Smith 1994, 351-356. Baʿlu drags the dead body of the sea monster on dry land, just as Marduk does with the corpse of Tiāmat: *šá-lam-ta id-da-a* UGU-*šá iz-ziza* 'he flung down her corpse, he took his stand on it' (En. el. IV.104).

320 From a philological point of view this is the best rendering. One should not bend the text to avoid this parallel to Lev. 24:11 (against Pardee 1980, 274; Smith 1994, 356). Deliberate anonymity to avoid blasphemy was quite normal (Brunner-Traut 1975). ʿAṯtartu and ʿAnatu correct Baʿlu also in KTU 1.2:I.40, but there they only grasp his hands and do not scold him.

321 Captives ought not be put to death (2 Kgs 6:22).

Fig. 30: Baʿlu standing on the serpentine body of Yammu, piercing him with his lightning spear. The artisan used the grain of the stone to suggest heavy rainfall (Musée du Louvre, AO 15 775).

When he was with Yammu Baʿlu himself confesses that all strength had left him (KTU 1.2:IV.1, 5). It was only through an automatically striking weapon provided by Kôṯaru that Baʿlu was able to knock out his opponent (KTU 1.2:IV.18-26). The artisan who made the stele must have exaggerated Baʿlu's power.

So the latter's victory over the Sea and his monsters had only been a Pyrrhic one and could certainly not be interpreted as a definitive elimination of his opponent. The Sea and his evil monsters continued to be a threat. Eventually the god of death Môtu exploits this fact to his advantage in his famous speech at the beginning of Tablet V,

KTU 1.5:I.1–5

(1) *k tmḫṣ ltn bṯn brḥ*	Although you defeated Lôtānu, the fleeing serpent,
(2) *tkly bṯn ʿqltn*	destroyed the coiling serpent,
(3) *šlyṭ d šbʿt rʾašm*	the Tyrant with the seven heads,
(4) *ṯṯkḥ ttrp šmm*	you were uncovered, the heaven came loose,
kr<k>s (5) *ʾipdk*	like the girdle of your cloak!

Maliciously Môtu reminds Baʿlu of the present status of Yammu: he is a cup-bearer of Death (KTU 1.5:I.21-22). Death and Sea are allies, both 'beloved' sons of Ilu, and they will attack Baʿlu again.

Therefore it is most remarkable that the myth ends with a prayer to Kôṯaru to assist (again!) in defeating Yammu's monsters Tunnanu and Arišu (KTU 1.6:VI.51-53). The struggle between the god of life, Baʿlu, and his formidable opponents representing chaos and death will never end. This continuing threat to ordered life explains ʿAnatu's explosive reaction to the mere arrival of messengers of Baʿlu at the beginning of the myth.[322] She displays a disproportionate apprehension that Yammu and his monsters might have mounted yet another attack on Baʿlu whereas she believed to have destroyed them all, including Tunnanu, Arišu and Lôtānu (KTU 1.3:III.32–IV.4).[323] Thus not even the gods could be certain that Yammu would not break loose again. As a consequence human beings still had to fear the god of the sea whose satellites might come along any time to take away not only a daring sailor, but also unsuspecting others, even pregnant women (KTU 1.14:I.14-15).

The same evil powers are warded off again and again in the Jewish Aramaic incantation bowls and amulets of a much later date. The Sea, the Leviathan, the Tannin, the Fog, we meet them all again here.[324] This folk religion apparently was a remnant of the ancient Canaanite belief that Yammu and his monsters had never been defeated in a really definitive way.

The same was true of the other arch-enemy of Baʿlu, the god of

---

[322] On the order of the tablets belonging to the *Myth of Baʿlu*, see De Moor 2012.

[323] In KTU 1.2:I.22-23 the fiery appearance of the monstrous (lines 12-13) messengers of Yammu is described. ʿAnatu claims to have defeated 'Fire' in KTU 1.3:III.45.

[324] Isbell 1975; 1976; Naveh & Shaked 1985; Müller-Kessler 2005; Bohak 2008.

death Môtu. Even though ʿAnatu did destroy him as effectively as she could,[325] after seven years Môtu rose to challenge Baʿlu again (KTU 1.6:V.7–VI.16). In the ensuing struggle the god of life and the god of death appear to be equally strong (KTU 1.6:VI.16-22). To human beings, however, it sometimes looked as if Môtu was the stronger.[326]

It should be noted that at the end of the myth the god of death does not succumb to Baʿlu. It is expressly stated that he only gives in because he fears the wrath of his father Ilu (KTU 1.6:VI.22-23). Neither in this case nor in the earlier episode describing the victory over Yammu is it Baʿlu himself who overpowers his opponent. Yammu is defeated only with the help of the automatic magical axe of Koṯaru. Môtu is forced to give up as a result of the intervention of the sun goddess. With such an unreliable champion, human beings had to fear that one time Baʿlu might fail again, leaving the earth to the god of death for seven or more consecutive years (KTU 1.19:I.39-46).

The equilibrium between life and death attained in the *Myth of Baʿlu* can hardly be called stable. People could derive very little reassurance from it. Therefore the turnabout of Ḥôrānu which ensured humanity at least eternal life as a genus was of vital importance. However, he could not undo all the damage his rebellion had caused, so his serpentine offspring remained a constant threat, both on earth and in the sea, because also in the animal world procreation started the eternal cycle of life. So there was always a new Leviathan or Tunnanu to be conquered. Ḥôrānu is a most ambiguous god whose revenge cost Adammu his immortality but whose turnabout let life proliferate.

2.11 *Conclusions*

At the head of the pantheon of Ugarit stood Ilu, the creator and father of all other deities. His main wife was Aṯiratu, mother of the seventy sons of Ilu who constituted the core of his family and a creatress in her own right. Creation by word or thought alone

---

[325] KTU 1.6:II.30-37. The passage was clearly inspired by the Egyptian cult of Osiris, cf. De Moor 1987, 87, n. 422; 88, n. 430; 89, n. 435; 90, n. 436.
[326] KTU 2.10:12-13, see e.g. Lipiński 1981; Pardee 1987.

is also attested for both of them. However, Ilu also 'created' by impregnating other goddesses and earthly women. On other occasions he creates by molding clay like a potter. This imagery is also attested for other creator deities in the ancient Near East. Ilu creates not merely at the beginning of the cosmos, but many times after. So also the Ugaritians believed in *creatio continua*.

It seems that Ilu has usurped the title of 'Ilu the Father' from an earlier, unnamed god who created heaven and earth. Ilu was thought to have separated heaven and earth with the help of two giant sons, *ṯkmn wšnm*, 'Shoulder-and-Middle-Point (of the earth)'.

At the time when the religious texts of Ugarit were written (late thirteenth century BCE) Ilu's son-in-law Baʿlu and the latter's father Daganu were clearly on the rise, adumbrating the dominance of Baal in the first millennium BCE. On a far smaller scale than Ilu Baʿlu and some other deities were able to create. However, even then El – the later form of his name – was still venerated as the creator of heaven and earth.

Ilu dwelt in a 'tent' at the headwaters of Euphrates and Tigris. Possibly this 'tent' was the heavenly firmament itself, but in any case it is also described as a luxurious palace. As in other creation myths of the ancient Near East the earth was probably raised from the primordial Flood. We have strong reasons to suppose that Ilu was thought to dwell on the mountain Ararat, the highest point of Turkey/Armenia and the mountain on which the ark presumably landed. The Ararat is an extinct volcano with two peaks, one of which is called a 'beaker, crater' in Ugaritic. Because Ilu was probably also identified with his mountain, just as Baʿlu was identified with his mountain Ṣapānu (Zaphon), these twin peaks explain the images of Ilu/El holding a beaker in his hand while blessing. Seen from Mesopotamia the sun went under between these two peaks. The 'vineyard of the great gods' seems to have been the predecessor of Paradise.

It has long been recognized that certain passages in the Hebrew Bible reflect what has been dubbed an 'Adamic Myth'[327] that is older than the Eden narrative of Genesis 2–3. Passages quoted in this connection are Isaiah 14:12-15, Ezekiel 28, Ezekiel 31, Psalm

[327] See e.g. Mettinger 2007, 81, n. 75; 87.

82 and Job 15:7-16.[328] In all these cases the story which seems to have inspired the authors must have related a rebellion of a human being or a god against the highest deity. As a result, the rebel is thrown out of heaven or paradise. However, thus far no convincing parallel from the ancient Near East has been adduced for this 'Adamic Myth'.[329] In our opinion KTU 1.107 and 1.100 provide this lacking background, although we have reason to suspect that a similar myth may have existed in the ancient Near East much earlier.

We think that this myth is also reflected in the Ugaritic *Legend of Aqhâtu* and in the Babylonian *Erra Poem* which seems to be a few centuries younger than the Ugaritic myth.[330] All these traditions relate that the original sin was committed by a god who aspired to replace the highest deity of the pantheon. In Ugarit this god was called Ḥôrānu, 'the blazing one'. Other names he bore in Ugarit are Hilālu, certainly identical to Hēlēl, the 'morning star' of Isa. 14:12-15,[331] Šarru, 'the (Evil) Prince', ʿAdû, 'the Enemy'. The latter two designations are still names of Iblīs, the Devil in Islam (see Section 5.18). In Egypt, Anatolia, Phoenicia and Israel the same god was called Ḥaurān, Ḥaurōn or Ḥôrōn.

Originally Adammu, the divine prototype of humanity, was a very ancient androgynous deity of huge proportions. It seems unlikely that he was the first sinner, the Ugaritic myth rather reveals that he was the victim of a decision of the divine council to send him to the vineyard of the great gods on the earth with the assignment to induce Ḥôrānu, the rebel god who had been thrown out of heaven, to alleviate his revenge on the gods. Ḥôrānu's revenge

---

[328] E.g. Wallace 1985, 78-79, 185-186; Barr 1992, 47-49; Callender 2000b; Mettinger 2007.

[329] See e.g. Saur 2008, 317: 'Die Suche nach den traditionsgeschichtlichen Hintergründen der Texte [Gen. 2–3 and Ezek. 28] in mythischen Überlieferungen aus der Umwelt Israels scheint letztlich zu keinem tragfähigen Fazit zu führen'. Similarly already Spronk 1986, 211-227 for Isa. 14. See further Sections 4.5-4.7.

[330] However, the date of the *Erra Poem* is disputed and might be earlier, especially if the circumstance that the Sea Peoples are designated simply as 'the Sea' in Erra IV.131 is taken into account (cf. De Moor 1997, 63, n. 126; 182, n. 391).

[331] Actually the bright star Aldebaran which is sometimes occulted by the moon thus creating the impression that he disappeared from the sky.

consisted in transforming the Tree of Life into a Tree of Death by encircling it in the shape of a giant poisonous serpent, probably identical to the Leviathan of the Bible, and by pouring his deadly venom on it. As a result the Tree of Life that granted immortality to the gods became inaccessible and the entire world was blanketed in a poisononous fog. However, the snake that guarded the Tree of Life bit Adammu, thus threatening to break the thread of life for all eternity. The sun goddess Šapšu laments about this disaster and mobilizes all major deities to show their determination to exterminate Ḥôrānu's serpentine brood. Since this would bring about the end of Ḥôrānu's own offspring – the venomous serpents – the evil god relented, uprooted the Tree of Death and pruned it. This removed the poison, but was only a partial solution. Therefore Ḥôrānu also fathered the divine midwives, the Kôṯarātu, to ensure that creation by procreation would go on infinitely. Because of these magnanimous acts which cleared the way for continuation of life on earth Ḥôrānu received the epithet 'long of mercy' (KTU 1.107:30') and the first human being Adammu got the proleptic surname Šarruġāzizu, 'the Prince (Šarru = Ḥôrānu) is generous'. Also Philo of Byblos seems to have known the myth of the rebellion and turnabout of Hôran (Ḥôrānu). This supplies us with the link that is missing in Ugarit because the tablet preceding KTU 1.107 was lost.

As for Eve, she was originally the mother goddess Kubaba who later became Kybele (see e.g. Haas 1982, 97-99). It may be assumed that she shared the fate of her husband and became a mortal, but 'good-natured' woman, as she seems to be called in KTU 1.107:27'. The circumstance that her role is not described in greater detail may be due to the fragmentary state of the tablet KTU 1.107. The importance of sexuality to procreation is underlined by a marriage ceremony at the end of the Ugaritic myth (KTU 1.100:70-76).

Remarkably, some of the scenes described in the Ugaritic myth seem to have been depicted on ancient seals from Cyprus and Syria. If we are right, the most ancient pictures of Adam, Eve and the Devil ever published are among them.

Ḥôrānu, the Devil, was an ambiguous god. On the one side he threatened to destroy all life, but he repented and provided a kind of surrogate: the renewal of life through procreation. By engendering the divine midwives he even offered protection to pregnant women and their babies. This double character made him the ideal patron of all healers and so he lived on in divine healers like the Phoenician Eshmun, the Greek Asclepios and the Roman Aesculapius. The serpent-entwined staff of Asclepios is still the symbol of the medical profession. It has also been found in the Ḥaurān, the god's homeland, on a basalt altar from the Roman period.[332]

Fig. 31: Drawing of the god Aesculapius as found on a basalt-altar from Kafr al-Mā, southern Syria (Gressmann 1909, Plate CLVII, No. 389). Especially interesting is the fact that he is feeding the serpent a leaf which is uncommon in the Greek and Roman representations of the god, but recalls the feeding of the venomenous serpent in KTU 1.100 (see Appendix 2).

[332] We are grateful to Meindert Dijkstra for pointing this out to us.

Fig. 32: The drawing of the basalt altar on the preceding page was made after the original object that is still preserved in the garden of the National Museum of Damascus, Syria (photograph courtesy Meindert Dijkstra).

The theme of the 'Adamic Myth' as we have elaborated it for Ugarit is partially present in the Babylonian poem of Erra and to an even lesser degree in some other ancient myths (Chapter 3 below). The material from the Hebrew Bible will be discussed in Chapter 4. Later pseudepigraphic and Islamic accounts of the Fall are evidently based on a mixture of data from the texts just quoted and Genesis 1–3. We will deal cursorily with the traditions preserved in these parabiblical texts (Chapter 5) and in the New Testament (Chapter 6), mainly to establish which elements were taken over and which elements were left out, or were modified.

3
Similar Motifs in the Ancient World

3.1 *Introduction*

In this chapter we will briefly discuss a number of ancient Near Eastern myths and epics that in some respects parallel the Ugaritic religious traditions about the creation of humankind and/or rebellion against the highest deity. We have added some Greek myths for two reasons:

1. It is becoming evermore clear that exchange of ideas between Greece and the Levant started as early as the second half of the second millennium BCE, and probably earlier.
2. The final redaction of the Hebrew Bible took place in the Hellenistic era.

Hittite and Hurrian parallels, in so far known to us, have been discussed in Section 2 because of their closeness to the kingdom of Ugarit the population of which comprised a significant Hurrian segment and which was under partial control of the Hittites when the Ugaritic myths were written down. In some Ugaritic cultic texts Hurrian passages have been incorporated, testifying to the close contacts between the two religions.

3.2 *Egyptian Myths*

3.2.1 *Creation Motifs in Egypt*

According to the creation theology of Heliopolis the primeval sun god Atum engendered a male-female twin Shu and Tefnut, symbols of duality in the world, by masturbation and/or sneezing.[1] Shu and Tefnut gave birth to Geb and Nut (Earth and Heaven). Geb and Nut produced Osiris (male) and Isis (female) as well as Seth (male) and Nephtys (female). Atum created in the primordial dark void and the primeval Flood. He also created by his word alone. Atum's son Shu is called 'Father of the gods' and 'Life, lord of years'.

---

[1] This section is based mainly on Allen 1997.

In Memphis the creator god was Ptah, 'the Lord of Life', the one 'who built people and gave birth to the gods'. Ptah creates through words spoken in his heart and uttered by his tongue. He makes everything, wood, minerals, plants.

The cosmology of Thebes concentrated on the sun god Amun-Re, the pre-existing and unknowable creator of everything. Amun-Re became the national god of Egypt during the New Kingdom and was also worshiped in Canaan toward the end of the second millenium BCE. Not surprisingly, the number of similarities with the religions of Canaan grew spectacularly in that period, also with regard to creation and procreation terminology (De Moor 1997, 41-58).

The Pyramid Texts ascribe the creation of the human species to Atum but do not contain any details about this act. Since the Middle Kingdom (1991-1786 BCE) the creation of humankind on a potter's wheel is attributed to the god Khnum. Since the New Kingdom he had to share this quality with Amun-Re, the almighty 'Creator of Creatures' (De Moor 1997, 47).

3.2.2 *Seth and Horus*

Seth was a god of disorder from the start. He was born abnormally, 'with a blow he broke through his mother's side and leapt forth' (Te Velde 1977, 27-28). Seth is the rebel among the Egyptian deities, he is associated with death and desert, he murdered his father Osiris, the ruler of the Netherworld and approached his friend Horus, son of Isis and Osiris, with homosexual intentions. This incident led to a struggle between Horus and Seth which cost Horus an eye and Seth the semen of his testicles (Te Velde 1977, 32-53).

However, Seth also had another side.[2] He stood in the prow of the bark in which the sun god Re travelled at night through the Netherworld and thrust his spear into the mouth of the great serpent Apophis, thus saving Re and his entourage from this terrible sea monster. (Fig. 31).[3]

---

[2] Cf. Cruz-Uribe 2009, especially 202: 'I am uncomfortable with the notion that Seth is uniformly portrayed as a negative character.'

[3] For more pictures of this scene see http://www.joanlansberry.com/setfind/stabapep.html

Fig. 33: The partly theriomorph Seth thrusts his spear into the mouth of Apophis (grayscale reproduction of photo Cairo Museum, public domain).

Seth's exuberant sexual activities earned him a place in erotic songs and personal names like 'Seth-is-gracious', 'Seth-is-kind', 'Seth-causes-to-live' testify to his friendliness (Te Velde 1984, 910). The reconciliation between Horus and Seth symbolized the unification of the Northern and the Southern part of ancient Egypt and was in this way crucial to the stability of the country (Mathieu 2011).

All this tallies more or less with the ambiguous character of the Ugaritic god Ḥôrānu with whom Seth seems to have been identified early on in Canaan (cf. Sections 2.6 and 2.9). 'Man's inclination to explain reality by means of binary oppositions or paired contrasts that complement each other is also evident in Ancient Egypt ..., and one of the forms in which it appeared was the divine pair Horus and Seth, who came into conflict and were reconciled, who were separated and united.' (Te Velde 1980, 25-26).

3.2.3 *The Myth of the Cow of Heaven*

The Egyptian *Myth of the Cow of Heaven*[4] starts in the era when the self-created sun god Re was king over humans and deities alike (*Cow of Heaven*, 3). However, the humans revolted against the old god Re (4-5) – no reason for their insurrection is mentioned in the text, but it may be assumed that they protested against the forced labor they were required to do for the higher deities. Fearing Re's wrath they fled into the desert. Re summons the deities he has generated, among them Shu, Tefnut, Geb, Nut and the primordial ocean Nun, the most ancient of the deities (8-28). Re asks Nun what he should do with the humans, because he hesitates to kill them since he had created them from the tears of his own eye (29-34). Nun and the other deities calm him by assuring him that his eye will now go out and smite them (35-47). This 'eye' appears to be the goddess Hathor (47-48).

Hathor kills humankind, wading in their blood in the shape of the cruel goddess Sachmet – the myth does not describe how the massacre takes place (49-60). However, this is too much for Re and he devises a ruse. He has 7000 jars of beer mixed with ochre so that the mixture poured out on the land looks like a flood of blood (61-86). The next morning Sachmet sees the red fluid and gulps it down, becoming so drunk that she does not recognize the humans anymore (87-91). She becomes the lovely Hathor again (92-100).

However, Re declares that he is too tired to endure humankind anymore and indicates that he yet wants to kill them all (104-106). The other deities in his retinue protest, whereupon Re copulates in the shape of a bull with Nut who has transformed herself into a cow (114-123) thus initiating another cycle of creation by procreation.

3.2.4 *The Repulsing of the Dragon*

The Egyptian coffin text 160 contains spells against the great serpent Apophis whom Seth had to conquer every night (Ritner 1997). The dragon is said to reside east of the mountain Bakhu upon which the sky leans. The length of the monster is 30 cubits (*c.* 15,25 meter). His forefront is flint and one of his names is 'he who is in burning'. Seth reminds the serpent that he has bound him earlier and will once again take its strength away.

[4] Cf. Hornung 1982; Lichtheim 1997a.

3.3 *Mesopotamian Myths and Epics*

Several Mesopotamian myths contain elements of a generation conflict in the divine world (Cassin 1973). In Ugarit we saw how the younger god Baʿlu rebels against the creator Ilu and how Kirtu's eldest son Yaṣṣibu challenges his father to abdicate.[5] Such generation conflicts occur in any society and they alone are not sufficient to suppose a direct relation between Ugaritic and other ancient Near Eastern myths. So we will try to identify more detailed similarities.

3.3.1 *Sumerian Concepts of Creation*

According to a Sumerian text from Abū Ṣalābīḫ dated *c.* 2500 BCE heaven (**an**) and earth (**ki**) were the first pair of deities.[6] They bring forth Enki and Ninki, the deities responsible for the precious gift of water. They engender seven ancestral deities, the last pair of which are Enlil and Ninlil (Lisman 2013, 23-25, 170-172). At first heaven and earth seem to have been inanimate but inseparably united in permanent intercourse. Jan Lisman suspects a link with the sacred marriage as an image for the primeval cosmic marriage, but has to admit that there is no conclusive evidence for this supposition (Lisman 2013, 28-39, 77-81). In any case there is sufficient reason to assume that just as in Ugarit the origin of sexuality as the driving force of procreation was an important element in Sumerian concepts of creation. Possibly also a talking snake plays a role at this early stage.[7] However, it is not necessary to postulate a direct link between the Sumerian and Ugaritic concepts because it is 'logical' to ask when and how the eternal cycle of procreation started.

According to other early Sumerian texts, especially *The Song of the Hoe*, it was Enlil who separated heaven and earth (Lisman 2013, 25-27, 57-59, 163-164, 324-329; Wiggermann 2013, 113-114).

---

[5] Sections 2.1-2.2.

[6] Since the Ur III period they are sometimes preceded by Namma, the primeval mother of all (Lisman 2013, 122-125, 164-165, 173-174, 196-200).

[7] Lisman 2013, 31-35, 159-160.

Fig. 34: Cylinder seal depicting Enlil as creator of the cosmos and human beings (*c.* 2300 BCE; after Wiggermann 2013, 117, Fig. 1a).

According to the Sumerian text called *The Disputation between Ewe and Wheat* the gods on the cosmic 'Hill of Heaven and Earth' created first of all ewe and wheat which they gave humankind as sustenance. The text does not indicate where these humans came from, but initially they were still very primitive beings who became civilized only after the great Anunna-gods had 'inspirited' them (Lisman 2013, 176-177, 262). Wheat and ewe start a quarrel about which one is the most beneficial to the world. The disputation is won by wheat.[8]

Since the Old Babylonian period the idea is attested that humankind was created from clay. One of the most relevant texts to the present investigation is the Sumerian myth *Enki and Ninmaḫ* which describes the creation of humankind.[9] It resembles *Atraḫasīs* (Section 3.3.2 below) in many respects. The younger gods complain about the heavy work the great gods have assigned to them. Enki is supposed to help them, but he sleeps on until his mother Namma wakes him and instructs him to create a human substitute for the gods.[10] Enki donates some of his own blood and asks his mother to mix it with clay and fashion the bodies of the first man and woman. The two marry and bring forth offspring. To celebrate the achievement, Enki arranges a banquet. When Enki and his companion Ninmaḫ are merry with beer, Ninmaḫ says to Enki,

[8] Vanstiphout 1997; Lisman 2013, 40-44, 256-281.

[9] Lambert 2013, 330-345; Lisman 2013, 48-53, 177-181, 293-309. See also Hess & Tsumura 1994; Batto 2013, 26-27.

[10] Another account of the creation of humankind (KAR 4) gives a similar reason and has two deities slaughtered to make humankind from their blood (Lambert 2013, 350-360; Lisman 2013, 60-64, 330-346).

> (17) "It is for me to decide whether a human body should be good or bad. (18) In accordance with my decision will I make a destiny good or bad." (19) Enki replied to Ninmaḫ, (20) "I shall assess the destiny you decide upon, whether it is good or bad."
> (*Enki and Ninmaḫ*, Section II, 17-20, transl. Lambert 2013, 339).

Ninmaḫ subsequently fashions seven humans, but they are all invalids. Enki, however, devises a sensible task for everyone of them. So Enki has won the contest and now proceeds to fashion a humanoid himself, offering Ninmaḫ the right to decree its fate. However, Enki's humanoid appears to be an even greater failure than Ninmaḫ's. She appears to be unable to improve the cripple's fate and becomes a refugee on earth.

In Sumerian mythology there is no rebellion in primordial times. To quote Jan Lisman,

> ...the relations within the Sumerian pantheon were generally peaceful; the rare conflicts were scarcely if ever solved through violence. The motif of theomachy, which is so conspicuous and prevalent on Sargonic seals, is completely unknown in Sumerian mythology (Lisman 2013, 63).

3.3.2 *Atraḫasīs*

A Babylonian composition that comes fairly close to the Ugaritic concept of the primordial history is *Atra-ḫasīs*.[11] This literary masterpiece has been handed down through at least a thousand years and has been transformed in the process several times. Presumably the Old Babylonian version was written by the scribe Ipiq-Aya in the seventeenth century BCE. The epic starts in the era 'when the gods were (still like) human beings' (I.1).

In these primordial times the Anunna-gods divided the cosmos that was evidently already there among themselves. Their king was Anu who got the heaven, their warrior was Enlil who took the earth, and the sea and the underworld were for Enki, the god of wisdom. The Anunna-gods under Enlil's leadership burdened the lower ranking Igigi-gods, who are called his offspring, with

[11] Text and translation Lambert & Millard 1969; other modern translations with comments are Dalley 1991, 1-38; Foster 2005, 227-280. See Kvanvig 2011, 13-82, for a fine summary of the tablets thus far discovered and the scholarly discussion about them to date.

forced labor on the earth, making them dig the two great rivers of Mesopotamia, Euphrates and Tigris.

After 2500 years of drudgery, the Igigi revolted under the leadership of a certain Awēla. His name resembles the Babylonian word for 'man' (*awīlu*),[12] but at this time he was still a god, be it a god doing forced labor like a human being. Awēla proposes to kill Enlil.

The rebels surround Enlil's abode, intending to remove him from office. Enlil sends them a messenger to inquire who the leader of their revolt is, but they answer that all of them are determined to make war on him. Enlil does not dare to resist and asks Anu to replace him. Eventually the gods decide to have a human being created to take over the forced labor.

The gods slaughter the rebel Awēla. The mother-goddess Mami (or Nintu) mixes his flesh and blood with clay.[13] She fashions the first human from this mixture, so that a divine spirit would dwell in human beings. Presumably the first humanoid was an androgynous creature, having both breasts and a beard. The male and female halves were split and the two mated. After nine months the womb of the woman was opened and the first human baby was born, with Mami (Nintu) acting as midwife. Human sexual reproduction could begin. The text seems to refer to a marriage ceremony that henceforth should be repeated by every couple.[14]

The humans started providing the gods with food, but eventually the world population became so enormous that its noise disturbed Enlil's sleep.[15] First the gods sent a plague, afterwards they sent severe droughts which deprived humans of their sustenace, but time and again their plan is frustrated by Enki who provides a ruse to obviate the curse. Finally the divine assembly decides to send the devastating Flood, but Enki instructs Atra-

---

[12] There are, however, other readings and interpretations of the god's name which most likely was *Wē* though even then ^{d}*we-e i-la* may be a deliberate pun on *awīlu*. Cf. Kvanvig 2011, 39-57; Oshima 2012, 416-417; Batto 2013, 201, n. 5.

[13] Also other Mesopotamian myths contain the motif that humankind was created from clay and the blood of a god, cf. Kvanvig 2011, 48-59; Oshima 2012; Lambert 2013.

[14] Foster 2005, 238, n. 5; Batto 2013, 86-95.

[15] The noise motif was also adopted in other Babylonian myths, cf. Lambert 2013, 301.

ḫasīs to build a boat in which he, his family and all kinds of animals survive the deluge. After disembarking, Atra-ḫasīs sacrifices to the gods who appreciate this gesture very much, sniffing the delicious smell of the offering.

The mother-goddess reproaches the great gods Anu and Enlil for not having prevented the destruction of humankind, her offspring, but at first these gods are only angry that Enki has spared some living creatures. Finally a compromise is reached. The mother-goddess must incorporate death in future births. An important role in keeping the growth of humanity within bounds is attributed to Lamaštu, a goddess who was thrown out of heaven because of unruly behaviour, probably an evil inclination to kill babies (Wiggermann 2000).

It has long been observed that originally the story of the Flood has been a separate, originally Sumerian epic that was later incorporated in both the Gilgameš epic and Atra-ḫasīs. The latter, however, bears the closest resemblance to the biblical account of the primeval history.

After the Flood a new order is established. Barrenness, stillbirth and diseases will henceforth curb any uncontrolled growth of human population. Death becomes the destiny of every human being.[16]

3.3.3 *The Gilgameš Epic*

An equally famous literary work is the *Epic of Gilgameš*. It too started its rise to glory far in the second millennium BCE in the form of unconnected Sumerian stories. It too is known in several reworked versions.[17]

The main character of the epic is Gilgameš, king of the city of Uruk. He terrorizes the inhabitants of Uruk, demands the *ius primae noctis* with brides and is described as a wild bull. His victims complain to the god Anu who orders the mother goddess Aruru to fashion an antipole for him, the wild and hairy Enkidu who

---

[16] There is considerable debate about the question whether or not primeval humankind was immortal. Cf. Kvanvig 2011, 31-39. We do not want to enter into this discussion here but simply note that according to all ancient mythologies deities too could die, and in some cases were resurrected miraculously. Cf. Korpel 2012.

[17] Tigay 1982; George 2003.

intially lives among animals. Gilgameš succeeds in making him a 'civilized' human being by instructing a whore to seduce him. The two become friends and embark upon adventurous journeys together. They go to a cedar forest in order to slay Ḫuwawa, a monster whose 'speech is fire and his breath is death'[18] guarding one particular cedar the top of which touches the heaven (Gilg. Ep. V.294). The Cedar Mountain is described as 'the dwelling of the gods, the throne-dais of the goddesses'.[19]

The Standard Babylonian text states that two-thirds of Gilgameš was a god but a third of him human (Gilg. Ep. I.48). He was very tall (I.29, 37) and his enormous proportions are described in I.56-58. Enkidu too was 'like a god'.[20] He was created from clay by the mother goddess Aruru herself (Gilg. Ep. I.99-106).

The *Epic of Gilgameš* has nothing to tell about the creation of the cosmos and of human beings, but it evidently describes events that were supposed to have taken place long ago. The great Flood is narrated as an event of the past by the immortal hero Ūta-napišti who survived it in a boat and was allowed to live on for ever at the mouth of the rivers (En. el. X–XI). So the Gilgameš Epic does not describe primordial times, since cities were already in place. But that is also the case in KTU 1.107. The epic is relevant to our investigation because one of its main themes is the inevitability of death, as in the Ugaritic texts we have discussed in Chapter 2. When Enkidu has learnt that he must die he calls out to his friend Gilgameš,

> My friend, [*my destiny is*] drawn,
> people do go prematurely to their fate.[21]

After the death of his friend Enkidu Gilgameš is inconsolable and starts a search for the plant that will enable him to renew his life infinitely, but a snake steals it from him.[22] Already the Old

[18] OB III.iii.111; v.198, translation George 2003, 199, 203. Standard version Gilg. Ep. II.292.

[19] Gilg. Ep. V.6, translation George 2003, 603.

[20] Old Babylonian version, OB II, col. ii.53, 73; v.194; Standard version Gilg. Ep. I.207.

[21] Gil. Ep. VII.88-89, tr. George 2003, 639.

[22] We have discussed this episode at length in Sections 2.2 and 2.4

Babylonian version of the epic states that the gods kept eternal life to themselves and created humankind as mortals,

> Who is there, my friend, that can climb to the sky?
> Only the gods have [dwelled] forever in sunlight.
> As for man, his days are numbered,
> whatever he may do, it is but wind.[23]
>
> O Gilgameš, where are you wandering?
> You cannot find the life that you seek.[24]
>
> The ale-wife spoke to him, to Gilgameš:
> 'O Gilgameš, where are you wandering?
>
> You cannot find the life that you seek:
> when the gods created mankind,
> for mankind they established death,
> life they kept for themselves.'[25]

No reason is given for the loss of the life-giving plant, but the unruly behavior of Gilgameš and especially his conflict with the goddess Ištar (Gilg. Ep. VI) may have been seen as rebellion against the established order.

3.3.4 *Adapa and the South Wind*

The concern of humans about their inevitable death is also expressed in the Babylonian *Tale of Adapa and the South Wind*, dating from the latter half of the second millennium BCE.[26] The god of wisdom Ea granted the human Adapa, citizen of the cult center Eridu, perfect wisdom, but 'eternal life he did not grant him' (A/A', line 4). Ea made him his viceroy over humans (A/A', line 6). One day the south wind causes Adapa's boat to capsize. At Adapa's command the wing of the south wind is broken. When the south wind has stopped blowing for seven days the highest god Anu notices it and instructs his courier Ilabrat to bring Adapa up to heaven. Arriving there Adapa is warned not to eat 'food of

---

[23] OBV III, iv.140-143, tr. George 2003, 201.
[24] OBVA+BM, i.7'-8', tr. George 2003, 277.
[25] OBVA+BM, ii.14'-iii.5, tr. George 2003, 279.
[26] Foster 2005, 525-532; Izreʾel 2001, 67-74.

death, water of death' (B. 36-37[29'-31']). When he is brought before Anu they offer him 'food of life, water of life', but because of the warning he has received he refuses it (B. 75-78[61'-63']); D.1-2). So Adapa misses his chance to become immortal because he was too apprehensive.

The similarity with the story in Genesis has been discussed by several scholars[27] but in our opinion it is rather remote. Of course it is interesting that Adapa is one of the semi-divine antediluvian sages (*apkallus*) and that Ea grants him rulership over his fellow humans, but he definitely was not an immortal god like Adammu. Also in other respects the similarities are rather remote.

3.3.5 *Anzû*

It is possible that the Babylonian myth of Anzû, another mythological bird of prey,[28] has influenced the Ugaritic mythological traditions about Ḥôrānu. Anzû was a rebel god who stole the tablets of destiny from the highest god Enlil. None of the great gods was willing to volunteer as his opponent, until Ninurta took up the challenge.

> When Anzu heard what he said,
> He let loose his piercing shriek within the mountain.
> It grew dark, the face of the mountain was enveloped,
> The sun, light of the gods, became dark.[29]

When the two are joined in battle it is said; 'clouds of death rained down' (Anzû II.55). This is an obvious parallel to the Ugaritic texts discussed in Section 2. However, in many other respects the two tales do not match. The resemblance may be explained by the shared imagery in ancient Near Eastern accounts of struggles of deities with all kinds of monstrous creatures, like the Sea with its helpers, such as the Leviathan, Tannin, Rahab (Wazana 2008). Often the darkening of the sky accompanies such conflicts. The mythographs situated these struggles in primordial times and predicted that they will happen again at the end of the world.

---

[27] Among them Draffkorn Kilmer 1987; Izre'el 2001, 126-128; Kvanvig 2011, 121.

[28] Another one in the Babylonian legend of *Etana*. Abraham Winitzer proposes multiple links with the biblical story of Eden (Winitzer 2013; 2014).

[29] Anzû II.48-51, tr. Foster 2005, 569.

3.3.6 *Enūma ēliš*

Ever since Hermann Gunkel published his epochal work *Schöpfung und Chaos*[30] the Babylonian creation myth *Enūma eliš* ('When up there ...')[31] has been the most cited parallel to biblical concepts of creation. In reality, however, Gunkel had to adduce other texts from the Bible to bolster up his thesis that also according to the Hebrew tradition the creation process started with a primordial combat between God and a sea monster. This could not be read into Genesis 1. Nowadays many scholars see Gunkel's idea as too simplistic, though others still support it in essence.[32]

According to the Babylonian creation myth *Enūma ēliš* giant serpents helped Tiāmat in her insurrection against the highest god Anu, his son Ea and his grandson Marduk.[33] Tiāmat made Qingu the leader of her insurrection and entrusted absolute divine power to him (En. el. I.147-160). When Marduk had defeated Tiāmat, he chained Qingu and reckoned him among the dead gods (En. el. IV.119-120). This struggle between Marduk and the serpentine sea monster Tiāmat was a popular motif among artisans cutting seals.[34] Marduk cleaves the primordial Sea 'like a dried fish' and creates the cosmos out of the two halves (En. el. IV.137-146). Later on Marduk created the first human beings from the blood of Qingu to labor for the gods (En. el. VI.29-34). The circumstance that Qingu is part of the human body suggests that rebellion runs in the blood of humankind, but no first transgression by human beings is related in the extant text of the myth and here too the first rebellion takes place in the divine world.

Also in other respects the Babylonian epic of creation is similar to Egyptian, Ugaritic and Hebrew concepts of creation. In this

---

[30] Gunkel 1895. The last reprint of this work known to us was published in 2012 by Ulan Press (sold by Amazon.com).

[31] Other scholars prefer to call this work an epic. We follow the superb edition of Lambert 2013. A much simpler but still useful edition is Talon 2005. Insightful comments on some relevant passages are provided by Lisman 2013, 186-195.

[32] See e.g. Tsumura 2005; Watson 2005; Whitney 2006, 11-18; Scurlock & Beal 2013, all with earlier literature.

[33] En. el. I.134-144; II.19-30; III.23-34, 81-92.

[34] See e.g. Fig. 17 in Section 2.8 and Teissier 1984, 168-169, no. 224; Ḫammade 1987, 116-117, No. 226; 1994, 99, No. 424.

myth Marduk is elevated to the highest level of godhead and is depicted as the creator of the cosmos.[35] Also the notion of creation by word alone is present. Marduk has to give proof of his superiority to the other gods by commanding an astral constellation to disappear and make it reappear again,

> They (the gods) set a constellation in the middle.
> And addresses Marduk, their son,
> "Your destiny, Bēl, is superior to that of all the gods,
> Command and bring about annihilation and re-creation.
> Let the constellation disappear at your utterance,
> With a second command let the constellation reappear."
> He gave the command and the constellation disappeared,
> With a second command the constellation came into being again.
> When the gods, his fathers, saw (the effect of) his utterance,
> They rejoiced and offered congratulation: 'Marduk is the king!'
> (En. el. IV.19-28, tr. Lambert 2013, 87.)

It is important to note that the conflict between Marduk and Tiāmat is not the first battle for supreme power recorded in *Enūma ēliš*. Earlier his father Ea had killed Apsû, the fresh water ocean (En. el. I.67-74). Nor are these gods the only ones to whom victories over monstrous enemies were ascribed. Ningirsu, a warrior god of the Sumerian city of Lagash, for example, defeated 'the Seven-headed Snake', among a host of other dragons (Lambert 2013, 202-204). In polytheism rebellion against the highest deity of the moment was as common as attempts to overthrow the sitting ruler in human societies. Only the time scale and the proportions of the antagonists were macrocosmic.

3.3.7 *Other Mesopotamian Creation Myths*

Lambert 2013, 279-526, treats quite a number of other Babylonian creation myths in which conflicts in the divine world precede the creative organization of an orderly world. In the text *Uraš and Marduk* the primordial god Uraš (Earth) seems to deplore the fact that he granted Marduk supremacy and seems to be called 'the Enemy' (Lambert 2013, 311-315),

---

[35] Cf. Lambert 2013, 147-277.

In *The Slaying of Labbu*, the high god Enlil cannot sleep because people lament about their diminishing numbers. He creates the Labbu, a huge snake, to silence them, but all gods are frightened by the monster and ask 'Who will go and kill Labbu?' One of them succeeds and the blood of Labbu flows for several years (Lambert 2013, 361-366).[36]

According to *The Founding of Eridu* (Lambert 2013, 366-375) all the lands were sea at first. Creation started with the founding of the city of Eridu and its temple Esagil by Lugaldukuga, the father of Marduk. This father god made all the great gods, among them Marduk who created humankind, animals, Tigris and Euphrates, and gave them all names. He then created the vegetation and cattle, among them the breeding ram. Next he builds the major cities of Babylonia.

Also according to another Babylonian myth humans were created to relieve the work of the gods (Mayer 1987). With the consent of her twin-brother Ea the mother goddess Bēlet-Ilī ('Mistress of the gods') fashions a human being from clay. The highest god Ellil approves the product and seems to bless it with the name of *lullû*, a primal human being. From this undifferentiated creature Bēlet-ilī forms the first intelligent and beautiful human, a king.[37] Here the tablet breaks off.

3.3.8 *The Poem of Erra*

It seems admissable to connect Ḥôrānu with the redoutable Babylonian god Erra whose name is derived from the same root *ḥwr/ḥrr*.[38] Part of the volcanic area of the Ḥaurān which we identified as the homebase of Ḥôrānu was called Ḥarra (see Section 2.6). This is the exact Northwest-Semitic equivalent of the name of Erra. The *Poem of Erra* was one of the most popular compositions in Babylonia, even more widely read than the *Epic of Gilgameš*. It is usually dated in the ninth or eighth century BCE, but certain elements, such as the designation of the Sea peoples with the singular 'Sea' (IV.131), just as in Ugarit and some old poems in the

[36] For yet another dragon slaying episode see Lambert 2013, 384-386.
[37] Van Seters 1989 recognized the importance of this text for the interpretation of the creation stories in the Bible.
[38] Roberts 1971; 1972, 24. Cf. Akkadian *erēru* D 'to make dry'; *erru* 'dry'.

Bible,[39] as well as the Sutaeans (IV.133), might point to older traditions incorporated in the work.

It is the merit of Helge Kvanvig to have recognized the similarity between the *Poem of Erra* and other ancient oriental accounts of the primeval history.[40] However, it is evident that at the beginning of the poem the created world is already there, including human beings. The Flood is referred to as an event in the past. The 'Weltbaum' whose roots reached into the Netherworld and whose top brushed the sky and from which the image Marduk had been made had become unattainable. The parallelism with the Ugaritic myth resides in the fact that Erra throws the world back into a state of chaos comparable to primordial times.

Erra instructs his seven helpers, the Sibitti, to smear their weapons with deadly venom (I.7, 38) and to blaze like fire (I.33). Also Erra himself is a flaming deity (I.113), as is his counselor Išum ('Fire').[41] Sometimes he is identified with Nergal, the ruler of the Netherworld.[42] Like the sun, Erra surveys the entire orbit of the world (I.116). He rises against the highest god Marduk and announces that he wants to rule heaven, earth and underworld in Marduk's stead (I.181-184; IV.127). Tablet II:6'-14' mention the brilliance of Erra's star[43]. In II.14-15 he threatens to obscure sun and moon. Erra merciless kills and destroys everything on earth because humanity has held him in contempt (I.120; also III.15; IV.113). According to Tablet IV Erra transforms himself into a human being and incites the inhabitants of Babylon to rebellion which results in more senseless massacre. Finally, however, Erra calms down and is convinced by his advisor Išum to stop the devastation (V.1-41), just as the Ugaritic god Ḥôrānu relents at the end of KTU 1.100.

The ambiguous character of Erra matches that of the serpentine god Ḥôrānu (cf. Section 2.9). The serpent is a phallic symbol expressing the double nature of the procreation process: danger-

[39] De Moor 1997, 182 *et passim* afterwards.

[40] Kvanvig 2011, 136-138, 158-176,

[41] In the poem *Erra and Naram-Sin*, 21, Erra says of himself, 'I am a [fla]me, I am [fi]re' (Westenholz 1997, 164-165). For a possible parallel see Hendel 1985.

[42] Von Weiher 1971, *passim*; Wiggermann 2008, 217-218.

[43] The 'Fox Star'. Cf. Al-Rawi & Black 1989, 112-113.

ous to the woman who in Antiquity often died in pregnancy or childbirth (Stol 2000, 27-48), but at the same time indispensable to the survival of the human race.[44] Peter Machinist has pointed out that the alternation between rest and violence in the Erra poem is reflected in the conflicting and intermingling characters of Erra and Išum (Machinist 1983). The turnabout of Erra and Ḥôrānu at the end of both the Babylonian and the Ugaritic texts expresses the conviction that excessive violence always must give way to pacification.

3.3.9 *Berossos*

Of the writings of the Babylonian historian Berossos (fourth century BCE) only fragments survive.[45] He relates the primeval history from the account of a marine monster called Oannes who taught humankind all skills necessary for civilization. In the primordial dark ocean all kinds of strange hybrids lived, among them horse-like, bull-like, fish-like and snake-like creatures. Over them ruled Thalath (Sea), apparently Tiāmat.

Afterwards Berossos gives a more or less accurate summary of the standard version of *Enūma ēliš* as well as a list of ten antedeluvian kings with extremely long regnal years. Subsequently he records the great Flood, more or less in accordance with the Mesopotamian accounts. What is important for our investigation is that Berossos is the only one who identified the place where the ark landed as 'the Korduain Mountains' in Armenia, i.e. in his time the Kurdish mountains in Armenia.[46] Of course he and others accepted the legend that on this mountain range still remnants of the ark could be found.

As John Day has demonstrated, Berossos's account of the Flood is remarkably in line with the biblical account of the Flood (Day 2013, 61-76), but as long as no Canaanite parallel has been found it has no relevance to our present investigation.

---

[44] This seemingly contradictory aspect is also present in the union between the destructive Babylonian god Erra and his wife Mamma who was reponsible for motherhood. Cf. Roberts 1971, 13, n. 35.

[45] The following is based on Verbrugghe & Wickersham 1996, 11-52.

[46] Cf. Verbrugghe & Wickersham 1996, 50, with note 20; Day 2011.

3.4 *Iranian Religions*

3.4.1 *Old Iranian Myths*

Mary Boyce gives this succinct description of the Old Iranian cosmogony,

> ...the gods created the world in seven stages. First they made the sky of stone, solid like a huge round shell. In the bottom half of this shell they put water. Next they created earth, resting on the water like a great flat dish; and then at the centre of the earth they fashioned the three animate creations in the form of a single plant, a single animal (the 'Uniquely-created Bull') and a single man (Gayo-maretan, 'Mortal Life'). Seventh, they created fire, both visibly as itself and also as an unseen, vital force pervading the animate creations. The sun, part of the creation of fire, stood still overhead as if it were always noon, for the world was brought into being motionless and unchanging. Then the gods offered a triple sacrifice: they crushed the plant, and slew the bull and man. From this beneficent sacrifice more plants, animals and men came into existence. The cycle of being was thus set in motion, with death followed by new life; and the sun began to move across the sky and to regulate the seasons in accordance with asha.[47]

Later Iranian traditions may still preserve parts of much older creation myths,[48] but we feel incompetent to assess the value of these often rather complicated theories.

3.4.2 *The Gāthās of Zoroaster*

According to some scholars Zoroaster seems to have lived somewhere between 1700 and 1500 BCE (Boyce 1979, 18), but others think of a later date: somewhere before 1000 BCE[49] in the seventh century BCE or even later.[50] Usually the study of Zoroastrianism starts with the *Gāthās*, mostly hymns and prayers, which are considered the most ancient Zoroastrian scriptures, though it is uncertain if all of them go back to the prophet himself. The high-

---

[47] Boyce 1979, 12. *Asha* is a difficult to translate word for natural order as well as truthfulness or justice if it is applied to moral issues. For a fuller treatment see Boyce 1975, 22-177.

[48] See Kreyenbroek 2013.

[49] Kreyenbroek 2013, 133.

[50] Humbach 1991, I, 24-30, 48-49; Ahn 2003, 123-124.

est divine being, Ahura Mazda, the sole Creator of all that is good, revealed himself to this prophet-priest Zoroaster.

Ahura Mazda (Pahlavi name: Ohrmazd) is his uncreated God,[51] existing eternally, Creator of all else that is good, including all other beneficent divinities. His opponent is Angra Maynu – Pahlavi name: Ahriman – the Devil in Zoroastrianism. Both are primal spirits who came together in the beginning to create life and death,

> Yasna 30:3-5
> [3] Yes, there are two fundamental spirits, twins which are renowned to be in conflict. In thought and in word, in action, they are two: the good and the bad. And between these two, the beneficent have correctly chosen, not the maleficent.
> [4] Furthermore, when these two spirits first came together, they created life and death, and how, at the end, the worst existence shall be for the deceitful but the best thinking for the truthful person.
> [5] Of these two spirits, the deceitful one chose to bring to realization the worst things. (But) the very virtuous spirit, who is clothed in the hardest stones, chose the truth, and (so shall those) who shall satisfy the Wise Lord continuously with true actions.[52]

The deceptive spirit succeeded in convincing the Old Iranian gods to choose his side (Yasna 30:6; 32:3-5). The evil spirit is sometimes called 'the enemy' (Yasna 28:6) and is the creator of the deceit that pervades the world (Yasna 51:10).

It is sometimes maintained that this dualistic view does not preclude that Zoroaster was in fact a monotheist, at least initially (Fox 1967). Indeed the rhetorical questions in Yasna 44 suggest that Ahura Mazda is the Creator of all, both luminous bodies and dark spaces, dawn, midday and evening. Zoroaster shrinks back from attributing evil to Ahura, but he does ask himself to which side Ahura will grant victory when it comes to a clash between the hosts of truth and deceit (Yasna 44:15). The same uncertainty transpires in Yasna 53:9,

> Poison adheres to those of evil preferences. They are decline and darkness, these furious violators of truth whose persons have been

[51] Which is not necessarily the only One, cf. Kellens 1994, 13, 118.

[52] Translation Insler 1975, 33. 'Hardest stones' is a metaphor for enduring truth. 'Best thinking' is a metaphor for heaven.

> condemned. Where is the truthful Lord who would expel them from life and liberty?[53]

In general, however, Zoroaster seems to have been convinced that ultimately the struggle between good and evil will be won by the former. His dualism is evident, but the two opponents are not equally strong.

In later Zoroastrian texts motifs occur that seem to come closer to what we found in Ugarit and other Semitic myths. For example, in a late Avestan text it is stated that Angra Mainyu had to flee from heaven when Ahura Mazda brought the good genius Asha-Vahishta into action against the forces of evil,

> Angra Mainyu, who is all death, the worst-lying of all Daevas, rushed from before him (Yašt 3:13).[54]

In the younger Avestan traditions many demons or, if one wants, deities are recognized[55] who have to be neutralized by magic rituals (Ahn 2003). It is questionable if this can still be called monotheism. Ahriman refuses to offer praise to Ohrmazd's very acute creatures[56] and is said to have generated offspring in the form of snakes, scorpions, lizards and frogs.[57] Ahriman also poisons the primordial Tree in the middle of the earth.[58] However, since it is impossible to date such passages with any degree of certainty the possibility remains that they were borrowed from other religions. In any case the Greater Bundahišn presupposes the existence of Islam already.

3.5 *Greek Myths*

3.5.1 *The Primeval Deities*

According to the *Theogony* of Hesiod[59] the first who came into being was Chaos, followed by Earth who brought forth Heaven.

[53] Translation Insler 1975, 113.
[54] Translation Joseph H. Peterson, www.avesta.org/ka/yt3_bi.htm.
[55] Kellens 1994, 121.
[56] Greater Bundahišn I, 19-22, ed. Anklesaria 1956, 6-9.
[57] Greater Bundahišn IV, 15, ed. Anklesaria 1956, 48-49.
[58] Greater Bundahišn, IV,17, ed. Anklesaria 1956, 50-51, cf. Greater Bundahišn Ia, 4, 11, 19.
[59] Hesiod lived somewhere between 750 and 650 BC.

From Chaos also came forth Erebus (Netherworld darkness) and Night. Night and Erebus subsequently engendered Aether and Day in love. Earth also brought forth Hills and the Deep with its raging swell, Pontus (*Theogony*, 116-133). Earth also lay with Heaven and bore other dyads of deities, among them Iapetus (*Theogony*, 134-138). They also engendered Kronos who according to Philo of Byblos was to be equated with the Canaanite supreme god El.[60]

At the urging of his mother Earth Kronos castrated his father Ouranos (Heaven). Earth absorbed the blood of her husband's testicles and bore the Giants from it. Kronos threw the bloody testicles into the sea and from the bloody foam Aphrodite was born on Kythera from where she went to Cyprus where she was also said to be born (*Theogony*, 147-206).

Kronos used to swallow his own children to prevent them from becoming threats to himself, but through a ruse of his mother Rhea, Zeus, 'the father of gods and humans', was saved (*Theogony*, 453-506). When Zeus had grown up he forced his father to give up the deities he had swallowed, among them Iapetus who became the father of Atlas and stole the fire from Zeus. As a price for the fire Zeus instructed Hephaistos to fashion the first human female, 'the beautiful evil'.[61]

Meanwhile Night too bore children, mostly evil deities like Fate and Death, Blame and Woe, Destinies and Fates who determine what will be the lot of every human being, good or bad, punishing the sinners for their transgressions. Night is also the mother of the Hesperides who guard the tree with the golden apples as well as other fruit-bearing trees beyond the Ocean.[62] Sun, Moon, Stars and Dawn were borne much later (*Theogony*, 371-382).

Earth bore another child, Typhon, engendered by Tartarus, the fathomless Deep. Typhon was a serpent with a hundred heads from which fire flashed and unspeakable sounds came forth which only the gods could understand. In a cosmic battle Zeus conquered this monster and threw him down into the Tartarus where he joined Kronos. A great part of the earth was scorched by the hot vapor

---

[60] *Theogony*, 134-138.

[61] *Theogony*, 558-589. Apparently 'mortal humans' existed already.

[62] *Theogony*, 211-225. Later on Hesiod mentions a terrible snake as guardian of the tree with the golden apples (*Theogony*, 333).

of the struggle between Zeus and Typhon and rocks melted.[63]

Evidently there are similarities between the Ugaritic myth and Hesiod's account, but it is difficult to say if any direct dependence may be assumed. The most obvious parallel are the primordial pairs of deities, but such pairs are also attested in Egypt and Mesopotamia. The closest parallel is found in KTU 1.179:9' and KTU 1.100:1 where the pair of deities *šmm wthm* 'Heaven and Flood' occurs at the beginning of some lists. Other lists of deities, however, pair Heaven with Earth,[64] so Ugarit seems to have known similar conflated accounts of the earliest history of the divine world. Also Hesiod's account of the tree with the golden apples seems to be a combination of different traditions.

3.5.2 *Phaeton*

As some have suspected,[65] the Greek myth of Phaeton ('the Luminous'), son of the sun god Helios and the human mother Clymene, shows some relationship with the myth laying behind Isa. 14. According to the account of Ovid (43 BCE–17/18 CE) in his *Metamorphoses* Phaeton badly wanted to drive the sun chariot of his father. Finally his father reluctantly agreed to let him use it, with a lot of paternal advice which Phaeton ignored as soon as he had leapt on the chariot. However, the horses sensed the different driver and bolted. The sun chariot then skimmed dangerously close over the earth, creating clouds of smoke and scorching enormous areas which became deserts. Zeus decided to intervene and threw a lightning bolt at Phaeton who toppled from the chariot, died and was bewailed by all (Ovid, *Metamorphoses* 2, 1-366). Now that it has become likely that according to the Canaanite myth Ḥôrānu, 'the Blazing One', once rebelled against Ilu and when he was thrown down from heaven took revenge by enveloping the earth in a poisonous fog, this seems a close enough parallel to assume that Ovid may have made use of some version of this oriental myth.[66]

---

[63] *Theogony*, 820-868. See also Aeschylus, *Prometheus Bound*, 365-366 (under the volcano Etna); Pseudo-Apollodorus, *Library*, 1.6.3.

[64] See Sections 2.1 and 2.7. This agrees with the theogony of Pseudo-Apollodorus (*Library*, 1.1.1).

[65] E.g. Wildberger 1978, 552-553.

3.6 *Conclusions*

In view of the longstanding debate about the different accounts of creation in the Bible it is a sobering observation that many other nations in the ancient world entertained multiple traditions about the primordial history. Apparently the differences were not experienced as excluding each other which allows for the conclusion that the ancients themselves were realizing that they were speculating when they were writing about events no living person could ever have witnessed.

Moreover, many of the parallels we found are of such a general nature that they can be explained as universal reactions to certain phenomena. For example, the fear of snakes is shared by all human beings. Exaggeration of this fear leads to speculations about serpentine monsters threatening the whole world. Rebellion against oppression by the ruling class is also a universal phenomenon, especially if a generation conflict is involved. Chagrin about the inevitablity of death is a feeling most humans share, so it is not surprising that it has found expression in various Mesopotamian myths.

The differences between the texts discussed are certainly too great to assume direct dependence in every respect but the parallels between accounts of creation and a rebellion against the deities that have emerged are sufficiently strong to assume partial dependence, possibly due to a common substratum of oral tradition. Creation by word alone and comparison with a potter's work are attested in several of the religious traditions discussed. Also the mixing of clay with the blood of a (rebel) god is attested several times and points to the semi-divine status of humankind.

There are also parallels that can hardly be attributed to common experience and primitive 'logic'. It is doubtlessly important that according to the Babylonian myth *The Founding of Eridu* humankind was created *before* all other creatures, just as in Ugarit and in Genesis 2. The narrative of the great Flood in the Sumerian Flood Story, *Atraḫasīs*, the *Gilgameš Epic* and *Berossos*[67]

[66] This becomes even more likely if one considers the possibility that it is an old myth with which another Phaeton mentioned by Hesiod, *Theogony*, 984-992, may be connected. Cf. Van der Sluijs 2008, who also indicates that there is a connection with marriage ceremonies.

may differ in many details from the Hebrew version, but direct depence on a common tradition is hard to deny. However, thus far no story of the Flood and its hero has been discovered in Egypt and Ugarit. Both *Atraḫasīs* and the Ugaritic myth end in a marriage ceremony which expresses the conviction that procreation ensures the immortality of the human race. Ultimately this may go back on Sumerian tradition.

Creation by procreation was also an option for deities in Egypt, Babylonia and Ugarit, but not in Israel. In the late second millennium Egypt, Babylonia and possibly Iran adopted the henotheistic principle, i.e. one creator god was elevated to the highest rank whereas the power of other deities was reduced. In Ugarit Ilu is still the nominal head of the pantheon, but his authority had probably been contested in the past by Ḥôrānu and is being challenged again at the end of the second millennium BCE by the younger god Baʿlu. The parallels between Kronos and Zeus on the one hand, Ilu and Baʿlu on the other are too obvious to be ignored.

Most of the religions discussed knew a capricious god who rebelled against the highest god, but who seems to have repented in the end. The Egyptian rebel god Seth was identified with the Canaanite god Ḥaurān/Ḥôrānu at least as early as the beginning of the second millennium BCE. However, the closest parallel to the Ugaritic divine offender Ḥôrānu is the Babylonian god Erra. Even their names are etymologically related. The two gods share several characteristics, e.g. their fiery looks and their initial determination to destroy the created world. Ḥôrānu, Erra and Ḥaurān/Seth finally regret their evil acts and for that reason were also venerated as friendly gods who were even invoked in connection with love songs and marriage ceremonies. This ambiguous character is an important aspect of their role in the inhabited world.

In contrast to KTU 1.107 the *Poem of Erra* does not start abruptly but has a proper preamble. It was not necessary to start with an account of creation because meanwhile the canonical version of the Babylonian creation myth *Enūma ēliš* had become available.

A more remote parallel is the Greek myth of the demigod Phaeton, the 'Luminous', whose disobedience to his father the sun

[67] See on the Mesopotamian Flood traditions now Chen 2013.

god Helios caused the chariot of the sun to skim dangerously close over the earth, scorching large areas that be became deserts.

It is a popular idea that dualistic concepts in Judaism and Christianity – God (or Jesus) *versus* the Devil – were inspired by Zoroastrianism,[68] but in our opinion this theory must be revised because the existence of inferior deities was not denied in Zoroastrianism and neither the Hebrew Bible nor the New Testament denies the existence of other spirits, good and bad. Moreover, our investigation has shown that the opposition Ilu–Ḥôrānu reflects an inequality that is similar to that in the Bible – ultimately, the Evil One has to give in. Just as Satan has to give in. In the texts of Ugarit one encounters a society struggling with a religious revolution. Baʿlu is trying to replace the old creator god Ilu as the head of the pantheon. However, this younger god had to copy the model laid down by his father-in-law Ilu: Baʿlu too defeated the evil powers of Yammu and Môtu, be it only by a very small margin.

A rebellion of primeval humans against the highest deity is possibly attested in the Egyptian myth *The Cow of Heaven* as well as in the Babylonian epics of *Atraḫasīs* and *Gilgameš*, but it should be remembered that these primeval human beings were seen as semi-divine in all three cases and that the created world apparently already existed. The first humanoid was androgynous and was split into a male and a female half who started the eternal cycle of procreation (Atraḫasīs; Mayer text), but death becomes the destiny of every individual human being (Atraḫasīs, Gilgameš, Adapa, Ugarit, Old Iran).

None of the myths discussed in this Chapter is as close to the biblical accounts of creation, rebellion and restoration of order as the Ugaritic myth. Only these two religions share the names of the divine Creator and the first human-like being. Only here the tree of life/death in the garden/vineyard of God or the Great Gods plays an important role, although Greece may have taken over the motif of a fruit-bearing tree guarded by a huge snake. More parallels as well as differences between the primordial history as narrated in Ugarit and the Bible will be discussed in the next Chapter.

---

68 Hultgård 2000, 76.

4
The Reception in the Hebrew Bible

4.1 *Preliminary Remarks*

'Die biblische Paradieserzählung Gen 2–3 ... gehört zu den *am meisten ausgelegten und wirkungsgeschichtlich wichtigsten Texten der Bibel*.'[1] Similar statements abound in the exegetical literature and have met general assent. While preparing this study we realized once more that it has become totally impossible to gain a comprehensive view of the entire history of research into these fateful chapters and so we feel the urge to apologize in advance for the omissions and mistakes that will no doubt be pointed out by our colleagues. Our only excuse is that in the absence of fresh data the discussion about the primordial history of humanity shows a tendency to endless repetition of the same arguments. Since we believe that the evidence we have presented in the previous chapters opens up new vistas and challenges to biblical scholarship we decided to speed up its publication. Hopefully specialists in other fields will find it worthwhile to investigate these matters further.

We want to state right away that we find ourselves in agreement with the current view that Genesis 1–11, and especially Genesis 1–4,[2] are late monotheistic reworkings of certain earlier, more mythological accounts of the creation of human beings and the primordial history.[3] As they stand now, these chapters have evidently served as an introduction to the Deuteronomistic History in which sin and retribution are the leading motifs. Genesis 1–4 in particular should be understood as the introduction to the whole Hebrew Bible in its canonical form since these chapters presup-

---

[1] Hartenstein 2009, 43.

[2] With Genesis 2–4 as a separate editorial unit. Cf. Peels 2009, 21; Gordon 2011, 206-207

[3] For a brief overview of the discussion see Ska 2008. Lateness does not preclude the adoption of earlier materials (Gertz 2004) and therefore we will devote attention to source critical aspects only when this seems expedient. For a presentation of the distinctive priestly and non-priestly layers in Gen. 1–11 see Arneth 2007.

pose Israels failure to keep the stipulations of the Sinai covenant throughout its early history.[4]

It has often been emphasized that the first chapters of the Bible want to be understood as history which would distinguish them clearly from the genre of 'myth'.[5] The problem with this kind of argument is that it rests on a supposed distinction between 'myth' as fiction and 'history' as an account of real events. This distinction cannot be maintained. The myths an epics of the ancient world were written in the past tense because they too wanted to be understood as 'history'. Historical records from the past were rarely accurate representations of what had really happened. They were colored by what their authors wanted to believe.[6] At the end of this book we will outline our own position in this debate (Section 7.3).

In most subdivisions of this chapter we will first discuss the main differences between the Ugaritic myth and the biblical passage, followed by an enumeration of possible similarities. Inevitably this is no more than a first rather superficial attempt to take stock.

4.2 *Genesis 1*

It has long been recognized that Genesis 1:1–2:3 belongs to the material written by a priestly writer at a relatively late date in the development of the Hebrew Bible. Several elements in the first creation story point to this late origin in priestly circles[7] and most differences between the Ugaritic myth and Genesis 1:1–2:3 are related to this priestly point of view. The circumstance that, as we hope to demonstrate, some similarities were allowed to remain may be explained by the fact that the author also had to reckon with originally Canaanite traditions which through folk religion had be-

---

[4] E.g. Schüle 2006; Postell 2011; Adamczewski 2012.

[5] Lately James Hoffmeier's contributions to Halton 2015.

[6] This was correctly observed by Kenton Sparks and to a lesser extent by Gordon Wenham in their contributions to the same volume.

[7] See for a lucid treatment of this priestly origin Smith 2010. It is possible that a redactor of the Holiness Code (H) was responsible for Gen. 1 as a complement of Gen. 2–3. Cf. Arnold 2012, with earlier literature. In any case it seems unwise to detach Gen. 1 from its traditional context. Cf. MacDonald 2013.

come generally accepted, just as they entered other late writings like pseudepigraphic works and the New Testament.

As John Day has pointed out recently, it is possible that the priestly writer was inspired by Ps. 104. Day admits that this Psalm too might have reached Israel through Canaanite channels which had adopted the hymn from Akhenaten (Day 2013, 19-23). If so, it is not easy to disentangle the tradition history of this impressive tribute to the Creator of all.

4.2.1 *Differences*

1. The Creator God is called אֱלֹהִים. The usage of the petrified plural for a singular deity is unattested in Ugarit (cf. Section 2.1). However, it has been argued that אֱלֹהִים replaces an earlier use of אֵל which is the Hebrew equivalent of Ugaritic Ilu.[8] No 'God-the-Father' (Ugaritic *ʾilʾib*) preceded אֱלֹהִים.

2. The importance attached to the Sabbath (Gen. 2:1-3) is distinctive.[9] Although sequences of seven days occur frequently in Ugaritic literature (see below), no concept comparable to the Sabbath seems to have developed there.

3. The use of the unique verb ברא which earlier probably meant 'to build, construct', but which is here reserved for the incomparable work of God's creation because the common verb בנה was felt to be too trivial and was used by Israel's neighbors to describe creation by their deities.[10]

4. In Ugarit the equivalent of Hebrew תְּהוֹם is masculine *thm* and feminine *thmt*. Both designate the primordial Flood, but in Ugarit *šmm wthm* 'Heaven and Flood' are deities.[11] The priestly writer

---

[8] See e.g. De Moor 1997 *passim*; Davies 2006, 186.

[9] Cf. Arnold 2012, 334-336.

[10] Becking & Korpel 2010 who reject the proposal of Van Wolde 2009a, 184-200 and Van Wolde 2009b to translate ברא in Gen. 1:1–2:4a by 'to distinguish' or 'to separate' instead of the customary 'to create'. See also the critical remarks by Walton 2011, 127-133 and Day 2013, 5-6. The rejoinder by Van Wolde & Rezetko 2011 does not convince the present writers.

[11] De Moor 2008, 181. A term *thw* 'steppe, desert' which might be thought to correspond to Hebrew תֹּהוּ, does not exist in Ugaritic (contra Del Olmo Lete & Sanmartín 2003, 864-865).

studiously avoids anything which might hint at such a divine status of these cosmic entities.[12]

5. The refusal to use the names of sun and moon which were quite innocently employed by earlier biblical writers (שֶׁמֶשׁ and יָרֵחַ) and their replacement by 'the great light' and 'the small light' (Gen. 1:14-18) reflects a strict monotheistic dogmatism that is foreign to most other biblical books.[13] The reason for this strictness is evidently that in the world around Israel sun and moon were venerated as deities However, this might be a later correction of an earlier version in which the names were still used, because even the priestly writer describes the task of the lights as 'rulership' (מֶמְשָׁלָה) over day and night, as if they were divine royal beings (Gen. 1:16).

6. The priestly writer wanted to avoid the impression that God would have created or even engendered other deities. Whereas in the surrounding cultures deities often transformed themselves into theriomorphic shapes so that animals in turn might resemble deities and were worshiped as deities, the priestly writer restricts the honor to resemble God to humankind alone (Gen. 1:26-27).[14]

7. Of course there was no room anymore for a creatress like Ilu's wife Aṯiratu or the sun goddess Šapšu in the priestly creation narrative.

8. One of the significant differences between Genesis 1 and myths about the creation of humankind in the cultures surrounding Israel is that God created humans in his image, whereas the surrounding cultures held that cult images of their gods were born in heaven, though made on earth.[15] In the Hebrew priestly tradition the direction of the act is opposite to that in other cultures. According to the priestly writer of Genesis 1 the likeness of God was conceived and made in heaven. A slight, but important difference.

[12] Tsumura 2005; Watson 2005, 269-272, both with earlier literature.

[13] See, however, Isa. 24:23; 30:26 הַלְּבָנָה 'the white one' for the moon and הַחַמָּה 'the hot one' for the sun.

[14] We disagree with James Barr who stated that אָדָם can only mean 'male human being'. Cf. De Moor 1999.

[15] Compare the aptly chosen title of the volume edited by Dick 1999 who cites the relevant ancient oriental texts.

9. In Gen. 2:1-2 the priestly writer emphasizes that God *finished* (כלה pi.) his work of creation on the seventh day. This implies that he opposed the idea of a *creatio continua*[16] which is attested all over the ancient Near East, including Ugarit (Sections 2.1 and 3), and also in many other passages in the Hebrew Bible.[17]

10. In other cultures of the ancient Near East dominion was considered a prerogative of deities and royalty. Since initially Adammu was a god it seems that the circumstance that he was given dominion over the earth before he was bitten by the serpent (KTU 1.107:3) remained in accordance with this ideology. However, in contrast to this Gen. 1:28-30 and 9:2 attribute the assignment to rule the world to the *entire* human race. This has rightly been described as a 'democratization' of the idea of dominion.[18]

11. Knowing that Gen. 2–6 would follow immediately, the priestly author confirms time and again that God's creation was good. Evilness was introduced by the failure of humans to always choose what is right and good. It is surely significant that after the creation of humankind the refrain 'And God saw that is was good' is missing between vv. 27 and 28, though v. 31 tries to remedy this, obviously because someone realized that also in this respect humans resembled God. In the polytheistic world around Israel the deities are unpredictable and ambiguous, sometimes good, sometimes bad.[19] As a result, not all aspects of creation are totally good. Malicious deities and evil spirits threaten the good life on earth. However, the evilness existing in this world continued to trouble Israel's stern monotheists.[20]

4.2.2 *Similarities*

While it is certainly true that the priestly writer of Gen. 1:1–2:3 composed a masterful, coherent creation story reflecting his

---

[16] An ongoing process of creation throughout history.
[17] Angerstorfer 1979, 224-225; Becking & Korpel 2010, 18.
[18] Cf. Middleton 2005, 121; Levenson 1988, 114, 116, but also the *caveat* of Moberly 2009, 53-54. A similar development took place with regard to beatific afterlife, cf. Spronk 1986, 91-92, 310.
[19] Cf. Batto 2013, 199-228 on the malevolence and capriciousness of deities in Mesopotamian myth.
[20] Countless studies, many of them in Laato & De Moor 2003.

own theological insights, it cannot be denied any longer that even he used older mythical traditions that were partially written in poetry. These older traditions agree in many respects with what we have found with regard to creation in the texts of Ugarit (mainly Section 2.1),

1. In Genesis 1 the Creator of all is אֱלֹהִים, a reverent plural of the elative form (אֱלוֹהַ) of the Ugaritic creator Ilu, El (אֵל) in the Hebrew Bible (Section 2.1). All three designations of God occur both in Ugarit and in the Hebrew Bible (cf. Section 2.1). This is a major difference with other ancient Near Eastern religions where the creator gods bear totally different names.

2. If one translates Gen. 1:1-2 'In the beginning[21] when God created heaven and earth, the earth was void and emptiness and darkness was over the the surface of the Flood' (or a similar rendering), as has been advocated by many scholars, the Flood was already there before God started his work of creation.[22] This would be in agreement with other Near Eastern creation myths, the Ugaritic one probably among them (Section 2.1).

3. Egypt, Babylonia, Ugarit and the Hebrew Bible appear to have known the concept of creation by word alone. The dogma of *creatio ex nihilo* (creation out of nothing) can no longer be regarded as a unique feature of Genesis 1.

4. It has long been observed that the seven day scheme of Genesis 1 is a literary form that was popular in ancient oriental literature and especially in Ugaritic myths and epics. The relevance of this datum for the interpretation of Genesis 1 was recognized by several scholars,[23] but is still unknown to many readers of the Bible.[24]

---

[21] *r'išyt* in the meaning of 'beginning, primordial time' does occur in Ugarit (KTU 1.119:25), but describes the beginning of kingship, not the beginning of creation.

[22] We are unconvinced by the objections to this interpretation (e.g. Walton 2011, 123-127; Day 2013, 6-7.).

[23] See e.g. Bauer 1935; Cassuto 1961, 167-168; Ridderbos 1963, 63-65; Loewenstamm 1980.

[24] Even to Collins 2013. The objection that other people in the ancient Near East also had a 'history' about the beginning of the world and humanity breaks down on the argument that all ancient civilizations (Egypt. Mesopotamia and also Israel) allowed several accounts of creation to exist

Of course the priestly writer used this literary ploy because he intended to make the Sabbath the crowning event of creation.

5. Although the division of the primordial flood of Gen. 1:2-8 into the waters above the firmament and the waters under the firmament is attested also in other ancient Near Eastern religions (Section 3.5.5), the Ugaritic descriptions are much closer to Genesis 1. The same terminology is used[25] and the same deity is responsible for this event, be it that in Ugarit the younger god Baʿlu (Baal) aspires to take over Ilu's role of the Creator who separated the primordial waters (Section 2.1).

6. Whereas the priestly writer avoided the names of sun and moon, he maintained the pair heaven and earth (Gen. 1:1-2, 8-10). Perhaps he did not know any longer that *ʾarṣ wšmm* 'Heaven and Earth' had been Canaanite deities.[26]

7. In Gen. 1:12 and 1:24 God orders the earth 'to bring forth' (יצא Hiph.) vegetation and all kinds of living animals. Since the same verb is used occasionally to describe the bringing forth of offspring,[27] this may be regarded as a faint echo of the concept of the earth as the mother of all.[28]

8. According to Gen. 1:20-22 God also created the sea-monsters[29] and all creatures swarming in the waters and the air. Remarkably enough the Priestly Writer does not differentiate between clean and unclean animals here, as in e.g. Lev. 11:10, 46; 20:25. On the contrary, God pronounces them all 'good', blesses them and orders them to multiply. This acceptance of the idea that God was also responsible for the existence of evil or abhorrent creatures may

side by side, testifying to their awareness of the conjectural nature of any 'history writing' about the beginnings of the cosmos and its inhabitants.

[25] רָקִיעַ is missing, but this is probably accidental, cf. Dijkstra 2011, 55, n. 6.

[26] Cf. Section 2.1. The reverse order of the names is unimportant, cf. De Moor 1970a, 227, and Gen. 2:4.

[27] Clines, *DCH*, vol. 4, 262-263.

[28] Cf. Dijkstra 1999; Kübel 2007, 123. It is no valid objection to this suggestion that God causes the earth *orally* to bring forth. The same concept existed in Ugarit, cf. Section 2.1.

[29] There is insufficient reason to deny the mythological nature of these animals, cf. Westermann 1974, 190-191; Korpel 1990, 555-558. Contrast Hendel 2013, 38.

seem a consequence of Israel's monotheistic faith, but it is not. In KTU 1.12:I.14-33 Ilu too creates horrible monsters by his word alone.

9. Although hitherto no equivalent of דְּמוּת has turned up in Ugarit, the terms describing the likeness to God of human beings in Gen. 1:26[30] are simply taken over from the same terms other Canaanites used to describe a cult image of a king.[31] In any case the idea that humankind reflected the physical appearance and spiritual excellence of the deity more than any other creature is definitely attested in the ancient Near East, also in Ugarit (Section 2.1).[32]

10. In Ugarit immortality by sexual intercourse was granted earlier to animals than to the first humanoids (Section 2.5). The same is the case in Genesis 1. This is expressed by the formula פְּרוּ וּרְבוּ 'be fruitful and multiply' which is used on the fifth day in the blessing of the animals (Gen. 1:22), and by the same formula in connection with human procreation on the sixth day (Gen. 1:28). The importance of this notion is underlined by its repetition in Gen. 8:17 and 9:1 when humanity is allowed to make a new start (Section 4.4).

11. The priestly writer did not erase entirely the androgynous nature of the first humanoid creatures before they were separated into man and woman because he deemed it logical to suppose that this had been the case and because it allowed him to reconcile his own view with that of the Yahwist (Gen. 1:26-27). To this end he adapted a poetic description of the first humanoid that concurs remarkably with what we found in Ugarit and elsewhere in the ancient Near East (Sections 2.3, 2.6; 3).[33]

---

[30] Repeated in Gen. 9:6, cf. Section 4.4.

[31] Aramaic *dmwt'* and *ṣlm'*, Abou-Assaf *et al.* 1982, 28, 33; Dietrich & Loretz 2003, 323, 40; Day 2013, 13-15.

[32] Therefore it is unwarranted to overemphasize the uniqueness and theological importance of Gen. 1:26-27, as is done by many colleagues, even by Middleton 2005. It is also unwarranted to reduce the likeness to purely functional similarity, cf. Schellenberg 2009, 100-101. In observing these points we do not want to deny at all that the reverse – the anthropomorphousness of deities – is far more prominent in the 'Umwelt' of Israel.

[33] This is elaborated in De Moor 1998a. See also Becking 2011, 8-9. The idea that God would be consulting other gods here in order to dismiss them immediately (so e.g. Carr 2003; Day 2013, 11-13) does not differ

12. According to Gen. 1:28-30 God gave Adam dominion over all parts of the cosmos and their inhabitants.[34] Especially Tryggve Mettinger has pointed to the fact that the idea of the *dominium terrae* has significant parallels in ancient Near Eastern descriptions of kingship.[35] Now it seems likely that in Ugarit the great gods exalted Adammu and gave the earth in his hand (Section 2.1). There is no mention of kingship in KTU 1.107 or KTU 1.100, but all the great deities of Ugarit were depicted as royalty, each with a specific domain. This warrants the question whether it was not the other way round – the high status of 'divine' royalty being derived from that of deities.[36]

4.3 *Genesis 2–4*

The story of Eden in Genesis 2–3 and the account of the first murder in Genesis 4 have fascinated readers of the Bible from Antiquity to our age. Modern research into the origin and development of these narratives indicates a long and complicated redactional development of the present text which ended only in the postexilic period.[37] We agree with that point of view. Impressive attempts

---

substantially from the old assumption that God would be addressing the heavenly court of angels here. The same objections remain in force. Clines 1990, 44 writes: 'To say, for example, that women as well as men are created as the image of God is to move beyond the horizon of the text.' We believe that P held that in the first human being both sexes were present, to be separated only later on. This idea too was borrowed from Mesopotamia (Section 3.3.10-12).

[34] This too is repeated when humanity is allowed to make a new start in Gen. 9:2. Cf. Section 4.4.

[35] Mettinger 2005. It is evident that this is meant as responsible stewardship of the king (Day 2013, 15-16).

[36] In KTU 1.14:VI.26-28 the beauty of princess Ḥariya is compared to that of the goddesses of love ʿAnatu and ʿAṯtartu. In Sumerian love songs bride and groom are compared to figurines of the beautiful deities Inanna and Dumuzi, cf. Uehlinger 1988; Sefati 1998, 92-93, 267-280.

[37] See e.g. Uehlinger 1988; Van Seters 1992, 128; Otto 1996; Kübel 2007; Arneth 2007, 97-147. After an evenhanded and sympathetic survey of the long recognized contradictions and tensions in Gen. 2–4 R.W.L. Moberly concludes, 'in analytical terms one should recognize that the narrative is, in a very real and important sense, artificial and constructed out of originally diverse material' (Moberly 2009, 28; similarly LaCocque 2006, 5-6). Becking 2011, 3-4 prefers a date in the late monarchic era.

to present a coherent synchronous reading of the text definitely have their merits[38] but cannot explain away the diversity of the sources that have been combined in Genesis 2–4.

We think that it requires too much modern ingenuity to eliminate the notion of a first or 'original' transgression from these chapters. The use of the term 'original sin' may be frowned upon by scholars who are of the opinion that Genesis 2–3 do not contain any indication of the so-called 'Fall'.[39] Not even the origin of death would have been meant by the author.[40] The Ugaritic myth renders the latter point of view highly unlikely.[41] In general it is difficult to believe that the first transgression of a divine command did not result in punishment in the form of death.[42] Deities and rulers of the ancient oriental world meted out capital punishment for far lesser offenses.[43]

The biblical account of the new start of humanity after the great Flood emphasizes Noah's obedience to God's commandments (Gen. 6:22; 7:5, 9, 16), thus creating a sharp contrast with Adam and Eve. Moreover, the Egyptian myth of the *Cow of Heaven* furnishes a convincing parallel of original sin by humanity in the

---

38 E.g. Van Wolde 1989; Mettinger 2007, 12-41.

39 E.g. Ricoeur 1969, 232-233; Levison 1988; Meyers 1988, 77; Barr 1992, ix, 5-6; Becking 2011, 9-12. Some feminist authors express themselves very strongly on this point, e.g. Carmichael 1992, 47, 'The later pious understanding of the story is in fact a classic example of how a text has been misinterpreted to mean the opposite of its originally intended meaning'.

40 Barr 1992b, 5-10; De Villiers 2009.

41 Contrast a statement like that of Ricoeur 1969, 233: 'All the speculations on the supernatural perfection of Adam before the fall are aventitious contrivances.' We now know that Adammu was indeed a god before he was bitten by the snake, but obviously divinity did not entail a continuous state of immortality in the ancient Near East as, among others, the Ugaritic *Myth of Baʿlu* demonstrates.

42 Cf. Mettinger 2007, 95: 'The fact that express terminology for "sin" ... does not appear in the Eden Narrative should not lead to premature conclusions.'; Gordon 2010, 14: 'The key point about the eating of the forbidden fruit is that it is an act of disobedience'; Day 2013, 45: 'The idea of sin is there, even if the word is absent'.

43 The goddess ʿAnatu, for example, has the young hero Aqhâtu murdered because he refuses to hand over his miraculous bow, a gift of a god, and spurns her offer of eternal life, calling her a liar (KTU 1.17:VI.25-39). The goddess characterizes this behavior as *pšʿ* 'transgression' and *gʾan* 'arrogance' (KTU 1.17:VI.43-44).

form of an insurrection against the highest god Re.[44] So it is certainly possible that such a concept was developed in Israel too. This is at least what Ben Sira (*ca.* 180 BCE) thought when he wrote in Sir. 25:24,

מאשה תחלת עון	By a woman was sin's beginning,
ובגללה גוענו יחד	and on her account we all die.[45]

However, whether a human being was the first to sin remains to be seen. The Ugaritic form of the 'Adamic Myth' seems to indicate that a *god* was the first rebel and this is in accordance with other traditions which we hope to discuss later on. This raises the question why the final form of Gen. 2–3 attributed the first transgression so emphatically to a woman.

4.3.1 *Differences*

1. Nowadays most scholars agree that Genesis 2:4–3:24 is a very late, but well-composed literary unit. Its author must have known the creation story of Genesis 1, the Deuteronomistic History and Ezekiel 28.[46] As compared to the Canaanite myth, the biblical story of Eden was adapted to the deuteronomistic doctrine of sin and retribution. Just as Israel as a people would not be able to keep God's commandments, Adam and Eve did not resist the provocation by the serpent and disobeyed the only command (צוה, Gen. 2:16) God had given them in the garden. The command 'you shall not eat' (Gen. 2:17) is formulated in the same categorical way as the ten commandments.[47] This is also evident in Genesis 4:3-4

---

[44] Hornung 1982; Lichtheim 1997, 36-37; see Section 3.2.3. Perhaps a human(oid) rebel occurs also in the Babylonian poem Atraḫasīs, cf. Section 3.3.1.

[45] Hebrew text according to manuscript C (Beentjes 1997, 99). For a broader discussion see Section 5.5.

[46] See e.g. Wyatt 1981; Stordalen 1992, 175-77; 2000, 213; Van Seters 1992, 124-126; LaCocque 2006, 5-8; Otto 1996; 2007; Mettinger 2007, 13, n. 8; 16-17; 59, 134-135; Kvanvig 2011, 189-190, 204–207. Some scholars regard Gen. 2:8, 9b, 10-14, 16-17 as later additions (Keel & Schroer 2002, 143). Becking 2000, 3-4 and Day 2013, 48-49 argue for a pre-exilic date.

[47] Cf. Postell 2011, 35. Already 4 Baruch 3:7 and the Targum noticed this allusion to the Law, the Targum by adding to Gen. 2:15 that God took Adam to dwell in the garden of Eden to toil *in the Law* and to observe *its commandments*, cf. Grossfeld 1988, 58.

where Cain and Abel fulfill the Law with regard to the first fruits, though Cain proleptically neglects a command like Exod. 23:7.

Although not the entire primordial story has been preserved in Ugaritic, nothing suggests that Adammu and his wife were condemned to death because of transgression of a divine commandment. Adammu has to die because in spite of the considerable powers the 'great gods' invested in him he appeared to be unable to avoid the poisonous bite of the primeval serpent.

2. The monotheistic principle of the final author of the biblical story constitutes a major step forward in the history of humanity because humans are no longer subjected to the whims of many unpredictable deities,[48] but become accountable to the one God and their fellow humans for their own choices between good and evil.[49] In Ugarit humans like Kirtu, Danīʾilu and Aqhâtu are righteous sufferers who have to pay heavy penalties inflicted by capricious deities even though they are guiltless (Danīʾilu) or because of relatively minor offenses (Kirtu and Aqhâtu). In the Bible the roles are reversed: the ambiguousness of the gods becomes the ambiguousness of human individuals. This is a fundamental shift in outlook to which we will come back in the epilogue to this book (Section 7.3).

3. Throughout Gen. 2:4–3:24 the divine name is יְהוָה אֱלֹהִים. John Day surmises that everywhere אֱלֹהִים has been added to יְהוָה by a later redactor 'to make it perfectly clear in the polytheistic environment of the ancient world that Yahweh was the same deity as Elohim referred to in the previous narrative of Gen. 1.1–2.4a.' (Day 2013, 25; see also MacDonald 2013). But why would a theological issue entirely up to Israel have bothered the polytheistic 'Umwelt'? In our opinion it is much more logical to suppose that יְהוָה אֱלֹהִים replaces the very old name of God יְהוָה אֵל.[50] This name even crops up in the *Apocalypse of Abraham* and the *Ladder of Jacob* as another name of El (Sections 5.12 and 5.13).

[48] See Sections 2.3 and 2.9 on the duplicity/ambiguity of certain Ugaritic deities.

[49] However, also in this respect a partial similarity may be observed (see below, Section 4.3.2 point 6).

[50] Cf. De Moor 1997, 310-369.

Thus far no comparable name has been found in Ugarit and for that reason we regard יְהוָה אֱלֹהִים or יְהוָה אֵל as a distinctive feature of the biblical description of the events in the garden of Eden. However, in KTU 1.1:IV.13-20 Ilu renames his son *Yw* 'Yammu' (Sea). The circumstance that the latter's servants refuse to bow to Ilu's pantheon has been adduced as an argument for the linguistically possible identification of *Yw* with the name of the God of Israel (De Moor 1997, 164-168).

4. There was no 'Tree of Knowledge of Good and Evil' in the Ugaritic vineyard of the gods. The similarity between the biblical and the Ugaritic account lays in the likelihood that the Tree of Life became a Tree of Death. However, we believe that there are good reasons to assume that the Tree of Knowledge was identical to the Tree of Life in Genesis so there may well have been only one tree in Eden (see below).

5. Whereas Kubaba and Adammu were regarded as deities before Adammu (nearly?) died of snakebite, the Hebrew writers make Adam and Eve humans from the start, although it is not always easy to choose between a proper name 'Adam' and a generic designation 'the human' or 'the male'.[51] However, these first humans desired to be like God (or: gods), but were duped (Gen. 3:5-7).

6. It is sometimes stated that the use of עָפָר 'dust' in Gen. 2:7 is a distinctive element in the Eden story, because it anticipates the עָפָר in Gen. 3:19, characterizing the first human being as mortal from the beginning. It is doubtful whether this is a cogent argument. At least in Job 10:9 and possibly also in Job 27:16 עָפָר 'dust' and חֹמֶר 'clay' seem to occur as synonyms.

No Canaanite myth relates that God himself blew his breath/spirit in the first humanoid being. In Gen. 2:7 it is God himself who blows the spirit of life into the first human being, in Ugarit it is a minor goddess – Tāqiʿatu, one of the Kôṯarātu, goddesses protecting conception to childbirth – who blows air into the lungs of babies (KTU 1.24:49). The major difference is of course that

---

[51] Hess 1990. Perhaps we should correct the Masoretic text of Gen. 2:20b; 3:17, 21 to make all occurrences of אָדָם before Gen. 4:25 appellatives (Mettinger 2007, 30; Day 2013, 24, 32).

according to Genesis a man had a part of God's breath/spirit, but a woman only indirectly through his 'flesh'.[52]

7. Adam's naming of the animals (Gen. 2:19-20) is lacking in the extant parts of the Ugaritic myth.

8. Although both stories emphasize the importance of procreation (see below) the explicit descriptions of sexuality in the Ugaritic texts are lacking in the Hebrew narrative. On the contrary, Gen. 3:7, 10 imply that nakedness became shameful (contrast Gen. 2:25) and Gen. 3:15-16 stresses the woman's pain in childbirth and ascribes only to her sensual desire.[53]

9. Whereas the serpent in the Ugaritic myth bites Adammu, the serpent in the biblical narrative only speaks to Eve.[54] However, Amos 9:3 suggests that God can command 'the serpent' (הַנָּחָשׁ) at the bottom of the sea to *bite* people. This indicates that in Israel too the concept of a biting Leviathan was known, be it fitted into the henotheistic principle.

Although a giant speaking serpent is attested in the Egyptian tale of *The Shipwrecked Sailor* and in Hesiod's description of Typhon,[55] no serpent speaks in the extant portions of the Ugaritic

[52] Cf. Uehlinger 1988, 93-94.

[53] Whatever translation one chooses for תְּשׁוּקָה, cf. Clines, *DCH*, Vol 8, 684. Beattie 2014 argues for an early, erroneous transposition of the male's lust (תְּשׁוּקָתוֹ) to Gen. 4:7. This is not impossible (cf. Song 7:11). According to the preserved part of the Ugaritic tablet KTU 1.107:46' female arousal is seen as the stimulus for male arousal, so there too a certain reciprocity is present. However, the emphasis on the shamefulness of nakedness in the canonical text of Gen. 3 casts doubt on Beattie's proposal. In our opinion the present text of Gen. 4:7 rather refers back to Gen. 3:15: it is the ardent wish of the serpent to bite the heel of humans, but both Gen. 3:15 and Gen. 4:7 state confidently that humankind will be able to prevail.

[54] The description of the natural enmity between the offspring of Adam and that of the serpent in Gen. 3:15 is commonly seen as a mutual instinct to destroy each other, on the part of the snakes by biting the human's heel. However, the interpretation of the verb שׁוּף is difficult. Cf. Clines, *DCH*, vol. 8, 308, 723. If it does mean something like 'destroy' it is significant that according to the Ugaritic myth the offspring of Ḥôrānu is threatened to be extinguished by the major deities of Ilu's pantheon whereas according to Gen. 3:15 the offspring of the woman will defeat the offspring of the serpent. But a different solution will be proposed in Section 4.8.

[55] Sections 2.8 and 3.5.1.

myth. Yet the speaking serpent in Eden may be regarded as a trace of its polytheistic background. In Ugaritic and other ancient Near Eastern myths deities could switch effortless between anthropomorphic and theriomorphic shapes.[56]

10. One of the most significant differences between the Ugaritic account and the biblical story of Eden is the evaluation of the first sin. In view of the fact that the ancient Near East, including Ugarit, held a very low opinion of women in general,[57] which resulted in an androcentric orientation in the world of the Bible[58] it is striking that in none of the other ancient Near Eastern creation narratives the negative role of the woman has got so much emphasis as in the biblical narrative (cf. Section 3). Many modern scholars have tried to nullify the idea that Genesis 2–3 would describe a human transgression but this is only possible when reading the text with a modern, western and maybe feminist point of view. We disagree with such strategies.[59] The curses in Gen. 3:14-19 are clearly intended as lasting punishment because of the transgression of God's command. The narrative is a story about the first man and his wife, but the text does not state that because of Eve *all* humans are doomed to wickedness. This would even be in contradiction to the basic principle of quasi-equality of man and woman the author accepted.[60] Also the references to Genesis 2–3 in the book of Job (e.g. Job 1:21; 5:7; 14:1; 15:7; 20:4; 31:33) confirm that the author was not aware of any narrative that blamed Eve for the origin of sin, otherwise he could have used this as an argument. On the contrary, Job questions whether he did any evil (Job 7:20) and stresses the fact that he did not hide any transgression, as Adam did (Job 31:33).[61] Nevertheless, compared to other ancient Near Eastern parallels the text of Genesis 2–3 seems to

---

[56] See e.g. Sections 2, 4.2 and 6.

[57] Marsman 2003.

[58] Clines 1990 is doubtlessly right in maintaining that one should not try to make Gen. 2–3 an exception.

[59] See Section 4.3 above. As Christoph Levin (2009, 92) points out, the story does not tell the story of the origin of sin in general, but it describes the first disobedience of human beings against God and its dire consequences.

[60] Cf. Otto 2007, 127-128, but note our observation above, point 6.

[61] There is no reason at all to suppress the name of 'Adam' in this verse. Cf. Tur-Sinai 1957, 446; Gordis 1978, 353; Clines 2006, 971-972, 1029-1030.

emphasize the negative role of Eve. The idea seems to be absent outside Israel, except for Greece (Pandora, see below). Even in the rest of the canonical Bible there seems to be no remembrance of the first woman as the first sinner, but just Adam.[62]

In the Ugaritic texts published to date there is no mention of any transgression by Adammu, and his wife even seems to be described as having a good character. It is the god Ḥôrānu who is the bad genius who causes death on earth. The Babylonian myth *Enūma ēliš* and the *Myth of the Creation of Humankind and the King*[63] describes the creation of humans as the result of the laziness of the gods. They were in need of helpers who could till the ground for them, and do the heavy work. The only 'mistake' of humankind is that they make too much noise, but there is no differentiation into male or female in this 'human transgression'. Also the Egyptian myth of *The Cow of Heaven* does not differentiate between the sexes of the human rebels (Section 3.2.3). So, why was Eve cast in such an exceptional, negative role in the biblical narrative? Why is it she who listens to the serpent and disobeys God's commandment not to eat from the Tree in the middle of the garden?

Now that the narrative of Gen. 2:4–3:22 is generally assumed to have its origin in exilic times or even later, it is quite clear that Hellenistic influence could have had an impact on the story. Several scholars have suggested that especially the focus on the bad behaviour of Eve in the story has its counterpart in the Greek story of Pandora. Her name can mean both 'present of all the gods' (Hesiod's etymology) as well as 'she who gives all things' (Philo Judaeus).[64] The latter strikingly resembles the etymology of Eve's name in Genesis 3:20, 'mother of all living'. In this respect it is interesting that the ancient poets used to name the earth 'Pandora' too, as noticed by Philo, in the description of 'mother of all, fruitbearing and giver of all'.[65]

---

62 Cf. Isa. 43:27; Job 31:33; Rom. 5:12; 1 Cor. 15:22. See also 4 Ezra 4:30; 7:116-119 (46-49). However, it is also possible that this reflects the idea that a man was responsible for all acts of his wife. 'Adam' in Hos. 6:7 is probably a place name. Cf. Macintosh 1997, 236; Metzger 2009, 530-531, 541; Becking 2011, 2.

63 Cf. Section 3 on the 'Mayer' text.

64 Cf. Bremmer 2000, 26-27.

Hesiod was the first to tell about the creation of the woman and he calls her καλόν κακόν 'the beautiful evil'.[66] He ends his story about her stating that Zeus made women to be an evil to mortal men, with a nature to do evil.[67] Utterances like these leave nothing to the imagination with regard to the view on women and it cannot be denied that the story of Genesis 2:4–3:22 with regard to the figure of Eve shows remarkable resemblance to the Pandora story.[68] Despite occasional praise for upper class women as managers of households[69] women remained subordinated to men and were often charged with a natural propensity to do wrong. All extremely negative verdicts on women are attested in postexilic and later texts when the impact of the Greek culture on Israel intensified.

Especially the Book of Ben Sira of the second century BCE reveals a rather negative attitude towards women. He keeps conspicuously silent on the role of Israel's matriarchs and heroines of the past and he devotes much more attention to evil than to good women.[70] Earlier we indicated already that Ben Sira attributes death to Eve's sin (Sir. 25:24), but one should read the entire context of that statement. We quote some verses in translation,[71]

> (25:15) No poison worse than that of a serpent,
> no venom greater than that of a woman.
> (25:16) With a dragon or a lion I would rather dwell
> than live with an evil woman.
> (26:7) A bad wife is a chafing yoke;
> whoever marries her has a scorpion in his grasp.

With regard to a man's unmarried daughter Ben Sira has a stern warning,

> כי מבגד יצא עש For as a moth comes out of a garment,

[65] Bremmer 2000, 32.
[66] Hesiod, *Theogony*, 585. Hesiod lived somewhere between 750 and 650 BCE.
[67] Hesiod, *Theogony*, 590-612. Some scholars regard this criticism as a later interpolation in the work of Hesiod, but that makes little difference for our investigation.
[68] Phipps 1989, 37-49; Van Seters 1992, 125, Blenkinsopp 2011, 9, 70-71.
[69] Xenophon, *Economics*, III.14-15; Prov. 31:10-31. Cf. Cohn Eskenazi 2013; Maier 2013.
[70] Schroer 1996, 96-101; Calduch-Benages 2013.
[71] Mainly following Skehan & Di Lella 1987, 343.

ומאשה רעת אשה	so a woman's wickedness (comes) out of a woman.
מטוב רוע	Better being wicked than good
איש מטיב אשה	when a man is making a woman good,[72]
ובית מחפרת	and better a family than the foul language
תביע אש	a woman pours forth.[73]

Also the *Testament of Reuben*, part of the Testament of the Twelve Patriarchs, dated in the second century BCE, contains a highly negative description of women, starting with the statement,

> For evil are women, my children, and by reason of their lacking authority or power over man, they scheme treacherously how they might entice him to themselves by means of their looks.[74]

Where did this misogyny originate? The prophets had often attributed idolatry – defined as whoring – to women and this may have been a reason why after the fall of Jerusalem especially women were blamed for the downfall of the holy city.[75] Ephraim Stern has surveyed the distribution of small female figurines in Judah that are dated from the late eighth century down to the beginning of the sixth century BCE. After the exile such figurines

---

[72] I.e. 'correcting, chastising her'. See also Sir. 26:10.

[73] Sir. 42:13-14. We follow MS B here. There are several variant readings in other manuscripts, the most interesting one coming from the Masada scroll, ובת מפחדת מכול חרפה. 'and a respectful daughter better than any disgrace', cf. Beentjes 1997, 74, 117. We have opted for the *lectio difficilior* of B which creates a kind of parallelism between vv. 13b and 14b.

[74] *Testament of Reuben*, 5:1, translation Kee 2009, 784. The Paragraphs 3 to 6 rant against sexual promiscuity. Apparently this was inspired by Gen. 49:4 according to which Reuben defiled his father's bed by sleeping with the latter's concubine (cf. De Hoop 1999, 86-97). Contrary to the Hebrew text and contrary to Reuben's own remorseful account of the incident in Paragraph 3, it is the woman who is apparently blamed here for the act. Later on Philo, Josephus and the author of 1 Tim. 2:13-14, all influenced by the Hellenistic culture, pass similar negative judgments on Eve and women in general. Cf. LaCocque 2006, 191; Zevit 2013, 8-14. Also the rabbinical exegesis kept to this negative view of Eve. According to Gen. R., XVII.6, Satan would have been created simultaneously with Eve.

[75] E.g. Jer. 44:15-30; Ezek. 13:17-23; Amos 4:1. Jeynes 2014, 8 objects that in Jer. 44 also men are involved, but v. 15 clearly indicates that the women took the initiative to sacrifice to the Queen of Heaven. Ezek. 13 and Amos 4 are even more convincing. As are Ezek. 16, 23 and Hos. 2.

seem to have been found only in areas outside Judah.[76] Furthermore, in the areas in Persia where Jews dwelt not a single cultic figurine has been found.[77] It is difficult to interpret the contradictory evidence from the Persian period, but it might well be that the religious leadership suppressed this form of *feminine* worship.[78] The Greek view on women as the root of all evil[79] may have provided a welcome background for the biblical Eden story in its final redaction.

11. After the expulsion of Adam and Eve God places two cherubs (winged lions) outside the garden of Eden to guard it (Gen. 3:24).[80] According to the Akkadian and Ugaritic tradition the two gatekeepers of the garden of the gods were scorpion-men (Section 2.4). However, both are mythological monsters and according to Ezek. 28:14 the king of Tyre saw himself as a winged cherub guarding Eden (Section 4.6). The Investiture Panel from the Amorite city of Mari shows two winged lions guarding both sides of the king's garden (Bradshaw & Head 2012). The difference is that according to the biblical account the guards are installed as punishment to deny humans access to the Tree of Life (Gen. 3:22, 24).

4.3.2 *Similarities*

1. The opening verse of the second creation account in the Bible is rather peculiar,

Gen. 2:4

אֵלֶּה תוֹלְדוֹת הַשָּׁמַיִם וְהָאָרֶץ בְּהִבָּרְאָם

These are the generations of heaven and earth when they were created,

בְּיוֹם עֲשׂוֹת יְהוָה אֱלֹהִים אֶרֶץ וְשָׁמָיִם

on the day that the LORD God made earth and heaven.

---

[76] Stern 1982, 171; 1999, 250. See, however, the judicious criticism of De Hulster 2012.

[77] Stern 1999, 254.

[78] If the account of Eve's creation was inspired by the making of images of goddesses, as Uehlinger 1988 proposed, the biblical writer's intention may have been negative rather than positive.

[79] Egyptian influence, considered possible by Schroer 1996, 101, is historically unlikely.

[80] On the function of cherubs as guards see Launderdale 2003.

The elaborate, rather cumbersone style alone betrays the late, redactional hand that composed this 'verse'. Normally the formula אֵלֶּה תּוֹלְדוֹת introduces lists of human generations.[81] Here inanimated parts of the cosmos would have been meant. However, the Ugaritic material we have assembled in Section 2.1 renders it highly likely that originally heaven and earth were seen as a pair of divine beings created by Ilu/El. Even the reversed order 'earth and heaven' of Gen. 2:4b is attested in Ugarit too. The verse in its present form looks like an unsuccessful attempt to mask its Canaanite origin.

2. The Ugaritic myth (Chapter 2) and similar Near Eastern traditions (Chapter 3) show that already much earlier than the composition of the story of Eden the motif of the loss of immortality and its replacement by procreation was incorporated into the history of humankind. Child-bearing was the primary function of women (Clines 1990) and since child-mortality was so enormous in those days, women were indispensable to the continuation of our genus.

3. The polytheistic Ugaritic myth lays the blame for the loss of the Tree of Life with a divine rebel. None of the great deities invoked to undo the damage he caused is able to provide an effective remedy, not even Ilu, the Creator of all. Only the turnabout of the rebel himself clears the way for a new beginning. The presence of a 'Tree of Death' in the doomed garden in the Ugaritic version of the myth allows for the hypothesis that it was originally the Tree of Life which lent the deities immortality. We agree with those scholars who stress the importance of this Tree.[82] In our opinion the Tree of the Knowledge of Good and Evil is the same as the Tree of Life since both are בְּתוֹךְ הַגָּן, 'in the middle of the garden' (Gen. 2:9; 3:3).[83] This observation would seem to have some relevance

---

[81] There are still scholars who take Gen. 2:4a as the conclusion of the priestly creation story, though they see it as a redactional addition (so e.g. Day 2013, 18-19). However, the Petuḥah before v. 4 constitutes an argument in favor of a fresh start.

[82] E.g. Wyatt 1981, 15-17 (though it is now clear that the serpent cannot be El), contrast Pfeiffer 2000; Wagner-Tsukamoto 2012, 109.

[83] The *waw* at the beginning of וְעֵץ הַדַּעַת טוֹב וָרָע in Gen. 2:9 may be understood as a so-called epexegetical *waw*, '*that is*, the Tree of the Knowledge of

to the long-standing debate about the question if there were two important trees in Eden (Gen. 2:9) or only one.[84] The iconographic evidence we have presented constitutes an argument in favor of only one 'Weltbaum' (Section 2.8).

Although the Hebrew Bible lays the blame evidently with the first pair of humans, the narrator does not exonerate the deity entirely. God himself knew good and evil, as the serpent points out (Gen. 3:5) and God himself admits it (Gen. 3:22). It is God who created the serpent (Gen. 3:1) as well as the woman who should have been Adam's helper (Gen. 2:18) which Adam does not fail to rub in (Gen. 3:12). Also in many other places in the Hebrew Bible and the New Testament God seems to act in an unpredictable and ambiguous way in his dealings with human beings, especially when innocent people have to suffer. Of course this contradiction was also felt in polytheism, especially in Ugarit, and led to all kinds of theodicean arguments.[85] Also the reverse occurs: like Ḥôrānu, the God of the Bible could regret an earlier decision and annul it.[86]

4. God forms the first human being from the dust of the earth like a potter forming a vessel.[87] The very same verb (*yṣr*) is used

Good and Evil' (cf. Waltke & O'Connor 1990, § 39.2.4). This explanation is in accordance with the interpretation of Gen. 2:9 in all the Targumim. If so, the Tree of Knowledge of Good and Evil is just another name of the Tree of Life. We interpret the גַּם of Gen. 3:22 as 'again', like גַּם in Num. 11:4. Also in view of a number of ancient attestations of a single hybrid tree in the middle of the Garden Zevit's attempt to keep both trees must be termed unsuccessful (Zevit 2013, 94-95).
Of course we are not the first to assume that there was only one all-important tree in Eden. LaCocque 2006. 68-79, for example, assumes that originally there was only one tree but that the Yahwist deliberately split it in two to emphasize that good and evil are two sides of the same reality. If we are right in assuming that the Tree of Life became a Tree of Death the same opposition was already present in Ugarit.

[84] Surveys of the discussion are found with Pfeiffer 2000; Mettinger 2007, 5-11, 39-41; Ska 2008, 10, with n. 25; Lanfer 2012, 33-65.

[85] Laato & De Moor 2003 (for Ugarit De Moor 2003); Korpel & De Moor 2012, 298-303.

[86] Jeremias 2003. This is not the same as repentenace from evil, cf. Gelston 2011.

[87] A common view in ancient creation stories, cf. Frymer-Kensky 2006, 19-20 and Sections 2.1 and 3.

with the Ugaritic supreme creator Ilu. It has often been observed that in contrast to the priestly writer the Yahwistic source used by the late author of Genesis 2–4 speaks about God in a rather anthropomorphic manner.[88] He forms the first human being as well as the animals from the soil of the earth (Gen. 2:7, 19); he plants the garden of Eden like a gardener (Gen. 2:8); he puts Adam like a little toy in the garden (Gen. 2:15); like a surgeon he takes one side from Adam (Gen. 2:21-23);[89] he strolls leisurely in the garden and addresses Adam, Eve and Cain directly (Gen. 4:8-19); he personally makes garments of skins for the pair (Gen. 3:21). This anthropomorphism is also a characteristic of Ugaritic religious texts.[90]

5. A remarkable correspondence between the Ugaritic concept of creation and Genesis 2:7 is the circumstance that in contrast to Genesis 1 the first human being is created *before* any other creature. This also agrees with the Babylonian creation myth *The Founding of Eridu* Obv. 20-30.[91] In the canonical form of the Bible where Genesis 1 precedes Genesis 2–4 this was no longer a big problem, but it definitely is one of the inconsistencies the final redactors were unable or unwilling to iron out. It must be remembered that also in the surrounding cultures, e.g. Egypt and Babylonia, multiple creation narratives were allowed to exist side by side.

6. The Ugaritic myth demonstrates for the first time that there is a correspondence between the first divine rebel (Ḥôrānu) and Adam in the biblical narrative: both had the capacity to choose between good and evil. As a result both were seen as ambiguous beings (cf. Sections 2.3 and 2.9). In this sense humans became like gods, knowing good and evil (Gen. 3:5).

7. Neither Adammu himself nor his divine patron Šapšu expected

[88] See e.g. Von Rad 1982, 162; Blenkinsopp 2011, 7.

[89] For the rendering 'side' instead of 'rib' see LaCocque 2006, 117-130.

[90] Compare for example how Kirtu's gatekeeper is able to prevent Ilu from leaving unless he blesses him (KTU 1.15:II; cf. Gen. 32) or the way in which the Ugaritic king Dani'ilu regales the god Koṯaru in KTU 1.17:V, just as Abraham regales God in Gen. 18.

[91] Lambert 2013, 372-373. Cf. Section 3.3.6.

him to die. Apparently they believed him to be an immortal god. Unfortunately, however, deities did sometimes die in polytheistic religions. The story of Eden too presupposes the possibility of eternal life in bliss for Adam and Eve.[92]

8. In contrast to many scholars who view Gen. 2:10-14 as a late addition to the story of Eden[93] the location of Paradise at the headwaters of four rivers, originally probably the four tributaries of Euphrates and Tigris, shows that the very late author of Genesis 2–3 still adopted ancient motifs from the surrounding world, but adapted them to his own world view.[94] The Ugaritic description seems to indicate that Ilu dwelt on the mountain range of Ararat at the sources of Euphrates and Tigris. In other words, the creator god Ilu was thought to live in what became the garden of Eden in the Hebrew tradition.[95]

9. The garden of God in Genesis and the vineyard of the great gods in the Ugarit myth are close enough to assume a direct relationship between the two. The name of Eden may be late,[96] but the concept of a garden or vineyard of God or the gods is not.[97]

---

[92] Rabbi Ḥana b. ḥanina held that 'Adam was predestined not to taste death' (Gen. R. 9:5). We disagree with statements like 'the story ... nowhere says that Adam, before his disobedience, was immortal, was never going to die' (Barr 1993, 5, accepted even by Moberly 2009, 83.), or 'death was thought to be an integral part of human life from the very beginning of creation' (Schmid 2008, 64, see also 73-74) or 'das sein zum Tode ist nicht mit der Sünde, sondern mit der Schöpfung gegeben.' (Levin 2009, 97). Such statements are only possible if one eliminates the Tree of Life and the first murder in Gen. 4 which according to the narrator followed immediately after the expulsion from the garden of Eden.

[93] E.g. Humbert 1940, 46-47; Westermann 1974, 293-294; Wyatt 1981, 12; Brueggemann 1982, 45; Pfeiffer 2000, 490; Stordalen 2000, 270; Blenkinsopp 2011, 56.

[94] Cf. LaCocque 2006, 79-81; Stordalen 2011, 276-281, but cf. Speiser 1994.

[95] This was already suspected by several scholars, e.g. Day 2000, 29-31; 2013, 27-28; Mettinger 2007, 16, 135; Zevit 2013, 96-113. This solution is definitely preferable to a location of Eden in the Jordan Valley (Lipiński 1971, 40; Hiebert 1996, 52-59), on Mt Hermon (Day 1985, 117, retracted in Day 2000), or even in Jerusalem (Wyatt 1996).

[96] Although its etymology may be old, cf. Greenberg 2005, 256, with earlier literature; Day 2013, 25-26.

[97] It should be noted that Eden and the vineyard seem to be identified in the Qumran document 4Q433a f2:3.

10. Both on textual and iconographic evidence we have had reason to postulate the existence of a Tree of Life in the Ugaritic version of Paradise.[98] This tree probably became a Tree of Death by the vindictive act of the rebel god Ḥôrānu. The Tree of Life of Genesis 2:9 became a Tree of Death by the transgression of Adam and Eve (Gen. 2:17; 3:3).

11. Many attempts have been made to eliminate the evilness of the serpent from the story of Eden. However, the Ugaritic material indicates that the original serpent was the evil Leviathan and that we have to take into account the macrocosmic proportions of the conflict between Adammu and the serpent.

12. In Gen. 2:18 God concludes that it is *not* good (לֹא־טוֹב) that the human should be alone. Following immediately after Gen. 2:17 where 'the Tree of the Knowledge of Good and Evil' is mentioned this statement points to divine wisdom. Of course it is a traditionally accepted truth that humans are better off together than alone.[99] However, exactly Gen. 2–4 demonstrate that not all humans are always good. So God decides to make a helper fit for Adam (עֵזֶר כְּנֶגְדּוֹ), literally, a helper as his counterpart. In other words, she should be a *good* partner. The word עֵזֶר is frequently used for the good God as a helper of someone in the image of God (Gen. 1:26-27).[100] It is interesting that in KTU 1.107:27' the only woman mentioned in the text – presumably the wife of Adammu – is described as 'a good-natured woman'.[101]

13. The promise of the sun goddess 'she will not die' (KTU 1.107: 53')[102] parallels the serpent's promise 'you will certainly not die'

[98] Sections 2.2; 2.4; 2.8. The attempt to remove the Tree of Life from the biblical account by means of literary criticism (e.g. Pfeiffer 2000) must be reevaluated in the light of what we have found.

[99] See also Qoh. 4:9 and its extrabiblical paralels, Seow 1997, 181-182.

[100] For discussions about the woman as a helper, see Clines 1990; Stratton 1995, 96-98; LaCocque 2006, 127-130; Day 2013, 33-15. After a lengthy duscussion of earlier proposals Zevit 2013, 127-136 suggests an alternative translation of עֵזֶר כְּנֶגְדּוֹ: 'a helper like his kin'. This proposal rests on etymologizing and is unlikely for the simple reason that the biblical Adam did not have kin.

[101] See our discussion above, Section 2.3, as well as our note on KTU 1.107:27' in Appendix 1.

(Gen. 3:4). In both cases this appeared to be a half-truth.[103] In the Ugaritic *Legend of Aqhâtu* the goddess ʿAnatu similarly promises Aqhâtu eternal life which the hero brusquely refuses to believe,

KTU 1.17:VI.34-38

(34) *ʾal.tšrgn.y btltm.*	Do not fabricate (lies), Oh Virgin,
dm.lġzr (35) *šrgk.ḫḫm.*	because to a hero your fabrications are rubbish!
mt!.ʾuḫryt.mh.yqḥ	Death in the future, what can take (it) away?
(36) *mh.yqḥ.mt.ʾaṯryt.*	What can take away death in days to come?
spsg.ysk (37) *[l]rʾiš.*	Glaze may be poured on my head[104]
ḥrṣ.lẓr.qdqdy	potash on top of my skull,[105]
(38) *[ʾap.] mt.kl.ʾamt.*	[but] I too shall die the death of everyman,
wʾan.mtm.ʾamt	yes, I too shall certainly die!

Such duplicity is ascribed to several important Ugaritic deities, including Ilu.[106] To choose freely between life or death was the prerogative of great deities like the Egyptian Amun-Re, the Babylonian Marduk and the Israelite YHWH-El.[107] One may not like this idea, but one should not attempt to explain it away, as Fredrik Lindström 1983 does.

KTU 1.100 seems to imply that though individual human life inevitably ends in death, humankind as a whole became immortal by procreation.[108] This element has also been preserved in the story of Eden, not only in Gen. 3:16 but also through the wordplay between עָרוּם, 'sly' (Gen. 3:1) and עָרוֹם, עֵירֹם 'naked' (Gen. 2:25; 3:7, 10). The nakedness of lovers will defeat the slyness of

---

102 Because of the broken context it is impossible to ascertain who the woman is: Kubaba, the mortal Eve of Ugarit, or any woman in childbirth. Grammatically also 'you (singular) will not die' is a possiblility, but the presence of the Kôṯarātu renders this less likely.

103 This became known as the 'Liar Argument', cf. Barr 2006b; Moberly 2008; 2009, 70-87; Gordon 2010; Day 2013, 38-41.

104 A metaphor for getting grey hair.

105 A metaphor for getting white hair.

106 See sections 2.4 and 2.9.

107 De Moor 1997, 52-53, 61-62, 252.

108 As far as we know this was first observed by Sasson 1980, 215, without any knowledge of the Ugaritic prehistory: 'Ejected from the garden of Eden where his access to the Tree of Life permitted him unending life, man was, however, granted immortality not for an individual, i.e., Adam and Eve, but for the whole seed through the gift of birth giving.'

the serpent.[109] KTU 1.107 seems to support the idea that death is defeated by women bearing children. This is also the main consolation of Genesis 2–3. The knowledge acquired by eating the fruit of the Tree brought the realization of their sexual difference (Gen. 3:7, 8-11) and the knowledge of the pleasure to know each other intimately (Gen. 4:1). The labor of women (Gen. 3:16) would inaugurate an endless chain of human generations (תּוֹלְדֹת, Gen. 4:17ff.).

14. Many scholars have observed that it is possible to translate Gen. 3:1 'Now the serpent was more naked than any other wild creature'. The serpent of KTU 1.100 and of the *Gilgameš Epic* is depicted as having sloughed its skin (*ʿqšr*).

15. In contrast to Gen.1 and in accordance with Babylonian and Ugaritic terminology Gen. 2:22 uses בנה 'to build' for the creation of Eve.[110] With regard to Amos 9:6 one might argue that it is a poetic, metaphorical description of the construction of the LORD's heavenly abode,[111] but here it is undoubtedly just as much as Adam's formation from dust of the earth meant in the sense of creation.[112]

16. After the creation of Eve from a side of Adam, the latter concludes that his counterpart is part from him, and calls her אִשָּׁה 'she-man' (Gen. 2:22), because she was taken out of the man (אִישׁ). This is a folk etymology that can no longer be sustained. However, in Genesis 3:20 Adam again named his wife, now with the name of Eve, a name which is presupposed in Gen. 4:1,[113] and seems to have ancient roots. This name חַוָּה is a noun of the qattāl-class designating a profession or function, meaning 'she-who-gives-life'.[114] This is confirmed by the explanation that Adam called her like this because she is the Mother of All the Living

---

[109] LaCocque 2006, 136-137, errs in seeing this as 'a gate open to deceit, adultery, mistrust, and dissolution.'

[110] Cf. Section 2.3. Among those who noticed this were Uehlinger 1988, 96; LaCocque 2006, 117.

[111] So e.g. Lessing 2009, 556-557, with earlier literature. An obvious parallel is the building of Baʿlu's heavenly abode in the Ugaritic myth, cf. Korpel 1990, 188, 384-385.

[112] See also the passive forms in Gen. 16:2; 30:3.

[113] Cf. Levin 2009, 86).

[114] Dijkstra & De Moor 1975, 188-189.

(אֵם כָּל־חָי). Several scholars have seen in this title a remniscence of either the concept of Mother Earth, or the primeval mother-goddess.[115] The latter possibility becomes more likely now that in Ugarit and elsewhere Adammu appears to be paired with Kubaba, the primordial mother goddess.[116] Although it was obviously not the intention of the final redactor to introduce Eve as a mother goddess he may certainly have wanted to redress these traditions by a deliberate hint in Gen. 3:20.[117]

17. Usually the identification of the serpent of the Eden story with Satan or the Devil is seen as a late development. It is assumed to pop up for the first time in the first century BCE, in Wisdom of Solomon 2:23-24. If the allusion here indeed is to Genesis 3, it would be 'one of the earliest extant Jewish texts to equate the serpent with the devil',[118]

> (23) But God created the human for immortality,
> and made him an image of his own eternality,[119]
> (24) it was through the devil's envy that death entered into the world,
> and they who are his own experience him.

It is surely remarkable that according to this wisdom text Adam was created as an immortal and therefore divine being and that death is said to have been introduced not by Adam and Eve, but by 'the devil's envy' which is in accordance with other traditions stating that the devil begrudged Adam his high position as ruler over the entire created world (Sections 3.3.7; 3.4; 5.14; 5.16; 5.18). In the New Testament serpent and devil are identified in Rev. 12:9, where it is said that the old serpent is called both the devil and Satan.[120]

---

[115] E.g. Dijkstra 1999; Kübel 2007, 123-124.
[116] Cf. Section 2.3.
[117] Cf. Hamilton 1990, 204-207. The idea that her epithet would be related to Aramaic חוה 'serpent' and to an alleged Phoenician snake-goddess *ḥwt* has been defended by several scholars, but has very little to recommend it. Cf. Westermann 1974, 364-365.
[118] Winston 1979, 121. See also Day 2013, 35.
[119] Greek ἀϊδιότητος, some manuscripts read only εἰκόνα τῆς ἰδίας 'an image of his own proper'.
[120] See further Chapter 5 and for the derivation of the name 'Satan', Section 2.6. So it is not so very surprising that Armenian Christians took the role

However, since in Ugarit the god Ḥôrānu seems to have poisoned the Tree of Life in the shape of a huge serpent and continued to guard it,[121] the theory of the late origin of the identification of the Devil and the serpent must be revisited too. Like the biblical Devil/Satan, Ḥôrānu was an ambiguous figure. He fathered both the serpents that threatened the world and killed the 'immortal' deity Adammu, but after his turnabout he also fathered the Kôṯarātu-midwives to ensure the immortality of the human race as such through procreation (Sections 2.5 and 2.9). It seems likely that he himself as the father of all serpents could take on the shape of a serpent too.[122] His Ugaritic epithets *šr* '(evil) Prince' and *ʿd* 'the enemy' are still names of the devil in Islam (Sections 2.6 and 5.18). His Ugaritic epithets *ġzz* 'the generous one' and *ʾark ḥnt* 'long of mercy' (reading not entirely certain) point to his better ego. Ḥôrānu shares this ambiguous character with other ancient Near Eastern deities like the Ugaritic Ilu, the Egyptian god Seth and the Babylonian god Erra (see Chapter 3).[123] It is not only because we have discovered this background that we refuse to accept Moberly's all to easy solution to understand 'life' and 'death' in the narrative in Genesis 2–3 in metaphorical ways.[124] James Charlesworth's massive monograph on the serpent as an ambiguous creature (Charlesworth 2010) comes closer to the truth although he overemphasizes the good side of the serpent[125] and understandably could not treat the Ugaritic material in depth.

18. The Hebrew tradition seems to have transferred some traits of Ḥôrānu to Cain. The latter shares the ambiguity just discussed with the Ugaritic god (cf. Section 2.9). Cain is the first to sacrifice

---

of Satan and the serpent in deceiving Adam and Eve for granted (Stone 2008a, 141.

[121] So it is not at all a rational supposition that the serpent was guarding the Tree on God's authority, contra Wagner-Tsukamoto 2012, 104.

[122] Westermann's claim that there is no mythological background to the serpent (Westermann 1974. 325) appears to be untenable.

[123] It is very peculiar that in late Armenian traditions Satan is called Sadayēl (Stone 2008a) which recalls one of El's epithets, שַׁדַּי. But perhaps it merely rests on an early error for Sariel.

[124] Moberly 2009, 83-87.

[125] Cf. Gordon 2010, 17: 'The serpent, far from being a neutral or in any way a positive, figure in the narrative, has led Adam and Eve to pain and loss.'

piously to the LORD (Gen. 4:3)[126] and God describes this act as 'good' (אִם־תֵּיטִיב, Gen. 4:7), adding immediately that Cain also has the possibility to do things that are 'not good' (אִם לֹא תֵיטִיב, cf. Gen. 3:5). Indeed Cain becomes the first murderer (Gen. 4:8-10), just as Ḥôrānu in the shape of a huge serpent almost kills the first divine humanoid Adammu. Also some New Testament and parabiblical texts betray awareness of the identification of Cain with the Devil.[127]

This also might be confirmed by Gen. 4:7 where it is said that sin is lurking at Cain's door, as if it were a snake. In the ancient Near East the differentiation between a deity and its theriomorphic manifestation did not preclude identity – Cain was his own enemy. The serpent is the personification of Cain's evil side. Whether or not חַטָּאת in Gen.4:7 is an explanatory gloss,[128] or a deliberate alteration of an original reading *חטא[129], or a convoluted designation of Abel,[130] or simply a metaphorical personification of sin,[131] or a corrupted text which has troubled translators from ancient times on,[132] it seems certain that the רֹבֵץ was the tempter, the trickster – in other words: the serpent of Gen. 3.

> Regardless of the linguistic specifics, the idea is clearly a warning: Cain is free to resist or to give in to sin. For the first time in the Bible, the word "sin" occurs (*ḥaṭṭāʾt*), which sheds light on the role of Gen 3 in Israelite conceptions of sin, in light of the many parallels between Gen 3 and 4. Like Eve before him, Cain is clearly in danger of another serious breach. But unlike Eve's conversation with the serpent, Cain's problems are arising from within himself. (Arnold 2009, 79).

In Akkadian the verb *rabāṣu* sometimes describes the lurking of snakes, including the *bašmu*, the giant serpent.[133] So Cain has to

---

126 Proleptically fulfilling the Law, cf. Exod. 22:28-29; 34:19-20; Lev. 3:16; Deut. 32:38; Ps. 147:14. Later interpretations discerned differences with Abel's offering which made the latter's more acceptable. Cf. Byron 2008.

127 See below, Chapters 5 and 6.

128 So Crouch 2011b who opts for a demon.

129 Meaning 'lurker', so Loiseau 2013 on the basis of Akkadian parallels.

130 So Janowski 2003, with the very unlikely rendering 'lagert er sich als (Öffnung >) Anlaß zu einer Verfehlung'.

131 So e.g. Gordon 2011. See also Schlimm 2012 and Vreugdenhil 2013, 130-131.

132 For an excellent survey see Scarlata 2012.

face a formidable opponent who is hiding in his own human soul. Cain seems to have taken over also some other characteristics of the Ugaritic god Ḥôrānu,

- After she conceived Cain his mother Eve said that she 'created' (קנה) a human with YHWH, a statement that recalls Aṯiratu's epithet 'Creatress of the gods' (*qnyt.ʾilym* (KTU 1.4:I.22; III.26, 30, 35; IV.32). Although the extant Ugaritic texts do not indicate if ʾAṯiratu was Ḥôrānu's mother this seems likely enough since her husband Ilu was father of all deities.

- Ḥôrānu is the 'blazing One' (*ḥrr*), of Cain it is said that he was 'burning' (חרה, Gen. 4:5) with jealousy against his brother.

- Ḥôrānu's face turned green (paled) because of anger when he realized that his own posterity would remain childless if he did not lift his curse on the Tree of Death (KTU 1.100:61). The face of Cain 'fell' (נפל, Gen. 4:5) when he suspected that God did not accept his sacrifice.[134]

- Ḥôrānu in the shape of a serpent was the first to kill the humanoid Adammu, Cain was the first to kill his fellow human (Gen. 4:8).

- Ḥôrānu was apparently banned from heaven and had to wander between heaven and Netherworld (Sections 2.2 and 2.6). Cain was banned from the presence of the LORD and became a restless wanderer on the earth (Gen. 4:12, 14, 16), as is said of Satan (Job 1:7, 12).

- The most simple solution to the problem of the rebel in heaven would have been for Ilu to kill him. Especially so

[133] *CAD* (R), 12b. Cf. Ezek. 29:3 הַתַּנִּים הַגָּדוֹל הָרֹבֵץ בְּתוֹךְ יְאֹרָיו, 'the giant tuna lurking in the middle of your delta'. See also our remarks on Ps. 68:6-7 in Section 2.8.

[134] It is a persistent misunderstanding that God did not accept Cain's offering. This is not what the text says. God did not seem to pay attention to Cain's offering (Gen. 4:5) and then *saw* how Cain's face 'fell'. Cf. Korpel & De Moor 2013, 171-172.

if Ḥôrānu took revenge by turning the Tree of Life into a Tree of Death. However, when Ḥôrānu repented, Ilu assigned him the task to act as an avenger between heaven and Netherworld (Section 2.2). Still a killer, but a 'licensed' executioner.[135] Cain was the first killer according to the Genesis story, but God did not kill him either and sevenfold revenge is announced to someone who would murder Cain (Gen. 4:14-15, cf. Gen. 4:23-25).

- Ḥôrānu left the city of the East (*ʿr.dqdm*, KTU 1.100:62), to partially restore the Tree of Life, whereas Cain went to dwell in the land of Nod, east of Eden (קִדְמַת־עֵדֶן, Gen. 4:16) where he founded a city (Gen. 4:17).

- The preserved parts of the Ugaritic myth do not resolve the riddle of the sign of Cain (Gen. 4:15), but it may be assumed that something similar guaranteed Ḥôrānu a safe-conduct in the space between heaven and Netherworld. One of the most attractive later solutions to the riddle is that the sign was the letter Taw (ancient Hebrew X) which might either be interpreted as תמות 'you must die' or as תחי 'you may live'.[136]

4.4 *Genesis 5–9*

In dealing with Genesis 5–9 in one subsection of this study we are by no means asserting that these chapters have a common origin. However, they do have one final redactor as, for example, the many links between Genesis 9:1-7 and the earlier chapters of the biblical primeval history demonstrate.[137] However, since we are merely trying to indicate the relevance of the Ugaritic material for the elucidation of certain biblical passages, we opted for this practical approach.

It has long been recognized that the genealogy of Adam in Genesis 5 may be compared with the lists and chronicles of primordial (deified) kings in the ancient Near East.[138] Extremely long

---

135 Compare the Egyptian etymology for 'Satan' proposed by Görg 1996. However, see also Section 2.6.

136 Van Staalduine 1993, 289-290. Note the ambiguity. For another attractive solution see Moberly 2007.

137 See e.g. Arneth 2007b.

lifespans are attested primarily with Mesopotamian antediluvian kings. After the Flood such long lifespans become rare. No list of antediluvian kings has been found at Ugarit, but some of the Ugaritic ancestral deities, like Ditānu and Gaṯru, are also attested in Mesopotamia and elsewhere. It seems likely that Ditānu and Gaṯru were regarded as Amorite forefathers of both the elite of Ugarit and the leaders of Israel.[139] In any case the kings of Ugarit were deified after their death and this will have entailed an increase in their post-mortem size.[140]

Genesis 6:1-4 is one of the most 'mythological', even 'polytheistic' texts in the Bible.[141] One quotation may suffice to illustrate the uneasiness this passage generates even in modern scholars,

> The strange story of the marriages between Sons of God and human women in Gen 6:1-4 is one of the most cryptic and obscure narratives of the Hebrew Bible (Hendel 2004, 11).

These much-discussed verses describe the birth of giants as a result of sexual intercourse between antediluvian divine males and human females.[142] The highest Ugaritic god Ilu sires seventy divine sons with his wife Aṯiratu,[143] but also two sons with *human* females (Section 2.1 on KTU 1.24). In Greek mythology intercourse between deities and humans is described more often.[144] However, this would run counter to the monotheistic principle. So

---

[138] See e.g. Jacobsen 1939; Finkelstein 1966; Edzard 1980; Grayson 1980; Verbrugghe & Wickersham 1996; Glassner 2004.

[139] De Moor 1997, 332, 355. Here we want to suggest a connection between Ditānu (also spelled Didānu) and the Greek god Titan. On other grounds also Bremmer 2004; 2012 suggests a Syrian background.

[140] De Moor 1997, 323-328.

[141] Although both the Masoretic text and the Samaritan Pentateuch start a new paragraph before Gen. 5:32, this was probably triggered by the end of Gen. 5:31 וַיָּמֹת. Cf. Gen. 5:5, 8, 11, 14, 17, 20, 27. Next to 6:9-19, 5:32 looks like a 'false start' and most scholars agree that a new section begins with 6:1.

[142] See for overviews of the discussion Westermann 1974, 491-517; Wright 2005; Kvanvig 2011, 274-310. The latter scholar provides an elaborate analysis based on a comparison with Atraḫasīs (cf. Section 3.3.1).

[143] Sections 2.1 and 4.5. For the traditional number of seventy sons, cf. De Moor 1998b. For the echo in Deut. 32:8b see e.g. Day 1996, 38-40; Sanders 1996, 155-159.

[144] So we disagree with Hendel 1987, 16, n. 16.

exegetes have tried to find explanations for the presence of this 'Fremdkörper' in the Hebrew Bible from Antiquity to our days.[145] It does not help to declare that these בְּנֵי־הָאֱלֹהִים 'sons of God' or 'sons of gods' were (fallen) angels. Nowhere in the preceding chapters the reader has been prepared for the existence of lower divine beings.[146]

We agree with scholars who see nothing negative in the behavior of either gods or women in Gen. 6:1-4.[147] Like Gen. 6:3, the Ugaritic tradition about Adammu stresses the perishable nature of human flesh ('the flesh of Šarruġāzizu fell', KTU 1.107:8). However, no parallel for the 'hundred and twenty years' is found in Ugarit. The comparison is with the perishable flesh of animals.[148] The negative interpretation of Gen. 6:1-4 started only with Gen. 6:5-7. Although nothing indicates that the human partners had been seducing the sons of God, the human side is punished there, not the divine side. It must be assumed that as in many parts of the world, even today, illicit sexual behavior was seen as the woman's fault unless convincing proof to the contrary could be furnished.[149] The point in Gen. 6:1-4 is merely that as humankind became too numerous[150] their lifespan had to be shortened, just as human mortality was the solution in the Babylonian *Atraḫasīs Epic*. Nothing in Gen. 6:1-4 indicates that God meant this reduction of life expectancy as punishment for rebellion.

This interpretation gains force as soon as one realizes that

---

145 See e.g. Alexander 1972; Walters & Gooding 1973, 255; Díez Merino 1984; Fernández Marcos 1998, 141.

146 Cooke 1964, 32 insists on their divine status. He also rightly suspected a Canaanite background of the passage (Cooke 1964, 34). Attempts to solve the problem without recourse to mythology (e.g. Fockner 2008) are actually in line with the old apologetics and neglect the Petuḥah before Gen. 6:5.

147 Attempts to read an indication of sin in the difficult בְּשַׁגָּם (by rendering 'by their roaring' or 'by their erring') are unconvincing. We prefer the usual interpretation 'since it (humankind) too is (perishable) flesh' which is already found in 𝔊. Cf. Vervenne 1995; Clines, *DCH*, Vol. s8, 204; Day 2013, 90-91.

148 Because the רוּחַ of God dwelling in humankind is the breath of life (Gen. 6:17; 7:15, 22), it is very likely that originally the text read ידור 'will remain', with 4Q252:I.2 and 𝔊.

149 In this respect too there was little difference between Ugarit and Israel. Cf. Marsman 2003, 168-191, 663-671.

150 וַיְהִי כִּי־הֵחֵל הָאָדָם לָרֹב, Gen. 6:1.

the *rp'um* in the Canaanite tradition were great heroes of yore. They took part in the deliberations of the present ruler on earth. They had been the 'Saviors' of their country once upon a time. With their offspring on earth they decided about difficult decisions of national importance. Their supernatural size was simply the consequence of the way they loved to have themselves depicted – as supernatural, supersized human beings. An example is found in Deut. 3:11 which describes the deathbed of Og, king of Bashan, one of the last Rephaim,[151]

> Look! His bed is a bed of iron
> Is it not in Rabbah of the Ammonites?
> Nine cubits is its length,
> and four cubits its breadth,
> according to the common cubit.

Although it is uncertain what exactly was a 'common cubit', it is usually estimated to be at least 50 cm. So the funerary bed of this king was at least 4.50 m long. Also the נְפִלִים of Gen. 6:4 were famous heroes of the past who had fallen in combat.[152] Now that we know that in the Canaanite tradition Adam and Eve themselves were seen as supernatural giants (Sections 2.7-8) it becomes possible to surmise that to some extent the antediluvian women of Genesis 6 still measured up physically to their divine partners so that they were supposed to be able to receive the huge members of their divine lovers and were able deliver their giant babies. In Chapter 2 we have demonstrated that the Canaanites imagined everything in the primeval world, including human beings, of gigantic proportions.

Genesis 6:4 itself correctly observes that wicked giants were born also in later times (Og king of Bashan, Goliath). So it is certainly not the case that only the disembodied spirits of the giants lived on, as might be surmised on the basis of 1 Enoch 15:8-9 and the fragment from the *Book of Giants* 4Q531, fr. 19:3-4.[153] The giants lived on in both forms, but henceforth they too were mortals (Og, Goliath). Only their immaterial spirit could live

151 Deut. 28:54; Josh. 12:4; 13:12.
152 Finkelstein 1966.
153 Cf. Stuckenbruck 2004, 102-109.

on endlessly because it was taken from an immortal god. Human bodies, however, returned to dust or clay.[154]

The continuity of the early human race is, as we have seen (Sections 2.5; 4.2-3), a concern of Akkadian, Ugaritic and biblical writers alike. The crucial role of women in the process of procreation is emphasized in all three traditions. Several scholars have proposed to render טֹבֹת in Gen. 6:2 not as 'fair, beautiful', but as 'good'.[155] We have interpreted KTU 1.107:27' [ʾaṯt.]ṭ*bt.* n*p*š as 'a good-natured [woman]' as a description of the first woman and 'goodness' may well have been the ideal characteristic of her successors too (cf. Prov. 18:22).

A story about the great Flood that wiped out all living beings except the Flood hero, his family and the animals in the ark has not been preserved among the hitherto excavated Ugaritic tablets. For this reason we shall skip it here. However, a Babylonian fragment of the story has been found at Ras Shamra[156] and in view of the considerable influence of Mesopotamia on the religion of Ugarit we do not exclude the possibility that one day a Canaanite version will crop up somewhere.[157]

Hitherto also no Canaanite parallel to the account of the covenant with all creatures and the rainbow as its sign has been discovered.[158] Both Atraḫasīs III.v.46–vi.4 and Gilg. Ep. XI.164-167 relate that when the deities gathered after the Flood the creatress Bēlet-ilī/Nintu showed a necklace of beads which should always remind her of the disastrous event. This vaguely recalls the function of the rainbow according to Gen. 9:12-17, but it is far from certain that the necklace of the goddess was a symbol of the rainbow. Ellen van Wolde sees the 'giving' of the bow as a symbolic gesture by which God shows his willingness to transfer his power to those living on the earth (Van Wolde 2013). If so, this is another link with Gen. 1:26.

---

154 So also in Mesopotamia, cf. Oshima 2012, 420-427, with earlier literature.
155 Cf. Kvanvig 2011, 278.
156 Lambert & Millard 1969, 131-133.
157 The latest work on the Mesopotamian Flood traditions is Chen 2013. For the biblical account see Day 2013, 61-76, 98-136.
158 There is, however, a letter in which a personal covenant with a god is mentioned. Cf. De Moor 1997, 367. For *brt* 'covenant' see KTU 1.82:5 as interpreted by De Moor & Spronk 1984, 240.

Obviously the 'vineyard of the great gods'[159] could not be accommodated in the canonical Hebrew Bible, but in a deluted form it was adopted in the Genesis narrative. When humanity was allowed to make a fresh start after the great Flood[160] Noah planted a vineyard (Gen. 9:20), presumably on the slopes of Mt Ararat where the ark had stranded (Gen. 8:4). Thus he became a successor of Adam who worked in the first garden (Gen. 2:15). Like Ilu according to KTU 1.114, Noah became very drunk of the wine he produced and two of his sons had to cover his nakedness (Gen. 9:21-27), just as the two sons of Ilu had to take care of their drunken father (Sections 2.1 and 2.4 above). So nakedness continued to be a reminder of Gen. 3:7, 10-11, and murder like Cain's murder would never more go unpunished, because 'God made humankind in his own image' (Gen. 9:6; cf. Gen. 1:26; 4:8-11, 23-24). A further parallel is that all the earth and the animals are given in Noah's hand (Gen. 9:2), just as the earth and its animals were given to Adam (Gen. 1:18) and as the whole earth was given in Adammu's hand (KTU 1.107:2-3). Noah and all who were saved with him are exhorted to breed abundantly on the earth (Gen. 8:17; 9:7), as it was in the beginning (Gen. 1:22, 28). And in the Ugaritic myth. Apparently the priestly writer wanted to describe Noah as a second Adam. This was already noticed by the author of Jubilees 4:28-29 who placed the birth of Noah immediately before the death of Adam, in this way making Noah a new Adam,[161]

> 28 And in the fifteenth jubilee in the third week, Lamech took for himself a wife. and her name was Betenos, the daughter of Baraki'il, the daughter of his father's brother, (as) a wife. And in that week she bore a son for him and he called him Noah, saying, "This one will console me from my grief and from all my labor and from the land which the LORD cursed."
> 29 And at the end of the nineteenth jubilee in the seventh week, in the sixth year, Adam died. And all of his children buried him in the land of his creation.[162]

159 KTU 1.107:2, cf. Appendix 1.

160 We are not as sure as others are that there is a fundamental difference between the position of humans as rulers over all other creatures in Genesis 1 and 9, as maintained by scholars like Schüle 2006, 113-115 and Schellenberg 2009, 101-103, with further references. The absence of the verb רדה in Genesis 9 is an *argumentum e silentio*. See below.

161 Cf. Peters 2008, 77, 81.

4.5 *Isaiah 14*

In its canonical version Isaiah 14:4-21 is a song on the king of Babylon who is criticized for his haughtiness. Several scholars take it as one of the two major parts of a larger section on Babylonia, Isa. 13:1–14:32.[163] Because in the time of Isaiah Judah's major enemy was Assyria, not Babylon, most scholars agree in taking Isaiah 14 as a later addition to the Book of Isaiah, as a dirge on the Babylonian king[164] or as a prophetic song orginally intended for the Assyrian king,[165] but actualized in later times (Van Keulen 2010). The introductory verses Isa. 14:1-3 lend support to the hypothesis that the final redaction of the chapter took place at a fairly late date.

Bernard Gosse 1988 argues that from Isaiah 14:9 on all associations with other parts from the Book of Isaiah are absent and that mythological themes from Canaan dominate this part of the song. Because of his comparison of Isaiah 14 with Ezekiel 32:17-32 he concludes that Phoenician traditions formed the mythological background for the description of the downfall of the king.

Already Origen concluded that Isaiah 14 which deals with a king who falls from heaven cannot be referring to a human being, not even to Nebuchadnezzar whom Origen supposed to be meant by 'the king of Babylon'. 'For no human being is said to have "fallen from heaven" or to have been "Lucifer" or the one who "arose in morning" '.[166] Also Augustine draws a similar conclusion: verses 12-14 which ostensibly refer to the Babylonian king 'are of course to be understood of the devil'. However, he also admits that the second half of the line ' "he that sent orders to all nations is crushed on the earth" does not fitly apply to the head itself' (McKinion 2004, 122). Also interesting is the commentary of Ambrose, who combines Isa. 14:12 with Gen. 3, stating,

---

162 Translation Wintermute 2009, 63.

163 E.g. Childs 2001, 117-128. Gosse 1988 and Blenkinsopp 2000, 282-293 end the song with 14:23).

164 E.g. Wildberger 1978, 538, 541f.; Shipp 2002; Beuken 2007, 51, 57. Gosse 1988 explicitly dates the text of Isaiah 14 to the early reign of Darius I who was, however, a king of Persia. Blenkinsopp 2000, 286-287 enumerates several other possibilities without committing himself.

165 Many scholars opt for Sargon II, e.g. Childs 2001, 127; Mizrahi 2013, 433.

166 Quotation from McKinion 2004, 121.

> When the Lord Jesus redeemed the human race through his obedience, he reformed justice. The serpent, however, introduced sin through his disobedience, a sin which we are now able to identify as pride, the author of which is the devil, whom the prophet portrayed as saying, "I will seat my throne above the clouds and I will be like the Most High" (tr. McKinion 2004, 123).

Nowadays, many commentators assume that a Canaanite myth[167] on the fall of a rebellious deity from heaven must have furnished the background for this satirical song on the Babylonian king.[168] In fact, the scribe would have updated the old myth for his contemporaries. However, hitherto such a Canaanite myth about the fall of Hēlēl the Morning Star has not been identified, to the great frustration of scholars.[169] Up till now, the closest parallel to the fall of Hēlēl in Isaiah 14 was seen in a passage in the Baal-Myth, where the god ʿAṯtaru tries to take over the vacant throne of Baal (KTU 1.6:I.53-65).[170] Klaas Spronk, however, was absolutely right when he pointed out the differences between this story about ʿAṯtaru and the fall of Hēlēl.[171]

The song starts with the cry 'how the oppressor has ceased, the מַדְהֵבָה has ceased' (Isa. 14:4b). The variant reading מרהבה in 1QIsa[a] which is also supported by several ancient versions apparently connects the word with the name of the sea monster Rahab (Mizrahi 2013). This means that already this opening line makes use of the well-known typology of the great oppressor of the entire world as a terrible monster. This is in line with Isa. 14:1-8 and 14:16-27 which envisage mighty Babylonian and Assyrian oppressors. The Phoenician kings may be assumed to have exploited their

[167] Because of references to Canaanite deities like El and Hēlēl as well as the use of specific words and other names known from Ugarit. See our discussion below.

[168] Cf. Wildberger 1978, 543f.; Spronk 1986, 220-221.

[169] See e.g. Wildberger 1978, 544; Spronk 1986, 221; Albani 2004, 63; Van der Sluijs 2009, 269.

[170] See e.g. Watson 1999; Beuken 2007, 91; Day 2013, 93.

[171] Spronk 1998. See also Albani 2004, 63 who argues that the descent of ʿAṯtaru from the throne of Baʿlu is not a downfall but just a voluntary descent without any humiliation or punishment. This too is an inaccurate representation of the Ugaritic evidence. ʿAṯtaru's descent from Baʿlu's throne is depicted as a humiliation. His legs are too short to reach the footstool, his head does not reach the upper edge of the back (KTU 1.6:I.57-64).

colonies,[172] but hardly have terrorized the whole world by making it into a desert, destroying many cities and deporting their citizens (Isa. 14:16-17). Isa. 14:9-11 make sense only if many kings slain by the oppressor rejoice now that he himself has died and is finally powerless like they themselves. All these verses belong to the actualization of the original taunt which targeted a far minor king, probably a Phoenician king. It seems likely that this actualization took place in two phases, one in Assyrian times, perhaps after the death of Sargon II on the battlefield.[173] one after the fall of the Neo-Babylonian empire.

So we regard only Isa. 14:12-15[174] as belonging to the original satire badgering a Phoenician king[175] who was ridiculed because he assumed to get a place among the celestials on the mountain of El after his death.

Isa. 14:12-15

אֵיךְ נָפַלְתָּ מִשָּׁמַיִם (12)	How have you fallen from heaven,
הֵילֵל בֶּן־שָׁחַר	Hēlēl, son of dawn!
נִגְדַּעְתָּ לָאָרֶץ	You are felled to the earth,
חוֹלֵשׁ עַל־גּוֹיִם׃	you who razed nations.[176]
וְאַתָּה אָמַרְתָּ בִלְבָבְךָ (13)	And you thought in your heart,
הַשָּׁמַיִם אֶעֱלֶה	'I will to go up to heaven,
מִמַּעַל לְכוֹכְבֵי־אֵל	above the stars of El
אָרִים כִּסְאִי	I want to set up my throne,
וְאֵשֵׁב בְּהַר־מוֹעֵד	and I want to sit down on the mountain of the Assembly,
בְּיַרְכְּתֵי צָפוֹן׃	on the mountain range in the North,[177]
אֶעֱלֶה עַל־בָּמֳתֵי עָב (14)	I want to go up to the heights in the cloud cover,
אֶדַּמֶּה לְעֶלְיוֹן׃	I want to match the Most High!'

[172] Cf. Isa. 23:3; Ezek. 27:3b-9; 28:16, 18.

[173] Van Keulen 2010, 118-119 reviews the evidence but deems it unlikely that Sargon II himself is the tyrant.

[174] It may be noted that these verses are delimited by small spaces in 1QIsa[a], Oesch 1979, Table 9*.

[175] See the helpful definitions of the genre in Amzallag & Avriel 2012, 643-645.

[176] The verb חלשׁ is often carelessly translated 'to defeat', but both here and in Exod. 17:13 'to raze' would be a more precise rendering. This also accords better with the cognates.

[177] Nowadays צָפוֹן is often interpreted here as '(Mt) Zaphon', because scholars were all too eager to discover a link with the Ugaritic *Myth of Baʿlu.*

אַךְ אֶל־שְׁאוֹל תּוּרָד (15) Instead you will be brought down to the Netherworld,
אֶל־יַרְכְּתֵי־בוֹר׃ to the mountain range of the Pit.

Originally this song may have been directed against a Phoenician king, like the song in Ezek. 28 (cf. Section 4.6). One of the strongest Phoenician kings who ruled over both Sidon and Tyre was Lūli. He reigned from 729-694 BCE, but the last seven years in exile. In 701 BCE Sennacherib destroyed his kingdom and Lūli had to flee overseas. In 701 his exact whereabouts remained unknown to the Assyrians. Only later on he was discovered on Cyprus where he died a violent death, presumably executed by the god Assur.[178] Because already in 708 BCE the kings on Cyprus had subjected to Sargon II[179] it is possible that he was discovered on the island only in 694 BCE. This interpretation would be in accordance with Isa. 23:12 where the 'violated virgin daughter of Sidon' is urged to cross over to Cyprus where, however, 'she will have no rest'. If so, the original kernel of Isaiah 14:12-15 might belong to early Isaian tradition, but obviously this remains completely uncertain.

Isaiah 14:12-13 mentions the fall of a certain Hēlēl from heaven. In parabiblical literature this fall of Hēlēl is interpreted as the fall of Satan and his angels.[180] Also the text of Luke 10:18 seems to equate Hēlēl with Satan. The Vulgate translates the name of Hēlēl in Isaiah 14:12 as *lucifer* which just means 'light-bringer', but was interpreted early on as 'morning star', sometimes specified as the planet Venus. Because of this connection with Isaiah 14 Christians have begun to use Lucifer as a designation of Satan. This has long been seen as a misinterpretation. But is it? In any case Matthias Albani would seem to exaggerate unduly when he writes, 'However, the figure of *Helel* in Isa 14:12 has nothing to do with *Satan*.'[181]

With regard to the mythological background of Isaiah 14 especially Mark Shipp is highly critical. He states that 'those who

[178] Cogan 2008, 115-116, 126.
[179] As testified by the Cyprus Stele, Cogan 2008, 98-100, with earlier literature.
[180] Possibly also Ps. 82:7 reflects the myth of the fallen 'princes', Sariel among them (see Sections 5.3 and 5.13). One of the names of Ḥôrānu was Šarru, 'Prince' (cf. Section 2.6).
[181] Albani 2004, 62.

suggest that a narrative myth or myths lie(s) behind the poem operate largely on the assumption that "myth" may be defined as a story about the gods and such a story is represented in our text. They admit that no narrative about the gods is extant relative to Isa. 14. They suggest, rather, that the poem reflects such a narrative myth.' (Shipp 2002, 10). Furthermore, after a short discussion with Marvin Pope who suggested that Isaiah 14 and some other passages in the Hebrew Bible reflect a myth about the fall of gods from heaven, Shipp denies this by stating that there is no evidence that Ilu 'ever suffered such a rebellion and fall from his status as head of the Ugaritic pantheon, but rather that he was relegated to a "semi-retired" status of 'head god emeritus' " (Shipp 2002, 14). Shipp continues with the conclusion that if 'a notion of a divine rebellion and attempted usurpation of the throne of heaven by upstart deities must be questioned in Ugaritic mythology, then the analogy of such a rebellion with Isa 14 must likewise be questioned' (Shipp 2002, 14). Finally, he rejects in fact any narrative myth approach, because this is

> ...subject to some of the same criticisms as the "mythological allusions" approach: there is no single, mythical narrative which has been discovered to date which actually mirrors the themes, terminology, and deities mentioned in Isa 14:12-15, let alone the entire poem ... While there may be a narrative myth behind the poem, ... none so far suggested closely resembles the terminology and motifs sufficiently to suggest it as its narrative background. Until and unless such a myth is discovered, therefore, judgment about assigning the poem to one of the current suggestions should be restrained' (Shipp 2002, 18).

We have shown that this hypercritical approach reveals an imperfect understanding of the Ugaritic literature. Ilu did suffer from an insurrection by Baʿlu and probably from an earlier one by Ḥôrānu (Section 2.2).

Margaret Barker states that although there may have been a Canaanite background for Isaiah 14 'the closest parallels are in the OT itself and suggest that it was the Hebrews who told of someone being thrown from God's presence because of his pride or sin.' She then refers to Gen. 3:4, Isa. 14:14; Ezek. 28:13 as well as Ezek. 28:2, 6, 17; Phil. 2:6, and continues, 'The context of this star myth is not the lost mythology of Canaan, although that might have been very similar; it is the lost mythology of Israel and its temple, some of which has survived in the Enochic tradition ... ' (Barker 2012, 511).

Though in his scholarly commentary of 1986 John Oswalt still admitted that Isaiah 14 is alluding to 'the great literature of his day' (321), in his application commentary on Isaiah he rejects this idea in rather strong terms,

> The language here has intriguing overtones of several ancient stories about both human and divine hubris, and scholars have expended a good deal of energy seeking for the original poem that the prophet supposedly makes use of. There seems to be a scholarly antipathy to the idea that anything in the Bible could be original. However the search has not paid off, and it still seems as if Isaiah has taken a number of themes familiar to his hearers and woven them together into a new creation to make his unique theological point (Oswalt 2003, 210).

We failed to identify scholars who propagate the view that nothing in the Bible is original. And is a writer who 'has taken a number of themes familiar to his hearers and woven them together into a new creation' original in an absolute sense?

We hope to have made clear that the findings we present in this book cast doubt on the justification of quotations like those we cited above.

4.5.1 *Differences*

1. Though it seems more likely now that elements of an originally Canaanite myth have been used in Isaiah 14, the character of the text has been changed completely and has been more or less historicized (Wildberger 1978, 550-551). Because Ilu (El) and Hēlēl (Hilālu) were *Canaanite* gods the application of the song to the Babylonian king must be secondary.[182]

---

[182] As candidates for the Babylonian king several names have been proposed, even Assyrian kings like Tiglath-Pileser III, Shalmaneser V, Sargon II and Sennacherib. Babylonian kings proposed are Nebuchadnezzar, Nabonidus and Alexander the Great. See overviews with Blenkinsopp 2000, 286-287; Beuken 2007, 58; Shipp 2002, 158-162; Van Keulen 2010. The 𝔊 would even support Antiochus IV (Van der Kooij 1981, 39-42).

Sometimes, the use of Hebrew נֵצֶר in verse 19 is taken as a wordplay with

It is most important to note that already the original song Isa. 14:12-15 mocks not only about the king, but also about his religion. The king wanted to be like El, in line with the Canaanite belief that after their death kings were united with the highest god El/Ilu. This knowledge could not have been derived from the Hebrew Bible in its canonical form. So it must have been acquired via different channels. Ugarit has produced important information with regard to the deification of kings and famous heroes in Canaan.[183] When a famous hero or king died, he was united with the god whose 'son' he was during his lifetime. When he died the king was united with his creator Ilu/El. This idea is clearly expressed in the Ugaritic *Legend of Kirtu*. When the king lies dying, his wife says to his friends,

KTU 1.15:V.16-17

[*l*] *qṣ.mtm.ʾuṣbʿ*[*t*]	[To] the end of mortals is only a finger (away),[184]
[*k*]*rt.šrk.ʾil*	Kirtu is going to join Ilu.

The term used for the unification of the king with his personal patron Ilu is a participle derived from the same root as the vehemently opposed heresy of *širk* in Islam. This is the sin of associating any other being with God. Especially the Christian trinitarian dogma is branded as *Širk*. It is most remarkable to see this term being used in a positive sense in an authentic polytheistic document from the Near East. Here it describes the merging of a human being as a lower deity – Kirtu was already a 'son' of Ilu – with his creator.[185]

The mockery about this belief in Isaiah 14 and Ezekiel 28 shows that such ideas were rejected far earlier in Israel than in the Muslim world. When the Phoenician king had died, the poet asserts

the name of Nebuchadnezzar (Gosse 1988, 239; Holladay 1999, 635, 638; Van Keulen 2010, 117). In the end Van Keulen opts for a typological interpretation, not an individual Assyrian monarch, but the Assyrian king as *typos* of any cruel and arrogant ruler (122).

[183] Actually such deification is attested from a much earlier date on. Cf. Finkelstein 1966.

[184] KTU reads [x]*qmṣ.mtm* here. Inspection of the Inscriptifact Database (courtesy Wayne T. Pitard) learned us that this is hardly correct. Since *šrk* in the parallel colon can only be a participle of the G-stem, I assume the same for *mtm*, 'those dying, mortals'.

[185] Cf. De Moor 1997, 328-331.

that he did not became enthroned with, or even higher than, El on the latter's lofty mountain, but has become demonized: he is the fallen god Hilālu whose name is deliberately corrupted to Hēlēl, 'Wail!' (see below). The circumstance that Canaanite kings expected to be deified and be united with El after their death is the best explanation for the scathing criticism in Isa. 14 as well as Ezek. 28. Of course this presupposes a form of henotheism, if not monotheism, but we are not as wary as others are to assume this for prophets like Isaiah and Ezekiel.

2. In vv. 12-15 the Phoenician king is said to have fallen from heaven like the star Hēlēl. We believe to have demonstrated the astral character of Ḥôrānu/Hilālu in Section 2.5. Although we have not been able to prove the downfall of Hilālu in a really conclusive way, we believe to have adduced sufficient circumstantial evidence to surmise that this probably happened in the now lost tablet preceding KTU 1.107.

3. In the song about the fall of Hēlēl no woman plays a role. Since this is also the case in Ezek. 28 (Section 4.6) we regard this as a strong indication that the underlying Adamic myth cannot be Gen. 2–3. Some other narrative must have inspired these writers.

4.5.2 *Similarities*

It is understandable that scholars were cautious in defining a mythical background for the song in Isaiah 14, because so many unsatisfactory parallels from both Canaan and Mesopotamia have been adduced. Interesting for our investigation of Isaiah 14 and the mythical data from KTU 1.100 and 1.107 is a conclusion made by John Barclay Burns 1989, 202,

> Despite considerable scholarly investigation the mythological background to Is 14:12-15 remains resolutely obscure. It is best to envisage it as a collection of fragmentary mythological references employed to illustrate the overweening *hubris* of the despot. Hēlēl is the bright morning-star who fells from heaven. However, there is no evidence that, like the king of Babylon, his fall was punishment, that he was banished to the underworld or that he oppressed the nations.

In our opinion we have been able to present Canaanite data suggesting that Hēlēl (Hilālu) was indeed a god punished for his attempt to dethrone Ilu/El and was punished by his removal from the higher echelons of the celestials. In revenge he enveloped the entire world in a poisonous fog and seems to have changed the Tree of Life in the garden of Ilu into a Tree of Death, taking on the shape of a huge poisonous snake, the Leviathan, who bit Adammu so that he was on the brink of dying. Eventually he repented and made the damage he had caused partly good by uprooting and trimming the Tree of Death. Hilālu, probably the bright star Aldebaran, was also called Ḥôrānu and was the antipode of Ilu/El.[186] Several elements in the song of Isaiah 14 fall into place now.

1. Isaiah 14:12 mentions Hēlēl 'son of Dawn' who fell from heaven. Although *šḥr* 'Dawn' was also a god in Ugarit, he was a son of Ilu, not a son of Dawn (Šaḥar). Therefore it is more likely that 'son' is used here in a transferred meaning: 'belonging to' since the reappearance of Aldebaran, Ḥôrānu in his astral form, was connected with dawn (Section 2.5). We assume that the name of *Hll* in Ugarit was vocalized in the same way as in Arabic: *Hilālu.* We explain the Hebrew vocalization as a deliberate taunt: הֵילֵל is the imperative of √ ילל 'Wail!' (Ezek. 21:17; Zech. 11:2; cf. Isa. 23:1, 6, 14.).

In Ugarit Hilālu was an alternative name of the god Ḥôrānu, the progenitor of evil serpents, among them the serpentine sea monster guarding the Tree of Life in the 'vineyard of the gods'. As a result heaven and earth suffered from his poison. However, when all deities joined forces to destroy the snake and his offspring, Ḥôrānu partially lifted his grip on the Tree of Death and allowed renewal of life through procreation to make a new start. He then fathered the Kôṯarātu, goddesses overseeing conception and childbirth (KTU 1.17:II.26-42; KTU 1.24:40-50; KTU 1.179). These goddesses seem to take part in the struggle against the serpent that endangered childbirth (see above Section 2.5). This suggests a link between these Kôṯarātu, as well as between Hēlēl and Ḥôrānu. As stated in Section 2.5, a Phoenician inscription designates these goddesses facilitating childbirth as the seven concu-

[186] See for all this Chapter 2.

bines of Ḥaurān. So the Phoenicians seem to have been acquainted with this part of Canaanite lore.

2. Because it is explicitly said in Isaiah 14:12 that Hēlēl has fallen *from heaven* there can be no doubt that his rebellion is supposed to have taken place in heaven, not on earth.[187] This suggests that Hēlēl must have been a deity too, or in any case a divine being.

3. Hēlēl is called בֶּן־שָׁחַר 'son of Dawn'. In several studies the name of Hēlēl is explained as 'the shining one', a designation of the morning star.[188] The god Hilālu appears to be a blazing star, in our opinion Aldebaran who was thought to control the crescent moon (see above, Section 2.5). This seems to support the translation of Hēlēl by 'morning star' because this star reappears at dawn after occultation by the moon. Šaḥar is attested also as a deity in the Hebrew Bible. Ps. 139:9 describes the wings of Šaḥar, and theophoric Phoenician names confirm Šaḥar as a god.[189] In Ugarit *šḥr* is known as the deity 'Sunrise red', brother of Šalimu 'Sunset red' and fathered by Ilu/El (KTU 1.23:46-54) and two unnamed women (cf. Section 2.1). *šḥr* is also known as *qdm*, Qadmu, the deified East (KTU 1.12:I.7-8). Hēlēl definitely refers to Canaanite Hilālu. His epithet 'son of Dawn' in Isa. 14:12 confirms that Hēlēl was not the moon, as was often suggested because of his Ugaritic epithet *bʿl gml* 'lord of the crescent moon', nor the planet Venus, but that he was the blazing star Aldebaran that can be seen at dawn and at certain times is accompanied by the crescent moon (see above, Section 2.5). The noun בֶּן in the phrase בֶּן־שָׁחַר has to be read as a kind of affiliation.[190] The Greek translation renders Hēlēl son of Šaḥar ὁ ἑωσφόρος ὁ πρωὶ ἀνατέλλων and Latin Vulgate translates similarly *lucifer qui mane oriebaris*, 'the light-bringer that rises in the morning".

4. The ruler of whom it is said that he wanted to set his throne above the stars of El (Isa. 14:13) thought that he was about to take over the position of the highest god Ilu of the Canaanite pan-

---

[187] For a similar observation see Wildberger 1978, 551.
[188] E.g. Gosse 1988, 219; Watson 1999, 392; Beuken 2007, 49.
[189] Cf. Wildberger 1978, 551.
[190] Like an expression such as בֶּן־מָוֶת in 1 Sam. 20:31; 26:16 and 2 Sam. 12:5, indicating that people are close to death.

theon. He also said that he wanted to go up to the heights of the clouds and to equate himself with the Most High עֶלְיוֹן (Isa. 14:14). In a pantheon lower deities could rise in rank, ultimately deposing even the highest deity. As we have seen in Section 2.1, *ʿly(w)n* 'Most High was a designation of *ʾilʾib*/Ilu as the Creator of All. Because of his rebellion Hēlēl is said to have fallen from heaven' (Isa. 14:12) and brought down to Sheol (Isa. 14:15). This tallies with the Ugaritic myth in which the Canaanite god Ḥôrānu was probably cast down into the Netherworld after his attempt to seize Ilu's throne. Ḥôrānu originally occupied a high position in the list of deities and finally ended up at the end of the god list of the Ugaritic pantheon (Section 2.1). This proves that something must has happened which caused his downfall in the ranking of gods. Because Ḥôrānu is closely related to other divine and human rebels, the conclusion is justified that he himself apparently rebelled against Ilu. Furthermore, also the fact that he is excluded from the sacrificial cult in Ugarit is an argument to asume his falling in disgrace. In our opinion this provides a better background for Hēlēl's downfall in Isaiah 14:12-14 than any other proposal hitherto made.

5. Hēlēl wished to sit on the mount of assembly, on the utmost heights in the north (Isa. 14:13). The mount of assembly was the mountain of the highest god Ilu/El, where the assembly of the gods gathered. The 'Mountain of the Assembly' can hardly be anything else than the mountain on which the Canaanite pantheon was thought to convene (KTU 1.2:I.14-16: *pḫr mʿd tk ġr ll* 'the Congregation assembled on the mountain of the Night' , cf. Section 2.4). In the Balaam text from Deir ʿAlla the gods and goddesses belonging to the divine Asembly are still called 'Šadday-gods and -goddesses' so they were seen as the family of El Shadday.[191]

The phrase בְּיַרְכְּתֵי צָפוֹן can be rendered both 'on the mountain range of Mt Zaphon' as well as 'on the mountain range of the north'.[192] The rendering 'on the mountain range of the north'

[191] Cf. Hoftijzer & Van der Kooij 1976. 275-276; Aḥhituv 2008, 445.

[192] Most translations opt for the north, e.g. LUTHER, KJV, RSV, ASV, NJB, TOB, NASB, WEB, NEG79, NR94, SCHLA. In favor of this choice is the circumstance that the Zaphon was the mountain of Baʿlu, not of Ilu. Also Isa. 14:31 supports this choice. In Ezek. 38:6, 15; 39:2 the same expression can only

might be a reference then to the two tops of Mt Ararat, formerly the mountain of the highest god El/Ilu (see above, Section 2.4).

6. Although it is far from certain that Isa. 14:19 still refers to the same events as the song Isa. 14:12-15, it is noteworthy that the king is said here to be cast out, away from his grave and compared to a body trampled underfoot (Isa. 14:19). Often this is taken as a reference to king Sargon II of whom it is said that he was slain on the battlefield and was left unburied (see above) It is certain that Lūli, the king of Tyrus and Sidon who had to flee to Cyprus, died in exile. It is possible that the writer of Isa. 14:19-20 refers to the fact that he was not buried in the grave that Phoenician kings used to build for themselves during their lifetimes.

Yet this too might be considered a far echo of the Canaanite myth. The giant serpent, embodiment of Ḥôrānu, was thought to have been thrown into the desert, as is confirmed by Ps. 74:14 and Ezek. 29:5[193] In Ezek 29:5, it is explicitly stated that after being thrown into the desert the serpent will *not* be gathered and will *not* be buried. Furthermore, in iconography this serpent is often depicted as 'trampled underfoot'[194] just as is said of the king in Isaiah 14.

7. Hēlēl = Lucifer. The Vulgate translates Hēlēl in Isaiah 14:12 as Lucifer and later NT texts (Section 6) seem to interpret the fallen Hēlēl as Satan. Because of the equation of Hilālu and Ḥôrānu in Canaan it becomes clear that the Latin translation 'Lucifer' is not just a later interpretation, but can be traced back to the figure of Hilālu/Ḥôrānu in Canaanite myth. The designation 'Satan' has not turned up in Ugarit or elsewhere in ancient Canaan. But contrary to what many have thought the serpent in the tree was definitely the father of all evil, but paradoxically also the protector of eternal life through procreation.

8. Also Ḥôrānu's epithets *šr* 'the (Evil) Prince', *ʿd* 'the Enemy' and *ʾabdy* 'Destroyer' which correspond to designations of the devil in some pseudepigraphic works[195], the New Testament and

---

mean 'the mountain range of the north'.

193 See Sections 2.8 and 4.7.

194 E.g. on the well-known cylinder seal showing Marduk trampling the ancient serpent. Section 2.8, Fig. 22.

Islam[196] prove the antiquity of the concept of a potentially evil adversary of God. This ambiguity between good and evil was experienced as a characteristic of rulership. The gloss Isa. 14:20b לֹא־יִקָּרֵא לְעוֹלָם זֶרַע מְרֵעִים 'let the brood of the evil ones never again be invoked' may originally have had the devil and his demons in mind because 𝔊 and 𝔖 read a singlar. 'The brood of the Evil One' would have been the serpentine offspring of Ḥôrānu then.[197]

4.6 *Ezekiel 28*

First we present our own translation of Ezekiel 28:1-19.

וַיְהִי דְבַר־יְהוָה אֵלַי	(1) And the word of the LORD came to me,
לֵאמֹר׃	saying,
בֶּן־אָדָם אֱמֹר לִנְגִיד צֹר	(2) Human, say to the ruler of Tyre,
כֹּה־אָמַר אֲדֹנָי יְהוִה	Thus says the Lord GOD:
יַעַן גָּבַהּ לִבְּךָ	Because you overestimated yourself
וַתֹּאמֶר אֵל אָנִי	and said, I am El,
מוֹשַׁב אֱלֹהִים יָשַׁבְתִּי	I dwell in the dwelling of God
בְּלֵב יַמִּים	in the wide sea,
וְאַתָּה אָדָם וְלֹא־אֵל	whereas you are a human and not El,
וַתִּתֵּן לִבְּךָ כְּלֵב אֱלֹהִים׃	but you fancied yourself to be like God himself.
הִנֵּה חָכָם אַתָּה מִדָּנְאֵל	(3) Look! You are wiser than Daniel,[198]
כָּל־סָתוּם לֹא עֲמָמוּךָ׃	no secret remains hidden from you.
בְּחָכְמָתְךָ וּבִתְבוּנָתְךָ	(4) By your wisdom and insight
עָשִׂיתָ לְּךָ חָיִל	you made yourself a fortune,
וַתַּעַשׂ זָהָב וָכֶסֶף בְּאוֹצְרוֹתֶיךָ׃	you made gold and silver (flow) into your treasuries.
בְּרֹב חָכְמָתְךָ בִּרְכֻלָּתְךָ	(5) By your great wisdom, by your trade
הִרְבִּיתָ חֵילֶךָ	you made your fortune greater,
וַיִּגְבַּהּ לְבָבְךָ בְּחֵילֶךָ׃	but you overestimated yourself because of your fortune.

---

195 Sections 5.3; 5.13.

196 Sections 2.6; 5.18; 6.

197 Also Isa. 14:21 is a later elaboration in our opinion because the singular אֲבִיהֶם deserves trust since it constitutes an allusion to Adam's sin. The plural, however, is supported by Mt. 3:7 par., cf. Section 6.2.

198 Ilu was seen as extremely wise, KTU 1.3:V.30-31 par. The Daniel mentioned here is not the Daniel of the biblical book, but a Canaanite hero who plays an important role as a righteous sufferer like Job in the Ugaritic *Legend of Aqhâtu*, cf. De Moor 2003, 147-148, with earlier literature.

ס

לָכֵן כֹּה אָמַר אֲדֹנָי יְהוִה	(6) Therefore, thus says the Lord GOD:
יַעַן תִּתְּךָ אֶת־לְבָבְךָ כְּלֵב אֱלֹהִים	because you fancied yourself to be like God himself,
לָכֵן הִנְנִי מֵבִיא עָלֶיךָ זָרִים	(7) Therefore, I am going to bring strangers upon you,
עָרִיצֵי גּוֹיִם	oppressors of nations,
וְהֵרִיקוּ חַרְבוֹתָם עַל־יְפִי חָכְמָתֶךָ	and they shall draw their swords against the beauty of your wisdom,
וְחִלְּלוּ יִפְעָתֶךָ׃	and they shall defile your splendor.
לַשַּׁחַת יוֹרִדוּךָ	(8) They shall force you to descend into the Pit,
וָמַתָּה מְמוֹתֵי חָלָל בְּלֵב יַמִּים׃	and you shall die (in) the places[199] for the slain dead in the wide sea.
הֶאָמֹר תֹּאמַר אֱלֹהִים אָנִי לִפְנֵי הֹרְגֶךָ	(9) Will you still say, 'I am God', in the face of your killers?
וְאַתָּה אָדָם וְלֹא־אֵל בְּיַד מְחַלְלֶיךָ	Whereas you are a human, and not El, in the hands of your slayers?
מוֹתֵי עֲרֵלִים תָּמוּת בְּיַד־זָרִים	(10) You will die the sorry death of the uncircumcised by the hand of strangers,
כִּי אֲנִי דִבַּרְתִּי נְאֻם אֲדֹנָי יְהוִה׃	for I have spoken, declares the Lord GOD.

ס

וַיְהִי דְבַר־יְהוָה אֵלַי	(11) And the word of the LORD came to me,
לֵאמֹר׃	saying,
בֶּן־אָדָם שָׂא קִינָה עַל־מֶלֶךְ צוֹר	(12) Human, raise a lament over the king of Tyre,
וְאָמַרְתָּ לּוֹ	and say to him,
כֹּה אָמַר אֲדֹנָי יְהוִה	Thus speaks the Lord GOD:
אַתָּה חוֹתֵם תָּכְנִית	You were a carefully worked[200] signet
מָלֵא חָכְמָה וּכְלִיל יֹפִי׃	filled with wisdom and perfect in beauty.

[199] Ugaritic *mmt* in KTU 1.5:V.19 and Job 33:22.

[200] Ezek. 28:12 (with the emendation חוֹתֵם instead of חוֹתָם adopted by the versions and a host of scholars) seems to compare the King of Tyre to 'a perfect signet' (חוֹתֵם תָּכְנִית, 𝔊 ἀποσφράγισμα ὁμοιώσεως, 'a signet of likeness') 'full of wisdom and perfect in beauty' (for different, but less likely solutions see Greenberg 254-255; Callender 2000a; Bunta 2007.). The rare word תָּכְנִית is no doubt the same word as Akkadian *taknītu* / *taknû* 'care, solicitude' (*CAD* (T), 84-85), also used of carefully worked gems. So the literal meaning is 'a signet of care'. The imagery behind this designation is the king as the signet with which the deity seals important decisions on earth (cf. Jer. 22:24; Hag. 2:23, cf. Korpel 2010).

בְּעֵדֶן גַּן־אֱלֹהִים הָיִיתָ	(13) You were in Eden, the Garden of God,
כָּל־אֶבֶן יְקָרָה מְסֻכָתֶךָ	with every precious stone you were covered,
אֹדֶם פִּטְדָה וְיָהֲלֹם	red jasper, chrysolite, green jasper,[201]
תַּרְשִׁישׁ שֹׁהַם וְיָשְׁפֵה	turquoise, chrysoprase, nephrite,
סַפִּיר נֹפֶךְ וּבָרְקַת וְזָהָב	lapislazuli, haematite, malachite, and gold,
מְלֶאכֶת תֻּפֶּיךָ וּנְקָבֶיךָ בָּךְ	the workmanship of your beauty,[202] with your inscription on you.[203]
בְּיוֹם הִבָּרַאֲךָ כּוֹנָנוּ׃	On the day of your creation they were manufactured.
אַתְּ־כְּרוּב מִמְשַׁח הַסּוֹכֵךְ	(14) You were a polished protecting cherub[204]
וּנְתַתִּיךָ בְּהַר קֹדֶשׁ	and I placed you on the holy mountain,
אֱלֹהִים הָיִיתָ	you were 'God',
בְּתוֹךְ אַבְנֵי־אֵשׁ הִתְהַלָּכְתָּ׃	you walked in the midst of the fiery stones.
תָּמִים אַתָּה בִּדְרָכֶיךָ	(15) You were blameless in your ways
מִיּוֹם הִבָּרְאָךְ	from the day you were created
עַד־נִמְצָא עַוְלָתָה בָּךְ׃	until iniquity was found in you.
בְּרֹב רְכֻלָּתְךָ	(16) By the greatness of your trade
מָלוּ תוֹכְךָ חָמָס וַתֶּחֱטָא	you became filled with crime and sinned,

[201] The identification of the gemstones is problematic (see e.g. Block 1997, 106-10; Houtman 2000, 497-503; Premstaller 2005, 110; Gathmann 2008, 536-547), although it is clear that the Hebrew scribe partially borrowed the names of the gems he knew from the breastplate of the high priest (Exod. 28:17-20; 39:10-13). Here we arbitrarily follow the excellent Dutch study by Bolman 1938.

[202] The word תֹּף does not mean 'tambourine' here, but might be related to Ugaritic *tp* 'beauty' (cf. KTU 1.96:2), as a parallel of 'יֹפִי' in v. 12. Possibly this refers to a portrayal of the king's profile on the signet.

[203] נֶקֶב is derived from the root נקב 'to perforate, to inscribe with a name', cf. KTU 1.17:V.35), also used for iconography (cf. Deutsch 2002). Modern usage would opt for 'in it', but the writer does not forget that he has identified the king with the signet.

[204] We agree with Mettinger 1976, 270-271 that one should not arbitrarily change the Masoretic vocalisation of אַתְּ which, as he demonstrates, can well be interpreted as a masculine form. In line with the preceding verse the king is described here as a glittering creature. The *hapax legomenon* מִמְשַׁח can hardly mean anything else than 'polishing, rubbing' (cf. Akad. *muššu'u* 'to rub'). So we translate: 'you were a polished protecting cherub'. This agrees with v. 16, 'so I destroyed you, protecting cherub, from the midst of the fiery stones.' For such protective hybrids see Akkadian *kurību* (*CAD* (K), 559b) and the Egyptian/Phoenician/Hebrew sphinxes which were often gold-plated (cf. Exod. 25:18-22; 1 Kgs 6:23-28, 32, 35; Hendel 1985, 671; Launderdale 2003; Bradshaw & Head 2012, 20.

וָאֲחַלֶּלְךָ מֵהַר אֱלֹהִים	so that I had to pierce you, away from the mountain of God,
וָאַבֶּדְךָ כְּרוּב הַסֹּכֵךְ	and had to destroy you, protecting cherub,
מִתּוֹךְ אַבְנֵי־אֵשׁ׃	away from amidst the fiery stones.
גָּבַהּ לִבְּךָ בְּיָפְיֶךָ	(17) You overestimated yourself with your beauties,
שִׁחַתָּ חָכְמָתְךָ עַל־יִפְעָתֶךָ	your wisdom sank down to the Pit[205] with your splendor.
עַל־אֶרֶץ הִשְׁלַכְתִּיךָ	I have thrown you down on the earth,
לִפְנֵי מְלָכִים נְתַתִּיךָ לְרַאֲוָה בָךְ׃	in front of kings I have made you a ridiculous sight.
מֵרֹב עֲוֺנֶיךָ בְּעֶוֶל רְכֻלָּתְךָ	(18) By the greatness of your transgressions, by the crookedness of your trade,
חִלַּלְתָּ מִקְדָּשֶׁיךָ	you have defiled your sanctuaries.
וָאוֹצִא־אֵשׁ מִתּוֹכְךָ	So I brought forth fire from your midst,
הִיא אֲכָלַתְךָ	that devoured you,
וָאֶתֶּנְךָ לְאֵפֶר עַל־הָאָרֶץ	and I made you ashes upon the earth
לְעֵינֵי כָּל־רֹאֶיךָ׃	in the sight of all who saw you.
כָּל־יוֹדְעֶיךָ בָּעַמִּים	(19) All those who have known you among the peoples
שָׁמְמוּ עָלֶיךָ	are appalled at you;
בַּלָּהוֹת הָיִיתָ	you have become an object of terror,
וְאֵינְךָ עַד־עוֹלָם׃	and will never be around anymore.

פ

Ezekiel 28 consists of two oracles against the king of Tyre (28:1-10, 11-19) and one oracle against Sidon (28:20-26).[206]

There is little reason to assume that Ezek. 28:1-19 was inspired by Isa. 14, or the other way round, although in both cases it is the intention of the prophet to ridicule a foreign ruler and his religion. It may seem a distinctive difference that the astral character of Isa. 14 is missing in Ezek. 28, but by this time the prophet may

---

205 Same root as in v. 8.

206 So e.g. Habel 1967, 516-517; Dijkstra 1989, 55; Block 1998, 87-128; Day 2000, 28-29; Premstaller 2005, 93-133; Kustár 2006; Mettinger 2007, 85. The form-historical solution to declare Ezek. 28:3-5 a later expansion of the original prophecy (so e.g. Zimmerli 1969, 665; Loretz 1989) is unsatisfactory because the Daniel of v. 3 can better be explained on the basis of the Ugaritic hero of that name (see below). Sedlmeier 2001, 276-277, 289-295 regards not only vv. 3-5 as a later expansion but also vv. 6, 7-10. We see also insufficient reason to follow Gathmann 2008, 535-554 in regarding Ezek. 28:1-10 as a 'relecture' of Ezek. 28:11-19.

have preferred to name a Phoenician deity. In Tyre a star that fell from heaven was worshiped and this star may well have been devoted to the rebel god Ḥôrān who had once attempted to depose Ilu/El (Section 2.6). This made Ezekiel's mockery even more effective. The satirical song of Ezek. 28 became popular because it is evidently alluded to in Ezek. 29–32 (below Section 4.7) and Dan. 4.[207]

It has long been recognized that Ezekiel makes use of some Canaanite myth here that must have been known to his Israelite audience.[208] This lends a sarcastic tone to his adhortation to raise a lament for this Tyrian king.[209] The author is probably the prophet Ezekiel himself because he wrote a similar ironic lamentation about Judahite royalty in Ezek. 19.[210] The interest in the lack of circumcision (Ezek. 28:10), the knowledge of the gems in the high priest's breastplate (Ezek. 28:13),[211] the use of תָּמִים 'without blemish' (Ezek. 28:15) and the interest in the profanation of Tyrian sanctuaries (Ezek. 28:18) reflect Ezekiel's priestly background. The use of the verb ברא 'to create' reveals knowledge of the priestly creation narrative of Gen. 1 (Section 4.2). The designation of the garden of God as 'Eden' points to the tradition that has been codified in Gen. 2.[212]

In the light of what we have found in Ugarit many earlier hypotheses about this chapter have become less likely. For example the idea that Ezekiel 28 reflects a myth about the fall of El.[213] As John Day has argued convincingly, it is true that Ezek. 28 is

---

[207] Díez Merino 1984; Sulzbach 2004.

[208] See e.g. LaCocque 2006, 47; Mettinger 2007, 85-98. Although May 1962 and Patmore 2012, 5-8 point out some limitations and weaknesses in the search for the myth underlying Ezek. 28, their objections are not decisive.

[209] Possibly Ittobaal III who ruled from 591 to 573 BCE. Cf. Katzenstein 1973, 324-332; Bonnet 1988, 42-46.
Obviously Origen's solution to assume that the ruler of Tyre was in reality an angel, a view for which Anderson 2000b still expresses sympathy, is no longer tenable now that the notion of divine kingship has been discovered in the ancient Near East.

[210] Cf. Korpel 2009.

[211] Cf. Block 1997, 106-10; Premstaller 2005, 110; Gathmann 2008, 536-547.

[212] For succinct surveys of the differences and similarities between Gen. 2–3 and Ezek. 28 see May 1962, 168-169; Tigchelaar 1999, 37-38; Hendel 2013, 19-20.

[213] Pope 1955, 98-103; Van Seters 1992, 119-122.

based on Canaanite El traditions,[214] but the chapter is more in the line of the 'strong' creator god El who still headed the Canaanite pantheon.

Also the possibility that the deified king was identified with the national god of Tyre Melqart[215] would be acceptable only if the 'King of the City' (as is the meaning of the name of Melqart) were a manifestation of El which at first sight may seem rather unlikely. There is hardly sufficient evidence for a 'cultic drama' during which Melqart, who rather resembles Baal, the *rpʾu* 'Healer', would have replaced El.[216] However, in the period of Ugarit's bloom Aṯiratu (Asherah) did have a temple in Tyre and Sidon (KTU 1.14:IV.35-36) and it is hardly imaginable that her husband Ilu (El) would not have been in these cities too. What happened was that a few centuries later Ilu had been replaced by Baʿlu in the Levant, a change in allegiance already adumbrated in Ugarit itself.[217] So Melqart may well have been Baal in his role as El's successor.

4.6.1 *Differences*

1. To the prophet Ezekiel it was unthinkable that a human being could imagine himself to be God's equal, even though traces of deification of royalty are discernable in the Hebrew Bible itself (see e.g. Korpel 2006). Time and again Ezekiel emphasizes that the king is a mere human being. For the much-discussed designation בֶּן־אָדָם (Ezek. 28:2) Ugaritic suggests that originally it meant 'normal human being, such as God had it meant to be' (Section 2.1). The parallelism with וְאַתָּה אָדָם וְלֹא־אֵל suggests that here it is used to underline that both the prophet and the king of Tyre were ordinary human beings.

2. The king of Tyre is said to dwell 'in the wide sea' (Ezek. 28:2) and with unmistakable irony the prophet announces that he will drown in the same wide sea, even though his country was a seagoing nation (Ezek. 28:8).[218]

[214] Day 1994; 2000, 26-28. See also Davies 2006.
[215] So e.g. Bonnet 1988, 42-46; Mettinger 2007, 88-89; Gathmann 2008, 474-477.
[216] Against Fechter 1992, 155; Sedlmeier 2001, 284.
[217] De Moor 1997, 71-102; Korpel 1998, 105-111; see Section 2.1 above.

3. Deified kings were thought to enjoy a certain amount of bliss in the hereafter.[219] The prophet brusquely robs the king of Tyre of this hope (Ezek. 28:8-10, 16-19). Habel 1967, 520 observes, 'The contrast between the clothing of this royal first man and the nakedness of the primeval pair in Gen. 2-3 is immediately obvious.' The king of Tyre was 'exposed' before other kings (Ezek. 28:17).

4.6.2 *Similarities*

1. The expression 'dwelling of God' or 'dwelling of the gods' (מוֹשַׁב אֱלֹהִים, Ezek. 28:2) is unique in the Hebrew Bible, but is paralleled by the Ugaritic designations *mṯb ʾil* 'the residence of Ilu' and *mṯbt ʾilm* 'the residences of the gods'.[220]

2. The circumstance that in contrast to Genesis no woman is mentioned in Ezek. 28 has sometimes led to the assumption that here we have a different version of the primordial history in which only a man figured (e.g. McKenzie 1956). This is by no means a conclusive argument. In Antiquity women, even queens, were mostly ignored in texts promoting royal ideology. Ḥôrānu did have offspring (Section 2.1) but the extant Ugaritic texts do not reveal with whom he sired it.

3. The garden of Eden, God's garden in Ezek. 28:13, is paralleled by God's mountain (Ezek. 28:14), thus paradise is assumed to be located on the mountain of God. Sometimes this is seen as contradicting the aquatic paradisiacal scenery in other biblical texts,[221] but this is not necessarily the case, as has been pointed out by several scholars.[222] Rivers rise in mountainous regions and the texts of Ugarit depict Ilu as dwelling 'at the fountain-head of the two Rivers' || 'the middle of the streambed of the two Floods' (KTU 1.3:V.5-7 par.) as well as dwelling on a mountain (e.g. KTU 1.1:III.12, see Section 2.4). Protective geniuses (scorpion-men) on the mountain of El are also discussed in Section 2.4. When she be-

[218] This obviously refers to Tyre's geographic location and not to the abode of El. Cf. Premstaller 2005, 101.
[219] Spronk 1986; De Moor 2014, 377-385.
[220] E.g. KTU 1.4:I.12; 1.23:19, cf. Del Olmo Lete & Sanmartín 2003, 604.
[221] Such as Gen. 2:10-14; Ezek. 47:1-12; Joel 4:18[3:18]; Zech. 14:8; Ps. 42:7-8; 46:5. Cf. Premstaller 2005, 118.
[222] E.g. Noort 1999, 27; Stordalen 2000, 363-372; Blenkinsopp 2011, 61.

came the ruling queen mother the Phoenician queen Jezebel had a seal made on which she was depicted as a cherub (Korpel 2006).

4. The prophet recognizes Tyre's cleverness ('wisdom') in trade (Ezek. 28:3-7, 12) and knows that its king regarded his wisdom superior to the wisdom of the legendary Canaanite king Daniel. It has long been demonstrated that this Daniel was known in Ugarit too,[223] but not as an extremely wise ruler. So the motif of the king's wisdom must have been derived from his identification with El in Ezek. 28. El's wisdom is often praised in the texts of Ugarit.[224]

5. As we have seen when dealing with Isaiah 14, Ugarit has produced important information with regard to the postmortem deification of kings and famous heroes in Canaan.[225]

6. The king's descent into the 'Pit' (abode of Death) is paralleled by his descent into the 'the places for the slain dead in the wide sea' (Ezek. 28:8). The term מְמוֹת is the equivalent of *mmt* in Ugarit where Yammu (Sea) and Môtu (Death) were both described as beloved sons of Ilu and as allies battling against the god of life Baʿlu. The king's descent into the Netherworld seems to parallel the downfall of Ḥôrānu from the mountain of El (cf. Ezek. 28:16 and Section 2.2). In Ezek. 28:17b and 18b the king is also said to be thrown down *on* the earth. This might be seen as incompatible with the verses 8 and 17 where he is thrown down into the Pit (Netherworld). However, both Netherworld and earth were the areas where the Canaanite rebel god Ḥôrānu was allowed to wander after his expulsion from heaven.

7. The description of the 'fiery stones' in the mountainous dwelling of El in Ezek. 28:14, 16 finds its easiest explanation in the volcanic nature of Mt Ararat (cf. Section 2.4). The king believed himself able to walk between these flaming stones unharmed, but was burnt to ashes (Ezek. 28:18). This fate indicates that these stones

---

223 Day 1980; 1994, 38; De Moor 1997, 149-150; Premstaller 2005, 99, all with earlier literature. Contrast May 1962, 167-168; Block 1998, 96.

224 De Moor 1997, 72-73. See also Job 32:13.

225 It is strange that many authors discussing the possibility of divine kingship in Ezek. 28 (e.g. Launderdale 2003) appear to be totally ignorant of the Ugaritic material.

were dangerous so that comparison with Akkadian *aban išāti* (a reddish semiprecious stone) is a less likely option.

4.7 *Ezekiel 29–32*

Ezekiel's oracles against Egypt exhibit many similarities with his oracles against Tyre.[226] Whereas the king of Tyre was described as a cherub, – a winged lion – the Pharaoh becomes an aquatic monster, a תַּנִּים (Ezek. 29:3). In both cases the imagery results in a contradiction. Whereas the lion has his den in mountain caves (Nah. 2:12-13), the king of Tyre is hurled down from the mountain of God. Whereas the crocodile's[227] habitat is water, the Pharaoh is thrown down in the desert (Ezek. 29:5; 32:3-6). Mostly the תַּנִּים or תַּנִּין is a marine animal[228] but the choice of metaphors is deliberately odd. Winged lions (sphinxes) would have been suitable symbols for Egypt where sculptures of sphinxes abounded (cf. Ezek. 32:2), whereas a seafaring nation like Tyre was proud to brave the huge monsters in the sea.[229] The cosmological myth about the defeat of the serpentine monster is apparently known to the prophet, but he defuses it by attributing the victory to his God who will fling the monster Pharaoh down in a similar way (Crouch 2011a; Marzouk 2014). The theme of the felled monster might have been derived from many other ancient Near Eastern myths, but the circumstance that its corpse is deposited in the desert definitely speaks in favor of the Canaanite background we have elucidated in Sections 2.8, 2.10 and 4.6 of this book.

In Ezekiel 31 the arrogant rulers of Assyria and Egypt are compared to a 'Weltbaum' that rivalled all the trees in the garden of God (Eden) in height. The prophet himself does not believe in such an enormous tree which would have given shadow to all animals and peoples of the world (Ezek. 31:5-6) and which would have surpassed even the trees of Eden in height (Ezek. 31:8). The

---

[226] Most authors are convinced that Ezek. 29–32 form a coherent collection of oracles against Egypt, be it with a small number of later expansions. See e,g, Zimmerli 1969, 697-702; Boadt 1980; Dijkstra 1989, 62-66; Block 1998, 128-134; Premstaller 2005, 134-207.

[227] The most likely identification here, cf. Zimmerli 1969, 707-708.

[228] KTU 1.6:VI.51; Isa. 27:1; Ezek. 32:2; Ps. 74:13; Job 7:12.

[229] See e.g. Krings 1993, Fig. 9/2-7, 9-14; Fig. 10/15-18, 20-22.

parallels with the *Poem of Erra* (Section 3.3.7) are obvious, but are not discussed in Bodi 1991. Yet they are important to our investigation because they confirm the supernatural dimensions of the Tree of Life in the garden of God (Sections 2.8 and 4.3).

Ezekiel observes that this mighty tree – the Assyrian king – has been cut down (Ezek. 31:10-18; see also Ezek. 17:22-24). Ultimately this motif may have been derived from the description of the downfall of the Assyrians in Isa. 10:33-34. The Pharaoh should have understood the unhappy fate of this tree as a warning (Ezek. 31:18b), but he did not. Therefore the prophet returns to his imagery of the Egyptian king as an aquatic monster that will be thrown down on dry land (Ezek. 32:1-15).

4.8 *The Serpent Tamed*

According to Gen. 3:14-15 God cursed the serpent in the Garden of Eden because he had beguiled Eve into eating from the fruit of the forbidden tree.

וַיֹּאמֶר יְהוָֹה אֱלֹהִים אֶל־הַנָּחָשׁ	3:14	And the LORD God said to the serpent,
כִּי עָשִׂיתָ זֹּאת		'Because you have done this,
אָרוּר אַתָּה מִכָּל־הַבְּהֵמָה		cursed are you above all cattle,
וּמִכֹּל חַיַּת הַשָּׂדֶה		and above all wild animals.
עַל־גְּחֹנְךָ תֵלֵךְ		On your belly you shall go,
וְעָפָר תֹּאכַל		and dust you will eat,
כָּל־יְמֵי חַיֶּיךָ׃		every day of your life.
וְאֵיבָה אָשִׁית	3:15	And I will put enmity
בֵּינְךָ וּבֵין הָאִשָּׁה		between you and the woman,
וּבֵין זַרְעֲךָ וּבֵין זַרְעָהּ		and between your seed and her seed.
הוּא יְשׁוּפְךָ רֹאשׁ		The latter will look for your head,[230]
וְאַתָּה תְּשׁוּפֶנּוּ עָקֵב׃		and you will look for its heel.'

With this understanding of the text both sides will always have to watch each other closely, looking for an opportunity to eliminate

[230] The verb שׁוּף is problematic, cf. Clines, *DCH*, vol. 8, 308. Provisionally, we opt for the meaning attested in the 𝔊 (τηρέω), Sabaean and Palestinian Arabic: 'watch intently, look for' (Kazimirski 1860, t. 2, 1288; Barthélemy 1965, 417; Copeland Biella 2004, 514; Muraoka 2009, 678). All ancient translations that want to attribute victory to the offspring of humans translate the first occurrence of the verb differently from the second.

the other's most dangerous limb. The humans know that they must crush or immobilize the serpent's head before it can bite them with its poisonous fangs. The serpents know that their best chance to immobilize their opponent is by biting the human's heel before it can trample them underfoot.[231] Neither side can be assured of victory.

The majority view in the Bible is that only God is able to slay the wicked serpent, both in the past and in the future.[232] However, some texts allow pious humans to participate in his victory, e.g. Psalm 91:13, alluded to in Luke 10:19 (cf. Section 6.4),

עַל־שַׁחַל וָפֶתֶן תִּדְרֹךְ	On lion and adder you will tread,
תִּרְמֹס כְּפִיר וְתַנִּין׃	you will trample young lion and tuna under foot.[233]

It has always been suspected that Psalm 91 has had an apotropaic function [234] and the Qumran florilegium of apocryphal Psalms 11Q11 that served the community as a collection of spells against demons confirms that this use of Psalm 91 rests on very old tradition.

How old? It may now be seen as established that the קטב 'Sting' of Ps. 91:6 occurs already in the thirteenth century BCE in Ugarit.[235] In a fragmentary passage of the *Myth of Baʿlu* it is related how the rain-god Baʿlu had to succumb to Môtu (Death).

KTU 1.5:II.20-24[236]

šmḫ.bn ʾilm.mt	Môtu, the son of Ilu rejoiced.
[21][*ytn.*]*gh.wʾaṣḥ.*	[He gave forth] his voice and cried:
ʾik.yṣḥn [22][*bʿl.*]	'How will [Baʿlu] like to call me (now)![237]
[*ʾik.hd.*]yq*rʾun* [.]	How will [Haddu][238] like to invite me!

[231] For the latter see Figs. 18, 24, 28, 30 in this book.

[232] Isa. 27:1; 51:9; Ps. 74:14; Job 26:13; 40:25[41:1]; Rev. 12:7, 9. Cf. Kaiser 1962; Day 1985.

[233] The Qumran manuscript 11Q11 has a slightly different text: 'On viper and adder you will tread, you will trample [serpent (?)] and tuna.' Cf. Isa. 27:1.

[234] See e.g. Cathcart 2011, 97-99; Vreugendhil 2013, 149-274, both with earlier literature.

[235] The following is loosely based on De Moor 1988a.

[236] We slightly correct the readings of KTU[3] after the Inscriptifact database (courtesy W.T. Pitard).

[237] The reference is to KTU 1.5:I where Môtu complains that was not invited to Baʿlu's housewarming party. Cf. KTU 1.4:VI.44-45.

[ ]	[ ][239]
[rš]*p.mlḥmy*	my warrior [Raš]pu(?),
24[ ]	[ ]
[*'an. š*]*lt.qẓb*	[I be]got the Sting,[240]
25 [ ]	[ ]
[ ].*šmḥ<z>y*	[ ] Šemiḥa<za>y[241]
26 [ ]	[ ]
[ ].*tb'*	[ ] he rebelled

So Môtu seems to have fathered this serpentine monster. We think that the stinging fangs of the primordial serpent that bit Adammu are also prominently present in KTU 1.107,[242]

KTU 1.107:4-6

h*n p bl.*	Look! The devouring mouth!
hn (5) [šnt(?)] qṯb*t.*	Look! The stinging [fangs(?)]!
pẓr.pẓr [.]	Frantically he tried to loosen (it),
w.*p nḥš* (6) ['aḫd(?)]	but the mouth of the serpent [stuck(?)]
[*yṯ*]q.nṯ*k.l yd'.*	He did not know how to bind the Biter,
l bn.lpq ḥmt	nor did he understand how to conquer the poison.

The Ugaritic *qẓb* is a variant spelling of *qṭb*,[243] as it is spelled in Hebrew. He appears to be a son of Death and this brings to mind Job 18:13 יֹאכַל בַּדָּיו בְּכוֹר מָוֶת, 'the first-born of Death will devour his limbs'. In KTU 1.107:35, 45 the primordial serpent Ḥôrānu is designated by the epithet *'akl*, 'Devourer' (|| *nṯk*, 'Biter'). One look at the terrible jaws of an attacking *Cerastes* suffices to understand that this is an apt description (Fig. 35).

---

238 The 'real' name of Ba'lu.

239 At least seven to eight signs are missing.

240 We assume **šôlittu* < **šawlidtu*, 1 sg perf. Š of √*yld*. The Sting was an evil demon according to Deut. 32:24; Ps. 91:6 and especially Hos. 13:14. Cf. Trachtenberg 1961, 36, as well as Job 18:13.

241 One expects the name of an evil deity here. Šemiḥazah was the leader of the rebelling angels according to the *Book of the Luminaries*, see Section 5.2. The Ugaritic sign *z* resembles the sign *y* so one may assume haplography.

242 See Appendix 1 for philological comments.

243 Cf. Freilich & Pardee 1984.

Fig. 35: Attacking *Cerastes Cerastes*(photograph Saša Lončarić, http://skorpac.deviantart.com/art/Cerastes-cerastes-151201599).

If the Sting was indeed the eldest son of Death he would be his crown prince which would explain Ḥôrānu's epithet *šr* 'Prince' if the two are identical.[244] The 'Sting' would be yet another name of Ḥôrānu/Ḥoron (cf. Section 2.6).

The literal meaning of *qṭb* may well be 'sting'. In Arabic *quṭb(ah)* denotes the point of an arrow,[245] but in view of what we have found hitherto it seems likely that it was originally a poison fang in Ugarit and Israel. In Ps. 91:5-6 we find the following external parallelism: פַּחַד לָיְלָה 'the terror of the night' ‖ דֶּבֶר בָּאֹפֶל 'the pestilence in the darkness' next to חֵץ יָעוּף יוֹמָם 'the arrow that flies by day' ‖ קֶטֶב וְשֵׁד צָהֳרָיִם 'the Sting and the demon of noonday' (so with 𝔊). So here too the Sting is compared to an arrow.

[244] In that case 'the King of Terrors' of Job 18:14 is rather Death himself than the Sting, the terrors being the dreadful phantoms of the night and Nether World. Cf. Isa. 17:14; Ezek. 26:36; 27:36; 28:19; Job 18:11; 24:17; 27:20; 30:15.

[245] Lane, 2541; Kazimirski, t. 2, 785.

In Deut. 32:23-24 רָעָב 'Hunger', רֶשֶׁף 'Rešeph' and קֶטֶב are the 'arrows' shot by God. In Israel these deities were demoted to the status of demons whom God could summon as his executioners if necessary. Assuming a slight re-vocalization of the consonantal text we might translate the whole passage as follows,[246]

(23)I will assemble evils against them,
 I will spend my arrows on them:
(24)Hunger, my Sucker,
 Resheph, my Warrior,
  and the Sting, my Poisonous One.
And I will send the teeth of beasts among them,
 with venom of creatures crawling in the dust.

This passage indicates that huge (בְּהֵמוֹת) poisonous serpents are among the executioners. The god Resheph was held responsible for deadly illnesses like pestilence and in this sense was an ally of Death (Môtu), like Ḥôrānu/Ḥôrōn.[247] Death and the Sting are also paired in Hos. 13:14 where God rebukes Ephraim for its sins,

(14)Shall I ransom them from the hand of Sheol?
 Shall I redeem them from Death (Māwet)?
O Death, where are your plagues?
 O Sheol, where is your Sting?
  Let compassion be hidden from my eyes!

The last line indicates that God uses these demons only reluctantly, as a last resort. In later Jewish literature they are still feared as malevolent spirits that must be kept under restraint,[248] but in the Bible itself they are clearly subordinate to God. The primordial Serpent has been muzzled.[249]

Possibly Ḥôrōn has been made subservient to God already within the Hebrew Bible itself. In Exod. 15:7 one may render תשלח חרנך יאכלמו כקש: 'you sent your Horon, he consumed them like stubble'. Suffixed personal pronouns with the names of deities are

---

[246] See for philological details De Moor 1988a; Sanders 1996, 193-200, 401-403; Laato 2015.

[247] See e.g. Blair 2009; Lipiński 2010; Münnich 2013.

[248] De Moor 1988, 101-102.

[249] See Section 2.8 on KTU 1.83:9 and Section 6.8 on 1 Cor. 15. Possiby also reflected in a conjectural reading of Ps. 68:23 (cf. Clines, *DCH*, vol.8, 238-239).

attested in Ugarit and ancient Hebrew inscriptions. And in Hos. 13:14 of course. Compare also Exod. 14:21: it is a strong wind from the *east* that dries up the sea.[250]

4.9 *Conclusions*

In this chapter we have discussed concepts of the primordial world as found in the first chapters of Genesis, Isaiah 14 and Ezekiel 28–32. Moreover we have described how the evil primordial serpent was tamed according to the Hebrew Bible. We might have included more,[251] but our sole purpose was to show that the Ugaritic material we have presented in Chapter 2 is highly relevant to the understanding of the biblical concepts of primordial times.

Most of the differences between the biblical accounts and the Canaanite myths have to do with the distinctiveness of Israel's faith. A special verb was coined for the incomparable activity of God's creating (4.2). The godhead of other deities was denied or ridiculed (4.5; 4.6), so there was also no room for a creatress anymore (4.2, but cf. 4.3). Serpentine monsters like Leviathan and Tannin become mere creatures of God (4.2) or metaphors representing evil rulers (4.5; 4.6; 4.7). Humankind is created in the image of God, not the other way round (4.2). Death entered the world as the result of Adam's failure to obey God's commandment (4.3). In no Ugaritic or other ancient Near Eastern narrative a woman is blamed for humanity's loss of immortality. This is exclusively the case in the Bible (4.3).

However, not all parts of the Hebrew Bible draw the same picture in this respect. For example with regard to the priority of Adam's creation (4.3). Or the idea hat God continues to create, often with human involvement (4.2).[252] A not unimportant question is: who was the first to rebel against God – Adam, Eve or the Devil? The Ugaritic texts discussed suggest it was the Devil (Ḥôrānu) rather than Adam and his wife. Certain biblical passages and some ancient Near Eastern myths seem to support this view.

One should not try to gloss over or harmonize such divergen-

[250] All this will be elaborated in a forthcoming article by Marjo Korpel.

[251] E.g. Psalms 82; Job 15; Dan. 4:4-18. For more possible allusions to the Garden Story see Zevit 2013, 251-259, 332-333.

[252] See also Korpel & De Moor 2012, 285-286.

cies and parallels, despite all the intelligent solutions scholars have thought up to get rid of them. The simple fact is that ancient humans were not interested in one dogmatic paradigm explaining everything in the world, as is demonstrated by Egypt and Babylonia where different creation stories were tolerated to exist side by side. As was the case in ancient Israel.

We mention a few points of accordance, or at least similarity, between the Ugaritic material and the Bible.

The Creator in the Hebrew Bible bears names that are identical to names of Ilu/El, the Creator of All in Ugarit and in some other Canaanite states (4.2).

As in other creation myths of the ancient Near East, Ugarit and Israel assumed that the primordial Flood was already there before creation started (4.2).

The separation of the primordial Flood into two bodies of water, one above and one below the firmament (sky), is a concept that Israel shared with many other religions, but originally the name of the deity responsible for this act was Ilu/El in Ugarit. However, the younger god Baʿlu disputed this all important position, adumbrating his dethronement of Ilu/El (first millennium BCE, 4.2).

Creation by word or thought alone (*creatio ex nihilo*) did occur in Egypt, Babylonia, Ugarit and Israel (4.2). The creation in seven days time of Genesis 1 should not be understood in a literal sense because framing a story in a seven day scheme was a common stylistic ploy in the ancient Near East, especially in Ugarit (4.2)

God forms the first human being from clay, like a potter. There exist many parallels for this imagery, also in Ugarit. The Ugaritic and Hebrew accounts of divine activity in times long past share an insouciant anthropomorphism (4.3.2.3).

As in certain other creation myths, the first human is created *before* any other creature according to Gen. 2:7 (4.3.2.4).

The idea that humankind reflected the physical appearance and spiritual excellence of the deity more than any other creature is definitely attested in the ancient Near East, also in Ugarit (4.2; 4.3.1.5). The Ugaritic tradition seems to attribute a good character to the first woman (4.3.2.11) which would seem to agree with Gen. 2:18.

The title 'Mother of All the Living' suits both Adammu's wife Kubaba and Eve (4.2.3.15). In Ugarit Adammu and his wife were initially immortal deities, but became mortals. Until Adam and his wife desired to become like God (or: gods) (4.3.1.4) they too were in principle immortal (4.3.2.16).

Also in Ugarit and Israel the first humanoids were thought to have been androgynous (4.2).

Both in Ugarit and Israel procreation became the consolation prize for the loss of immortality (4.2; 4.3.2.1; 4.3.2.11; 4.3.2.16), though in Israel sexuality is described in far less explicit terms than in Ugarit (4.3.1.7)

The location of the garden of the gods in Ugarit is remarkably similar to that of Eden in the Bible. Both point to the headwaters of Euphrates and Tigris descending from the Ararat mountains (4.3.2.7-8). Noah's vineyard is a replacement of the garden of Eden and is paralleled by the Ugaritic 'vineyard of the great gods' which was probably located on the slopes of the mountain of Ilu (Ararat). The creator god became very drunk of the wine it produced (4.5), like Noah when he drank the first wine from his vineyard.

There was probably only one tree in Eden, the very tall Tree of Life that later became a Tree of Knowledge (4.3). This tree became a Tree of Death by an act of hubris of a god in Ugarit or by humans who wanted to be like God in Israel (4.3.2; 4.7).

In accordance with the macrocosmic dimensions of the garden and its inhabitants the serpent seems to have been an evil monster, probably the Leviathan of the Hebrew Bible (4.3.2.10). The serpent in Eden did not bite Adammu, as did the big serpent in the Ugaritic 'vineyard of the great gods', but Amos 9:3 proves that also the Israelites assumed that the great sea serpent could bite people (4.3.1.8) and we will see later that traces of a tradition according to which Adam was bitten do occur in parabiblical literature (Sections 5.11; 5.14; 5.15 below).

A certain ambiguity in the behavior of deities and humans is the consequence of the freedom to choose between good and evil (4.3.1.2; 4.3.2.2; 4.3.2.5; 4.3.2.16). The Hebrew tradition seems to have transferred some traits of the 'devil' Ḥôrānu to Cain (4.3.2.17).

The giant proportions of the offspring from intercourse between gods and human females is attested both in Ugarit and Genesis 6.

The longevity of the antediluvian humans and the narrative of the Great Flood are hitherto missing in Ugarit, but on comparative grounds it may be expected that these traditions were known there too (4.4).

The myth alluded to in Isaiah 14 has long been elusive and certain scholars made eagerly use of this circumstance to reject any connection with extrabiblical lore. However, now that Hilālu appears to be an alternative name of Ḥôrānu, the Ugaritic predecessor of the Devil, and that the Phoenicians did know his consorts as goddesses facilitating childbirth, nothing prevents us anymore to accept that Isaiah used a satirical poem circulating in his days which ridiculed an unknown ruler, possibly the Phoenician king Lūli who was a contemporary of Isaiah and who had to fly to Cyprus when Sennacherib conquered Phoenicia in 701 BCE. A few years later he died in exile and in line with Canaanite mythology known from Ugarit the Phoenician king believed to be posthumously united with El, the highest deity of the Canaanite pantheon in his days.

Ezekiel 28 is a similar, but independent satyrical song about the king of Tyre (and Sidon). The location of garden of Eden mentioned in the song agrees in many respects with a location on the volcanic mountain of El, the Ararat. The king's hope to dwell there in bliss among the deities of the pantheon after his death is ridiculed ruthlessly by the Israelite prophet. He will be thrown down into the bottomless Pit.

In Ezekiel 29–32 Egypt is depicted in terms resembling the demise of the primordial serpentine monster that was thrown down into the desert. Also the idea of a gigantic 'Weltbaum' in the garden of God is rejected by Ezekiel.

According to the Hebrew Bible God has tamed the serpentine Devil and his offspring in primordial times. They are allowed to live on, but they do not constitute a real threat anymore to the pious. Humans can master them by invoking God's help (Psalm 91 and related texts), unless God himself reluctantly uses the evil demons to punish his people for its sins (Section 4.8).

5
The Reception in Parabiblical Literature

5.1 *Introduction*

Possibly Job 31:33 is the oldest reflection on the biblical story of Adam's transgression,[1] but we now know several extra-canonical elaborations of the primordial history that are possibly just as old or even older. It is too early for an exhaustive evaluation of the parabiblical literature on Adam, Eve, and the Devil in this study.[2] Our only goal here is to indicate that the ancient Near Eastern and especially the Ugaritic evidence collected in this book helps to understand some themes in this kind of literature which are unattested in the canonical accounts of creation and the early history of humankind. Our findings suggest that through extra-biblical channels of transmission, either oral or written, very ancient Canaanite lore has found its way into these parabiblical writings.

We might have included rabbinic traditions in this chapter, but decided to deal with these in the previous chapters where this seemed appropriate because in Judaism the written and oral Torah form an inseparable whole, even though many modern Jewish scholars are prepared to acknowledge the relatively late dates of their written rabbinic traditions.

5.2 *The Book of the Luminaries*

The oldest part of the pseudepigraphical work commonly called 1 Enoch is probably 1 Enoch 72–82. It is often called *The Astronomical Book*, but *The Book of the Luminaries* would seem a better title. It may date from before the third century BCE and was written in Aramaic.[3]

---

[1] On the translation see Clines 2006, 1030. With regard to Hos. 6:7, see Section 4.3.

[2] The literature on this subject is enormous and a full discussion would far excede our competences. Useful surveys are found with Stone 1992; Van Ruiten 2000a; Reed 2005. We confine ourselves to the older pseudepigrapha, but of course production of visionary encounters with Adam, Eve and the Devil did not stop. Cf. Bauckham 2013.

[3] Nickelsburg & VanderKam 2004, 6.

In it Enoch recounts the revelations of the archangel Uriel on a tour of heaven. He starts with the sun and its gates in east and west (72:2-37), followed by the moon and its phases (73). In 1 En. 77:3 he describes a northern quarter of the earth which is divided into three parts, one of which is 'the Garden of Righteousness'. Immediately after he continues,

> (4) I saw seven lofty mountains which are higher than all the mountains on the earth; from them snow emerges, and days, seasons, and years pass by (tr. Nickelsburg & VanderKam 2004, 107).

These seven mountains recur in *The Book of the Watchers* (1 En. 18:6-11; 22:1-13) and appear to be volcanic mountains in Urarṭu on the highest of which Ilu/El is said to dwell (see Section 5.3 below). From the viewpoint of the author these snowcapped mountains were situated in the north. Apparently he situated 'the Garden of Righteousness' with its Tree of Life in this region.

The author nust have known the Priestly creation narrative of Genesis 1 since he calls the sun 'the great luminary' (1 En. 72:4, 35-36) and the moon 'the smaller luminary (1 En. 73:1).

5.3 *The Book of the Watchers*

The greater part of *Book of the Watchers* (1 Enoch 1–36) dates from the third century BCE.[4] It describes the visions of the patriarch Enoch who was 'taken up in heaven' (Gen. 5:21-24), announcing doom for the sinners and bliss for the righteous.

In 1 Enoch 6–11 the rebellion of the Watchers is described.[5] The Watchers are fallen angels who have intercourse with mortal women who bear giants to them according to 1 Enoch (cf. Gen. 6:1-4). As Helge Kvanvig has shown, the Watchers have been derived from the Mesopotamian *apkallu*-tradition.[6] However, in contrast to these antediluvian sages who were seen as protective agents in Mesopotamia, the Watchers in pseudepigraphic literature are

---

[4] This is accepted by most scholars, e.g. Tigchelaar 1996, 141; 1999, 38; Nickelsburg 2001, 7, 169-171; Stuckenbruck 2004, 99; Reid 2005, 17; Kvanvig 2011, 347-361. There is much difference of opinion, however, on the extent of 'the greater part'. Cf. Tigchelaar 1996, 152-164.

[5] A number of inconsistencies points to unfinished redactional processes (Tigchelaar 1996, 166-182; Nickelsburg 2001, 165).

[6] Kvanvig 2011, 107-158.

negative powers, probably because they were seen as too divine by Jewish monotheists. However, in the light of the ambiguous nature of some ancient Near Eastern deities, among them the Ugaritic god Ḥôrānu, one is inclined to ask if the one excludes the other.

The leader of the Watchers was שמיחזה, Šemiḥazah.[7] All in all there were twenty Watchers and most of their names end in *el* 'god' reflecting a tradition of designating angels as divine (1 En. 6:7; later also inserted in 69:2). According to some textual witnesses the height of the giants who were born from intercourse with human daughters was three thousand cubits (1 En. 7:12, cf. Nickelsburg 2001, 182). They committed all kinds of sins, devouring living creatures, including human beings, and made the earth desolate.[8]

Against them rose the archangels Michael, Sariel, Raphael and Gabriel (1 En. 9).[9] They had to remove the perversity spread by the Watchers and had to restore lush vegetation on the desolate earth (1 En. 10). In 1 En. 20:6 the task of Sariel is described as being in charge of 'the spirits who sin against the Spirit'. On the basis of Mark 3:29 par., George Nickelsburg (2001, 298), considers the possibility that this is a Christian interpolation, but it may just as well be that – like Ḥôrānu/Šarru in Ugarit, – Sariel originally had belonged to the rebels whose accursed fate he appears to know well (1 En. 27:2-4).

Quite probably, the name of Sariel originally was Šarʾel, 'Prince of God',[10] or 'The Divine Prince'. This brings him close to the alternative Ugaritic name of Ḥôrānu, viz. Šarru 'the Prince'. It is remarkable that later on Sariel is replaced by Phanuel or Uriel (1 En. 27:2; 40:9: 54:6; 70:8-9, 13). In 1 En. 20:1-8, however, Uriel and Sariel occur side by side. According to Targum Neofiti on Gen. 32:25 Jacob's opponent would have been Sariel. Possibly this was

---

[7] 1 En. 6:3, 7; 69:2. The meaning of this name is unclear, cf. Knibb 1978, 67-68; Nickelsburg 2001, 179; Wright 2005, 120-122. It is possibhle that he too occurs already in Ugarit, see Section 4.8.

[8] Evidently the union between the angels as heavenly beings and the women on earth was taken from Gen. 6:1-6 and was seen as the cause of humanity's depravation. The giants who were their offspring were seen as bastards and misfits. Cf. Stuckenbruck 2004, 101-103.

[9] In 1 En. 20–36 their number is expanded to seven.

[10] Nickelsburg 2001, 220.

derived from *Ladder of Jacob* 4:1-3 (Lunt 2009, 408-409). The name of Phanuel may have been derived from Penuel or Pniel in Gen. 32. This link is important because it shows Sariel's good side.

Gabriel was 'in charge of paradise and the serpents and the cherubim' (1 En. 20:7). Even if 'the serpents' are seen as seraphim representing the flaming sword,[11] the plural is remarkable in view of what we found in Ugarit and on Cyprus.

On his westward journey Enoch sees 'a place that was burning night and day, where (there were) seven mountains of precious stones' (1 En. 18:6), some of them of 'flame-colored stone' (1 En. 18:7),

> (18:8) And the middle one of them reached to heaven like the Throne of God—of antimony; and the top of the throne was of lapis lazuli. (18:9) And I saw a burning fire. (18:10) And beyond these mountains is a place, the edge of the great earth; there the heavens come to an end. (18:11) And I saw a great chasm among pillars of heavenly fire. And I saw in it pillars of fire descending; and they were immeasurable toward the depth and toward the height' (tr. Nickelsburg & VanderKam 2004, 39).

This description agrees surprisingly well with the mountainous volcanic region where the Canaanite high god Ilu/El was supposed to dwell at the confluence of the upper and the lower Floods at the end of the earth (cf. Section 2.4). The author of this passage must have had a vague knowledge of the Canaanite mythological traditions about the dwelling of Ilu/El.

Further on his journey Enoch sees seven stars of heaven, bound and cast into the fire of hell. When Enoch asks why they have been cast there Uriel answers him that these stars have transgressed the command of the Lord and will remain bound there for ten thousand years (1 En. 21:1-6).

In 1 En. 22 the Mountain of the Dead is described. Since everywhere in the ancient Near East the entrance of the realm of death was thought to be located in the west at the place where the sun went under, this mountain must have been part of the same mountain range as the abode of Ilu/El. We quote some lines from the translation of George Nickelsburg and James VanderKam,

---

[11] Nickelsburg 2001, 296.

> (22:1) From there I traveled to another place. And he showed me to the west a great and high mountain of hard rock. (22:2) And there were four hollow places in it, deep and very smooth. Three of them were dark and one, illuminated; and a fountain of water was in the middle of it.
>
> And I said, "How smooth are these hollows and altogether deep and dark to view."
>
> (22:3) Then Raphael answered me, one of the holy angels who were with me, "These hollow places (are intended) that the spirits of the souls of the dead might be gathered into them. For this very (purpose) they were created, (that) here the souls of all human beings should be gathered. (22:4) And look, these are the pits for the place of their confinement. Thus they were made until the day (on) which they will be judged, and until the time of the day of the end of the great judgment that will be exacted from them." (tr. Nickelsburg & VanderKam 2004, 42).

The description of the volcanic area is continued in 1 En. 23 where a stream of fire is described. Chapter 24 starts with, 'And he showed me mountains of fire that burned day and night.' Again the number of mountains is seven, the middle one rising above all others 'like the seat of a throne' (1 En. 24:2-3; see also 1 En. 25:3). Subsequently 1 En. 24:3–25:6 describes a beautiful fragrant tree, growing on the mountain of God, 'its fruit (is) good, and its fruit (is) like the bunches of dates on a palm tree' (1 En. 24:4). No creature has authority to touch this tree until the great judgment day when its fruit will be given to the righteous and humble (1 En. 25:4-6). Clearly this is a description of the restored paradisiacal garden with its Tree of Life awaiting the righteous.[12]

According to 1 En 32:3-6 Enoch was allowed to see the Tree of Wisdom in the 'Paradise of Righteousness' from which Adam and Eve had eaten. It is situated in the east. Evidently this was an early attempt to harmonize the Tree of the Knowledge of Good and Evil with the Tree of Life, but significantly it was as high as a fir and looked like a carob tree and a vine, so it was a hybrid tree.

---

[12] According to Song of Songs 7:8-9 the bride is a tree of life, both date palm and vine.

5.4 *Jubilees*

The *Book of Jubilees* which was originally written in Hebrew in the second century BCE[13] more or less follows the antediluvian narrative of Genesis.[14] However, on the first day God creates a great number of angels and spirits, among them 'the angels of the spirit of fire' (Jub. 2:2), which recalls Ḥôrānu's fiery nature.

The author of *Jubilees* was not the first one to supply information about the creation of the angels. Usually it is assumed that he and others inserted this because they missed it in Genesis 1. However, Jacques Van Ruiten has pointed out that the author understood אֱלֹהִים in certain cases as a plural: 'gods'.[15] The Ugaritic narrative confirms that the angels and spirits replaced the deities of an earlier version of the creation story.

According to the best text of Jubilees humankind was created on the sixth day as 'one (person),[16] man and woman', which might imply that the first human was seen as an androgynous being, as we had reason to suspect earlier.[17] God gave her/him dominion over everything which was upon the earth and which was in the seas and over everything which flies, and over beasts and cattle and everything which moves upon the earth or above the whole earth. Over all this he gave her/him dominion (Jub. 2:14). In the Ugaritic myth the great gods gave the earth in the hand of Adammu.

However, just as in Genesis 2:18, 21-25 the LORD builds Eve from a rib of Adam and closes the wound with flesh (Jub. 3:4-7). Adam and Eve were tilling the garden of Eden peacefully for seven years (Jub. 3:15-16). Significantly, the prohibition to eat from the Tree of Knowledge of Good and Evil (Gen. 2:9, 16-17; 3:3-5) is missing in *Jubilees*. Also the Tree of Life (Gen. 2:9; 3:22, 24) is conspicuously absent. However, the Tree of Knowledge is present (Jub. 4:30). Perhaps the author saw no possibility to harmonize the conflicting accounts. In its account of the Fall itself *Jubilees* follows Genesis closely, although several ancient witnesses attest

---

[13] However, it is necessary to discern a later redactional layer, cf. Segal 2007.

[14] For a meticulous comparison of the Eden narratives in Genesis and Jubillees see Van Ruiten 1999; 2000b.

[15] Van Ruiten 2000b, 25.

[16] Jubilees 3:3-4 emphasizes that Adam was alone.

[17] See Section 4.2.

that the serpent had four legs which were cut off to punish it.[18]

Enoch was the first who learned to write and was allowed to dwell in Eden forever,[19] writing down everything he saw, also the pollution of the human daughters by the Watchers (Jub. 4:16-26). Jared's name was chosen 'because in his days the angels of the LORD, who were called Watchers, came down to the earth in order to teach the human sons and perform judgment and uprightness upon the earth' (Jub. 4:15).[20] According to this tradition the Watchers originally were good angels. However, it seems likely that this was a later redactional attempt to reconcile conflicting theological views.[21] Jub. 5:1 replaces 'the sons of God' by 'the angels of the Lord' – possibly the oldest interpretation of Gen. 6:2, 4.[22] Only later, when they had mated with the human daughters, the Watchers were punished by mutual killing, were bound and thrown into the depths of the earth (Jub. 5:6-11).[23]

5.5 *The Wisdom of Ben Sira*

In the *Wisdom of Ben Sira*[24] 40:1 (MS B) Eve seems to be regarded as Mother Earth and the sage seems to allude to Gen. 3:20,

> A great task it is that God apportions,
> and a heavy yoke he imposes on the children of Adam,
> from the day one leaves the womb of one's mother
> to the day one returns to the Mother of all living.[25]

Perhaps the sage refers to one's burial in the earth here[26] and to the well-known view of the earth as the Mother goddess. However,

---

18 Wintermute 2009, 60, note d.
19 Compare Section 3.3.3.
20 Cf. Wintermute 2009, 62.
21 Segal 2007,125-132.
22 Van Ruiten 2000b, 188.
23 Cf. Gen. 6:7-13 and on the parallel in the *Damascus Document*, Van Ruiten 2000b, 195-196.
24 The work originated *ca.* 180 BCE. Legarreta Castillo 2014, 38-47 summarizes the views on Adam in Ben Sira.
25 A marginal reading reads ארץ כל חי instead of אם כל חי. Cf. Beentjes 1997, 69. This might mean that he was aware of the reference either to a deified Eve, or to the earth as a mother goddess, but deemed this too blasphemous and corrected it to the more neutral 'earth'.
26 So Skehan & Di Lella 1987, 469, on the basis of Gen. 2:7 and 3:19.

the external parallelism with Adam suggests that 'the Mother of all living' merely denotes Eve (Gen. 3:20). In that case he would have entertained the notion that in the hereafter Eve and her offspring would be reunited. This is a far cry from the divine status of the first pair of human beings, but it still implies some kind of restful afterlife that contrasts favourably with the burdensome existence on earth.

Ben Sira then continues with the fate of bad people, and verse 11 states that 'All that comes from the earth returns to the earth, and what comes from above returns to above' (𝔊 renders 'what comes from the water returns to the sea'). This might be seen as a parallel to verse 1.[27] However, it also might be taken as the specific punishment for the bad ones (Sir. 40:12-16), whereas for the righteous ones (Sir. 40:18-27), a life is promised that is like 'a Garden with Blessings'.[28] Parallel to 40:11 where it is said that what comes from the earth returns to the earth and what comes from above returns to above.

Also Job 1:21 seems to describe a similar view,

> Naked I came from my mothers womb,
> and naked I will return there.

Several scholars have tried to mitigate the idea that Job would return to the womb of his mother,[29] but the parallelism in this verse leaves no doubt that indeed the poet must have had the idea that Job would return to his (apparently) eternal 'mother'. It is clear that the scribe does not mean Job's real mother, but because there are more references to the Genesis 2–3 narrative in the Book of Job (e.g. Job 5:7; 14:1; 15:7; 20:4; 31:33) it is more likely that the scribe refers to Eve as the mother of all living. This text then might contain reminiscences of the idea of deification of the first woman. The fact that the epithet Mother of All the Living comes quite close to Mother Earth is obvious.[30] Also Kübel comes to the conclusion that in the texts listed above the epithet 'Mother

---

[27] So Kübel 2007, 125,

[28] παράδεισος ἐν εὐλογίαις. (Sir. 40:17, 27).

[29] Cf. Kübel 2007, 125-126.

[30] Cf. the discussion of 'there' in Job 1:21 by Clines 1989, 36-37, who shows two possibilities: 1. the mother's womb is the womb of Mother Earth, and 2. it is a euphemism for the Netherworld. Clines prefers reading it as a

of All the Living' has been transposed from the earth to Eve as the universal Mother, and he argues: 'Because man is no longer thought to have been brought forth from the dust of the earth, but is *created* from it, it is no longer possible to take the earth as the universal mother. It can only have been used as a title for the first woman.'[31]

Remarkably enough Ben Sira makes God co-responsible for Adam's transgression, as if he agrees with Adam's excuse in Gen. 3:12,

אלהים מבראשית ברא אדם
וישתיהו ביד חותפו
ויתנהו ביד יצרו

God created Adam in the beginning,
and put him in the power of his death,[32]
and gave him in the power of his desire (Sira 15:14).

However, one might also consider the possibility of an emendation, reading חופתו 'his bridal chamber' which produces a better parallelism with יצרו 'his desire' instead of חותפו 'his death'. If so, Ben Sira suggests that Adam accepted the fruit from Eve because she aroused him. Ben Sira blamed Eve for this act (see Section 4.3).

In Section 4.3 we discussed Ben Sira's extremely negative view of women, and especially of Eve.[33] His opinion is shared later on by Philo of Alexandria[34] and other Hellenistic Jews.

---

reference to Mother Earth, as in Sir. 40:1. The same view is defended by Keel & Schroer 2002, 57. The concepts of Eve and Mother Earth as Mother of All the Living seem to be intertwined, humankind is made from dust of the earth and created in the mother's womb as in the earth (Ps. 139:13, 15) and will return to the earth (Gen. 3:19). Clines 1989, 37, duly notes that it is quite difficult to discern between related metaphors like these.

[31] Kübel 2007, 127, who stresses the fact that Mother Earth only could bring forth creatures when she was a goddess. This idea would have been abandoned deliberately by the author of Genesis 2–3.

[32] We interpret חותף after Arabic *ḥatf*, a designation of a natural death. However, the second line is mostly regarded as a gloss because it would be at variance with Ben Sira's view of God's omnipotence and the free will of humans (Beentjes 2003, 510-514).

[33] Legarreta Castillo 2014, 45 wrongly denies that Sira 25:24 has anything to do with Eve.

[34] *De opificio mundi*, 151b-c. Cf. Legarreta Castillo 2014, 59-60. In this re-

5.6 *The Animal Apocalypse*

The *Animal Apocalypse* (1 Enoch 85–90, dated between 165 and 161 BCE) that is the second part of the *Book of Dreams* (1 Enoch 83–90) is usually regarded as an allegory and no doubt its Jewish author meant it to be understood in this way. We find Olson's theory that the *Animal Apocalypse* should be understood as a sophisticated theological interpretation of human history in the past, present and future quite attractive.[35] However, in view of the universal salvation of the world the author of this apocalypse envisages, including the gentiles in the Abrahamic covenant, as Paul would do later, Olson might have elaborated on the author's criticism of the pagan world. In view of what we have found in Ugaritic mythology it seems likely that he rejected certain Canaanite concepts which he may have known through the channels of folk religion.

For example, Adam and Eve are compared to a white bull and a young heifer (1 En. 85:3-8). Their offspring is also described as cattle. Here the fall of the Watchers starts with the fall from heaven of one star which joins the cattle to pasture among them (1 En. 86:1). So the fall of the morning star (Isa. 14) is inserted here *after* the creation of Adam which is in accordance with the Ugaritic myth. The union between the sons of God who are also described as stars and human daughters (Gen. 6) is narrated as follows,

> I looked at them and I saw and behold, all of them let out their organs like horses, and they began to mount the cows of the bulls, and they all conceived and bore elephants and camels and asses (1 En. 85:4).

The plasticity of this description cannot be explained by reference to certain biblical passages alone.[36] It reflects criticism of what Jews saw as sexual depravity among their Canaanite neighbors (cf. Section 2.5). In Enoch's vision all of these lusty animals are bound and thrown into the abyss of the earth (1 En. 88:1-3). This may

---

spect Philo deliberately deviated from Plato's *Timaeus* which otherwise he admired and used frequently (Runia 1986, 345-346).

[35] Olson 2013, who reviews earlier interpretations on pp. 2-13.

[36] Olson 2013, 134-136 mentions Ezek. 23:20 and Gen. 6:4.

reflect the binding of the Titans as related in Hesiod's *Theogony*, 713-721[37] and/or the binding of rebels in 1 En. 18:6-14 and Jub. 5:6-11, but the prominence of the binding of the evil Leviathan-serpent in Ugaritic myth may have been the ultimate model for all these traditions.[38]

5.7 *The Similitudes*

In the *Similitudes* (1 Enoch 37–71, first century BCE or first century CE) it is stated that Eve was led astray by Gadre'el who was responsable for the discovery of all kinds of murder weapons (1 Enoch 69:6). This would seem a reworking of the account in the *Book of the Watchers* (1 Enoch 8:1) which attributes the making of weapons [for men] and jewelry for women to Asael. So 'Eve' in the *Similitudes* seems to have become a generalized term for the 'women' of 1 Enoch 8:1.[39]

Enoch describes a large house made of hailstones in heaven that was at the same time filled by fire (1 En. 14:8-13; 70:5-6). Such a description would seem to fit the snowcapped volcanic area where Ilu/El was said to have his abode (Section 2.5).

In 1 Enoch 60:7-8 a primordial monster is cleaved into two halves,[40] one of which is thrown down into a desert,

> And on that day two monsters will be separated from one other: a female monster whose name (is) Leviathan, to dwell in the depth of the sea above the springs of the waters; and the name of the male (is) Behemot who occupies with his breast an immense desert,

[37] So Stuckenbruck 2004, 109-110.

[38] Sections 2.3-4, 2.8, 5.3 and 5.4. See also the chaining of Tiāmat's evil helper Kingu in the Babylonian Creation Epic (En. el. IV.119-120).

[39] We fail to see that Asael is blamed for the seduction of Eve 'in a manner that evokes the equation of the Serpent with Satan in later literature.' (Reed 2005, 114). Or, that we have here 'an interesting development, namely, the gradual transference of traditions about the antediluvian descent of the angels onto the figure of the Serpent/Satan.' (Reed 2005, 115). Neither the serpent nor Satan is mentioned. The evidence we have assembled suggests that the identification of the primordial serpent with the forces of evil took place much earlier. Rather women in general are blamed here for taking an interest in the jewelry made by the descendants of Tubal-Cain (Gen. 4:22). Prophetic criticism like that of Isaiah (3:16-24) had made craving for jewels a sin in Judaism (cf. Küchler 1986).

[40] Compare En. el. IV.137-146, Section 3.3.5.

> named Dendayn, on the east of the garden where the chosen and righteous dwell (tr. Kvanvig 1988, 250).[41]

Now that we have reason to assume that according to Canaanite mythology the great sea serpent was thrown down into the desert (Section 2.8) there is no need to speculate about the meaning of 'Dendayn' (other spellings do exist) anymore.[42] It is simply a name based on the desert state called דְּדָן 'Dedan' in Hebrew.

1 En. 60:23 mentions a 'Garden of the Righteous' which is probably identical to the 'Garden of Life'[43] in 1 En. 61:12. The righteous are allowed to live their after their death until the final judgment when Eden will be restored for them in full glory.

5.8 *Testaments of the Twelve Patriarchs*

With the exception of a number of Christian interpolations, the *Testaments* date from the early second century BCE (Kee 2009, 777-778). The *Testament of Levi* 18:10-14 envisions the future restoration of paradise[44] where the saints will eat of the Tree of Life.[45] The Tree of Knowledge is not mentioned and Beliar shall be bound. For the latter promise Kee refers to Isa. 24:22-23 (Kee 2009, 795, n. c), but 'binding' is not mentioned there whereas the Ugaritic myth explicitly mentions the binding of the evil serpent. See Section 5.6 above. In our opinion the promise that also the LORD's children will trample on the wicked serpent might be a Christian interpretation.[46]

5.9 *Qumran*

Many religious writings were found in and around Qumran, the site of a Jewish sectarian community in the Judean Desert. Some of the scrolls their scribes produced have been preserved relatively intact, but most of the Qumran texts are very fragmentary. This

---

41 A similar description is found in 4 Ezra 6:49-52, cf. Metzger 2009, 536.

42 For such learned attempts see Kvanvig 1988, 246-253; Tigchelaar 1999, 48.

43 One wonders whether the rendering 'Garden of the Living' would be possible. See below Section 5.9 on 4Q385c:3.

44 See also *Testament of Levi* 5:10-12.

45 Also in the Greek *Apocalypse of Ezra* 2:11 only the Tree of Life is mentioned.

46 Cf. Mark 3:7; Luke 11:14-22.

renders identification of passages dealing with the primordial history sometimes difficult. However, because the date of these Hebrew and Aramaic texts is fairly certain (first century BCE to first century CE) they constitute an important anchor point for research into the history of parabiblical writings. Some of the works we discussed earlier are also represented among these scrolls.

The Aramaic *Genesis Apocryphon* is clearly dependent on the *Book of Jubilees* and its composition is mostly dated in the first century BCE. When Lamech sees that his wife Bit-enosh[47] has given birth to an abnormal baby he starts to suspect her of intercourse with one of the Watchers (עירין), the Holy Ones (קדישין) who begot giants (נפילים) (1QapGen II.1).[48] He urges her to tell him the truth about her pregnancy. She tries to mollify him by recalling her sexual pleasure with him, Lamech, and assures him that the child is his (1QapGen II.9-18). In a fragmentary passage the boy seems to be described as 'a fire'[49] – 'fire' is more aptly applied to Ḥôrānu than to any other 'son of God'.

The *Genesis Apocryphon* goes on to describe the violence committed by the giants and the landing of the ark 'on one of the mountains of Hurarṭ and eternal fire [...]' ([...] חד מן טורי הוררט ונור עלמא, 1QapGen X.12). The circumstance that the vocalization of the name is closer to 'Urarṭu' then that of the Masoretic text suggests that this is an independent tradition. Although unfortunately the text breaks off, the association with 'eternal fire' is definitely suggestive.

Noah praises God for the Flood which also destroyed 'all workers of violence, wickedness and deceit' (1QapGen XI.13-14). Noah plants his vineyard on Mount Lubar (cf. Steiner 1991) and drinks its wine with his whole family after four years (1QapGen XII.13-16).

---

47 Her name means 'Daughter of the Human'. She does not occur in the Hebrew Bible.

48 Elsewhere these Watchers are called בני שמיא 'sons of heaven' (1QapGen II.6; V.3-4), a clear circumlocution of the 'sons of God' of Gen. 6:2. See also the illicit union of human daughters with ʿAzazʾel in 4Q180, Frag. 1.7. Other Qumran fragments speculating about the giants are 1Q23, 1Q24, 4Q203, 4Q532-533.

49 עולימא דן נור 'this boy is a fire' (1QapGen V.13).

In 1QH^{a} the hymnodist compares himself to a woman giving birth. He describes her labor-pains as a כור הריה, 'crucible of the pregnant woman' (1QH^{a} XI.8, 10, 12)[50] and he knows full well that a woman in labor may die (1QH^{a} XI.8-10, 12). Especially a woman who is pregnant with a viper[51] will suffer horrible pains (1QH^{a} XI.12). The great Sea (ימים, III.15) and the Netherworld (שאול ואבדון, III.16) conspire against her.[52] This reminds us of the alliance between Death and Sea in the texts of Ugarit (Section 2.10). In accordance with the typical prejudice against women of the time it is she who is held responsible for the birth of the 'serpent',

> ... and the gates of the Netherworld (Sheol) will open for all viper-works (18) and the doors of the Pit will close behind her who is pregnant of wickedness and the eternal bolts behind viper-spirits (1QH^{a} XI.17-18).

The imagery of this passage can hardly be derived from the canonical Hebrew Bible.[53] Rather 'viper' is a designation of a devil with whom the woman is supposed to have had intercourse. The fiery crucible, the connection with death and procreation are reminiscent of the role played by the ophidian god Ḥôrānu/Horon in Ugaritic and Phoenician texts, but deliberately omitting his positive role in protecting pregnant women (Section 2.5).

According to 4Q225, Frag. 2, II.9-10 'the Prince of Accusation' (שר המ[ש]טמה) approached God after the birth of Isaac and accused (ישטים) Abraham with regard to Isaac. It is generally assumed that this 'Prince of Accusation' is another name of Satan and that he was an ally of Belial (cf. Section 2.6).

The eschatological battle between the righteous under the command of Michael and the evil forces of Belial is described in 1QM. Belial is called שר ממשלת רשע, 'the Prince of the dominion of wickedness' (1QM XVII.5-6) which recalls Ḥôrānu's epithet *šr*, 'Prince'.

---

[50] Also said of Noah's mother in 1QapGen VI.1 and of both parents in 4Q416, Frag. 2, III.17 = 4Q418, Frag. 9:18.

[51] Others translate 'nothingness', but this is less likely because of what follows.

[52] Also in the longer version of the *Testament of Abraham* 19 Death and Sea are allies using venomenous vipers against mortals.

[53] Charlesworth 2010, 427 refers to Isa. 30:6 but this is a rather remote parallel.

A *pesher*-commentary on the Book of Hosea interprets Hos. 6:7 evidently as referring to Adam's transgression (4Q167, Frags. 7-8). 4Q381, Frag. 10+11 seems to acknowledge that the original blissful state of Adam and Eve described in Frag. 1 came to an end because they did what was evil in the eyes of the Lord so that he had to banish them to the deep Sheol (Netherworld), perhaps until he would grant them mercy at the end of times (4Q381, Frags 10+11:3). Because of Adam's transgression his days were shortened (CD-A X.8-9). However, the community foresaw the eschatological restoration of 'the glory of Adam',[54] 'eternal glory and everlasting peace' for 'all the children of Eve',[55] and the restoration of Eden with the gigantic Tree of Life for the pious.[56] and the restoration of the גן החיים, 'the Garden of the Living' (4Q385c:3).

A very interesting florilegium of apocryphal Psalms (11Q11) mentions שדים 'demons' next to the שר המשטמה 'the Prince of Accusation' (II.3-4) which confirms that the latter was their leader. The demons wear horns (V.7), like the Leviathan-viper Ḥôrānu (Section 2.7), and since they are the offspring of an illicit union of humans and holy ones (V.6) it may be assumed that they were the giants of Gen. 6:4. Of course YHWH will defeat them and rescue the faithfull, in accordance with the canonical Psalm 91 which is quoted here in a slightly deviant form. In view of the other parts of this collection it may be assumed that Psalm 91 was used as an apotropaic text by the community of Qurmran.

5.10 *2 Enoch*

2 Enoch[57] gives the following account of the second day of creation,

---

54 1QS IV.23; see also CD-A, III.20; 1QH^{a} 4:27; 4Q171:II.1-2; 4Q265, Frag. 7, col II.14.

55 4Q418, Frag. 126, II.11-12.

56 1QH^{a} XIV.16-18; XVI.5-26. Literally 'trees of life' as in *Psalm of Solomon* 14:2, but in our opinion this plural or dual must be interpreted as an attempt to harmonize the 'two' trees in paradise because Qumran also refers to the עץ הדעת 'the Tree of the Knowledge (of good and evil)', 4Q422 I.10; 11Q12, frag. 5:3.

57 The book dates from the first century CE, but many scholars believe that 2 Enoch is based at least in part on prechristian Semitic sources. Cf. Andersen 2009, 94-97; Böttrich 2012, 64-65; Macaskill 2012, 101. It is no longer justified to call the work 'Slavonic', cf. Hagen 2012.

2 Enoch 29:1-5 (J)[58]

> (29:1) And for all my own heavens I shaped a shape from the fiery substance. My eye looked at the solid and very hard rock. And from the flash of my eye I took the [marvellous] substance of lightning, both fire in water and water in fire;
> (29:2) neither does this one extinguish that one, nor does that one dry out this one. That is why lightning is sharper and brighter than the shining of the sun, and softer than water, more solid than the hardest rock. (29:3) And from the rock I cut offf a great fire, from the fire I created the ranks of the bodiless armies–ten myriad angels–and their weapons are fiery and their clothes are burning flames. And I gave orders that each should stand in his own rank.
>
> [Here Satanail was hurled from the height, together with his angels. See also chapters 7 and 18 of 2 Enoch.]
>
> (29:4) But one from the order of the archangels deviated, together with the division that was under his authority. He thought up the impossible idea, that he might place his throne higher than the clouds which are above the earth, and that he might become equal to my power. (29:5) And I hurled him out from the height, together with his angels. And he was flying around in the air, ceaselessly, above the Bottomless.

The spirit of God of Gen. 1:2 has become the first angel here and this angel fell earlier than Adam. Also interesting is the fact that he was created from fire and stone.[59] Francis Andersen draws attention to the fact that fire is not present in the account of the creation in Genesis 1. 'But Ezek. 28:16 has a connection between stones and fire, and the myth behind this could have Canaanite connections'.[60] The Ugaritic myth studied in this book seems to be at least one of the Canaanite sources which were incorporated in 2 Enoch by someone who knew them either by oral tradition or

---

58 Translation Andersen 2009, 152; cf. Orlov 2012 on the intrusion of Adamic traditions into the Enochic corpus.

59 God formed rocks from water on the first day of creation. This calls to mind the Ugaritic pair of primordial deified *ʾabn* 'Stone' (masculine) and *ʿn* 'Source' (feminine) (KTU 1.100:1).

60 Andersen 2009, 148, n. f. Andersen does not give his reasons for this hypothesis.

in the form of elaborations of secondary texts like Isaiah 14 and Ezekekiel 28.

It is long known that 2 Enoch mixes the biblical account of creation with other material that can only partially be traced back to known sources.[61] Remarkably enough 2 Enoch attributes also to Adam an *angelic* status before his fall and allows him to reign on earth like a king. Adam is created on the sixth day,[62]

> 2 Enoch 30:11-12 (J)
> (30:11) And on the earth I assigned him to be a second angel, honored and great and glorious.
> (30:12) And I assigned him to be a king, to reign on the earth, and to have my wisdom. And there was nothing comparable to him on the earth, even among my creatures that exist.[63]

2 Enoch 31:3-6 (J) gives a very truncated account of the sin of the Devil, Adam and Eve in paradise,

> 2 Enoch 31:3-6 (J)
> (31:3) And the devil understood how I wished to create another world, so that everything could be subjected to Adam on earth, to rule and reign over it.
> (31:4) The devil is of the lowest places. And he will become a demon, because he fled from heaven; Sotona, because his name was Satanail.
> (31:5) In this way he became different from the angels. His nature did not change, <but> his thought did, since his consciousness of righteous and sinful things changed.
> (31:6) And he became aware of his condemnation and of the sin which he sinned previously. And that is why he thought up the scheme against Adam. In such a form he entered paradise, and corrupted Eve. But Adam he did not contact.[64]

The phrase 'because he fled from heaven' is clearly inspired by the Ugaritic and biblical epithet of the Leviathan, 'the fugitive serpent' (*nḥš bryḥ*) (cf. Section 2.8). So even here we still find a connection between the Great Serpent encircling the earth and

[61] Van Ruiten 2000a, 55-60, provides a detailed comparison.
[62] This is in accordance with Gen. 1:26, Jub. 3:3-4, as well as with Jewish (b. Sanh., 38a) and Islamic tradition (Schöck 1993, 63-64).
[63] Translation Andersen 2009, 152.
[64] Translation Andersen 2009, 154.

the paradise story. We think that the phrases 'And that is why he thought up the scheme against Adam. In such a form he entered paradise, and corrupted Eve' refer to the metamorphosis of the Devil. The description 'in such a form' might go back to a similar tradition as that preserved in 3 Baruch 9:7 where the devil dons the garment of the serpent (its sloughed skin).[65]

2 Enoch mentions a Tree of Life which Enoch saw from the third heaven. This pleasant, fragrant tree stood in the middle of Paradise and was a hybrid tree (2 Enoch 8 [J, A]). 2 Enoch portrays Enoch as a second Adam who will restore the paradisiacal condition of humanity.[66]

5.11 *The Wisdom of Solomon*

The mainly Jewish apocryphal work *Wisdom of Solomon* (first half of the first century CE) contains a number of remarkable passages relevant to our study. In the first chapter the author states right away,

> (12) Do not court death through a deviant way of life,
> nor draw down destruction by your own actions,
> (13) For God did not make death,
> nor does he take delight in the destruction of the living;
> (14) he created all things that they might endure,
> All that has come into existence preserves its being,
> and there is no deadly poison in it.
> Death's rulership is not on earth,
> (15) for justice is immortal.[67]

This is a remarkable statement because it seems that death has entered the world not by the speech of the serpent or by human disobedience to God's commandment or by a deadly snakebite, but by injustice. The author seems to polemicize here against several current interpretations of Genesis 3, among them one close to the

65 We see insufficient reason to assume that Satan had intercourse with Eve according to this text, as is surmised by Van Ruiten 2000a, 59-60. However, in 4 Macc. 18:6-8 a mother of seven sons declares, 'No seducer of the desert nor deceiver in the field corrupted me, nor did the seducing and beguiling serpent defile my maidenly purity.' (Anderson 2009, 563). So the concept of illicit intercourse with the devil in the shape of a serpent did exist.

66 Orlov 2012, 152-153.

67 Translation Winston 1979, 100.

Canaanite myth about the biting snake in the vineyard of the gods. In Section 4.3 we already discussed Wisd. 2:23-24 which confirms that humankind was created for immortality but was the victim of the Devil's envy. The two texts taken together seem to imply that the Devil's envy was seen as injustice by this author.

Immortality is not regained by mere procreation, but by virtue (Wisd. 4:1),

> (1) It is better to be childless, provided one is virtuous,
> for in virtue's remembrance there is immortality[68]

The just will obtain immortality in the hereafter (Wisd. 5:15). Therefore the sage does not deplore his mortal entry in this world (Wisd. 7:1-6), for wisdom extricates him from Adam's sin,

> Wisdom 10:1-2
> (1) It was Wisdom who closely guarded
> the first-fashioned father of the world, created alone,
> she extricated him from his own blunder,
> (2) and gave him the power to master all things.[69]

5.12 *The Apocalypse of Abraham*

This work has only survived in Old Slavonic translation. The Hebrew original may have been written at the end of the first century or the early second century.[70] Abraham rebukes his father Terah for the images of gods the latter had made (*Ap. Abraham* 1–3, cf. Josh. 24:2). One of them was the god Barisat[71] who seems to have been cut from the wood of the 'Weltbaum' in paradise (*Ap. Abraham* 6:10-17), but was burnt to ashes through his own fault (*Ap. Abraham* 5:6-12). Before that happened, however, the wooden image 'fell from the height to the earth, he became from greatness to smallness, and the appearance of his face wasted away' (*Ap. Abraham* 6:14-15, tr. Rubinkiewicz 2009, 691). Could this be a

[68] Translation Winston 1979, 130. Cf. Legarreta Castillo 2014, 46. According to Wisd. 8:17 there is immortality in befriending wisdom.

[69] Translation Winston 1979, 210.

[70] Rubinkiewicz 2009, 682-683. Even a retroversion has been attempted, cf. Kulik 2004.

[71] בָּרֵאשִׁית? Cf. Gen. 1:1.

reminiscence of the fall of Ḥôrānu whose face paled when he realized that his rebellion had been stopped?[72]

God appoints the angel Iaoel[73] to accompany Abraham. This Iaoel says of himself,

> *Apocalypse of Abraham* 10:10-11, tr. Rubinkiewicz 2009, 694:
> (10) I am appointed to hold the Leviathans, because through me is subjugated the attack and menace of every reptile. (11) I am ordered to loosen Hades and to destroy those who wondered at the dead.

It is rather remarkable that as in the iconography we have discussed in Section 2.8 there appear to have been more than one Leviathan. Strengthened by the sight and speech of the angel, Abraham embarks upon a journey of forty days to Horeb, the mountain of God (*Ap. Abraham* 12, cf. 1 Kgs 19:5-8).

When Abraham sacrifices (as in Gen. 15), an unclean bird of prey descends on the carcasses, but the patriarch chases him away (cf. Gen. 15:11 where, however, a plural is used). Apparently Azazel could take on the shape of a raptor, like Ḥôrānu (Section 2.2).The bird speaks to Abraham, urging him to abandon his angelic companion and trying to discourage him to ascend to the holy heights, pretending that if Abraham does, he will be consumed by fire. So the bird is a liar. Abraham asks his protecting angel what this is and the angel replies: 'This is disgrace, this is Azazel!'. In early Judaism Azazel, the goat sent away into the desert for the atonement of the people of God according to Lev. 16, became a manifestation of the Devil.[74] The angel addresses the bird,

> *Apocalypse of Abraham* 13:7-9, 11b-14, tr. Rubinkiewicz 2009, 695:
> "Shame on you, Azazel! For Abraham's portion is in heaven, and

[72] KTU 1.100:61, Appendix 2.

[73] No doubt *yw'l* or *yhw'l*, not *yhwh'l* as proposed by Rubinkiewicz 2009, 693, note 10b.

[74] If our supposition that Ugaritic *ġzz* 'generous one' is a name or epithet of Ḥôrānu, the Devil (cf. Appendix 1, n. 15), the connection between the two is immediately clear, because Ugaritic *ġ* equals Hebrew ʿ and many angels got names ending in El. In that case the sending away of the goat in the desert might be a vague recollection of the banishment of Ḥôrānu to the Ḥaurān. On Azazel see e.g. Loretz 1985; Janowski 1999; Orlov 2003.

> yours is on earth, (8) for you have selected here, (and) become enamored of the dwelling place of your blemish. Therefore the Eternal Ruler, the Mighty One, has given you a dwelling on earth. (9) Through you the all-evil spirit (is) a liar, and through you (are) wrath and trials on the generations of men who live impiously. [...] You have no permission to tempt all the righteous. (12) Depart from this man! (13)You cannot deceive him, because he is the enemy of you and of those who follow you and who love what you wish. (14) For behold, the garment which in heaven was formerly yours has been set aside for him, and the corruption which was on him has gone over to you."'

This too is an important passage because it demonstrates that Azazel (the Devil) wanted to dwell on height which brought shame on him. Therefore God assigned him a place on earth. He has no permission to tempt righteous people who are his enemies. They may hope to receive the garment of the celestials, but not Azazel himself. Apparently the writer assumes that Azazel sinned earlier than Adam.[75] The angel orders Abraham to address Azazel as follows, 'May you be the firebrand[76] of the furnace of the earth! Go, Azazel, into the untrodden parts of the earth!' (*Ap. Abraham* 14:5). The fiery nature of Azazel matches that of Ḥôrānu (Section 2.6).

On his journey to the top of the mountain of God Abraham is allowed to have a look at the fiery flames separating it from the throne of God,

> *Apocalypse of Abraham* 15:5-7, tr. Rubinkiewicz 2009, 696:
> (5) And I saw on the air to whose height we had ascended a strong light which can not be described. (6) And behold, in this light a fiery Gehenna was enkindled, and a great crowd in the likeness of men.

This agrees with the volcanic background of the dwelling of Ilu/El as we described it in Section 2.4. What is most remarkable is that when he is allowed to approach the throne of God the angel

[75] In *Ap. Abraham* 14:4 the angel reproaches Azazel to have scattered the secrets of heaven and to have taken counsel against the Mighty One (God).
[76] Or 'torch' or 'burning coal'.

instructs Abraham to recite a hymn to 'Holy El' among whose epithets are 'benevolent' and 'merciful', well-known epithets of the Ugaritic Ilu/El (*Ap. Abraham* 17:8-12). The angelic hymn continues with a kind of doxology,

> *Apocalypse of Abraham* 17:15, tr. Rubinkiewicz 2009, 697:
> (15) Eli, eternal, mighty one, holy, Sabaoth,
> most glorious El, El, El, El, Iaoel

Suddenly Iaoel is no longer an angel, but El himself.[77] It seems that the writer of this apocalypse has tried to reconcile Canaanite traditions that were still fairly close to those of Ugarit with themes from the Hebrew Bible.

Subsequently Abraham is allowed to have a look at the garden of Eden. In a sort of flashback he may see Adam, Eve and the Devil in the garden,

> *Apocalypse of Abraham* 23:4-11. tr. Rubinkiewicz 2009, 700:
> (4) And I looked at the picture, and my eyes ran to the side of the garden of Eden. (5) And I saw there a man very great in height and terrible in breadth, incomparable in aspect, entwined with a woman who was also equal to the man in aspect and size. (6) And they were standing under a tree of Eden, and the fruit of the tree was like the appearance of a bunch of grapes of the vine. And behind the tree was standing (something) like a dragon in form, but having hands and feet like a man's, on his back six wings on the right and six on the left. (8) And he was holding the grapes of the tree and feeding them to the two I saw entwined with each other. (9) And I said, "Who are these two entwined with each other, or who is this between them, and what is the fruit which they are eating, Mighty One, Eternal?" (10) And he said, "This is the world of men,[78] this is Adam and this is their thought on earth, this is Eve. (11) And he who is between them is the impiety of their behavior unto perdition, Azazel himself."

Again this account resembles Canaanite mythology in several respects. The first human beings were of giant proportions (cf. Section 2.8) and initially they were one androgynous being, the more

[77] See also *Ladder of Jacob* 2:18 (Lunt 2009, 408). This text dates from the first century CE.
[78] Rubinkiewicz 2009, 700, note 23j: 'Or "of man, human." '.

or less male half strongly fused to the female half.[79] The Tree in the garden of Eden was similar to a vine, as in Ugarit (cf. Section 2.4). The serpent does not speak to Eve here, but hands a bunch of grapes to the 'entwined' humanoid whose sin consisted in accepting and eating it. So both halves were equally responsible. In *Apocalypse of Abraham* 24:5 'the crafty adversary', apparently the Serpent (Gen. 3:1), is the main culprit.

5.13 *The Ladder of Jacob*

The pseudepigraphic text *Ladder of Jacob* has been preserved only in Old Church Slavonic but seems to go back to a Greek original dated in the first century BCE (Lunt 2009, 403-405). As in other pseudepigrapha, the throne of God is described as 'fiery' (2:7). The opening hymn addresses God with many names, among them Yaoil (2:18), which recalls the Iaoel of the *Apaocalypse of Abraham* (section 5.12).

In 3:2 Sariel is described as 'leader of the beguiled', apparently a circumscription of Satan (Lunt 2009, 408). Interestingly, Sariel is depicted here as an angel who initially was evil, as in the *Book of the Watchers* (Section 5.3), but apparently is assumed to have repented. It is predicted that at the end of times God will destroy the Leviathan because he has risen against God and his people,

> *Ladder of Jacob* 6:11-13. tr. Lunt 2009, 410:
> (11) Their land swarmed with reptiles and all sorts of deadly things. (12) There will be earthquakes and much destruction. (13) And the LORD will pour out his wrath against Leviathan the sea-dragon; he will kill the lawless Falkon with the sword, because he will raise the wrath of the God of gods by his pride.

Several elements in this passage are highly interesting. Volcanic areas are still prone to tectonic movement causing earthquakes. The homeland of the Devil swarms with serpents and he himself seems to be equated with the great sea serpent Leviathan as well as with an evil falcon. Both descriptions fit Ḥôrānu, the serpentine falcon god (Sections 2.2; 2.8; 2.9). There is no need anymore to speculate about the origin of the epithet 'falcon'[80] because it

[79] Cf. Sections 2.7; 3.3.1; 5.4; 5.16.

[80] See Lunt 2009, 403-405, 409, note 5m.

belongs to the original Canaanite traditions about Ḥôrānu.

This background also explains the rather unorthodox description of the eschatological theophany,

> *Ladder of Jacob* 7:20-22. tr. Lunt 2009, 410-411:
> (20) Then the Almighty will be on earth in body, and, embraced by corporeal arms, he will restore human matter. (21) And he will revive Eve, who died by the fruit of the tree. (22) Then the deceit of the impious will be exposed and all the idols will fall face down.

An anthropomorphic God being embraced by corporeal arms and restoring human matter – such imagery is understandable in the context of Canaanite myth (cf. Section 2.2), but is hardly compatible with the canonical books of the Bible. The reference to Eve eating the forbidden fruit in Eden emboldens us to ask if 'the deceit of the impious' should not be understood as the deceit of the serpent in Eden. The falling down of the 'idols' might be a reference to the fall of Satan and his wicked angels.

5.14 *The Life of Adam and Eve*

According to *The Life of Adam and Eve* [*Vita*], 12-16[81] Satan refused to worship Adam whom God had created in his image.[82] When God had threatened to elevate Adam, Satan had answered resentfully that he was higher in rank than Adam and that he would place his throne above that of God if the latter would carry out this plan. For this arrogance he was was thrown out of heaven, away from the fellowship of heavenly angels (*Vita* 12–16).[83]

However, this story which might perhaps date from the first century CE,[84] gives a rather fuzzy account of the original sin. The

---

[81] There exist various forms of this text, cf. De Jonge & Tromp 1997; Stone 1999; Levison 2000; Knittel 2002; Tromp 2005. We use the easily accessible translation of the *Vita* by Johnson 2009, whom we also follow with regard to the numbering of verses. The synoptic problem has been expounded by Knittel 2002, 36-37. For treatments of all kinds of problems in this text we refer the reader to Anderson 2000a; Legarreta Castillo 2014, 88-96.

[82] Obviously this echoes Gen. 1:26.

[83] This crucial passage is missing in the partially parallel *Apocalypse of Adam* (see below).

[84] Johnson 2009, 252; Knittel 2002, 53-63. However, De Jonge & Tromp 1997, 75-77, emphasize the dificulty of dating the text and cautiously assign it

book starts with 'When they were driven out of Paradise', without mentioning the reason for their expulsion, but later on Eve recounts that Satan climbed the Tree of Life in the form of a serpent and sprinkled his evil poison on the fruit he gave Eve to eat (*Vita* 19:2-3).[85] It is not unimportant that according to this rewritten account Satan did not leave Eve the choice.

According to Adam's story of the Fall the tree in the middle of Paradise was the Tree of the Knowledge of Good and Evil (*Vita* 32). The pains its fruit caused Adam to suffer at the end of his life could only be relieved by the tree of God's mercy 'from which flows the oil of life' (*Vita* 36). Eve and her son Seth return to the earthly paradise to procure this precious antidote and though they are not allowed to enter, the archangel Michael allows them to take with them some soothing aromatics (*Vita* 40-43).[86] According to some of the textual witnesses Seth was wounded by the teeth of the beast (*Vita* 39:3; 44:1), but how this came about is unclear. Obviously this episode might be a remnant of the Canaanite myth relating that Adam was *bitten* by the serpent.

At the end of his life Adam was taken up in the heavenly Paradise of Righteousness (*Vita* 25), which indicated that his repentance was accepted. So Satan was the first to sin. Eve and Adam were deceived by him. Some scholars distrust the repentence of Adam and Eve as narrated in the *Vita* and argue that it might be a Christian attempt to partially exonerate the first Adam and his wife. However, the parallels with the Ugaritic myth and the Erra epic are so obvious that this has become an unlikely hypothesis. The first rebellion against the highest deity took place in the realm of the primordial gods.

5.15 *The Apocalypse of Moses*

The *Apocalypse of Moses*, dating from the end of the first century or the early second century CE, partially parallels *The Life*

a date between the second and fourth centuries CE. In De Jonge 2003, 181-200, this scholar opts decidedly for a Christian, anti-jewish origin.

[85] This passage is missing in the partially parallel *Apocalypse of Adam* (see below).

[86] In this connection it is significant that Eve is partly exonerated in some of the text forms of *The Life of Adam and Eve*, cf. Levison 2000, 39-46.

of Adam and Eve.[87] The work probably originated in Jewish-Palestinian circles.[88] In this case too the author embellishes and explains the Genesis narrative in a midrashic way, for example by making Satan let pour the poison of his lust on the fruit before Eve ate it. At the end of his life Adam falls ill and asks Eve to return to the paradise in order to obtain the oil that runs from the Tree of Life.[89] He expects to be cured by it (*Ap. Mos.* 5–9). Seth and Eve go to the paradise together and encounter an animal, obviously the serpent, and Eve blows up at it,

> Oh you evil beast!
> Do you not fear the image of God
>   that you attacked him?
> How did you open your mouth!
>   How strong were your teeth!
> How is it possible that you do not recall
>   your subordinate position?
> That you were subordinate to the image of God? (*Ap. Mos.* 10:3)

Here it seems that Adam was bitten by the serpent, as in the Ugaritic myth. The animal promises Seth not to bother the image of God anymore, although it does appear to have wounded Seth (*Ap. Mos.* 12:2). Seth and Eve proceed to the paradise and pray God to give them the oil of mercy, but God sends the archangel Michael to them with the message that this is impossible, but that at the end of times all flesh, including Adam, will rise and enjoy all the pleasures of paradise (*Ap. Mos.* 13).[90]

---

87 See for a synopsis Anderson & Stone 1999. Some scholars, especially Tromp 2005, regard it as an early recension of the *Life of Adam and Eve* (*Vita*).

88 For this work we follow the excellent edition and commentary of Dochhorn 2005. His conclusion with regard to the date and place of origin is found on page 172. See also Tromp 2005.

89 It seems that some regarded Eden as a the prototype of the temple and the seven-armed (?) candle (menorah) as the Tree of Life (Dochhorn 2005, 262-263, nn. 14, 15).

90 See on this subject and is relevance for the concept of the Second Adam, Sharpe 1973. The *Testament of Adam*, dating from somewhere between the second and fifth century CE, mentions the future deification of Adam (3:3). However, since this is connected with the godhead of Christ as the resurrected Second Adam it has little relevance to our inquiry.

5.16 *The Apocalypse of Baruch*

The *Apocalypse of Baruch* (3 Baruch) is difficult to date because it is apparently reworked by Christians. Most scholars date it between the first and third century CE. It exists in a Greek and a shortened Slavonic version. It is unique in that it links up Adam's sin with the moon.

3 Baruch 9:1-7 Greek version:[91]

> (9:1) And when they had withdrawn, night arrived, and with it the moon and the stars. (9:2) And I Baruch said, 'Lord, explain this also to me, please. How does it depart and where is it going, and in what pattern does it travel?' (9:3) And the angel said, 'Wait and you will see this shortly.' And on the morrow I saw this also in the form of a woman, seated in a wheeled chariot. And in front of it were oxen and lambs near the chariot, and also many angels. (9:4) And I said, 'Lord, what are the oxen and lambs?' And he said to me, 'These are angels also.' (9:5) And again I asked, 'Why does it sometimes grow larger and sometimes grow smaller?' (9:6) 'Listen, O Baruch: This which you see was designed by God to be beautiful without peer. (9:7) And during the transgression of the first Adam, she gave light to Samael when he took the serpent as a garment, and did not hide, but on the contrary, waxed. And God was angered with her, and diminished her and shortened her days.'

3 Baruch 9:1-7 Slavonic version:[92]

> (9:2) And I said to the angel of the Lord, 'Teach me what the moon is." (9:3) And he said to me, 'it is like a woman, sitting on a chariot, and twenty angels are leading the chariot by means of oxen, and the oxen are angels. The form of the moon is like a woman.' (9:5) And I Baruch said, 'Lord, why does it sometimes wax and sometimes wane?' (9:6) And he said to me, 'Listen, Baruch, it was beautiful.
> (9:7) But when the first-created Adam sinned, having listened to Satanael, when he covered himself with the serpent, it (i.e. the moon) did not hide but shone forth, and God was angered by it. He lay bare its days to affliction.

[91] Translation Gaylord 2009, 673.
[92] Translation Gaylord 2009, 672.

5.17 *The Apocalypse of Adam*

The Coptic *Apocalypse of Adam* reveals none of the typically christian intrusions that characterize many other pseudepigraphic writings. There is some affinity with Jewish apocalyptic traditions, but the work as a whole is clearly produced in gnostic circles. Its date is difficult to establish, but it might have originated in the first or second century CE.[93] The work presents itself as the revelation which Adam taught to his son Seth 'in the seven hundredth year' (64:2-3).

Adam narrates the creation of Eve and himself as follows,

> When God had created me out of the earth along with Eve, your mother, I went about with her in a glory that she had seen in the aeon from which we had come forth. She taught me a word of knowledge of the eternal God. And we resembled the great eternal angels, for we were higher than the God who had created us and the powers with him, whom we did not know. Then God, the ruler of the aeons and the powers, divided us in wrath. Then we became two aeons. And the glory in our heart(s) left us, me and your mother Eve, along with the first knowledge that breathed within us.[94]

This account was apparently based on Genesis, but was transformed into the gnostic doctrine of the origin of γνῶσις, knowledge. The text deviates in several aspects from Genesis: Adam and Eve are created simultaneously as one androgynous being.[95] Eve shared her special knowledge with Adam.[96] The serpent is not mentioned at all.[97] Initially Adam and Eve were divine beings like the great eternal angels and purportedly were even higher than

---

[93] MacRae 2000, 152. However, in MacRae 2009, 707-708, he broadens the timespan to the first to fourth century. Böhlig & Labib 1963, 95, stated confidently, 'Die Schrift stammt aus vorchristlicher Gnosis.'

[94] *Ap. Adam*, 1:2-5, MacRae 2000, 155, 157. We follow MacRae's translation except with regard to his spelling 'god' instead of God in lines 7, 17, 20. In MacRae 2009, 712, he himself corrected this to 'God'.

[95] This concept occurs more often in gnostic literature, but has very ancient oriental roots. Cf. De Moor 1998a.

[96] This may rest on Jewish-Aramaic teaching, cf. Ber. R. XX.11, with Dochhorn 2005, 357-358, n. 7.

[97] In other Sethian lore such as the *Secret John* the serpent is even a positive figure. Cf. Rasimus 2009, 65-101. Ḥôrānu's name may live on in Ophite speculations recorded by Origen: (H)Oraios, the seventh of the Archons. In our opinion this is more likely than a derivation from the name of the Egyp-

God. The fall came about because Adam started to feel 'a sweet desire' for his wife. It seems therefore that Eve is exonerated here by making Adam co-responsible in a physical way and attributing the rebellion against the highest deity to both of them. The division of man and woman is not an act of grace towards Adam, as in Genesis, but an act of wrath which cost them their divine status and made them mortal (cf. *Ap. Adam*, 65:15-16; 67:10-14).

5.18 *The Primordial History in Islam*

Obviously the only Creator of all in Islam is Allāh, clearly differentiated from *ʾilāh*, any deity, and *ʾālih*, a pagan god. Yet all three names are evidently related to Ugaritic *ʾilh* and Hebrew אֱלוֹהַּ. Like all henotheistic and monotheistic religions, Islam struggles with the origin of evil. According to the Qurʾān the Devil (Iblīs)[98] was created earlier than Adam. Originally he was one of the angels in the heavenly paradise. However, when God had created Adam as his viceroy to rule in God's place on earth (Sura 2,30) and demanded that all angels would prostrate themselves before Adam,[99] Iblīs refused to do so.[100] Iblīs argued that he had a higher status than Adam because he was created from fire, whereas Adam was shaped from ordinary clay. For this rebellion Iblīs is sent away from the heavenly paradise (Sura 7,12; 17,66), but is not executed and is granted respite to the end of times.[101]

Other early Arabic traditions state that before God created

tian god Horus, as proposed by Rasimus 2009, 104-105. See Sections 2.6 and 2.9. Finally the demon Ornias of the undatable *Testament of Solomon* 1:10-12 ought to be mentioned: he is 'like a flaming fire' and promises the boy whom he is troubling 'all the silver and gold of the earth'. He and his allies fly around without rest and, exhausted, fall down from heaven like stars (*Test. Sol.* 20:14-17).

98 The name is supposed to be derived from the Greek διάβολος (Martinek 1996, 165, n. 1). According to many Muslim scholars his other name is *Šayṭān*. This is no doubt a loan from Hebrew שָׂטָן, Satan (but cf. Section 2.6 on the etymology of the name). It is well-known that Muslim scholars were acquainted with Jewish literature, including pseudepigrapha (Wasserstrom 1994). Other scholars distinguish Iblīs from Šayṭān.

99 Out of deference, not to worship him. Cf. Schöck 2001, 24.

100 Sura 2,34; 7,11-24; 15,28-44; 17,61-63; 18,50; 20,116-123.

101 For heretical elaboration of the motif of the fallen angel ʿAzāzʾil in the Shia Islam, see Beinhauer-Köhler 2004. Stone 2008 overlooks the possibility that his Armenian sources may have been influenced by Islam.

the angels and Adam there had been *ǧinn*, spirits.The *ǧinn* were created by God from smokeless fire (Sura 55,15). According to Sura 18,50 Iblīs had been such a *ǧinn*. The Muslim tradition resolved this problem by asserting that God sent Iblīs with an army of angels to the earth to annihilate the *ǧinn*.[102] So Iblīs/Šayṭān did have a good side too.[103] Especially in Ṣūfism the ambiguous nature of the Iblīs comes to the fore.[104] Iblīs did have offspring, but the faithful are discouraged to befriend them (Sura 18,50).

Before the Fall Adam was a beautifull, beardless youth.[105] Although later tradition naturally did not recognize the divine status of Adam, his status as *ḫalīfa*, 'viceroy, substitute (of God or as successor of corrupted angels)' (Sura 2,30) is no doubt unique.[106] Also traces of his gigantic dimensions are still found in Islamic tradition[107] Later Muslim tradition attributed to Adam an offspring of forty thousand children.[108] Like Jewish and Christian interpreters before them, Muslim scholars speculated about the species of the tree in paradise. Next to date palm, vine, fig and carob-tree, a special kind of wheat is mentioned.[109] The angels can eat its fruit because they are immortal.[110]

The name of Eve does not occur in the Qur'ān, but in Sura 4,1 it is intimated that God created a single person and created from him his wife. Early commentators state that she was created from the lowest of Adam's ribs or from a rib on his left side.[111]

At Satan's prompting, Adam and Eve eat the forbidden fruit and have to descend from the heavenly paradise to the earth (Sura 7,20-22). However, if they follow God's guidance and repent, God will forgive them and allow them to return to paradise (Sura 2,37-38; 7,23; 20,122).

---

[102] Schöck 1993, 18-19, n. 95; 98-99, with n. 551; Rippin 2001, 527.
[103] So also Fahd 1997, 407.
[104] Rippin 1997, 408; 2001, 526.
[105] Schöck 1993, 69, 86.
[106] Schöck 2001, 23.
[107] Schöck 1993, 69-73, 83, 119, with footnote 679.
[108] Steenbrink 2011, 180.
[109] Schöck 1993, 109-110; 2001, 25. Probably this too was derived from Jewish sources, cf. Sections 2.4 and 2.8.
[110] Sura 20,120-123; cf. Schöck 2001, 25; Rippin 2001, 525.
[111] Schöck 2001, 24. According to the Jewish Targum Pseudo-Jonathan on Gen. 2:21 the rib was taken from Adam's *right* side.

5.19 *Conclusions on Parabiblical Literature*

In the parabiblical texts we have discussed in this chapter it is not always clear whether they refer to the distant past, the immediate present, or the distant future. However, since it is obvious that the future is depicted as the restoration of the paradisiacal past, it is yet possible to draw some conclusions about motifs shared with the ancient Near Eastern, especially the Ugaritic and Hebrew texts discussed thus far.

It is evident that the canonical tradition about Adam and Eve has had an overbearing influence on apocryphal, sectarian and pseudepigraphic works. Yet we believe that some Canaanite Adam-traditions that were omitted from the Hebrew Bible were reintegrated in these parabiblical compositions. Whether this came about via oral tradition or by consulting now lost Canaanite sources is still a moot question. In any case the Ugaritic material throws new light on the parabiblical Adam-traditions.

5.19.1 *The Location of Paradise*

Paradise is situated at the headwaters of Euphrates and Tigris, on a very high, snow-capped mountain of volcanic origin.[112] There is a well-watered garden or vineyard on its slopes where the Tree of Life grows.[113]

5.19.2 *Divine Sinners*

The first rebellion against the Creator is not ascribed to humans, as in Genesis, but to lower divine beings (angels, demons). Evidently the seventy sons of El and Asherah became seventy angels later on, as in Canaanite mythology.[114] The leader of the evil angels sometimes bears names that resemble epithets of Ḥôrān, e.g. Sariel who originally seems to have been an evil god.[115]

---

[112] 1 En. 14:8-13; 18:6-7, 9-11; 22:2-4; 70:5-6; 77:3-4; Ap. Abraham 15:5-7; Ladder of Jacob 2:7. The Genesis Apocryphon refers to the mountains of Hurarṭ where eternal fire (is burning), 1QapGen X.12.

[113] 1 En. 22:3-4; 77:3; Wisd. b. Sira 40:17, 27; Test. Levi 18:10-14; 1QH[a] XIV.16-18; XVI.5-26; 2 En. 8; Ap. Abraham 23:4-11; Life of Adam and Eve 25.

[114] 1 En. 1–36 (the Watchers); 69:6; 86:1; Jub. 2:2; Wisd. Solomon 2:23-24; Ladder of Jacob 3:2; Qur'ān, Sura 2,34; 7,11-24; 15,28-44; 17,61-63; 18,50; 20,116-123. Cf. Sanders 1996, 155-160. 363-374; De Moor 1998b.

In Ugarit the Devil was also called *ġzz* (Ugaritic *ġ* = Hebrew ʿ), 'the generous one' which suggests a solution for the hitherto enigmatic name of ʿAzazel in the Bible and parabiblical literature.[116] Apparently Sariel repented, like Ḥôrōn/Šar. The ambiguity in the character of the wicked angels reflects the character of Ḥôrōn and his serpentine brood in Ugaritic myth. In accordance with the testimony of the Hebrew Bible the wicked angels are subordinated to God and pious human beings are able to master the demons (11Q11).

5.19.3 *Human Sinners*

The first humanoids were androgynous beings of gigantic dimensions,[117] thus coming close to divine status.[118] They are given complete control over the earth or even the whole creation.[119] The leader of the evil spirits is jealous of them and disguises himself as a huge speaking serpent who poisons the fruit of the Tree of Life with his spittle,[120] thus partly reducing the responsibility of the first human sinners. We have found only vague indications that Adam was bitten by the snake,[121] but Seth is said to have been wounded by it when he returned to the garden. Possibly this replaces an earlier version in which Adam was bitten. However, because of Adam's sin the lifespan of humans was reduced (CD-A X.8-9). Only one parabiblical text from the Hellenistic era explicitly lays the guilt totally with Eve (Wisd. b. Sira 25:24).

The 'sons of God' of Gen. 6 become fallen angels and their sexual intercourse with earthly women is seen as unnatural depravity resulting in all kinds of misdeeds (Sections 5.3; 5.6; 5.9).

---

115 According to Targum Neofiti on Gen. 32:25 he was Jacob's opponent at the Jabbok river. According to the *Ladder of Jacob* 3:2 Sariel was the 'leader of the beguiled'. In the Jerusalem Talmud (j. Sanh. 25d (VII.9) and in Aramaic incantation bowls the evil angel who repented to become a guardian angel is called שר or סר, 'the Prince'.

116 Ugaritic *ġ* equals Hebrew ע. For earlier attempts to solve the riddle of the name ʿAzazel see Clines, *DCH*, vol. 6, 326, 864.

117 E.g. Midr. Gen. R. I.26; VIII.1; Lev. R. XIV.1; XX.2; Apoc. Abraham 6:14-15; 23:5; Apoc. Adam 1:2-5; Odes Solomon 8:16-17.

118 E.g. 2 En. 30:11-12; Qurʾān, Sura 2,30.

119 E.g. Jub. 2:14; 2 En. 30:11-12.

120 E.g. Apoc. Abraham 23:7-8; Life of Adam and Eve, 19:2-3.

121 Especially Apoc. of Moses 10:3.

5.19.4 *The Renewal of Life*

The restoration of paradise for the pious is a theme in parabiblical literature and the New Testament.[122] Already the *Book of the Luminaries* (4th century BCE) 77:3 mentions the Garden of Righteousness situated in the north from the author's point of view. The *Book of the Watchers* (3rd century BCE) describes a beautiful fragrant tree, growing on the mountain of God. Its fruit will be given to the righteous at the end of times (1 En. 24:3–25:6). Afterwards many other parabiblical and New Testament writings mention a paradisiacal garden in which the righteous will be allowed to live after their death.[123]

As we have seen, the story of Adam was connected with the renewal of life during the Ugaritic New Year festival. In this connection it is interesting that even a version of the late rabbinic work known as the Abot de-Rabbi Nathan states 'On New Year's Day, the first man was created. In the first hour, he came into existence as a thought in God's mind'.[124] Although obviously the eternal renewal of life through procreation is seen as a divine gift in Judaism too, the sexual license of the Canaanite myths is firmly rejected.

---

[122] For the latter see Chapter 8.

[123] E.g. Sir. 40:17, 27; 1 En. 60:23; 61:12; 1QH[a] XIV.16-18; XVI. 5-26; 4Q385c:3; 2 En. 8 [J, A]; Ap. Abraham 23:4-11; Life of Adam and Eve, 25; Ap. Mos., 13; Luke 23:43; 2 Cor.12:4; Rev. 2:7; 21–22; Koran, Sura 2,37-38; 7,23; 20,122.

[124] PesK 23:1, M. 334, as translated by Günther Stemberger (oral communication). Creation by thought alone is also attested for the Ugaritic deities El and Asherah, cf. Section 2.1.

6
The Reception in the New Testament

6.1 *Preliminary Remarks*

In this chapter we only discuss passages in the New Testament that might be further elucidated by the knowledge about Canaanite traditions acquired in Chapter 2 of this book, referring back only occasionally to its reception in the Hebrew Bible and the parabiblical literature treated in Chapters 4 and 5. We will discuss passages per book of the New Testament, not in a chronological or thematic order, because of the great differences of opinion with regard to dating and thematic threading.

6.2 *The Gospel According to Matthew*

In Matthew 4:1-11 Jesus is led up by the Spirit into the desert to be tempted by the Devil (διάβολος). This introduction suggests that through his Spirit God himself was involved in the temptation of Jesus, just as God had allowed Satan to put Job to the test. In both cases God apparently knew beforehand that they would prevail, in contrast to Elijah in 1 Kgs 19. The confrontation between the two opponents reads like a rabbinic dispute, each of them quoting effortless from the Hebrew Bible which both apparently knew by heart. This alone demonstrates that there was little room here for introducing traditions outside the Hebrew canon.

Yet a number of parallels may be noted. The Devil was supposed to dwell in the desert,[1] just as the Canaanite god Ḥôrānu would have been thrown down into the desert where he and his serpentine brood lived most of the time.[2]

The Devil takes Jesus to a very high mountain, and showed him all the kingdoms of the world, saying to him, 'All these I will give you, if you will fall down and worship me.' (Mt. 4:8-9). This recalls the high mountain of Ilu/El (Sections 2.4 and 4.6) from which the rebelling god was thrown down (2.6) as well as the parabiblical accounts of the Devil's envy of Adam and his refusal

[1] Compare the parallel texts Mk 1:12-13; Lk. 4:1.

[2] As is confirmed by Ps. 74:14 and Ezek. 29:5. See Sections 2.8 and 4.7.

to worship Adam (Sections 5.10-17). His envy was caused by the fact that Adam was given dominion over the whole earth (Sections 2.2; 4.2; 5.4; 5.13; 5.14; 5.18). Satan's generosity brings to mind Adammu's alternative name in Ugarit: Šarruġāzizu, 'the Prince is generous' (Section 2.6).

Finally Satan also does a good deed. When it has become clear that Jesus will not submit to him, he just leaves Jesus without harming him in any way (Mt. 4:11, par. Lk. 4:13).[3]

When Jesus heals a blind and dumb demoniac the people around him are astonished. Some conclude that Jesus only could do this by the help of Satan/Be-elzebul, 'the Prince of Demons' (Mt. 12:24, par. Mk 3:22; Lk. 11:15).[4] This suggests that it was a common idea that Satan not only was an evil demon, but also possessed healing powers. Though Jesus himself concludes that if Satan casts out (ἐκβάλλω)[5] Satan, he is divided against himself (Mt. 12:26, par. Mk 3:23; Lk. 11:17-18), he does not deny the ambiguity in Satan's character, but only argues that a split-up ruler always will cause his own downfall.

In the same passage Jesus calls the Pharisees 'brood/offspring of vipers' (γεννήματα ἐχιδνῶν, Mt. 12:34; see also Mt. 3:7; 23:33 and Section 4.5 on Isa. 14:20b). Generally this phrase is attributed to Q, because it is also used by Luke and in the Q sermon of John the Baptist in Mt. 3:7.[6] If this is correct, the phrase goes back to fairly old sayings. The noun γέννημα is related to the verb γεννάω 'to father'. The verb is used in 𝔊 especially in genealogies and seems to be exchangeable with γίνομαι (cf. Gen. 4:18; 25:3; Isa. 9:5; Tob. 1:9; 1 Bar. 3:26). This related verb forms the keyword in Genesis 1, describing the creation of the world. Of the Canaanite god Ḥôrānu it was said[7] that he had *bnwt* 'things built/created, offspring', which appear to be serpents, so he fathered serpentine offspring. The word *bnwt* has the same double meaning as the

[3] See Sections 2.3; 2.39; 3.2.2; 3.3.7; 4.3; 4.5; 5.3; 5.18 on this kind of ambiguiity.

[4] In Judaism Satan and Be-elzebul were seen as allies or were even identified. In Ugarit *zbl bʿl*, 'his Highness Baʿlu', was seen as the great exorcist (De Moor 1987, 183-184, n. 6).

[5] The verb ἐκβάλλω is the keyword in Mt. 12:20-35, cf. Luz 1990, 258.

[6] Luz 1985, 147; Meier 1980, 390; Hagner 1993, 45.

[7] KTU 1.100:62, see Section 2.8.

Greek γεννήματα, it can mean both 'offspring' as well as 'fruit, product' (Liddell & Scott 1968, 844). The origin and meaning of the phrase 'offspring of vipers' have often been discussed. A major question has been why the Pharisees were adressed here specifically as the *offspring* of vipers, and not only as 'you vipers'.[8] Nestle concludes that though it is true that the Greek ἔχιδνα 'viper' outside the New Testament only occurs in Aquila (Isa. 59:5), a comparable expression ἐκγόνων ἀσπίδων 'offspring of asps' has been used in Isa. 11:8; 14:29 and 30:6.[9]

In this connection a passage in the Qumran Thanksgiving Hymns is interesting,

> ... and the gates of the Netherworld (Sheol) will open for all viper-works (18) and the doors of the Pit will close behind her who is pregnant of wickedness and the eternal bolts behind viper-spirits (1QH[a] XI.17-18).[10]

Hebrew מעשׂה ('deeds' or 'creations') in the expression מעשׂה אפעה ('viperworks') is a synonym of Greek γέννημα and Ugaritic *bnwt*. The Qumran text no doubt refers to the offspring of the primeval serpent.[11]

So in Matthew 12:34 Jesus uses the same kind of imagery that was already known from Canaanite texts and probably also is referred to in the three 𝔊 Isaiah texts. In fact Jesus reverses the

[8] Nestle 1912; Charlesworth 2010, 358.

[9] In Isa. 11:8 a paradisiacal scene is described where evil does not reign anymore, and the brood of vipers stands for the offspring of the serpent of Gen. 3. Isa. 14:29 is preceded by the song on the Fall of Hēlēl (see Section 4.5) and thus also is related to serpents as offspring of Satan. Isa. 30:6 𝔊 enumerates both 'asps and the offspring of flying asps', which must refer to mythological evil creatures.

[10] Charlesworth 2010, 359 already referrred to this passage in his discussion of Mt. 3:7. See also our remarks in Section 6.9.

[11] Similarly Charlesworth 2010, 359, with reference to Betz 1958.
Also in Rabbinic texts similar expressions and phrases do occur. In m. Abot 2:10 Rabbi Eliezer adhorts his students to listen to their masters with a critical ear. They may warm themselves by their fire, but should look out for the coals, because they can be like a bite of a fox, a sting of a scorpion, or the hissing of a venomous viper. Thus, the teachers were partly described as vipers, be it not as a viper's offspring (Strack & Billerbeck, Bd. 1, 1926, 114-115).

Pharisees' argument: not Jesus is serving Satan, but the Pharisees are serving him and behave themselves as were they Satan's own ophidian offspring.

In Matthew 23:33 Jesus addresses the Pharisees again as the offspring of vipers, but then adds the question 'how can you flee for the judgment of Gehenna?'[12] This combination of themes is interesting because in the dragon myths of Canaan already a serpentine, devil-like figure was known who was punished and thrown down in the Ḥaurān, a volcanic region in the Syrian desert.[13] This primeval serpent was the Leviathan encircling the habitable world and perpetually fleeing from its own biting mouth (Section 2.8). One of the earliest apocalypses, Isaiah 27:1, describes how this serpent will be defeated at the end of times.

6.3 *The Gospel According to Mark*

In Ugarit the god of the life-giving rain Baʿlu (Baal) was seen as the Savior (*rpʾu*) who defeated Yammu (Sea) and his monsters. This explains his prominent role in incantations against evil spirits and poisonous snakes who were held responsible for all kinds of mental diseases (De Moor 1987, 175-190). It is definitely suggestive that in Mk 4:35-41 Jesus stills the raging sea and in the next passage 5:1–20 heals a demoniac whom nobody had been able to bind.[14] The demoniac is said to live in tombs 'in the land of the Gerasenes'. The exact location of this region is unknown (Taylor 1955, 278), but it is certain that it must be sought in the Bashan area, the region where the great sea-serpent had been thrown down (Section 2.4). There are many megalithic monuments on the heights of Bashan, nowadays Golan, which were supposed to be tombs (μνήματα, Mk 5:3, 5).[15] The disturbed man calls Jesus a son of the Most

---

[12] Cf. Mt. 3:7, 'offspring of vipers, who informed you how to flee from the coming wrath?'

[13] See Sections 2.4. and 6.12.

[14] Compare what is said about Adammu in KTU 1.107:6, 'he did not know how to bind the Biter', cf. Appendix 1. See also the sequence in Mk 6:45-52 par. about Jesus treading the sea like Baʿlu (cf. Fig. 29), followed by the passage about Jesus healing people in the region of Gennesaret.

[15] See e.g. Epstein 1972-1973; Kochavi 1989. Note the play on words when the possessed urges Jesus not to 'torture' him (μή με βασανίσῃς, v. 7). According to Ps. 68:6-7 there were 'burial grounds' on the Bashan, cf.

High God (Mk 5:7), a title of Ilu/El.[16] He says his own name is 'Legion', a designation of demons in Ugarit which occurs together with the 'Ḥôrānites', offspring of Ḥôrānu, the master of serpents.[17] The name 'Gerasenes' resembles the verb *grš* which is used in connection with Ba'lu's battle against the Sea (KTU 1.2:IV.11-12; see also Isa. 57:20).

Mark goes on to narrate how Jesus revived the daughter of Jairus (Mk 5:21-43). This combination of themes renders it likely that Mark is hinting at popular Canaanite traditions about the victory of life over death, substituting the name of the pagan god Baal by that of his own champion, Jesus.

We discussed Mk 3:22 (where Jesus is supposed to cooperate with Be-elzebul) already under Section 6.2. According to Mk 8:33 (par. Mt. 16:23) Satan can also be active through a human person, like Peter. When Peter tries to prevent Jesus from accepting his suffering, Jesus' response is rather harsh, 'Get behind me, Satan! You are thinking not as God thinks but as human beings do.' In the Ugaritic incantation KTU 1.82 demons are summoned 'to go back'.[18] For Jesus, Peter's protest 'implies the same kind of temptation which presented itself in the desert that of accepting the popularly expected Messianic role' (Taylor 1955, 379-380). The parallel text in the gospel of Matthew adds that Satan is an obstacle or even a cause to sin (σκάνδαλον). Also other texts emphasize that Satan can seize human beings and get them in his power (Mk 4:15; Lk. 22:3 (Judas), 31; Jn 13:27 (Judas); Acts 5:3; 10:38; 26:18; 1 Tim. 3:6-7; 2 Tim. 2:26) and even can chain them by disease (Lk. 13:16).[19]

6.4 *The Gospel According to Luke*

As observed above, the fall of Hēlēl in Isaiah 14 seems to go back to the fall of the Canaanite god Hilālu/Ḥôrānu. This god was also known as the 'the (evil) Prince' and 'the Enemy' and therefore may

---

Section 2.8.

[16] Section 2.1, also for the healing by touching the robe of Ilu, KTU 1.169:12-15 with Mk 5:25-34 and 6:56.

[17] Ugaritic *pg*, KTU 1.82:26-27, cf. De Moor & Spronk 1984, 245-246.

[18] Cf. De Moor & Spronk 1984, 243, 245.

[19] See also our discussion on the personified view of Satan in Section 6.8 below.

be compared with the later ideas about Satan. Up till now, the identification of Hēlēl with Satan was observed only in later Jewish texts like *The Life of Adam and Eve* (dating from somewhere between the 1st and 4th century CE)[20] and 2 Enoch (most likely from the first century CE), as well as the Vulgate by its rendering *lucifer* 'light-bringer, morning star' as a translation for Hēlēl. So, when in the New Testament mention is made of the Fall of Satan that seems to parallel the Fall of Hēlēl in Isaiah 14, some scholars nowadays deny that there would have been any relationship between the two because

> Despite the long history of linking this verse [Luke 10:18] with Isa 14:12 as applied to the fall of Satan (...) there is finally no adequate basis for such a connection, or for any early Jewish interpretation of the text from Isaiah as referring to the primordial fall of Satan from heaven.'[21]

According to John Nolland the closest parallel to the imagery is provided by Test. Sol. 20:16-17: 'we [demons] ... fall ... like flashes of lightning to the earth' (Nolland 1989, 563). However, the *Book of the Watchers* (3rd century BCE), also deals with the fall of a number of angels, among them Sariel, who might be the same as Ḥôrānu/Satan[22] and our research with regard to the Canaanite background of Isaiah 14 (see Section 4.5) leaves no doubt that the idea of a fall of Satan from heaven might well be part of a residue of popular Canaanite traditions.

We discuss the text of Luke 10:15-20 briefly, because the fall of Satan as described in Isaiah 14:12-13 and 14:15 seems to be referred to in this passage.[23] In Luke 10:15,[24] Jesus said to Capernaum,

> And you, Capernaum,
> will you be exalted to heaven?
> You shall be brought down to the Netherworld.

---

[20] See Section 5.14 above.
[21] Nolland 1989, 563.
[22] See our discussion on this 'bad' Sariel in Sections 5.3 and 5.13.
[23] For a discussion of the genre of 'vision' and the structure of this text, see Humphrey 2006. Dochhorn (2010, 257) denies reference to the past.
[24] See also the parallel text Mt. 11:23.

Just as the fall of the king of Babylon in Isaiah 14 was compared to the the fall of Hilālu/Ḥôrānu from heaven, Jesus adopts similar imagery to describe the fall of the city of Capernaum.[25] Though some scholars doubt the connection with Isaiah 14, because Jesus does not mention a falling star, but just the lightning (Lk. 10:18),[26] the reference to Tyre and Sidon in Lk. 10:13-14 suggests rather strongly that Luke was aware of the link with Isa. 14 and Ezek. 28.[27] In Lk. 10:18-19 Jesus continues,

> (18b) 'I saw Satan like lightning
> falling from heaven.
> (19) Behold, I have given you authority
> to tread upon serpents and scorpions,
> and over all the power of the Enemy;
> and nothing shall hurt you.'

Whether this saying should be taken as a real statement by Jesus or not is a hotly discussed question.[28] Also whether Jesus is referring here to an event in the past, present or future is uncertain.[29] Most scholars nowadays seem to tend to a visionary experience of Jesus with regard to the past.[30] The falling of Satan is also narrated as a past event in rabbinic literature. According to Pirqe de Rabbi Eliezer, 14, God cursed the serpent (Gen. 3:14) by casting down Sammael[31] and his troop from their holy place in heaven, and cutting off the feet of the serpent (Friedlander 1916, 99).

If Jesus and his disciples were acquainted with the ancient

---

25 The parallel between Lk. 10:15 and Isa. 14:13 and 14:15 has been noticed by e.g. Nolland 1989, 557; Bovon 1996, 57.

26 E.g. Vollenweider 1988, 192-196; Humphrey 2006.

27 The possibility of a link with Isa. 14 has been acknowledged by many scholars, see e.g. Bovon 1996, 57; Hultgård 2000, 72; Marx 2000; Gathercole 2006, esp. 148 (against Nolland 1989).

28 Theobald 2005, 174.

29 Cf. Hultgård 2000, 71; Theobald 2005, 178.

30 Vollenweider 1988, 190, 196, 199; Theobald 2005. 178. The fall of Satan in the aorist form refers to a definitive fall, not a temporary fall (Nolland 1989, 563). Gathercole 2003, refers to several ancient interpretations referring to the past, but finally takes it as an eschatological view of Jesus in the future.

31 Who had disguised himself as the serpent in paradise (cf. Section 5.15). The name Sammael seems to contain the element *sammā*, in Aramaic 'drug, poison'.

Canaanite tradition about the fall of Ḥôrānu, the (evil) serpent-Prince, at the beginning of the world, the treading on serpents (plural!)[32] and scorpions in verse 19 makes sense. Serpents and scorpions were seen as demonic creatures which humans and their divine patrons had to combat eternally.[33] So there is no contradiction between past and future. The treading upon serpents and scorpions is symbolic for the battle against demonic powers, like the casting out of demons by the disciples (cf. Mk 16:18).[34]

When Luke suggests that Jesus saw Satan fall from heaven, he implicitly suggests Jesus was preexistent with God, present from the beginning of creation and thus able to witness the punishment of the Rebel. This would be in accordance with some parabiblical traditions that situate the fall of the rebel star from heaven *before* Adam's fall (Sections 5.6; 5.10; 5.12; 5.14; 5.18). The designation of the Devil as 'the enemy' in Lk. 10:19 is not a late development in postbiblical Judaism, as some would have it (e.g. Foerster 1935, 814). Already in Ugarit *ʿd* (*ʿadû*) 'the enemy' and *ʾabdy* 'Destroyer' were designations of Ḥôrānu, the serpent-god who rose up against the Creator (Section 2.6).

However, the primordial fall of Satan apparently was not a definitive one. Alfred Marx (2000, 171) in his discussion of Lk. 10:18 refers to Mk 13:25 and its parallel Mt. 24:29, both describing

---

[32] Compare our findings on the role of the serpents in Ugarit, esp. Fig. 27, the seals from Cyprus, as well our discussion of *The Book of the Watchers* in Section 5.3.

[33] Compare for example Gen. 3:15 about the enmity between the woman and the serpent, and Fig. 14, where procreation seems to be threatened by the scorpion under the bed. See also the parallelism between serpents and scorpions in Deut. 8:15.

[34] Similarly Charlesworth 2010, 357, who considers the serpents and scorpions in Luke 10:19 as 'something negative, perhaps the Destroyer, God's Antagonist, and the Devil.'
Hitherto many scholars were of the opinion that the role of Satan in Lk. 10 is that of the prosecutor, similar to the figure of Satan in Job 1:6-12 (cf. Theobald 2005, 181). They based themselves on v. 20 that is thought to refer to a kind of final judgment. Satan would have been thrown from heaven because he prosecuted people falsely. After Satan's fall these people can be recorded in the heavenly book of the righteous. However, no final judgment is mentioned in v. 20 and it seems more likely that it is meant as a consolation for those who partake in the battle against evil, despite all the risks.

the eschatological event of Jesus' arrival on the clouds. At that moment the stars will fall from heaven. A similar event is described in Rev. 6:13, as well as in 8:10. All these texts seem to describe an event similar to the fall of Hēlēl/Satan in Isa. 14 and Lk. 10:18.[35] The stars might be a reference to angels (Koch 2004, 256-258). So also in this sense the final phase of history was thought to repeat its beginning.

6.5 *The Gospel According to John*

Bordreuil 2007 has pointed out that according to Num. 21:4-9 the poison of snakes by which some of the Israelites were bitten was deactivated by the bronze serpent erected by Moses, a clear example of apotropaic magic that bears some similarity to the magic use of the text of KTU 1.100 as an incantation against snakebite. The staff of Moses evidently represents the Tree of Life around which the serpent is coiled, as with the staff of Asclepius. The turnabout of Ḥôrānu in the Ugaritic myth which restored the cosmic order by neutralising the serpent's poison by which the Tree of Life had become deformed renders the positive application of this symbol understandable. In Jn 3:14-15 the healing power of the serpent staff of Moses is referred to and compared to the elevation of Christ which brings eternal life. In fact this text compares Jesus to the healing serpent[36] and so the text also recalls the promise to the Mother of All Living in Gen. 3:15 (Ronning 1997, iv; 358-359). The Son of Humankind would be lifted up just as Moses lifted up the serpent in the desert. Ronning concludes that as the curse in Gen. 3:15 was on the serpent, the curse is applied to Jesus in his crucifixion (Ronning 1997, 360).

The comparison of the staff of Moses to Christ on the cross suggests that people who are in need of Christ's elevation have been 'bitten' like the Israelites in Num. 21:6, 9.[37] Because of the

---

[35] That Jesus will be the definitive conqueror of Satan is said also in Jn 12:31, a text probably influenced by Rev. 12:9, cf. Aune 1997b, 695.

[36] Martinek 1996, 101, 139; Ronning 1997, 358; McCord Adams 2006; Charlesworth 2010, 1-15, 352-420. Also the Apostle Paul uses a reference to Num. 21:4-9 in 1 Cor. 10:9. See the brief summary of the discussion in Charlesworth 2010, 354.

[37] McCord Adams suggests that not the people are 'bitten' in Jn 3:14, but Jesus' enemies shoot their poison into his body. This, however, requests an

relation between Moses' staff to Genesis 3 one might assume that John was acquainted with a story in which Adam was bitten by the serpent. Traces of the story that the first human was bitten by a primordial snake, as in the Ugaritic myth, are also found in parabiblical traditions (Sections 5.11; 5.14; 5.15).

As we argued in Section 4.3 the role of Ḥôrānu seems to have been taken over by Cain in the biblical account of Genesis 4. In the New Testament some texts seem to support this idea. In Jn 8:44 it is said,

> You are from your father, the Devil,
> and you want to do your father's desire.
> He was a murderer from the beginning
> and he does not stand in the truth,
> for there is no truth in him.

Jesus addresses here especially the Pharisees[38] who devise plans to put him to death. Just as in Mt. 3:7 (and comparable texts Mt. 12:34; 23:33; Lk. 3:7) where Jesus calls the Pharisees 'offspring of vipers' in the sense of offspring of Satan/Devil, he describes them here implicitly as children of the Devil.

De Bondt considers the possibility that the 'murderer from the beginning' might refer to Cain (Gen. 4).[39] With other scholars, however, he finally prefers to read it as a reference to Genesis 3, the Devil as the one who from the beginning tells lies, thus bringing death into the world.[40] This interpretation is based on *Wisdom of Solomon* 2:24, where it is said that the Devil brought death into the world.[41] It is questionable whether this theory is tenable.[42] Genesis 3 tells how death came into the world, but one cannot conclude from this text that the serpent *causes* the death

---

unlikely shift in the comparison and therefore does not convince us.

[38] 'Jews' is a shorter designation of the same persons addressed in Jn. 8:1-20. See v. 21 'them' and the continuing learned disputation style.

[39] De Bondt 1947, 142.

[40] Similarly Ridderbos 1987, 364, 'Uiteraard wordt hiermee op het paradijsgebeuren gedoeld, waarin de duivel door leugen en list de dood over de mensen heeft gebracht.' (Of course, this refers to the paradise-event, in which the Devil through lies and deceit has inflicted death on humankind).

[41] Beasley-Murray 1999, 135. Cf. Sections 4.3; 5.11; 5.12 of this study.

[42] See now also our discussion of the comparable text in 1 Jn 3:11-12 below.

of humans, let alone that he was a 'murderer' (Greek ἀνθρωποκτόνος). In the *Apocalypse of Abraham* 24:5 Abraham is described viewing the 'adversary' in the Garden of Eden,[43] together with Adam, Eve and Cain, and it is Satan who leads Cain to murder his brother Abel. So this text too connects Satan and Cain.

Martin Hasitschka does not see any necessity to refer back to the Hebrew Bible. He takes only the immediate context to explain Jn 8:44, suggesting that the Devil as a murderer is related to his killing of the Son of Humankind (Hasitschka 2005, 113-114). The Devil as a liar in his view forms just a contrast to Jesus as the one who brings the truth. However, in this interpretation the expression ἀπ' ἀρχῆς is not explained.[44] In general, interpreters of Jn 8:44 are more concerned with the question to whom Jesus is speaking than to who was meant by the 'murderer' and the 'liar'. In the Hebrew Bible it is said of Cain in Gen. 4:8 that he murders (𝔊: ἀποκτείνω), and he is the only one in the Bible of whom it can be said that he murders from the beginning (ἀπ' ἀρχῆς), an expression especially linked to the very beginning of the world.[45] Furthermore Cain is clearly lying when after the murder of his brother he replies to God's question 'where is your brother' with 'I do not know; am I my brothers keeper?' (Gen. 4:9). That Satan (not Adam!) has been sinning 'from the beginning' (ἀπ' ἀρχῆς) also is attested in 1 Jn 3:8.[46]

A reminiscence of the fall of Satan (as in Lk. 10:18) is found also in Jn 12:31,

> Now is the time for judgment on this world,
> now the ruler of this world will be be cast out.

---

[43] See Section 5.12.

[44] The interpretation of ἀπ' ἀρχῆς in Jn 8:44 is also skipped by Dennis 2007, 681.

[45] Cf. Mt. 19:4; 24:21; Mk 13:19, as well as 𝔊 of Isa. 22:11; 42:9; 43:13; 45:21, as well as Gen. 1:11 (𝔊) and Jn 1:1-2.

[46] Also noted by Smalley 1984, 168, who emphasizes that the presence of sin in the world from the start is presented by John 'as a result of the Devil's own rebellious activity and incitement'. In contrast to Paul who blames Adam for sin in the world. For Satan as the primordial source of all sin in Jewish apocalyptic literature, see also Dennis 2007, 683-685.

Again an eschatological repetition of the primeval history is connected with the casting out (ἐκβάλλω) of Satan, similar to the ruler in Isaiah 14, who was said to have fallen from heaven (Isa. 14:12) brought down (Isa. 14:15) and cast out (Isa. 14:19). Euphemistically Satan is called the ruler of this world (ὁ ἄρχων τοῦ κόσμου τούτου),[47] whereas the text obviously means that only God is the ruler of the world. In Isa. 14:5 it was said that the LORD has broken de scepter of the ruler (ἄρχων). Jn 12:31 clearly presupposes the theme of an ancient myth of a cosmic combat that has been reworked into an apocalyptic tradition, as was described in detail by Judith Kovacs.[48] As we have expounded in Chapters 2 and 3 of this study, already in ancient times the theme of a rebellious god who was about to take over the rulership of the cosmos by rebelling against the old ruler was widespread (we encountered these thoughts also in Egypt, Canaan and Mesopotamia (Chapter 3) as well as in Isaiah 14 and Ezekiel 28. Kovacs stresses that the cosmic combat and the casting out of Satan is not just a remnant of an ancient myth, but in Jn 12:31 arrives at the turning point by the crucifixion of Jesus, 'On the cosmic level, this moment brings the decisive victory over the evil ruler of this world'.[49] However, the struggle will go on with Jesus' followers (Kovacs 1995, 234). Kovacs admits that the dualism present in the book of John (the combat between light and darkness, the children of God and and the children of Satan) is an ancient theme that 'goes back to Canaanite, Mesopotamian and Greco-Roman texts' (Kovacs 1995, 236).

6.6 *The Book of Acts*

More or less parallel to the expression of source Q 'offspring of vipers', denoting children of Satan/Devil,[50] the author of Acts describes how Paul (Acts 13:10) addresses Elymas the magician – who tried to turn the proconsul Sergius Paulus away from the

---

[47] For a discussion of this term which also occurs in Jn 14:30 and 16:11, see Kovacs 1995, 230.

[48] Kovacs 1995, 228-229, 236; see also Beasley-Murray 1999, 211, as well as Dennis 2007.

[49] Kovacs 1995, 233. Similarly Dennis 2007, 682.

[50] See Section 6.2 on the Gospel of Matthew.

faith in God – by the epithet of 'son of the Devil' (υἱος διαβόλου). This phrase is not used elsewhere in the New Testament, although comparable phrases are attested.[51] According to Canaanite lore even evil deities like Môtu (Death) and the Devil Ḥôrānu did have offspring (Sections 2.1; 2.10; 4.8).

A text that still lacks a full explanation is the story of Paul's shipwreck on the island of Malta (Acts 28:1-10).[52] At first the local people are friendly to Paul and his companions. They welcome them and make a fire so they can warm themselves. Paul gathers a bundle of branches and puts them on the fire, but because of the heat a snake (ἔχιδνα) comes out of the wood and fastens itself on his hand. The people then become afraid and think Paul is a murderer (φονεύς), but Paul shakes off the serpent into the fire, and he himself is not harmed at all. The people are still waiting for his arm to swell, but nothing happens. Their conclusion is that Paul must be a god. Paul and his companions then are invited by a person from the island to stay for a few days with him. His father is very ill. Paul heals him and during the rest of his stay heals all other ill people on the island.

Noteworthy in this text are the following events,

1. A biting serpent in the wood[54]
2. Paul does not fall dead by the bite, a circumstance causing the locals to call him a 'god'.

---

[51] See our discussion of Jn 8:44 and 1 Jn 3:12 in Sections 5.3 and 5.11.

[52] The rendering Malta for Greek Μελίτη still represents the general consensus among scholars,[53] though also the possibility of Dalmatia has been suggested, as well as the specific island of Mljet in Dalmatia (Meinardus 1976).

[54] Charlesworth notices that the text does not mention the biting of the serpent and concludes that from the view of ophiology it is likely that the viper did not bite but only tried to escape the fire by climbing in Paul's arm, Charlesworth 2010, 355. Similarly Pesch 1986, 298, who states that the viper probably has not bitten, but only entwined Paul's hand. According to the Greek text the snake 'fastens' to his hand (καθῆψεν τῆς χειρὸς αὐτοῦ). However, if this were true and there was no real snakebite, the islanders too could have seen that nothing serious had happened, would not have been astonished and would not have been waiting for the swelling (Acts 28:6).

3. Like the first disciples of Jesus Paul appears able to heal suffering people on the island.

Especially remarkable is the fact that in the New Testament the word ἔχιδνα 'viper' only occurs in four other texts, namely in the expression 'offspring of vipers' as an epithet for the Pharisees.[55] The word as used by Matthew and Luke clearly refers to Satan as the 'father' of the Pharisees. No doubt, Luke uses the word also in this text of Acts deliberately.[56] According to Joshuah Jipp Luke's description of Paul as a godly human being is in agreement with other descriptions of charismatic figures (Jipp 2013, 4). Paul is described here as a man who defeats the Devil and as a man who appears to be immune to the snakebite (Jipp 2013, 6-7). Furthermore, it is remarkable that Paul does not invoke the name of Jesus, after he has been bitten, causing some scholars to conclude that Acts 28:1-6 contains a secular anecdote which is used only to glorify Paul (Jipp 2013, 4).

The Adamic Myth tells about the god Adammu, bitten by a serpent who guarded the Tree of Life. Only the progenitor of the serpents, Ḥôrānu, appeared to be able to detoxify the poison. Adammu survives and all the people that were doomed to death by the poisonous serpent(s) in the Tree of Life are rescued and do not die immediately but live on as a genus, be it as mortals. Acts 28 is interesting, not only because of the order of similar events, but also because it is situated on the island of Malta, well-known for its Semitic background. Archaeological excavations have revealed remnants of Phoenician settlements from the 8th century until the 6th century BCE. Also the name of the island seems to be related to a Semitic word *meliṭa*, a safe harbor (Ward Gasque 1992, 490-491).

Acts 28 as worded by Luke recalls the text of Lk. 10:19 where Jesus promises the seventy two elders that they will not be harmed by snakes and scorpions.[57]

6.7 *The Letter of Paul to the Romans*

Manuela Martinek states about Rom. 3:13 that the apostle Paul

[55] See our discussion above with Mt. 3:7 par.
[56] Luke also knows other words for serpent or viper, see Lk. 11:11, ὄφις.
[57] Pesch 1986, 298; Jipp 2013, 6. For Lk. 10:15-19, see our discussion above.

seems to mention the serpent in a similar way as he elsewhere adduces the Devil/Satan, namely as a threat to the young community of Christians. Paul worries about the ability of the new believers to withstand the temptations of evil (Martinek 1996, 87-93). In Rom. 3:13 Paul describes evil people as having the poison of vipers on their lips, quoting a text from the Hebrew Bible.[58] In the Hebrew Bible the phrase is used for evil people and for the danger of wine. If Martinek is right in this respect[59] and Paul indeed uses the image of the serpent here as a reference to Satan/Devil, Paul must have been acquainted with a version of the Paradise story in which the serpent administered his poison to the first human being by biting him.

In contrast to John who ascribes the origin of sin to Satan (see above) the apostle Paul makes Adam reponsible for the original sin. He does so explicitly in Rom. 5:12-14,[60]

> (12) Therefore as through one human being
> sin came into the world,
> and death through sin,
> so death came to all human beings,
> because all sinned –
> (13) Before the law sin was in the world,
> but sin is not counted when there is no law.
> (14) Yet death reigned from Adam to Moses,
> and over those who did not sin after the likeness of the transgression of Adam,
> who is a type of the one to come.

In contrast to Ben Sira,[61] Paul does not accuse Eve of the original sin. One might ask if in early Judaism creation stories were known in which either Satan or Adam committed the first sin, without mentioning Eve, or without a specific role for Eve.[62] The text sug-

---

[58] Ps. 58:5; 140:4; Prov. 23:32, cf. Martinek 1996, 101.

[59] Also Charlesworth 2010, 354, suggests a reference to the serpent as the symbol of the Liar or Deceiver.

[60] For a full discussion of this text see Legarreta Castillo 2014, esp.150-159.

[61] Cf. Section 4.3.

[62] In two texts ascribed to Paul Eve is mentioned as the first sinner however: 2 Cor. 11:3 and 1 Tim. 2:13-14, see our disccusion below. Wilckens 1987, 315 concludes that in Rom. 5:12 no mythic background can be discerned.

gests that death did not belong to the original life of humans, but that it entered the world through sin (Dunn 1988a, 289). Although Paul first states that the sin of one man caused death he continues with the conclusion that finally all humans are condemned to die because they sinned no less than the first human.[63] Furthermore, Paul calls the sin of Adam in verse 14 a 'transgression' as if he had transgressed God's commandments (Dunn 1988a, 290) which in our opinion is implied in the wording of Gen. 2:16 and 3:11, 17 (Section 4.3).

In Rom. 16:17-18, after a long list of greetings, the apostle Paul warns the Romans to watch out for those who cause divisions and put obstacles (σκάνδαλα)[64] in their way. He comforts the Romans by announcing that soon God will trample Satan under their feet (Rom. 16:20).[65] In oriental iconography the evil serpent was often depicted as trampled underfoot (see Sections 4.5; 4.8). Furthermore, Paul's statement seems to echo Gen. 3:15 about the serpent whose head will be crushed.[66] Thus also Paul seems to combine designations of both Satan/Devil and the primordial serpent.

6.8 *The Letters of Paul to the Corinthians*

A text clearly referring to Genesis 2 is 1 Corinthians 11:7-9 where Paul seems to describe just the facts about the order between man and woman in his discussion of the need for women to wear a veil,

---

Paul just refers to Gen. 3. Death and sin are no mythic powers for him anymore. However, the language used points to personification.

[63] Generally scholars nowadays are of the opinion that Paul did not hold a doctrine of original guilt, but only a doctrine of original sin. See e.g. Brandenburger 1962, 169-180; Wilckens 1987, 317; Dunn 1988a, 291; Black 1989, 79-80; Rapinchuk 1999; Bormann 2007, 74; Legarreta Castillo 2014, 158. They argue against inherited sin because ἐφ' ᾧ has to be read as 'because' and not as Augustine did on the basis of the Vulgate text (*in quo*) 'through him (= Adam)'. Others hold to the more traditional view that Paul indeed meant 'original sin' in Rom. 5:12, e.g. Kline 1991.

[64] The same was said of Satan in Mk 8:33; Mt. 16:23, causing obstacles for Jesus, see our discussion above on Mark. The word σκάνδαλον has demonic implications, cf. Müller 1969, 61-66; Wilckens 1982, 143.

[65] See also 1 Cor. 15:25, 27.

[66] Wilckens 1982, 143; Dunn 1988b, 907. See also Lk. 10:19: Jesus' disciples will tread upon serpents and scorpions. Perhaps both texts might be taken as references to Gen. 3:15, as suggested by Aune 1997b, 697.

but not for men, 'since man is the image and glory of God; but woman is the glory of man. For man was not made from woman (ἐκ γυναικὸς), but woman from man (ἐξ ἀνδρός). Neither was man created for woman, but woman for man.' As Schrage formulates it, Paul reads Genesis 1 through the lens of Genesis 2 and seems to use a Jewish tradition that related Gen. 1:27 to just one human being, namely a man (Schrage 1995, 509), although Paul clarifies himself later by stating that men are not independent of women (1 Cor. 11:11-12).

When Paul refers to creation history, he only seems to mention Adam, as the one who sinned and transgressed God's commandment. Not only in the Letter to the Romans is this the case, also in the first Letter to the Corinthians he presents Adam as the first human by whom all human beings die (1 Cor. 15:22).[67]

In 1 Cor. 15:45-47 he again takes up the image of Adam as the first man and contrasts him to Christ whom he takes as the second human being or the second Adam. The contrast between Adam in whom all die and Christ in whom all are made alive implicitly accuses Adam of the first sin. No Eve is mentioned. Wilckens states that the text of Rom. 5:12 cannot be read without these verses from 1 Corinthians, for Paul clearly takes the thought worked out in 1 Corinthians as presupposition for his letter to the Romans (Wilckens 1987, 308). In 1 Corinthians Paul elaborates the contrast between Adam and Christ.

In New Testament scholarship the origin of Paul's doctrine of the two Adams is a much discussed topic and up till now no convincing background for Paul's view has been presented (Hultgren 2003, 343). Paul seems to polemicize against views that were common in those days in Corinth. Tuomas Rasimus summarizes the three major views among scholars,

1. Paul does not polemicize at all, and therefore does not oppose anything.

[67] According to Legarreta Castillo 2014, Paul relied on earlier Jewish interpretations of Genesis 1–3 of which some attributed to Adam (and/or Eve) original sin and death, and others distinguished an earthly and a heavenly man. Lee 2012, however, argues that Paul used early church tradition for his Adam Christology.

2. Paul opposes an Adam mythology in which the heavenly man is placed before the earthly one.

3. Paul opposes a dualistic anthropology overemphasizing the spiritual element.[68]

It has been argued that Paul polemicizes against a scheme of the two Adams as known from Philo who *ontologically* distinguishes a *first* heavenly Adam (ὁ οὐράνιος ἄνθρωπος) in Gen. 1:26 and a *second* earthly Adam (ὁ γήινος ἄνθρωπος) in Gen. 2:7.[69] Most scholars take 1 Cor. 15:46 as polemic.[70]

Another major background for Paul's polemic in 1 Cor. 15:46 that sometimes has been proposed is Gnosticism and its *Urmensch* myth, in which there is a belief in a primodial ἄνθρωπος from heaven and in contrast to this heavenly man there should have been an earthly man. In a primordial Fall Myth the heavenly man fell into the earthly world and became an earthly being, the earthly Adam. The idea is that the heavenly and the earthly man were one and the same (Hultgren 2003, 357-358). Most scholars, however, deny a gnostic background of 1 Cor. 15:46, according to Hultgren for good reasons, because

> ... it is highly doubtful that there was in the first century (or perhaps ever) a widespread and unified Oriental Urmensch myth.[71]

Egon Brandenburger, however, has defended the thesis that Gnosticism is pre-Christian and that it played a role in Corinth.[72] According to Brandenburger the gnostic Adam originally has been

[68] Rasimus 2009, 160-161, with earlier literature.
[69] *Legum allegoriae* 1.31, see the discussion in Hultgren 2003, 343-354, esp. 343-345.
[70] E.g. Wilckens 1987, 308; Schrage 2001, 306. Hultgren 2003, 355-356, however, denies the polemical character of the verse and takes the supposed order merely as a description of what he calls *futurity* of the spiritual body: 'Paul is not polemically reversing the order of the two men but simply emphasizing the qualitative and temporal distance between them as a way of explaining how resurrection is even possible. Paul is not reversing Philo here.' (Hultgren 2003, 356).
[71] Hultgren 2003, 358.
[72] Brandenburger 1962, 68-157. See also our remarks on the *Apocalypse of Adam* in Section 5.17.

a divine being who has descended to the earth to act as a savior (Brandenburger 1962, 153-157). He concludes that there must have existed a so-called primordial human savior myth (*Urmensch-Erlöser-Mythos*) containing foreign and non-Jewish elements that up till now has remained a mystery with regard to its origin. In this myth Adam already existed before the creation of the world, but he did not take part in creation (Brandenburger 1962, 132). Nevertheless, Adam plays a major role in the myth as a heavenly (not only divine) being, a figure who also was standing above the angels. By his very nature this heavenly human had shown himself having anthropological as well as related cosmological significance.[73] Brandenburger suggests Indo-iranian influence for the latter concept (Brandenburger 1962, 136).[74]

Another origin that has been proposed for the first and second human being (Adam) in 1 Corinthians is the so-called Ophite Myth (cf. Rasimus 2009). Tuomas Rasimus defends this thesis especially by bringing Irenaeus' Ophite account of *Adversus Haereses* to the fore, where also a first and a second Adam are described.[75] The first Adam is created as a heavenly being, be it only mentally. He is described as gigantic (just as in the rabbinic sources) and receives a mind and thought and the knowledge of the supreme God. After Adam has eaten from the forbidden tree the god Ialdabaoth[76] casts him and Eve down to the earth. Only then their bodies become corporeal and mortal (Rasimus 2009, 163-164). Also in *The Apocryphon of John* the earthly Adam is created second, after a first heavenly Adam. The idea of this earthly Adam apparently originates in the 'garments of skins' of Gen. 3:21 (Rasimus 2009, 165). In *The Apocryphon of John* Adam explicitly has been expelled from his earlier heavenly dwelling place where he was created anew from earth.[77]

---

[73] Brandenburger 1962, 134, 'Und dieser himmlische Mensch hatte seinem Wesen nach betont anthropologische Bedeutung, wenn sich auch damit z.T. eine kosmologische verbinden konnte.'

[74] The theory of Brandenburger has been severely ciriticized, especially because of the supposed gnostic background. See the overview with Legarreta Castillo 2014, 7-12.

[75] Irenaeus, *Adv. Haer.* 1.30.

[76] The Jewish creator God that was seen as an inferior god with a false monotheistic claim, cf. Rasimus 2009, 171-174.

[77] Ap. John II. 20:35–21:14, cf. Rasimus 2009, 165.

In our opinion the discovery of the Canaanite background of the Adamic Myth can shed new light on the statements of Paul and on Brandenburger's suggested 'primordial human myth'.[78] The use of ἀλλ' 'but' at the beginning of 1 Cor. 15:46 seems to introduce a contrasting view[79] in Paul's argument against an apparently notorious creation story or doctrine in which the first Adam was known as 'a human from heaven' (ὁ ἄνθρωπος ἐξ οὐρανοῦ) and the second Adam was known as 'the first human from the earth' (ὁ πρῶτος ἄνθρωπος ἐκ γῆς χοϊκός, 1 Cor. 15:47). The Adamic Myth indeed describes Adammu as a heavenly being who had a high position in the pantheon, but no role in creation. He appears at the top of the god list in KTU 1.179:8'-9', even before the deities 'Heaven and Flood' (see Section 2.5) and according to KTU 1.107 he appears to be chosen as the one who was supposed to act as a Savior of both the heavenly and earthly world. The 'foreign' and 'non-Jewish' aspects observed by Brandenburger possibly entered the gnostic and pre-christian Adam views through the channel of popular religion which often pops up in later speculations about the primeval world and its future restoration. Apparently, also Jesus was aware of popular belief, referring to it occasionally.[80]

A remarkable element in the *Letters to the Corinthians* is the personified view of Satan. Several times he is depicted as a real person.[81] In the Hebrew Bible this personified view on Evil is known only from the Book of Job 1–2, Zech. 3:2 and 1 Chron. 21:1. In all other cases where שׂטן as a noun or verb is used it

[78] Also others suggested a kind of redeemer myth as the background for Paul's Adam motif, see the overviews by Legarreta Castillo 2014, 1 and Lee 2012, 3, who writes: 'The existence of the Primal Man myth in the first century AD has been largely rejected by English-speaking New Testament scholarship due to its lack of evidence'.

[79] *Pace* Hultgren 2003, who does not pay attention to this particle.

[80] E.g. Lk. 10:15-19, see also our discussion above.

[81] E.g. 1 Cor. 5:5; 7:5; 2 Cor. 2:11; 11:14 and 12:7. See also 1 Thess. 2:18; 2 Thess. 2:9; 1 Tim. 1:20; 1 Tim. 5:5 and the texts on the person of Satan/Devil in the Book of Revelation, Rev. 2:8-9 and 2:13. In the latter text Satan is even said to have a throne in the city of Pergamon. Though meant metaphorically, the imagery is described quite realistic and personal. For this throne of Satan several possibillities have been raised, both specific and general, cf. Aune 1997a, 182. For Satan as a person, see also Rev. 2:24; 3:9; 20:7.

merely means 'adversary'. In parabiblical literature personified evil angels, including Satan(ael), are much more common. The Ugaritic myth provides insight in the prehistory of the figure of the Devil in Canaan. Apparently, this view was banned by the rabbis who were responsible for the canonical Hebrew Bible because it suggested a dualistic view of divine power. In folk religion, however, much of the original Canaanite ideas of a demonic personality survived. Also Jesus was acquainted with this personal view of Satan.[82]

1 Corinthians 15 has always been a mighty consolation to Christians confronted with the relentlessness of death.[83] Here the apostle Paul, with the absolutre confidence of the truly faithful, triumphantly announced Christ's victory over death, a victory in which ultimatley all his followers may share.

However, even if one does not experience any difficulty in sharing the emotional content of Paul's defiant question 'O Death, where is your sting?' (1 Cor. 15:55), it is still the exegete's duty to ask: What exactly do these words mean?

According to Paul the sting is sin,ʽαμαρτία (1 Cor. 15:56). One may be inclined to regard this as an abstract concept, but to Paul it was a personified, demonic power. It 'lives' (Rom. 7:9) to work 'death' in people who are subjected to its tyranny (Rom. 7:13). Is the 'Sting' a demonic power then? In Section 4.8 we have shown that in Ugarit he was a son of Môtu (Death) and that his name 'Sting' derives from the poisonous fangs of the big primordial serpent Ḥôrānu.

In 1 Cor. 15 Paul uses elements of the belief in resurrection that became increasingly popular in Palestine during the intertestamental period. We now know why this belief hardly ever found expression in the canonical books of the Hebrew Bible. It appears to have been one of the fundamental concepts of Baalism.[84] Traces of Canaanite mythology are present in the folk religions of Palestine and Paul assumes that his readers are acquainted with these traditions.The metaphor of the seed in 1 Cor. 15:42-44 derives from the so-called 'Gardens of Adonis', pots in which grains of wheat

---

[82] E.g. Mt. 4:1-10, Mk 1:12-13; Lk. 4:1-13, also Mk 8:33 par. Mt. 16:23 (Peter = Satan).

[83] The following lines are partly taken from De Moor 1988a.

[84] Cf. Spronk 1986; De Moor 2014.

were sown after the harvest to demonstrate the vitality of the seed that germinated in just a few days (De Moor 1987, 88-90, 266.) In 1 Cor. 15:4 Paul refers to Hos. 6:2 when he says that Christ was raised 'on the third day in accordance with the Scriptures'. Hosea himself, however, was far from accepting the idea of resurrection. On the contrary, with heavy irony he quotes from the mouth of idolaters who thought they could represent his God in Baalistic terms. What had been unacceptable to the Hebrew prophet was adopted by Paul in the light of the resurrection of Christ. In 1 Cor. 15:55 Paul is quoting again from the book of Hosea. In this case too the prophet did not mean to pronounce a message of hope.

However, already in the Hebrew Bible itself these demoniacal forces were subordinated to the God of Israel (Section 4.8). They do no longer constitute a menace to his faithful servants. Psalm 95:5 assures them,

לֹא־תִירָא מִפַּחַד לָיְלָה	You need not fear for the terror of the night,
מֵחֵץ יָעוּף יוֹמָם	for the arrow that flies by day,
מִדֶּבֶר בָּאֹפֶל יַהֲלֹךְ	for the pestilence that walks around by night,
מִקֶּטֶב יָשׁוּד צָהֳרָיִם	for the Sting that destroys at noonday.

' 'You need not fear ...' – Death lost his Sting already in the Hebrew Bible itself. In this respect there is no real tension between Paul's interpretation in 1 Corinthians 15 and the message of the prophet Hosea.

In his *Second Letter to the Corinthians* Paul seems to assume that the serpent deceived Eve in Eden, for in 2 Cor. 11:3 he says, 'But I am afraid that just as the serpent deceived Eve by his craftiness (his work), your thoughts will be led astray from a sincere and pure devotion to Christ.' Paul uses the narrative of Genesis 3,[85] but apparently also a rabbinical legend of the snake according to which Satan seduced Eve sexually in the garden.[86] In fact he does not state that any man or woman is related to Eve in their very nature, but that they have to be aware of the danger that the

---

[85] See the short discussion in Charlesworth 2010, 354. By a comparison of the specific words used in 2 Cor. 11:3 and Gen. 3 (𝔊) Ralph Martin has shown convincingly that Gen. 3 formed the major background for Paul in this specific verse (Martin 1986, 334).

[86] b. Yeb. 103b; ʿAbod. Zar. 22b; Shab. 146a, as noticed by Martin 1986, 333.

same fate may overcome them if they do not withstand the false teachers (cf. Beattie 2007, 211).

The emphasis on the seducing serpent might go back at least to 4 Macc. 18:8 where in an ambiguous parallelism the seduction of the snake is mentioned within the context of marriage. In 4 Macc. 18:6-8 a mother of seven sons declares, 'No seducer of the desert nor deceiver in the field corrupted me, nor did the seducing and beguiling serpent defile my maidenly purity' (Anderson 2009, 563). The parallelism between the seducer in the desert and the deceitful serpent no doubt have a sexual connotation, just as in Genesis 3. This ambiguity of the serpent metaphor also seems to be used by Paul, for in 2 Cor. 11:2 he describes his audience as a pure bride (παρθένος ἁγνή), who may be seduced by a serpent, just as Eve was seduced.[87] In this text Paul does mention seduction but he does not directly accuse Eve of any transgression, in contrast to his accusation of Adam in Rom. 5:12.

6.9 *The Letter to the Hebrews*

In this letter it is said that the Devil has the power of death, suggesting that he is a kind of deity who had the power to meet out death (Heb. 2:14). It is the only time in the New Testament that Satan/Devil is connected with death.[88] Where does this idea come from? It might be from the fact that Satan also was related to demons and illnesses, but one would expect more attestations if indeed his demoniacal character was related to death. According to the Ugaritic Adamic Myth the fallen god Ḥôrānu probably turned the Tree of Life in the vineyard of the gods into a Tree of Death, and in this way made death enter the world. Ḥôrānu was evidently associated with Death, but was not identical to him (Section 2.6).

[87] Cf. Beattie 2007, 212; Charlesworth 2010, 217.

[88] According to William Lane the Devil originally had no power over death, but gained control over death when he seduced humankind to rebel against God. Probably the relationship between Devil and death came into New Testament tradition through the text of Wisdom 2:23-24 (Lane 1991, 61). Grässer 1990, 147, argues the opposite position stating that Jewish traditions already formed the basis for the relationship of Devil and death. The texts he mentions, however, are not very convincing (Gen. 3:1-6; Rev. 20:10, 13).

6.10 *The First Letter to Timothy*

The first Letter to Timothy contains a view of women that contradicts other utterances of Paul, as well as what is known of Paul from *The Acts of Paul and Thecla*. Therefore, most scholars nowadays take the letters to Timothy and some other Paulinic texts as pseudo-Paulinian, probably meant to counteract the more friendly behavior of Paul towards women.[89] In 1 Tim. 2:13-15 the transgression of Eve is described rather bluntly,[90]

> (13) For Adam was formed first, then Eve;
> (14) and Adam was not deceived,
> but the woman was deceived and became a transgressor.
> (15) But she will be saved through childbearing,
> if she continues in faith and love and holiness, with modesty.

The author uses an interpretation of Genesis 3 that was current in a very restricted circle (Section 5.5)[91] to bolster up his claim that women have to keep silent in the congregations. In his opinion Adam was not deceived, but only Eve, though Genesis 3 tells the story differently. Adam tries to blame Eve for the transgression, whereas Eve tries to accuse the serpent. The deception of the serpent (though even this is not mentioned explicitly) might be interpreted also as seduction in Greek.[92] Several solutions have been given to this rather misogynistic statement. Bruce Barron points to the fact that in Romans 5 it is Paul himself who describes the fall as a deed of Adam, not of Eve, and therefore could hardly have argued for any male superiority. Furthermore, Paul emphasizes that all human beings sin, not only Adam. In Barron's opinion Paul addresses here the heretic (gnostic) women in Ephesus.[93] The author of 1 Timothy clearly builds his view on the text of Genesis 2–3, and starts from the fall. Not Adam was deceived, but his wife was.[94]

---

[89] Ehrman ^{2}2000, 369; Beattie 2007, 208.

[90] For a discussion of the question whether women were allowed to speak in church according to 1 Tim. 2, see Moo 1980; Moo 1981; Barron 1990; Perriman 1993.

[91] See also Beattie 2007, 210.

[92] Just as in 2 Cor. 11:3, see above, as well as Beattie 2007, 211-213.

[93] Barron 1990, 455; similarly Holtz 1980, 72.

Interesting with regard to the themes in the Adamic Myth is the meaning of childbearing (τεκνογονία) in this text. Whereas Genesis 3:16 announces labor as a kind of punishment, the author of 1 Timothy 2:15 promises the woman that she will be saved (σωθήσεται) by childbearing. Presumably this also formed the conclusion of the Canaanite Adamic Myth. A different interpretation of the verse is given by Kenneth Waters who defends the idea that 'childbearing' has to be read metaphorically, referring to the bearing of virtues.[95] Waters bases himself on the incongruence of grammatical numbers in verse 15, starting with a singular for the 'she' that will be saved, and the continuation with a third person plural in the second half of the verse. He lists three possibilities of which for our purpose the second is most interesting,

> If "they" refers to "Adam and Eve," then Eve's salvation becomes dependent on childbearing and on both her piety and Adams piety. Meanwhile, Adams salvation is dependent only on his own piety. These also are ideas that have no precedent in biblical tradition.'[96]

Waters' metaphorical reading is based on a lot of examples where words for children refer to virtues. However, it remains difficult to reconcile a metaphorical interpretation of 'childbearing' with the clear references to Genesis 3 in this text.[97] Also Stanley Porter comes to the conclusion that the woman who abides in faith, love and holiness, will be saved by the bearing of children.[98] The problem of the non-biblical utterance that a woman can be *saved* by

---

[94] Davidson 1988, 190, who stresses the fact that Gen. 3:16 is about a man and his wife, not about any man and any wife, and therefore also in 1 Tim. 2:14 γυνὴ 'woman' has to be read as a designation of the wife belonging to the husband. The reading '(any) woman' in verse 15 in that view is not justified.

[95] Waters 2004, esp. 705-710.

[96] Waters 2004, 709.

[97] Similarly William Mounce, who argues that Paul continues his treatment of Gen. 3 in verse 15. He even calls verse 15 a qualification of verse 14 (Mounce 2000).

[98] Porter 1993. Mounce 2000, 147 finally concludes, somewhat unsatisfactory, in reaction to those who refer to the serpent from which Eve has to be saved, 'The problem with placing too much emphasis on the serpent (...) is that Paul never mentions it here; it must be surmised from the analogy to Gen 3. And Eve was not saved from the serpent; she and the Ephesian women will be saved from sin.'

childbearing therefore still remains unsolved.[99] Another suggestion, often proposed is that τεκνογονία should not be rendered 'childbearing', but 'childbirth', thus referring to the birth of Jesus.[100] The problem with this text could be explained by the salvation of the human race from the poisonous snake in the Tree of Life by procreation (Section 2.5).

6.11 *The First Letter of John*

In the Johannine letter of 1 John the author adhorts his addressees to love each other and warns them not to follow the example of Cain, as it is said in 3:11-12,

> For this is the message which you have heard from the beginning, that we should love one another, and not be like Cain who was of the Evil One (ἐκ τοῦ πονηροῦ) and murdered his brother.

The word πονηρὸς 'the Evil One' is known as a designation for Satan/ Devil in Mt. 13:19.[101] The author refers back to the creation story by using the phrase ἀπ' ἀρχῆς 'from the beginning'. Furthermore, in verse 15, the author concludes that anyone who hates his brother is a murderer of a human being (ἀνθρωποκτόνος). The same word was used in John 8:44, where the Devil is called a murderer of humans from the beginning. So it can be concluded that just as in Jn 8:44,[102] 1 John relates Cain to the Devil and states that he has come from (ἐκ) 'the Evil One'. In the Bible Cain seems to have taken over some features of Ḥôrānu (see Section 4.3), which is confirmed by these Johannine texts relating Cain explicitly to the Evil One/Devil.

---

[99] See the different interpretations in the overviews and discussions by Porter 1993; Mounce 2000, 144-147; Schwartz 2011, 54-59.

[100] Cf. Mounce 2000, 145; Waters 2004, 711.

[101] The parallel text in Mk 4:15 uses 'Satan' and the parallel text in Lk. 8:12 'the Devil'. The text of Mt. 3:19 confirms that also in the Lord's Prayer (Mt. 6:13) πονηρὸς has to be taken as a designation of Satan/Devil. See also the use of πονηρὸς in Mt. 12:34 where the Pharisees are addressed as offspring of vipers. See our discussion of this text in Section 6.2. Other texts relating πονηρὸς to the Devil/Satan are Mt. 13:38; Jn 17:15; Eph. 6:12 (πονηρία, Achilles 1986, 566); 2 Thess. 3:3; 1 Jn 2:13-14; 5:18-19.

[102] See our discussion above, Section 6.5.

Already in 1 John 3:8 sinning from the beginning is ascribed to the Devil,

> He who commits sin is of the Devil (ἐκ τοῦ διαβόλου); for the Devil has sinned from the beginning (ἀπ' ἀρχῆς). The reason the Son of God appeared was to destroy the works of the Devil.

Also in 1 John 3:10 the author stresses the fact that one who sins is not of the children of God, but of the children of the Devil (τὰ τέκνα τοῦ διαβόλου). These verses confirm that in 1 John 3:11-12 Cain is seen as a child of the Devil, one of his offspring.

6.12 *The Book of Revelation*

In the apocalyptic Book of Revelation the fall of Satan is described in chapter 9 as the fall of a 'star' (Rev. 9:1), as also Ḥôrānu was known as the star Hilālu (the star Aldebaran) who fell from heaven. In a second verse it is described how the Abyss opened and smoke rose from it like the smoke from a gigantic furnace. The sun and the sky were darkened by this smoke. This recalls the fog on the mountains that obscured the sun according to KTU 1.107:44'.[103] In the Ugaritic text the poisonous fog is caused by the giant Bashan serpent that is cast from heaven on the earth. In fact, these descriptions go back to the interpretation of volcanoes the ancients gave when looking at the craters and evidently melted rocks in the Ḥaurān.

In verses 3-10 the army of the fallen star is described and in verse 11 it is concluded that they had as king over them the angel of the Abyss, and it is explained further that in Hebrew he was called Abbadon (the Destroyer) and similarly in Greek, Apollyon. Of Ḥôrānu it also was said that he was a Destroyer (*'abd*, *'abdy*) because he let loose the destructive poison (*'abd*).[104]

Finally in verses 16-17 the horses are described on which the army rides that has to kill the evil people. Especially interesting is the description of the breath from their mouths, 'out of their mouths came fire, smoke and sulfur'. There is a striking similar-

---

[103] See Sections 2.2 and 2.8.

[104] See our discussion of Abbadon in Sections 2.6; 4.5; 6.4). See also 1 QH[a] 11:16 where Abbadon (אבדון) is used either as a synonym of Sheol, the Pit and the abyss, or as the epithet of the Master of Sheol.

ity with the poisonous fog issuing from the poison-lips/mouth of Ḥôrānu, the fiery Leviathan.[105]

Revelation 12 suggests that the defeat of Satan was not complete and the struggle with him is still going on, and only at the end of times a definitive defeat of Satan will take place. It is generally agreed that ancient mythological traditions about a combat myth form the background of Revelation 12.[106]

A different view is defended by Jan Dochhorn (2010) who denies any myth about a Fall of Satan in primeval times, because this would neither have been attested in the Septuagint, nor in the Hebrew Bible nor in the New Testament (Dochhorn 2010, 257) and even the apostolic Fathers would be unaware of such a story. Also Isaiah 14 about the fall of Hellel does not refer to such a story in his view for it refers to a historical king. Of Lk. 10:18 he states that this text is no doubt eschatological. The idea of Dochhorn is that those who assume a myth about the fall of Satan in primeval times turn the relationships over time upside down. He is of the opinion that all descriptions of a Fall of Satan were meant to be read eschatologically. Only in the third century CE the church fathers would have developed an idea of a primeval Fall of Satan on the basis of the eschatological texts that were there earlier (Dochhorn 2010, 258-259).

Since the writers of apocalyptic literature often addressed questions of their own time in narratives formulated in the past or future tense it is questionable whether Dochhorn's argument can be sustained. Moreover, we have shown that passges like Isa. 14 and

---

[105] See also Job 41:11-13[19-21], and the iconography of dragons depicted as flaming creatures. See Section 2.8.

[106] Collins 1976, esp. 57-100; Busch 1996. esp. 26 who enumerates Persian, Greek, Babylonian and Egyptian parallels as possible background, but does not mention any Ugaritic or Old Testament parallels. See also Nanz 2001 who discusses Isa. 14 as well as quite a number of pseudepigraphic works that point to a fall of Satan in primordial times; Koch 2004, 138-157, who enumerates ten specific features as so-called *Mythologemen*, among them the red seven-headed dragon, the combat with the dragon and the miraculous salvation by the newborn child, and the fall of Satan. Cf. Koch 2004, 139; also Van Henten 2006, esp. 182, 184, who refers to both the Hellenistic myth about Python and his slayers, and the Egyptian myth of Seth (Van Henten 2006, 185-186), that also contain the theme of the pregnant woman.

Ezek. 28 polemicize with religious concepts of Israel's neighbors (Sections 4.5-7). Our theory about the Canaanite background of the Adamic myth helps to understand so many elements in the Book of Revelation that the whole issue must be re-examined. In the Adamic Myth humanity is threatened by the venomous serpentine offspring of the Evil One, Ḥôrānu the Leviathan, the serpent in the macrocosmic Garden of God. After his turn about he fathered the Kôṯarātu-midwives to ensure that procreation of mortal humans would continue, even though the threat of death to life on earth would remain forever.[107] This myth was actualized in the ritual for the Ugaritic New Year festival (Section 2.5) which shows that past, present and future were interwoven in Canaanite religion.

Rev. 12:9 (par. 20:2) describes Satan as the great dragon and the ancient serpent[108] who is said to be the same as the Devil and Satan. Therefore this text has often been taken as the first text identifying the serpent in Genesis 3 with Satan/Devil.[109] However, as we have demonstrated above, the equation goes back to Canaanite mythological texts dating from the thirteenth century BCE which were probably transmitted through the channel of folk tradition.

The dragon in Revelation 12 has features of both the monster Leviathan with its seven heads (Rev. 12:3, par. Rev. 13:1; 17:1, 7, 9) [110] and of the Devil/Satan. This agrees with the figure of

---

[107] Section 2.8 (Fig. 14) and Section 2.10.

[108] John N. Day 1998, 431, adopting a proposal of Albright, renders the Hebrew expression נחש בריח in Job 26:13 and Isa. 27:1 'ancient serpent', thus creating Old Testament support for the expression in Rev. 12:9 and 20:2. This reading is based on Arabic *bāriḥ* 'yesterday, past'. However, if this were true, one would expect the rendering 'ancient serpent' also in the Greek and Latin translations of Job 26:13 and Isa. 27:1, not 'the fleeing one'. Also in Ugaritic and Hebrew the meaning 'fleeing' is widely accepted, cf. Del Olmo Lete & Sanmartín 2003, 236-237; *HAHAT*, 175; *DCH*, vol. 2, 263, and rightly so, because 'to flee' is the normal meaning of the verb *brḥ*. See Section 2.8 where we explain the background of this 'flight'.

[109] Cf. Martinek 1996, 101; Fabry 1986, 392; Aune 1997b, 696; Koch 2004, 247-252, often with bold statements and references to both Rev. 12:9 and *Wisdom of Solomon* 2:24 as the earliest proofs of the identification of Satan with the serpent/dragon.

[110] Cf. KTU 1.5:I.3, see Section 2.10, with Rev. 12:3, see also 13:1 and 17:3. Koester 2014, 545, seems to be unaware of the fact that the sea monster

Hilālu/Ḥôrānu described in Ch. 2 above, who also is the Evil One and could take on the shape of the primordial serpent threatening the world. Both seem to have been cast out of heaven onto the earth, and they are even said to be thrown down in the (Syrian) desert.[111] Revelation 12 emphasizes that the dragon is cast down, as it is said in v. 9 (cf. Rev. 8:10; 9:1; 12:3-4, 10, 12, 13),

> And the great dragon was thrown down, that ancient serpent, who is called the Devil and Satan, the deceiver of the whole world – he was thrown down to the earth, and his angels were thrown down with him.

The author of Revelation 12 also seems to be aware of the dwelling place of the dragon in the desert (Rev. 12:6, 14; 17:3). Revelation 2:13 refers to Satan's sanctuary as positioned in Pergamon, well-known in the first and second century CE for its Asclepion, the healing center of the god Asclepius (Potter 1992, 230), who is linked to Apollo and was also known under the name of Apolyon.[112] Asclepios was the god related to the serpent by his serpent-entwined rod. He is a late manifestation of Ḥôrānu/Ḥôrōnu (Section 2.11).

The great dragon is horned, like the huge serpent in the Ugaritic myth (Sections 2.8 and 4.8), and since he is ancient and has deceived the whole world he must be the primordial serpent of Gen. 3 who lives in enmity with the woman (Gen. 3:15). Since the woman

---

Leviathan that in the Old Testament has only 'many heads' (Ps. 74:14) in Ugarit definitely was described with 'seven heads', under the names of Lôtānu (Hebrew Liwyātān) and Tunnānu (Hebrew Tannīn). He therefore relates the monster merely to Typhon with a hundred heads and the Hydra with nine heads, and to the four beasts in Dan. 7:2-8 that have a total of seven heads and he concludes that the number seven in Rev. 12:3 would be just a literary device, pointing to a complete set.

[111] Ps. 74:14; Ezek. 29:5; 32:3-6 and see Sections 2.4 to the end and 2.8. Contrast Koester 2014, 568, who states that the beast coming from the sea is Satan's agent. He relates the beast to the four beasts of Dan. 7:2-8, and takes it as an animal that only replicates the dragon of 12:3 (Koester 2014, 569). On the basis of the Ugaritic Myth and imagery, however, it seems more likely that both the sevenheaded dragon as well as the beast and Satan are descriptions of one and the same Evil Power, who was able to transform himself in many disguises.

[112] Meaning 'destroyer', see Rev. 9:11. For Apolyon/Apollos, see Aune 1997b, 535.

of Rev. 12 is pregnant it is also remarkable that she and her child are saved (Rev. 12:5, 14-16). After his repentance Ḥôrānu became a protector of marriage and childbirth. According to Rev. 12:17 the dragon becomes furious about the rescue of the woman and therefore strides forward to make war to the rest of her offspring. This reminds us of Ḥôrānu's threat to the entire world of the living. In the Canaanite myth the continuation of life on earth can only be guaranteed by procreation.[113]

David Aune sees it as problematic that Revelation 12 starts in heaven whereas in v. 6 the woman first mentioned in v. 1 is said to have fled into the desert. In his opinion this contradicts the fact that the scene described takes place in heaven. However, Revelation 12 depicts the fall of the seven-headed dragon when he is thrown down on the earth. From the Canaanite as well as the Old Testament texts it appears that he is thrown specifically into the desert. So, if it is stated that the woman fled into the desert, hearers who were acquainted with the ancient myth of the fall of the Evil One into the desert could have known that the woman would not be safe, especially not in the desert. Generally, the desert was seen as a place that formed a safe haven for people who were threatened and pursued (Aune 1997b, 691), but this does not count for the woman in Revelation 12.[114] Especially Rev. 12:14 makes sense, where it is explicitly said that the woman was kept away from the serpent. In the light of the ancient Near Eastern material it is likely that in Revelation 12 there is no clear difference between the seven-headed dragon,[115] the ancient serpent[116] and the Devil[117] or Satan.[118] All are manifestations of the same being.

---

[113] See Section 2.5, as well as our discussion of 1 Timothy 2:15 above. See also our discussion of the Qumran text 1 QH[a] 11:8-18 in Section 5.9. It might be that in 1 QH[a] 11:16 'the S[heo]l [of A]bbad[on]' has to be read, instead of the generally proposed reading 'S[heo]l [and A]bbad[on]'.

[114] Similarly Giesen 1990, 272-273, who states that it is most probable that the dragon already has fallen on the earth before the birth of the child, so that the dragon can threaten both the woman and the child. In his opinion it is in any case clear that the fight in heaven has taken place before the flight of the woman into the desert.

[115] Greek δράκων, 12:3, 4, 7, 9, 13, 16, 17; 13:2, 4, 11; 16:13 and 20:2.

[116] Greek ὄφις, Rev. 12:9, 14, 15; 20:2.

[117] Greek Διάβολος, Rev. 12:9.

[118] Greek Σατανᾶς, Rev. 12:9.

Several texts in the Book of Revelation mention regions of fire and sulfur as the places where the dragon and his companions will be judged.[119] They will be cast into the lake of fire that burns with sulfur (Rev. 19:20; 20:10; 21:8.). Furthermore Rev. 15:2 states that those who conquered the dragon and the evil people were standing on something which looked like a sea of glass mingled with fire. Also Rev. 4:6 mentions this sea of glass, looking like crystal and describes it as laying before the throne of God.

In our opinion the writer of Revelation exploited the volcanic nature of mountains of Ilu/El and Ḥôrānu for his imagery,

1. The Ararat region was a volcanic region. The Book of Revelation describes the place *before* the throne of God as a sea of glass mingled with fire (Rev. 4:6). A 'sea of crystal' is mentioned in *Mek. de-Rabbi Ishmael*, Beshallah 5 on Exodus 15:8, 'The sea congealed on both sides and became a sort of glass crystal'. In the Ugaritic text KTU 1.83:5-6, it was said that the sea monster Yammu should be freezed (solidified, see our discussion in Section 2.8). Could it be that Revelation 4:6 describes a region with solidified lava (fire!) and ice?

2. The region at the feet of the mountain of El was the vineyard of the Gods, most probably the fertile grounds around Mt Ararat (El's mountain) where viticulture began (Section 2.4). Rev. 14:18-19 speaks of the vineyard on earth where the fruit is gathered. At first sight this image seems to refer back to Isa. 27:1-5 where both God's victory over the great dragon or serpent Leviathan is described, as well as God's vineyard as the place where the final judgment of the world will take place, but as we have seen Isa. 27 itself was dependent on Canaanite mythological tradition.

3. The place of judgment is a place of fire and sulfur, in other New Testament texts this place is called Gehenna. According to Mt. 5:22 it is the Gehenna of fire.[120] This is always

[119] Rev. 14:10; 19:20; 20:10; 21:8, see also Rev. 9:17-18, about certain 'horses' spitting fire.

[120] Gehenna as the place of judgment also is mentioned in Mt. 5:22, 29-30; 10:28; 18:9; 23:33: Mk 9:43, 45, 47; Lk. 12:5; Jas 3:6.

related to the valley of Hinnom where the refuse of the city of Jerusalem was burned. However, this does not explain the 'sulfur'. The desert area of Bashan and Ḥaurān where the great sea serpent was thought to have been thrown down was a volcanic region and even today sulfuric vents abound in the region.

4. In Rev. 9:14 the sixth angel is said to release the four killer-angels that were bound above the great river Euphrates. The binding of the serpent-demons was a theme both in Ugarit and in pseudepigraphic literature. Rev. 9:14 too refers to a scenery at the location of Eden, at the feet of Mt Ararat. This might be compared to Isa. 27:12 where the final judgment also starts from the region of the Euphrates and where in the same chapter also the fall of the dragon/serpent is announced (Isa. 27:1) and the vineyard of YHWH is foreseen(Isa. 27:2-6).

5. Rev. 22:1-2 describes the place of the throne as positioned on a mountain where rivers spring. Generally, this is taken as a reference to Ezek. 47:1-12, but in the wider context of the Book of Revelation one might ask whether the author was also acquainted with a broader tradition that also had knowledge of the mountain of God in the Ararat region where the four tributaries of Euphrates and Tigris sprang (Section 2.4). The Tree of Life (Rev. 2:7) will serve the pious who attain God's Paradise. According to Rev. 22:1 Trees of Life line both sides of the river in Paradise and since they yield fruit each month, it might be hybrids.

In his dissertation on Revelation 12 Michael Koch did a lot of research into myth and mythic themes in the Book of Revelation and concludes for Chapter 12 that the author, although using well-known traditions of myth, nevertheless combined several themes into what he calls a *Panopticum* of Evil.[121] He sees a fascinating composition in which originally separate components were integrated into a completely new image and warns that this is an artificial product that runs the risk to be splitted up into separate images. Koch provides schemes[122] in which he visualizes the

[121] 'Apk. 12 als Panoptikum des Bösen' (Koch 2004, 274-280).

images that would have been combined in a unique way by the author of Revelation 12. Of course, Koch is right in stating that the author of the Book of Revelation constructed a fully new literary text including a new description of Evil, using well-known ancient imagery. However, the combination of several features he mentions could already be observed with the figure of Ḥôrānu in the Adamic Myth. Especially the equation of serpent, dragon and Satan/Devil as mentioned in Rev. 12:9 also argues in favor of Ḥôrānu, who is both the Evil Prince, as well as a serpent, a sea monster and the star Aldebaran. Deities could manifest themselves in different forms, sometimes in more than one form at the same time. In dealing with these ancient mythological narratives one should keep in mind the capacity of metamorphosis which implies that one and the same personage could appear in many different shapes. Koch shows that evil angels were often seen as stars that fell from heaven (Koch 2004, 256-258). The texts of Ugarit use the same word for angels as the Hebrew Bible (*ml'ak*) and the pantheon consisted of many divine beings, with different ranking. The systematic differentiation between 'God' and 'angels' seems to be a typically Jewish invention to safeguard God from any competitor. Ḥôrānu was a divine being who originally belonged to the Canaanite host of heaven.

Koch separates the idea of the dragon from that of the serpent, and that of the deceiving serpent from the accusing Satan, but the circumstance that both the serpent and the Evil One were already combined in Ḥôrānu makes it impossible to separate the serpent of Genesis 3 from Satan the accuser in Job. In folk tradition they already must have been known as one and the same Evil One.[123] Koch calls it the double look of Revelation 12 and is of the opinion that in this text different traditions have been glued together. By this clever artificial combination of both Jewish and pagan traditons the dragon would have become a universalistic threatening power. Koch has the idea that the combination of serpent, dragon and Satan/Devil took place for the first time in Rev. 12:9 (repeated in Rev. 20:2) and is connected here with the name of Abbadon for the first time (Koch 2004, 316-317). However, as we

---

[122] Koch 2004, 249, 252, 263, 276.
[123] Cf. Section 2.3 and Appendix 1 on Abbadon.

have shown above, all these combinations were already present in the ancient Canaanite Myth of Adammu and the Fall of Ḥôrānu.

Rev. 2:7 (repeated in 2:11 and 2:17) declares that all those who conquered evil will be granted access to 'the Tree of Life which is in the paradise of God'. Revelation 22 also gives a description of God's dwelling place, situated in a well-watered region (Rev. 22:1-2). The river sprang from the throne of God, a description reminding us of the description of paradise in Gen. 2:9-14 and of the abode of the Ugaritic god El, both situated at the sources of the two rivers Euphrates and Tigris. On ancient cylinder seals the deity is depicted enthroned on his mountain (Sections 2.4 and 2.8). According to Rev. 22:2 there are special trees on both sides of the river that gave their fruit monthly. These trees also provide healing. The motifs given in Revelation 22 clearly refer to a restoration of Paradise (Aune 1998, 1178) where renewed access to the Tree of Life forms a symbol of eternal life (Aune 1998, 1222).

6.13 *Conclusions on New Testament*

Also in the New Testament traces of ancient myths seem to have been preserved, be it in patches, and we will list them here more or less categorized.

1. Satan is seen as the 'Enemy' as well as the 'Destroyer' (6.4; 6.12) just as Ḥôrānu. He was rebelling against the divine ruler of the world and therefore punished (6.5). He is described as a person who can seize human beings. This personified view of Satan/Devil presupposes a mythological view on the Evil One. Evil apparently is not yet entirely demythologized in the New Testament (6.3; 6.7; 6.8; 6.11).

2. Just like Ḥôrānu was the father of snakes and vipers, this idea also appears to be known among the New Testament authors, as well as by Jesus and his contemporaries. Jesus calls the Pharisees the brood of vipers in the context of a talk about Satan (6.2; 6.4), and implicitly, children of the Devil (6.5). A magician thus could be named a son of the Devil too (6.5) and even all people who sin could be called children of the Devil (6.11). Contrary to this view on evil people, people who did not sin, like Jesus and his followers, were said to be able to fight what was produced by the Devil, namely serpents, scorpions and demons (6.4).

The identification of Satan/Devil with the primordial serpent is attested several times in the New Testament (6.2; 6.4; 6.6; 6.7; 6.12), not only in the explicit texts of Rev. 12:9 and 20:2 (6.12). Thus, these texts cannot be taken as the first references to this identification. As shown above (Section 2.8) already in Canaan a Devil was known who could manifest himself in the form of a giant serpent/dragon with seven heads who threatens the entire world (6.12).

3. The fall of Satan as described by Jesus shows many similarities with the fall of Hēlēl in Isaiah 14 and the reconstructed fall of the Canaanite Ḥôrānu/Hilālu (6.4; 6.5; 6.12). It is suggested that Jesus was present from the beginning of creation and witnessed the punishment of Satan, still before the transgression of Adam (6.4). Satan just as Ḥôrānu also was described as a star who fell from heaven (6.12).

4. In the Old Testament the role of Ḥôrānu seems to be taken over by Cain in Genesis 4 (Section 4.3). This idea occurs also a few times in the New Testament (6.5; 6.11).

5. The New Testament ascribes the first sin to Satan/Devil (6.5) as well as to Adam (6.7; 6.8) and, to a lesser extent, also to Eve (6.8; 6.10).

6. Several New Testament texts relate Satan/Devil to the desert (6.2; 6.12) as well as to a place of fire, sulfur and judgment, like the volcanic desert region in which the Canaanite rebel god Ḥôrānu had been thrown down in his manifestation as a huge sea dragon. In the New Testament the place is called Gehenna[124] or just the Abyss where smoke rose from it (6.2; 6.12). Just like Ḥôrānu Satan/Devil is depicted as both a serpent as well as a sevenheaded dragon, comparable to the sevenheaded Lôtānu/Leviathan in ancient Ugarit (6.2; see Section 2.8).

7. It is not impossible that a myth about a heavenly, primordial human being was known to scribes of the New Testament (6.8).

[124] Later to be thought located near Jerusalem, after 2 Kgs 23:10.

This Adam was present before the creation of the world, but did not take part in creation (6.8). The second Adam has to act as a savior of the earth, just like the Canaanite Adammu who was sacrificed to lift the curse of Ḥôrānu, the Evil One (2.3). However, in Ugarit Adammu was reduced to mortal human proportions. The difference is that in the New Testament this Adam understandably has no role as a savior for the heavenly world (6.8) and that the second Adam regains his divine status, as was thought earlier about the archangels (5.3) and Enoch (5.10), but is also promised to all righteous people who persevere to the end (5.8; 5.9; 5.10).

8. Also the New Testament seems to be acquainted with a tradition about first human beings bitten by a venomous serpent (6.5; 6.6). The heavenly rebel Ḥôrānu made life on earth impossible by turning the Tree of Life into a Tree of Death by sending a serpent with a deadly poison into the tree. Thus Ḥôrānu was also related to Death. The two are even explicitly paired there (Section 2.1). In the New Testament the relationship between Satan/Devil and Death is mentioned rarely (6.9), but like Satan Death is sometimes personified (6.7).

9. The ambiguity of the serpent in the Adamic myth also occurs in Paul's letter to the Corinthians, where sexuality is presupposed in the ambiguous language about Eve's seduction by the primordial snake (6.8). This too is not new since it is already attested in Qumran (5.9). The idea that the human race was threatened by Satan from the beginning and has to to be saved by procreation not only is suggested in the Ugaritic Adamic myth and other oriental myths (Section 2.5 and Chapter 3) but also in the New Testament (6.10; 6.12).

10. According to the New Testament Satan could do evil as well as good, like Ḥôrānu who repented. He was even supposed to have healing powers (6.2; 6.5). Jesus is even compared to this healing serpent, as the one who finally defeats the venomous poison of the primordial serpent (6.5).

11. According to the Canaanite texts as well as some other ancient Near Eastern texts the mountain of El originally was Mt Ararat. The region below it was a paradisiacal vineyard (2.4). Traces of this concept are also present in the New Testament. The throne of God stands at a sea of glass mingled with fire and the final judgment takes place in a vineyard which no doubt must have been God's vineyard (6.12). In paradise, described as a well-watered region, there once has been a Tree of Life and at the end of times those who conquered evil get access to this restored Tree of Life (6.12).

12. Folk religion in New Testament times seems to have preserved some features of the Canaanite god Baʿlu (Baal) as the conqueror of the dangerous sea and the monsters in it. Just like Baʿlu, Jesus defeats these demonic powers (6.3). Jesus binds the demon who could not be bound by the Canaanite Adammu (6.3). The demons living in the land of the Gerasenes (Bashan region) are called 'Legion', a name also known from Ugarit for demons related to the offspring of Ḥôrānu. The tradition about the victory of life over death as known from the Ugaritic god Baʿlu is ascribed to Jesus, as the ultimate conqueror of demons and death (6.3). Also the disciples of Jesus are said to have the power to defeat the demonic powers, symbolized by the treading on serpents and scorpions (6.4).

As compared to the Hebrew Bible the New Testament takes the personifications of evil more seriously, including the Devil, the Prince of Evil. Only in some very late passages the Hebrew Bible itself seems to admit that only at the end of times the evil powers of this world will be defeated for good. This line appears to have been developed further in parabiblical literature and in the New Testament. As we have indicated several times before in this book, we suspect that the Canaanite Adamic Myth we recovered lived on among the ordinary people to whom Jesus' message appealed, despite official criticism as voiced in Isaiah 14, Ezekiel 28 and similar texts. Jewish magical texts dating from many centuries later demonstrate that also in Judaism this kind of popular religion was never totally repressed (Section 2.10).

7
General Conclusions

7.1 *Introduction*

Actually no conclusions to this book should have been written, because it is only the first attempt to formulate a new inroad into problems that have vexed interpreters of the Bible for at least two millennia. Once again we point out the need for a theory which might help to solve these problems.[1] It has long been suspected that biblical accounts of the primeval history partially rest on Canaanite mythology, but to the frustration (or relief) of scholars such a myth has not been identified hitherto. We quote some of them,

> The Canaanite Eden or First Man myth is yet to be recovered (May 1962, 167).
>
> Die zahlreichen Spekulationen über den mutmaßlichen mythologischen Hintergrund der Totenklage Ez 28 haben zu keinem schlüssigen Ergebnis geführt (Greenberg 2005, 252).
>
> There is no evidence that the paradise motif was borrowed from extrabiblical literature (Batto 2013, 83).

Let it be clear from the outset that we do not at all imagine to have presented the kind of fast and easy solution that is considered 'cool' nowadays. We go the difficult road of trying to disentangle the often conflicting evidence we found in literature and iconography from times long gone by.[2] We think it is important to view the solutions those people envisaged with a certain amount of sympathy and perhaps a fleeting moment of recognition. We may think that they lived in utterly primitive times, but on the timescale of the evolution of the human race they lived only yesterday.

---

1 See already Sections 2.11; 4.5; 4.6.

2 'The language of a literary composition must be understood in the light of its cultural milieu, for words and phrases carry significant overtones that are missed if one interprets them exclusively in terms of what their translated equivalents mean in a contemporary setting' (May 1962, 166).

The basis for the theory we develop in this work rests on admittedly fragile evidence: primarily one exceptionally well preserved Ugaritic tablet (KTU 1.100, Appendix 2), a second one which is so badly damaged that large parts of it can only be translated on a conjectural basis (KTU 1.107, Appendix 1), and a third one the existence of which we suspect even though not a single fragment of it seems to have been discovered so far. However, we were able to reconstruct its contents partially, primarily on the basis of a passage in the *Phoenician History* of Philo of Byblos. Anyone who feels that one should not launch a theory on such a narrow basis definitely has a valid point. However, if such a theory appears to solve a number of long-standing problems, it deserves to be tested in future research. This is an established procedure which in many cases has proved to be benificial to the further development of branches of scholarship. So we feel free to summarize our theory here.

7.2 *Summary of the Results*

7.2.1 *El the Creator*

In Chapter 2 we demonstrated that in Ugarit and other Canaanite states the Creator of All was El who in Ugarit was still called Ilu.[3] No other great creator or creatress in the ancient Near East bore the same name, with the exception of the God of Israel (Chapter 3). So it seems logical to surmise that the religion of Israel should be seen as rooted in its Canaanite environment.[4]

El created in various manners. His main wife was Ashera, mother of his seventy children and a creatress in her own right. Creation by word or thought alone is attested for both of them. However, like other creators in the ancient Near East, El also 'created' by impregnating other goddesses and earthly women. On other occasions he creates by molding clay like a potter. El creates not merely at the beginning of the cosmos, but many times after. So the Canaanites believed in *creatio continua*, as did some

[3] The ending *u* was a case ending which disappeared in the first millennium BCE. In order to avoid cumbersome repetition we shall cite names in this Chapter according to their later Hebrew form where this is possible.
[4] Cf. Korpel 1990; De Moor 1997.

biblical writers. Some lesser deities in the Ugaritic pantheon were also able to create, be it on a lower level.

Here it becomes clear already that at a certain moment the Hebrew concept of the Creator must have split off from its Canaanite roots. In a henotheistic or monotheistic theology there was no room anymore for worship of a female deity and for sexual reproduction of deities. Scholars are deeply divided over the date and reasons for this rupture, but in our opinion it must have taken place fairly early. However, we shall not pursue this issue here. It is possible that the name *Yw* in a Ugaritic myth designates the God of Israel, but not as a Creator. On the contrary, he is ridiculed there, just as Israel would ridicule the deities of Canaan later on.

El dwelt in a 'tent' at the four headwaters of the Euphrates and Tigris. Possibly this 'tent' was the heavenly firmament itself, but in any case it is also described as a luxurious palace,[5] both in the Ugarit and in the Bible. We have strong reasons to surmise that El was thought to dwell on Mt Ararat, the highest point of Turkey/Armenia and the mountain on which according to biblical and Mesopotamian accounts the ark presumably landed. This background explains a biblical name of God, El Shadday, 'El the Mountain-dweller'.[6] Mt Ararat is an extinct volcano with two peaks, one of which is called a 'beaker, crater' in Ugaritic. People believed that the sun went under between these two peaks, taking the dead along. The Ugaritic tablet KTU 1.107 mentions a 'vineyard of the great gods' which seems to have been the predecessor of the garden of Eden.

7.2.2 *Rebellion against El*

Our investigation has resulted in the conclusion that according to all major religions of the ancient Near East the first rebellion against the Creator took place in the divine world (Chapter 3).[7]

---

[5] Like the palace of Baal on Mt Zaphon which in reality was just a gold-edged mass of clouds. Cf. Korpel 1990, 82-83.

[6] Traditionally, but erroneously translated as 'God Almighty'.

[7] Many scholars have considered the possibility that the biblical accounts of the primeval history as well as parabiblical traditions like the *Book of the Watchers* were ultimately derived from ancient Near Eastern myths, e.g. Hess & Tsumura 1994; Kvanvig 1988; 2011; Wright 2005, 48-49; Walton 2011. In our opinion the Ugaritic material we presented here provides the

In the few cases where primeval humans were involved in rebellions against the highest deity they were still divine or semi-divine beings. This is an important point to comprehend the Canaanite concept of the garden of the gods. Divine status implied enormous proportions, also of their environment. The garden must have been thought of as covering the entire country of Armenia, and possibly more. Initially there was probably one Tree of Life[8] in the Canaanite version of Paradise, an enormously tall 'Weltbaum', the top of which touched heaven.

In Ugarit the rebel god was Ḥôrānu, known in Phoenician, Egyptian and Hebrew as Ḥaurān or Ḥôrōn. There are strong indications that in the lost first tablet of the Ugaritic myth he rebelled against El and was punished by expulsion from the volcanic mountain of El and thrown down in the Ḥaurān, part of the Syrian desert, where he started his own volcanic activity. His revenge seems to have consisted in making the Tree of Life inaccessible to the gods by positing himself as a huge serpent in the tree,[9] a monster resembling the biblical Leviathan, whose poison turned the Tree of Life into a Tree of Death. As a result the whole world started to wither and a poisonous fog enveloped everything. So the identification of the Devil with a poisonous serpent has a very long history. The great gods decided to send one of them, Adam, to the earth with the assignment to undo this deplorable situation. They gave him total power over the earth, but when he arrived at the tree, the serpent bit him immediately and he started to die. However, the sun goddess took pity on Adam and summoned all the great deities to charm the serpent before it would be too late. Because his own offspring, the serpents, would also be destroyed by such a massive alliance, Ḥôrōn enters the garden, uproots the Tree of Death and detoxifies it by removing its morbid growths.

---

hitherto missing link between Mesopotamia and Israel.

[8] One might ask why it is so often a plant or the fruit of a tree which was thought to have the potential of providing eternal life (Gilgamesh, Adamic Myth, Bible, etc.). The answer is simple: magicians and doctors in Antiquity performed 'miracles' with botanical medicines. It is somewhat ironic that to this very day some people still hope that one day medicines will help us to prolong life infinitely.

[9] Metamorphosis, which did not preclude that he manifested himself at the same time in other shapes.

Life can resume its course, be it in a reduced, mortal state. Though the Tree of Life was never restored in full, Ḥôrān became the licensed executioner of other rebels on earth and in heaven.

In his astral manifestation Ḥôrōn was Hilāl, the bright star Aldebaran which is sometimes occulted by the crescent moon in the early morning so that the star seems to disappear from the night sky. The well-known symbolism of the Ottoman-Turkish flag is derived from the phenomenon of Aldebaran reappearing next to the crescent. Iconographic representations of this happening are already found on artefacts from the second millenium BCE, also from Ugarit. Isaiah 14 mocks at Hilāl, mangling his name to Hēlēl, 'Wail!'.

7.2.3 *Adam's Wife*

As for Adam's wife, she too was a goddess in Ugarit (and many other countries) under the name of Kubaba who in the Greek tradition became Kybele, the mother of all. In the preserved parts of the Ugaritic myth no transgression of a divine commandment by either Adam or his wife is mentioned. We have given our reasons to believe that the inculpation of Eve in Genesis 3 was the consequence of putting the blame for the fall of Jerusalem on idolatry by women (Section 4.3, differences No. 10). After Adam has received the lethal bite, the sun goddess seems to promise him 'a good-natured woman' to start the cycle of procreation with her, thus ensuring the preservation of human life despite the inevitable death of every individual (KTU 1.107:27'). In his astral manifestation as the morning star Hilāl, Ḥôrān fathered the Kôṯarāt, seven divine midwives who became responsible for the preservation of life through conception and childbirth. So Ḥôrān was an ambiguous god whose character also had a positive side. This ambiguity is also discernable in later representations of the Devil.[10]

7.2.4 *Critical Reception in the Hebrew Bible*

The differences with the canonical Hebrew tradition, discussed in Chapter 4, are vast. The name of Ḥôrōn survives in geographical names only,[11] apparently because no divine rival of God was tol-

---

[10] Many examples in Charlesworth 2010.

[11] Among them 3Q15 (Copper Scroll) where 'cellars of Ḥôrōn' are mentioned

erated anymore. Yet even Genesis 1 contains some traces of its Canaanite background, for example the androgynic nature of the first humanoids.[12] The location and description of Eden matches the Canaanite concept of the garden or vineyard of El in so many respects that its location at the headwaters of Euphrates and Tigris cannot be doubted anymore, but the Hebrew writers adapted the account to their own world view. In Genesis too the loss of eternal life is replaced by procreation, but the explicit descriptions of sexuality in the Ugaritic myths are missing in Genesis 3 where the discovery of nakedness generates shame (Gen. 3:7).

There are no indications in Ugarit that Adam and his wife died because they had transgressed a commandment of a deity. However, Genesis 3 makes normal humans responsible for the choice between good and evil. No experience, not even the extraordinary event of meeting a speaking serpent, should deflect humankind from obeying God's commandment. Human beings can no longer hide behind some offense committed by a divine being in primordial times, but have to face the consequences of the fact that they themselves are responsible for the choice between good or evil.

In our opinion this too was the inevitable consequence of the adoption of a rather strict definition of henotheism or monotheism in postexilic Judaism. If no deity can be blamed for the origin of evil, humankind itself, being so close to godhead, must have comitted the first sin. The grand idea of Judaism was to attribute this not to fate or divine providence, but to allow human beings a free choice between good and evil. Obviously humans will always try to make their Maker co–reponsible, as Adam attempts to do in Eden (Gen. 3:12) and as some manuscripts of the *Wisdom of Ben Sira* state as a fact (cf. Section 5.5).

It has become clear that chapters like Isaiah 14 and Ezekiel 28–32 ridicule the religion of Israel's Canaanite neighbors, in particular their belief that after their death kings and great heroes would be united with El in his superb garden of delight. Later on this concept would be democratized so that all righteous people

(3Q15:IX.7). However, see Korpel's proposal at the end of Section 4.8.

[12] We agree with Rebecca Watson that in the wake of Hermann Gunkel's epochal work *Schöpfung and Chaos* (Gunkel 1895) scholars have all too eagerly sought for chaos motifs in the Hebrew Bible (Watson 2005).

attain this blissful state. The expulsion of the Canaanite Devil Ḥôrōn, the antipole of El, from the mountain of the great gods offered Israelite prophets a perfect argument against the idea that divine status could guarantee indemnity against punishment for sins committed.

7.2.5 *Reintegration of Mythical Motives Later On*

Despite this polemic against the religions of their neighbors, Canaanite traditions continue to glimmer through in the later parts of the Hebrew Bible and in parabiblical literature. Especially in the parabiblical literature and the New Testament which we discussed in Chapters 5 and 6 the number of apparent parallels, adopted or disputed, becomes so great that it is impossible to repeat them all in this final summary. We suspect that these parallels reached Judaism through channels of folk religion which also explains the presence of vestiges of Canaanite lore in rabbinical literature (Sections 2.3; 2.8; 6.8).

Some examples of this reintegration of Canaanite mythical motives must suffice here. Although the evil primordial serpent is said to have been defeated by God in texts like Ps. 74:14 and Job 26:13, the Isaiah Apocalypse states that his final defeat will take place only in a remote future (Isa. 27:1). This is in line with the Ugaritic belief that the powers of evil can never be mastered in any definitive way (Section 2.10). This return to a fundamental religious concept of the Canaanites gave rise to an enormous proliferation of apocalyptic literature and a renewed interest in the Devil and his demonic helpers. In its final shape the Hebrew Bible takes the demonic powers of this world seriously, but they are no longer a real threat for those who trust in the LORD (Ps. 91).[13]

As further examples of reintegration of Canaanite mythical motives in parabiblical literature we mention the location of the dwelling of El in the volcanic region of Urarṭu, the idea that not humans but gods or angels were the first rebels against God, the gigantic proportions of the garden and its tall Tree of Life, Eve as the universal mother who aroused the first man, procreation as the consolation prize for the loss of immortality (Gen. 2–3), the metamorphosis of the Ugaritic Devil into a huge serpent who

---

[13] Cf. Vreugdenhil 2013.

spoiled the Tree of Life, and in some sources even names, epithets and characteristics of the Canaanite Devil Ḥôrōn.

The New Testament goes a step further by also reintroducing the kind of exorcism we encountered in Ugaritic incantations (Sections 6.2; 6.3) and in extrabiblical Jewish magic (2.10). Like Ḥôrōn, the Devil is at home in the desert (6.2; 6.3; 6.12). Further parallels are his ambiguity (6.2) and his association with Death (6.9). The dragon of Revelation 12 is apparently the Canaanite sea serpent Leviathan who will be defeated by childbearing (6.10; 6.12).

To some extent also the role of Jesus as the Savior is comparable to that of the first Adam as described in the Ugaritic myth. It seems relevant to the discussion about the first and the second Adam in the letters of Paul, for it explains not only Paul's imagery, but also the gnostic pre-christian views on the first and second Adam, the first of which is always depicted as a heavenly being. One might say that in fact Jesus elaborated the ancient myth by becoming an ἄνθρωπος (human being) from heaven again. However, the Ugaritic Adam does not save the world and does not accept his death as an inevitable self-sacrifice.

7.3 *Epilogue*

We can imagine readers asking: Why bother with all this pagan mythology? The infallable Word of God was inspired by the Holy Spirit. Human considerations or foreign myths had nothing to do with this unique verbal inspiration.

This severe restriction of the influence of the human mediators on the text of the Bible has estranged many people from the Word of God. It is our conviction that God spoke and speaks through human intermediaries who were/are as much children of their times as children of God.[14] It cannot be denied anymore that the writers of the first chapters of Genesis made extensive use of myths and legends of the world in which they lived. But they did not leave these sources untouched.

No doubt the writers and editors of the first chapters of Genesis intended their work to be understood as a description of the first phase of world history,[15] but like all good historians each of

[14] Korpel & De Moor 2012; 2013.

these ancient scribes wrote with a purpose. The purpose of modern historians may be to give a more or less verifiable account of what really happened, although even then there can arise huge differences in interpretation of the available data as, for example, the national historiographies of the Second World War illustrate. Ancient historians were even less interested in factual history. They wrote history to propagate their worldview, their hopes and beliefs. Far more often than is commonly realized they gave indications that they did not know exactly what was the objective truth.[16]

This uncertainty pertained especially to the primordial history for which they had no records to go on before the art of writing had been mastered. This explains why the Hebrew scribes made extensive use of extrabiblical written sources for their reconstruction of the beginning of history, but adapted them to their own faith and circumstances.[17] They had no difficulty to allow different stories about the primordial history to coexist, repairing only the most glaring contradictions. They *expected* the readers to pick and choose what was good for them (cf. 1 Thess. 5:21).

Biblical history is like an extensive parable. Parables are also formulated as if they were history, but at their end the reader is urged explicitly to learn a lesson from the story. Most of the narratives in the Hebrew Bible got their final shape after the collapse of the nation and the destruction of the temple in 587 BCE. At first this disaster was incomprehensible because for many centuries the leadership of Israel – kings, priests and prophets – had believed that God would protect Zion and the Davidic dynasty for ever. The only possible explanation for the fall of Jerusalem and the destruction of the temple was that the whole nation had sinned

[15] Cf. Day 2013, 1-5.

[16] To give just one example: the symbolic function of names in the Hebrew story about the primeval world (see e.g. Mettinger 2007, 30, 66-67) is an indication that we are not dealing with an attempt to write factual history in the modern sense. The same kind of pointers is found in Ugaritic narratives which are characterized in this way as *legends*, not as factual history (De Moor 1987, 390-40, 243, n. 130, with further references).

[17] Hendel 2013, 24-32 uses the felicitous formulation that the stories of Genesis 1–11 belong to a wider family of ancient near eastern traditions, but reorient them to create distinctive ways of understanding and representing reality.

gravely and therefore had to suffer God's wrath. The general message of the so-called Deuteronomistic History was that this should happen never again.[18]

For this reason many of the stories in the first chapters of the Book of Genesis must be read as parables that raise questions like: Would I be able to create such a wondrous cosmos? Is there some truth to be discerned in the affirmation that it is 'good' as it is, even with its built-in 'evil' aspects? What would I have done if a serpent had said such seductive things to me? Is murder ever excusable? Should we not realize that the Creator of All can just as well become the Destroyer of All? As formulated by André LaCocque,

> Adam and Eve's story in Eden is *paradigmatic*. In it, all humans are invited to recognize themselves. There is nothing mechanical in the perpetuation of sin.[19]

The henotheistic or monotheistic reinterpretation of the primeval history in early Judaism has opened up a more detached view of nature which enabled people to abandon the mythical background that continued to burden other religious systems of the ancient world.[20] Obviously this was still far removed from a detached 'objective' view of the origin of the world and humanity, let alone from an explanation of the origin of evil – if such an explanation is possible at all. It is the merit of the Greeks to have produced the first philosophers, first among them Anaximander (611 – 546 BCE), who tried to think beyond the boundaries of a world that seemed to them a world governed by the caprices of deities.[21]

We have seen that in all polytheistic religions around Israel the deities act in unpredictable, ambiguous ways. Not only pre-

---

[18] Cf. Mettinger 2007, xii: 'The thesis of the Eden author is that obedience to the divine commandment leads to life, and disobedience to the forfeiture of the possibility of immortality. In important respects, the Eden Narrative repristinates significant elements of Deuteronomistic theology (the Law and obedience).'

[19] LaCocque 2006, 254. Similarly Wenham 1987, 90; Mettinger 2007, 67.

[20] So we do not think that it is correct to state that the first chapters of Genesis 'have a mythical rather than an historical character.' (O'Collins 2011, 80).

[21] Cf. the two questions for myths formulated concisely by Gregory 2012, 18.

dominantly evil gods like Ḥôrān, Môt, Erra and Seth have their amiable and horrible sides, the same is true of Canaanite deities like El, Baal and ʿAnat. Righteous human beings have to suffer from their capriciousness.

In Israel the roles are reversed: human beings themselves are confronted with their ambiguous behavior. Sometimes they do good, at other times they appear to be evil, or even cruel.[22] Whereas God is reliable and fundamentally good as long as humans obey his commandments. Sometimes it may look different, as in the cases of Noah, Abraham, Ruth, Job, but this does not detract from God's basic goodness. In all these cases the final outcome is positive. In the covenant God promises to support his people as long as they remain his faithful partners.

This is a fundamental shift which has no parallel in the biblical world. It has had enormous consequences for the historiography of ancient Israel. More than any other religious document of Antiquity the Bible depicts its heroes as flawed human beings in need of divine grace. Both Testaments state that the death of extremely righteous sufferers like the Servant of Isaiah 53 or Jesus Christ may serve vicariously to save flawed others.

Essentially, the first chapters of Genesis remain paradigmatic history meant to warn its readers not to make the same mistakes all over again. One should not use such history writing as an authoritative source on the laws of astronomy, physics or biology, as many creationists do.[23] Many modern scientists reject the idea of creation by a superior being and accept that the cosmos is governed by random and aimless processes which we are yet able to predict to an ever increasing degree. It becomes difficult then to apply ethical concepts such as good and evil to what is happening in and around us. In fact this line of reasoning is not at all so different from ascribing good and evil to the acts of capricious deities, as was the case in the world around Israel. Or we may

---

[22] In rabbinic teaching this is conceptualized as יצר הרע 'the evil inclination' and יצר הטוב 'the good inclination' that struggle in mankind. See e.g. Urbach 1975, 471-483.

[23] A recent overview of the current positions of creationists and evolutionists is found in Barrett & Caneday 2013. The volume shows that the relative opinions on these matters are nearing. However, none of those who contributed to it could take notice of the evidence assmbled in this volume.

prefer to believe in a purposeful creation by a superior Being we call God and accept the responsibility to choose between good and evil guided by what his servants have transmitted as his words.

In his impressive novel *And the Mountains Echoed* the writer Khaled Hosseini relates a story a father tells to his son. It contains this quotation,

> When you have lived as long as I have, the *div* replied, you find that cruelty and benevolence are but shades of the same color (Hosseini 2013, 12).

If that were true, a choice between good and evil would not make much difference, especially not if one is lucky enough to attain great age. However, it should not be glossed over that Hosseini puts these words in the mouth of a *div*, a huge devil ...

Appendix 1: *Text and Translation of* KTU 1.107

Obverse

[(1)]	[ ]
[m]*n.b*[ʾarṣ]*.hl*[k.ln]	[‘Whoever is] go[ing] on [the earth for us?][1]
(2) [b(?)]krm ʾil*m.rb*m.	[into(?)] the vineyard of the great gods?’[2]
nʿ*l*[*y.g*]m*r*	The champion was exalted,[3]
(3) [yt]n [.ʾa]r*ṣ.bdh.*	[they gave the e]arth in his hand.[4]
*yd*r*m*[.]pʾ*it*[.]ʾ*adm*	The brow of Adammu flowed,[5]
(4) [nḥ]š ʾ*iṯ*[l]*.yšql.yṯk*[*h*]	[the serpent] let fall spitt[le], it bit [him]![6]
h*n p bl.*	Look! The devouring mouth![7]
hn (5) [šnt(?)] q*ṭ*b*t.*	Look! The stinging [fangs]![8]
pẓr.pẓr [.]	Frantically he tried to loosen (it),[9]

---

1 Admittedly, the restoration is hazardous but it is in line with the sequel. For התהלך בארץ in the sense of going on the earth see Gen. 13:17; Josh. 18:8; 24:3; Zech. 1:10-11; Ps. 116:9; Job 1:7; 2:2. Cf. Isa. 6:8 מִי יֵלֶךְ־לָנוּ, ‘who will go for us?’.

2 Cf. גַּן־אֱלֹהִים in Ezek. 28:13; 31:8-9, Eden as גַּן־יְהוָה in Gen. 13:10, as well as כֶּרֶם יְהוָה in Isa. 5:7 and 27:2-3. For vineyards of deities in Ugarit, cf. Korpel 1990, 437. For orchards of deities in Babylonia, see *CAD* (K), 413-415.

3 For *gmr* see Del Olmo Lete & Sanmartín 2003, 301. Tentatively we take *nʿl*[y] as a perfect of the N-stem of *ʿly*, cf. En. el. I.99 and Clines, *DCH*, vol. 6, 408b. Possibly line 21 refers back to this event.

4 Cf. Gen. 9:2 בְּיֶדְכֶם נִתָּנוּ, ‘in your hand they are delivered’; Job 9:24 אֶרֶץ נִתְּנָה בְיַד־רָשָׁע, ‘the earth is given in the hand of the wicked.’ See also Gen. 9:2; Judg. 1:2.

5 On Adammu see our remarks in the main text. The form *ydrm* is derived from the attested Ugaritic root *drr* ‘to flow copiously ’ (Del Olmo Lete & Sanmartín 2003, 282, 946), in Arabic also said of beads of sweat (Lane, 862). Cf. KTU 1.13:15 as interpreted in *UF* 12 (1980), 306, 308. *pʾit* is also constructed as a masculine in KTU 1.17:II.9. For a possible parallel of beads of sweat covering the forehead see *CAD* (P), 518a, 548b.

6 So the antagonists both showed apprehension by exuding fluids.

7 The form *bl* is interpreted as an infinitive G of *bly*, like *hr* from *hry*, *ʿn* from *ʿny*, *ṯn* from *ṯny*, etc. The feminine form of the infinitive *blt* is attested in KTU 1.5:I.18 where it describes the gluttony of the god of death. Cf. Ps. 49:15.

8 Mouth and teeth are often used in parallelism. The trace before the *ṭ* can hardly be anything else than a *q*. We regard the resulting q*ṭ*b*t* as a participle of a verb *qṭb* related to the Ugaritic name of the demon *qẓb* ‘poison fang’. Cf. Tropper 2012, § 32.144.23. For ‘fangs’, see Deut. 32:24.

9 Cf. Del Olmo Lete & Sanmartín 2003, 690.

w.*p nḥš* (6) [ʾaḫd(?)]	but the mouth of the serpent [stuck(?)][10]
[*yṯ*]q.nṯ*k.l yd*ʿ.	He did not know how to bind the Biter,[11]
l bn.lpq ḥmt	nor did he understand how to conquer the poison.[12]
(7)[tml]ʾu*nh.ḥmt.*	The poison [filled(?)] him,[13]
*wt*ʿ*btnh.*ʾ*abdy*	yea, the Destroyer made him twist.[14]
(8)[tpl.bš]r.*šrġzz.*	The flesh of Šarruġāzizu [fell].[15]
*ybky.km n*ʿ*r*	He wept like a boy,
(9) [*wydm*ʿ.] k*m.ṣgr.*	[and shed tears] like a little one.
*š*pš.*bšmm tqr*ʾ*u*	Šapšu[16] called from heaven,
[(10) *hn.md*ʿ.]*nplt.yṭ*[b]y	[ʻLook! Why] did it fall, Oh my fr[iend?][17]
*md*ʿ*.nplt.bšr* (11) [š]rġzz.	Why did the flesh of [Š]arruġāzizu fall?
w*tpky.*k[*m.*]nʿr.	And (why) do you weep like a boy,

---

[10] Cf. *CAD* (A) 3, 48a.

[11] Cf. KTU 1.100:11 (par.) *yṯq nḥš*. For the binding of (the mouth of) snakes, see Pientka-Hinz 2009, 214; Miglio 2013, 44-45. For the binding of demons see Lambert 2013, 209-217.

[12] The Ugaritic verb *pwq* which usually has the meaning ʻto acquire, obtainʼ, might well have developed a meaning like ʻto be superior to, to surpassʼ, as in Arabic *fwq* (Lane, 2460).

[13] The tiny trace before *nh* accords best with ʾ*u*, cf. *CAD* (I/J), 140a.

[14] The word ʾ*abdy* ʻDestroyerʼ is a designation of the serpent, cf. Ethiopic (Geʼez) ʾ*abādon* ʻdevilʼ (cf. Hutter 1999a; Meier 1999). ʾ*abd* is his destructive poison. With regard to the verb ʿ*bt*, cf. Hebrew עבת Piʿel, ʻto twistʼ and עֲבֹת ʻtwisted cordsʼ.

[15] The restoration of this line is practically certain because of lines 10-11. This means that the lacuna at the beginning of line 8 must be wider than Pardeeʼs copy suggests. Also lines 9, 11 and 12 where Pardee himself accepts the self-evident restorations presuppose some more room.
The expression ʻhis flesh fellʼ parallels the Akkadian phrase *šīru maqātu* which describes the collapse of parts of the body (*CAD* (M) 1, 245b).
In our opinion *šrġzz* is a proleptic nickname of Adammu (line 3) who in that case bore two names, like many other Ugaritic deities. Šarruġāzizu means ʻthe Prince (Devil) is generousʼ, cf. De Moor 1987, 109, n. 26 and our comments in Section 2.6.

[16] Sun goddess of justice.

[17] Admittedly, the reading is uncertain but in any case it is likely that the *y* is the vocative particle. We have taken *ṭby* in the sense of ʻmy friendʼ, cf. Nougayrol 1970, 21, n. 4 and Akkadian *ṭābūtu* ʻfriendshipʼ.
A rather intriguing correspondence between the *Genealogy of Ḫammurapi*, 2, and the *Assyrian Kinglist*, 1, is *Ṭu-ub-ti-ya-mu-ta* = *Ṭu-*<*ub*>*-ti-ya A-da-mu* which might be interpreted as ʻMy friend(ship) is the Manʼ = ʻMy friend(ship) is Adammuʼ, cf. Finkelstein 1966, 98-99.

*tdm*ʿ*.km* (12) [ṣ]ġ*r.*	do you shed tears like a little one?'
*bkm.y*ʿ*ny*[*.šrġzz.*]	Thereupon [Šarruġāzizu] answered,
[yṯb.lh]*wth*	[he came back to her w]ords,[18]
(13) [*t*]ʿ*nn.bnty š*[*pš*].	'Please answer me, my creatress Šapšu:[19]
[lm.ʾan.lmt.] h*lk*	[Why am I] on my way [to death?][20]
[(14)ṯ]*b.kmm.lk*l[.]m*s*p[*r*]	Return ditto to the whole recitation.

---

(15) [*šp*]š *bš*m*m* tqrʾu.	Šapšu called from heaven,
m[.] nṣ*rt*	x [ ] shrieking[21]
(16) [ʾu.] h*t*m.ʾ*amn*[y.]	[Woe!] Now let me recite [a lament(?)]![22]
[ ]	[ ]
[*y*ʿ]*n*.k *mr*	[they will answe]r, 'How bitter!'[23]
(17) [b]š*l ytk.b*lt[n(?)]	[boi]ling liquid pours forth from Lôt[ānu (?)[24]]
[ ]	[ ]
[ ].*mr*. *hwt*	[ ] the bitterness of the word
(18) [ ]h.*ṯllt.khn*[*m*]	his [ ] you/she has stripped the priests [ ][25]

---

18 Restored on the basis of KTU 1.4:VI.15 (par.) *ṯṯb.b*ʿ*l. lhwty* 'you will come back, Baʿlu, to my words'.

19 Apparently Šarruġāzizu makes an appeal to the sun goddess Šapšu in her role of his creatress: **bānîtaya* (accusative because there is a complement). The weak *qātilt*-form of the participle is normal, cf. Tropper 2012, §§ 73.412, 75.535. The title 'creatress' may simply be honorific, like Ištar's title *bānât tēnēšēti* 'she who created humankind'. Also 'mother' must also be an epithet there, as *ummu* 'mother' is a divine epithet in Akkadian, cf. *CAD* (U), 128b-129b.

20 Compare Gen. 25:32 אָנֹכִי הוֹלֵךְ לָמוּת, 'I am on my way to death' as well as Gen. 47:15, 19; Deut. 5:25 לָמָּה נָמוּת; Jer. 27:13 לָמָּה תָמוּתוּ; Ezek. 33:11 לָמָּה תָמוּתוּ; Qoh. 7:17 לָמָּה תָמוּת.

21 The broken condition of the tablet makes any attempt at reconstructing lines 15-25 extremely hazardous, but Šapšu seems to lament about the impending death of Adammu. For the verb *nṣr* see KTU 1.16:II.25-26 describing the shrieking of a mourning oriental woman. See also the next verse-line and Tropper 2008, 91.

22 Compare the description of the lamenting two attendants about their murdered master in KTU 1.19:I.11-12: *wṯn gprm mn / gprh šr* ʾ*aqht / y*ʿ*n kmr kmrm* 'And the two attendants recite, his attendants sing about Aqhâtu, they answer, 'How bitter! How very bitter!'

23 Cf. the laments in KTU 1.19:I.7, 12, with De Moor 1987, 247-248, and the closing words of line 17.

24 Lôtānu (Leviathan) was the great sea serpent encircling the world. He was associated with evil. See for further comments Section 2.8. Would even the great serpent show regret in this weird manner?

25 In Job 12:19 the same is said of God. See also Joel 1:9. Since the priests were

[t]l*k pʿn*	[ ] they walk on foot.[26]
(19) [nš(?)]y.*yd.nšy*.p[ʿn(?).]	[He forg]ot(?)] the hand, forgot the f[oot (?)][27]
[*tṣḫ*.šp]*š.lmdb*	[Šap]šu [cried] to the Flood[28]
(20) [yd(?)]h.*mḫlpt*[.rʾišh(?)]	her [hands(?)] the locks [of her head(?).[29]]
[bb(?)]kt.ʾamr	[in wee]ping let me be bitter![30]
(21) [lm(?)].*nʿlm.*ʾa[dm(?)]	[Why(?)] was A[dammu(?)] exalted?[31]
[ ]	[ ]
(22) [ ]ʿ(?).*hn.*ʾ*a*l[ ]	[ ]x Look! Do not [ ]
[ ]	[ ]
(23) [. *l*]t*t.bn*.m[t.]l[y(?)]	[to] give [me(?)] someone who is bound to die[32]
[ ]	[ ]
(24) [ ].ḥmt [ ]	[ ] poison [ ]
[ ]	[ ]
(25) [ ] *x* [ ]	[ ] x [ ]
[ ]	[ ]

[broken, about 46 lines missing]

---

the recipients of donations to deities this line might imply that Adammu and his offspring had been providing the deities with food, just like the *lullû*-men in Mesopotamian myths, e.g. En. el. VI.5-8; Mayer 1987; Lambert & Millard 1969, 56-57. For the *ṯ* of the verb see Sabaean *ṯll* 'to plunder, take as booty' (Copeland Biella 2004, 544, who also cites cognates). For other possibilities see Pardee 1988, 246.

26 Walking naked and unshod were signs of mourning (e.g. Mic. 1:8).

27 For *nšy*, cf. Del Olmo Lete & Sanmartín 2003, 650-651; Tropper 2008, 91. The frequent parallelism in Semitic poetry between 'hand' and 'foot' as well as Ps. 137:5 suggested this proposal. Possibly this verse describes the sorry state of Adammu/Šarruġāzizu.

28 The Flood (freshwater ocean) formed the cold bottom of the Netherworld. Cf. De Moor 2008, 180. It was dreaded as a demoniacal power (KTU 1.82:27).

29 The loosening of the locks of one's head was a mourning gesture, cf. KTU 1.19:II.31-33 with De Moor 1987, 254; Gilg. Ep. VIII.39, 63.

30 Compare Isa. 22:4 אֲמָרֵר בַּבֶּכִי, 'let me be bitter in weeping'.

31 With most other Ugaritologists we assume a connection with line 2, cf. Pardee 1988, 247. For the form without *-y* see Tropper 2012, § 75.534. We interpret the enclitic *mem* as an emphasizing particle, cf. Tropper 2012, § 89.23.

32 Šapšu does not seem to resign herself to the death of Adammu, but 'son' need not be taken literally. See our comment on line 13. For the expression בֶּן־מָוֶת, 'someone who is bound to die' see 1 Sam. 20:31; 26:16; 2 Sam. 12:5.

Reverse

(26′) .*ʾa* [ ]	xx [ ]
[ ]	[ ]
(27′) [*ʾatt.*]*ṯbt.*n*pš* [ ]	a good-natured w[oman.][33] [ ]
[ ]r	[ ]x

(28′) [l'i]*l šd.ql.*	Run [to the g]od Šēdu,[34]
ṯ[n.lh.y.šd.]h*t.* ʾaṯr	re[peat to him, 'Oh Šēdu,] now follow![35]
(29′) [š'a(?).]*ġrm.y* ['il(?)]	[Lift up(?)] the two mountains, Oh [god!(?)][36]
[*wrd.bt.*]ḥ*rn*	[and descend into the house] of Ḥôrānu.[37]
(30′) [w'a*(?)*]*rk.ḥ*n[t(?).]	[and] lon[g] of merc[y](?)[38]
[ ] *ʿlk*	[ ] on you.
(31′) ['i]s*r.n*[ḥš.] [ ]	[b]ind the ser[pent][39]

---

[33] The reading is practically certain. Similar constructions are found in Gen. 24:16; 26:7; 1 Sam. 25:3; 2 Sam. 11:2; Est. 1:11; 2:3, 7. Cf. Gen. 6:2 וַיִּרְאוּ בְנֵי־הָאֱלֹהִים אֶת־בְּנוֹת הָאָדָם כִּי טֹבֹת הֵנָּה, 'the sons of God saw that the daughters of the human were good'. Compare also Akkadian *siništum damiqtum* 'the good woman', *CAD* (S), 286b-287a. It is interesting to see what the Rabbis understood to be a אשה טובה, 'good woman', b. Sanh., 100b; b. Yeb., 63a-b.; Midr. Teh., 59b.

In the ancient world men hated quarrelsome and ill-tempered women, cf. Prov. 21:9, 19; 25:24; 27:15. For Ugarit, compare Marsman 2003, especially 668. See also *The Instruction of Ankhsheshonq*, 25:14: 'May the heart of a wife be the heart of her husband, that they may be free of strife.' (Lichtheim 1980, 178); *The Instruction of Papyrus Insinger*, 18:22: 'As for a good woman of proven good character, you will not be able to blame her on acccount of it.' (Lichtheim 1980, 200).

It seems that Adammu and his wife were a good match since both were called *ṭb* 'good', cf. line 10.

[34] A protective genius. Cf. Lipínski 1995, 329-332. In Egypt he and Ḥaurōn are depicted as subduers of snakes. Cf. Section 2.9, Fig. 26.

[35] Assuming equivalence of *ʾaṯr* and *ʾiṯr*. Cf. *yʾarš* next to *yʾirš*, Del Olmo Lete & Sanmartín 2003, 108.

[36] The two mountains at the entrance of the Netherworld. Cf. KTU 1.4:VIII.1-6.

[37] The first part of the restoration has been derived from KTU 1.4:VIII.7. Ḥôrānu recurs in lines 31', 32', 38', and in KTU 1.100. According to KTU 1.100:67-68 and KTU 1.179 he possessed at least one house in the Netherworld (De Moor 2008). See also line 16.

[38] Cf. Exod. 34:6 (par.) and Healey 1998; Day 2000, 26. El's epithet רַחוּם is reflected in Ugaritic *rḫnt*, Korpel 1990, 165, n. 576.

[39] Assuming a variant wording of *yṯq nḥš*, line 6.

[ ] y(?).*ḥrn*	[ ] Oh(?) Ḥôrānu!
(32′) [w'i]s*p.ḫph*.ḫm[n(?).]	Collect its covering, Oh Ḫamanu(?),[40]
['isp.y.š]p*š.lhrm* (33′) [ḥmt.]	[collect, Oh Ša]pšu, [the poison] from the mountains![41]
ʿl.ʾar[*ṣ.lʾan.*]	(its) power on the earth.[42]
[*ʾisp.ḥ*]*mt* (34′) [y.*š*]p*š* .*lhr*[*m.*]	Collect the poison, Oh Šapšu, from the mountains,
ġr*pl.ʿl.ʾarṣ*	the fog on the earth.
(35′) [*ʾisp.*]*ḥmt.lp*[*.n*]*ṯk.*	[Collect] the poison from the mouth of the Biter,
*ʾab*d*.lpʾak*[*l*]	the destruction from the mouth of the Devourer.
(36′) ['ab(?).y]'asp.ḥmt	[May the Father(?)] collect the poison,[43]
[*ʾil*]*hm.yʾasp*[.]ḥ*mt*	may the Ilāhūma collect the poison.
(37′) [*tasp.*][*š*]*pš.l*hr[*m.*]. *ġr*[*p*]l	May Šapšu [collect] the fog on the mountains
ʿl.ʾarṣ.lʾan (38′) [*špt.*ḥ]*mt.*	on the earth the power of the poison-lips.[44]
'i[*l.*]w*ḥrn.*y*ʾisp.ḥmt*	May Ilu and Ḥôrānu collect the poison,
(39′) [*bʿl*] w*dgn.*y[*ʾi*]*sp.ḥmt.*	may Baʿlu and Daganu collect the poison.
ʿnt.wʿṯtrt (40′) [*tʾi*]s*p.ḥmt*	May ʿAnatu and ʿAṯtartu collect the poison,
yr*ḫ.wršp y!ʾisp. dhmt*	may Yariḫu and Rašpu collect the poison,

[40] We propose to view [w'i]s*p.ḫph* as a variant of *ʾisp ... ġrpl* (line 44' par.) and to connect *ḫp* with Hebrew *ḥph* and *ḥpp* and their cognates (cf. *HAHAT*, 379-380). Cf. Isa. 4:5.
At the end of the colon the name of a deity is expected. Perhaps Hurrian Ḫamanu? Cf. Del Olmo Lete & Sanmartín 2003, 395; Haas 1994, 427, 485. In Akkadian lexical lists Ḫamanu is described as a 'cedar mountain'. It follows immediately after Mt Buduḫdug, the mountain where the sun sets (cf. George 2003, 863 and Del Olmo Lete & Sanmartín 2003, 229).

[41] Restored after the sequel. At the beginning of line 33' there seems to be insufficient room for *ġrpl*.

[42] The restoration follows lines 37' and 44'. For *lʾan* 'power' see KTU 1.108:24-25. There it is used in a positive sense, here in a negative sense because it equals *ḥmt* 'poison', *ḫp* 'covering' and *ġrpl* 'fog' enclosing the earth. Because in line 37' *ḥmt* must be a genitive with *lʾan* the power intended here is the power of the poison.

[43] The tentative restoration is based on KTU 1.123:1 *ʾab wʾilm*. Because of the self-evident restorations at the beginning of lines 39', 41', 43', 44' there is definitely sufficient room for this restoration at the beginning of line 36'.

[44] The restoration of the beginning of this colon is based on line 45'. Because the following pair of deities heads the next colon, *ḥmt* must be in the genitive state here. Cf. Ps. 140:4.

(41′) [*ʿṯt*]*r wʿṯtpr.yʾisp.ḥmt.*	May ʿAṯtaru and ʿAṯtapiru collect the poison,
ẓẓ.wkm!ṯ (42′) [*yʾi*]*sp. ḥmt.*	may Ẓiẓẓu and Kamāṯu collect the poison.
mlk.bʿṯtrt.yʾisp.ḥmt	May Māliku in ʿAṯtartu collect the poison,
(43′) [*kṯ*]*r wḫss.y*[*ʾi*]*sp.ḥmt.*	may Kôṯaru and Ḫasīsu collect the poison,
šḥr. wšlm [*yʾis*]p. (44′) *ḥmt.*	may Šaḥaru and Šalimu collect the poison.
*ʾisp.*špš *lhrm.ġrpl.*	Collect, (Oh) Šapšu, the fog from the mountains,
ʿl ʾarṣ (45′) [*š*]p*t.ḥmt.*	on the earth the poison-lips,
lp[*.n*]*ṯk.ʾabd.*	from the mouth of the Biter the destruction,
*lp.ʾakl.ṯm d*l	from the mouth of the Devourer the paralysis of the lame one.[45]
(46′) [tqb(?)]*l.bl tb*ḥ[l]l	[May you be recepti]ve, may you arouse the male breeding animal,[46]
tzd.ʿrq.dm	may you be hot, exude blood![47]
(47′) [ ]	[ ]
*ʿ*rq[. n]*pš*	exude life![48]
(48′) [ ]	[ ]
*mšḥt.kṯpm.ʾ*ak*ṯ*n	I will make lean the destroyer of healthy babies.[49]

---

[45] For *ṯm* see Akkad. *šamāmu* ‘to lame, paralyse’ and *šimmatu* ‘paralysis’, often from snakebite (*CAD* (Š) 1, 295; (Š) 2, 7-8; Pientka-Hinz 2009, 213). For *dl* see Hebr. דלל II ‘to hang down’, said of lameness, and דַּל ‘weak, listless’. Apparently ‘the lame one’ is Adammu. Other proposals, like that of Watson 2007, are far less convincing.

[46] At the beginning of the line three or four signs are missing (Pardee 1988, 254). For [tqb(?)]*l.bl* see *qblbl* ‘receptor, headrest’ (De Moor 2010, 290). We assume that in these lines the bride is addressed as the human being who guarantees the continuation of the human species on earth. Both bride and groom are also addressed at the end of KTU 1.100. The word *bḥl* seems to be an allophone for *pḥl* ‘male breeding animal, stallion’ (Del Olmo Lete & Sanmartín 2003, 219, 668; cf. *CAD* (P), 479-481; Lane, 2345-2346; Leslau 1991, 156-157; Sokoloff 2009, 1178). Cf. *wtpky* for *wtbky* in line 11. Cf. KTU 1.100:1 *ʾum.pḥl.pḥlt* ‘The Mother of the male breeding animal (and) the female breeding animal’. As a verb in the L-stem *bḥl* might mean ‘to excite the male breeding animal’ (cf. the G-stem *faḥala* in Ethiopic ‘to be sexually aroused’, said of males), because the bride is the subject of all *tqtl*-forms in this verse.

[47] In KTU 1.24:8 the verb *zwd* describes the sexual arousal of the bride. See also the end of line 49’ where the day when she will bear is mentioned. The exudation of blood may refer to the blood of defloration.

[48] The external parallelism between *dm* ‘blood’ and *npš* ‘soul, life’ is also found in Gen. 9:4-5 and many other such texts in the Hebrew Bible.

(49′) [ ]	[ ]
ʾank[.*ʾa*]š*ḥ.bym.tld*	I myself will bow down on the day you bear.[50]
(50′) [ ]	[ ]
[ ] *bry*.[ ]	[ ] he eats/he fed [ ][51]
(51′) [ ]	[ ]
[ʾ*i*]l*m.r*bm [ ] t*š*t[*n*]	[ ] the great gods [ ] will put
(52′) [ ]	[ ]
[bn]*t.nš.bḥ*[y.tky(?).]*mt*	[ ] by li[fe] [the daughte]rs of mankind will [defeat(?)] Death.[52]
(53′) [ ]	[ ]
[ ]l.*tmt* [ ]kṯ[*rt*]	[ ] she will not die [ ] Kōtharātu[53]
(54′) [ ]	[ ]
[ ].ʾ*ak*l [ ]	[ ] food [ ]

Postscript:

In our opinion autopsy of the fragment KTU 7.163 should reveal whether it might belong to KTU 1.107. It was found in the same room as 1.107. Note the following possible parallels:

7.163:1 *ṣġr* 'little one' || 1.107:9, 12 *ṣġr* 'little one'.
7.163:3 ʾi*ṣr.k*d[ʾiy(?)] 'I will shriek like a b[lack kite(?)]' || 1.107:15 n*ṣrt* '(Šapšu) was shrieking'.
7.163:4 [ʾa]*ṯbṯ.kṯṯ*b[.mtm(?)] '[I will] give substance as with the bringing back of [the dead(?)]', cf. 1.22:I.6 *ṯm.yṯ!bš.šm.ʾil.mtm* 'there the name of Ilu gave

[49] For various possibilities see Pardee 1988, 254-255. The one chosen here presupposes a kind of *ius talionis*. The demon destroying podgy, healthy children will be punished by emaciation.

[50] Possibly said by Šapšu who promises to thank the other deities invoked for their protection of the child.

[51] Since no photograph of the lower edge of the tablet has been provided by Pardee 1988 we have to rely entirely on his copy of the few remaining signs. For *bry*, cf. Hebr. ברה.

[52] For *bnt nš* see Gen. 24:13 בְּנוֹת אַנְשֵׁי הָעִיר, 'the daughters of the men of the town'. Pardee discerned a tiny trace after the *b* and in view of its position it could well be a remnant of a *ḥ*. The conjecture *tk* was chosen because there is hardly room for more signs. In our opinion the verb *nky* occurs in KTU 1.16:II.27, cf. De Moor 1987, 215; De Moor & Spronk 1987, 154.

[53] We accept Pardee's tentative readings (Pardee 1988, 233, 255), but assume that the Kōtharātu are mentioned at the end of the line. Also in KTU 1.179 the Kōtharātu play a role as the goddesses assisting a woman in childbirth. The names of four of the Kōtharātu have to do with midwifery (KTU 1.24:48-49).

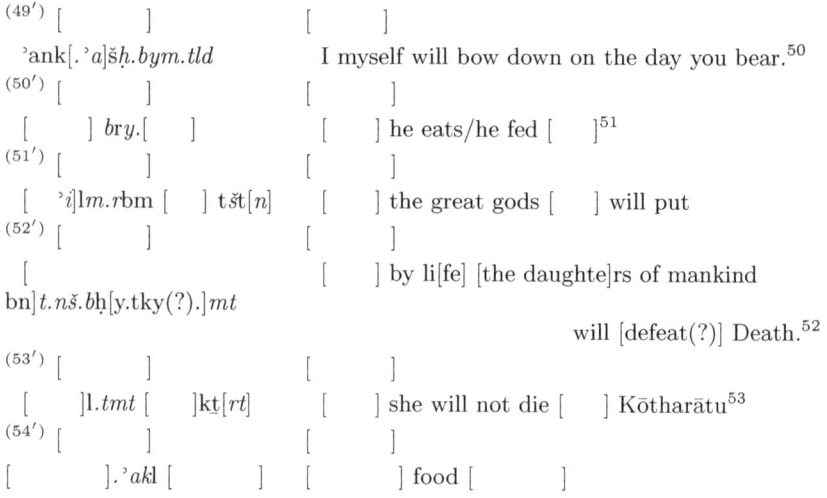

substance to the dead'. See for this translation p. 13, n. 48.
7.163:6 [ ] *'lk.'ig'.ṯ*[m dl(?)] 'because of you I will touch (verb *ng'*) the para[lysis of the lame one(?)]'. Healing by touching was a common practice.

If this very conjectural interpretation turns out to be acceptable, Šapšu seems to promise to revive Adammu.

Appendix 2: *Text and Translation of* KTU 1.100[1]

Obverse

(1) *ʾum.pḥl.pḥlt*	The Mother of the male breeding animal, (and) the female breeding animal,[2]
bt.ʿn.bt.ʾabn.	the daughter of the Source (and) the daughter of the Stone,
bt.šmm.wthm	the daughter of Heaven and Flood,
(2) *qrʾit.lšpv.ʾumh.*	called to Šapšu, her mother,[3]
špš.ʾum.ql.bl.	Šapšu, my mother, carry my voice
ʿm (3) *ʾil.mbk nhrm.*	to Ilu at the fountain-head of the two Rivers,
bʿdt.thmtm	at the confluence of the two Floods.[4]
(4) *mnt.*	My incantation is:[5]
nṯk.nḥš.šmrr	A poisonous serpent has bitten,
nḥš (5) *ʿqšr.*	a serpent that has sloughed its skin![6]
lnh.mlḫš ʾabd.	Let there be a charmer of the Destroyer for it,[7]
lnh.ydy (6) *ḥmt.*	let there be an expeller of poison for it!
hlm.yṯq.nḥš	Let him hit, let him bind the serpent,[8]
yšlḥm.<nḥš> ʿqšr	let him feed the serpent that has sloughed its skin,

[1] For the text see Bordreuil & Pardee 2004, 36-41. The interpretation of this tablet too is highly controversial, cf. lately Loretz 2011, 242-258. We present our own rendering here.

[2] See for this rendering Section 2.5.

[3] Šapšu was the Sun goddess. Her name is etymologically the same as that of the Babylonian sun god Šamaš and the Hebrew שֶׁמֶשׁ. Because she travelled through the sky and the Netherworld she was able to deliver the message of the Mother of the primordial animated creatures to all deities wherever they dwelt.

[4] The Upper Flood above the firmament of heaven and the Lower Flood beneath the earth.

[5] Every one of the twelve deities invoked against the poisonous serpent uses the same formula. Because of *mnty* in line 9 it is certain that a pronominal suffix of the first person singular is attached to *mnt* 'conjuration'.

[6] When a serpent sloughs its skin in spring it is at its most venomenous. Cf. Bordreuil 1985.

[7] We take the line as a precative noun phrase. Cf. Tropper 2012, § 92,52.

[8] We take *hlm* and *yṯq* as precative perfects balancing the jussives *yšlḥm* and *yʿdb*. Cf. Tropper 2012, § 77.34. For the binding of a monstrous serpent see Hoffner 1990, 12.

(7) *y'db.ks'a.wyṯb*	let him place a chair and sit down![9]

---

(8) *tqr'u.lšpš.'umh.*	She called to Šapšu, her mother,
špš.'um.ql.bl.	Šapšu, my mother, carry my voice
(9) *'m.b'l.mrym.ṣpn*	to Baʿlu on the heights of Ṣapānu,[10]
mnty.	My incantation is:
nṯk (10) *nḥš.šmrr*	A poisonous serpent has bitten,
nḥš 'qšr.	a serpent that has sloughed its skin!
lnh (11) *mlḫš.'abd.*	Let there be a charmer of the Destroyer for it,
lnh.ydy.ḥmt.	let there be an expeller of poison for it!
hlm.yṯq (12) *nḥš*	Let him hit, let him bind the serpent,
yšlḥm.nḥš.'qšr.	let him feed the serpent that has sloughed its skin,
y'db.ks'a (13) *wyṯb*	let him place a chair and sit down!

---

(14) *tqr'u lšpš.'u<m>h.*	She called to Šapšu, her mother,
špš.'um.ql.bl.	Šapšu, my mother, carry my voice
'm (15) *dgn.ttlh.*	to Daganu in Tuttul[11]
mnt.	My incantation is:
nṯk nḥš.šmrr	A poisonous serpent has bitten,
(16) *nḥš.'qšr.*	a serpent that has sloughed its skin!
lnh.mlḫš.'abd.	Let there be a charmer of the Destroyer for it,
lnh (17) *ydy.ḥmt.*	let there be an expeller of poison for it!
hlm.yṯq.nḥš.	Let him hit, let him bind the serpent,
yšlḥm (18) *nḥš.'qšr.*	let him feed the serpent that has sloughed its skin,
y'db.ks'a.wyṯb	let him place a chair and sit down!

---

(19) *tqr'u lšpš.'umh.*	She called to Šapšu, her mother,
špš.'um.ql.bl.	Šapšu, my mother, carry my voice
'm! (20) *'nt w'{.}ṯtrt 'inbbh.*	to ʿAnatu-and-ʿAṯtartu on Inbabe.[12]

---

[9] For this act see Caplice 1974, 18.

[10] Mt Zaphon, present day Jebel Akra, about 40 km north of Ugarit. This was Baʿlu's mountain.

[11] A city in northern Mesopotamia. Many Babylonian texts, especially from the city of Mari, confirm that Dagan(u) was the main god of Tuttul. It is noteworthy that Daganu is mentioned *after* his son Baʿlu here.

[12] ʿAnatu-and-ʿAṯtartu were consorts of Baʿlu and goddesses of love, hunting and war, like the Babylonian goddess Ištar. *Inbabe*, Hurrian for 'Mountain

mnt.	My incantation is:
nṯk (21) *nḥš.šmrr.*	A poisonous serpent has bitten,
nḥš.ʿqšr.	a serpent that has sloughed its skin!
lnh.ml(22)*ḫš.ʾabd.*	Let there be a charmer of the Destroyer for it,
lnh.ydy.ḥmt.	let there be an expeller of poison for it!
hlm.yṯq (23) *nḥš.*	Let him hit, let him bind the serpent,
yšlḥm.nḥš ʿqšr.	let him feed the serpent that has sloughed its skin,
yʿdb.ksʾa wyṯb	let him place a chair and sit down!

---

(25) *tqrʾu.lšpš.ʾumh.*	She called to Šapšu, her mother,
špš.ʾum.q[l] *bl.*	Šapšu, my mother, carry my voice
ʿm (26) *yrḫ.lrgth.*	to Yariḫu in Larugatu.[13]
mnt.	My incantation is:
*nṯk.*n[*ḥ*]š.*šmrr.*	A poisonous serpent has bitten,
(27) *nḥš.ʿqšr.*	a serpent that has sloughed its skin!
lnh.mlḫš.ʾabd.	Let there be a charmer of the Destroyer for it,
lnh.ydy (28) *ḥmt.*	let there be an expeller of poison for it!
hlm.yṯq.nḥš.	Let him hit, let him bind the serpent,
yšlḥm.nḥš (29) *ʿqšr.*	let him feed the serpent that has sloughed its skin,
yʿdb.ksʾa.wyṯb	let him place a chair and sit down!

---

(30) *tqrʾu.lšpš.ʾumh.*	She called to Šapšu, her mother,
špš.ʾum.ql b<*l.*>	Šapšu, my mother, carry my voice
ʿm (31) *ršp.bbth.*	to Rašpu in Bibite.[14]
mnt.	My incantation is:
nṯk.nḥvs.šmrr	A poisonous serpent has bitten,
(32) *nḥš.ʿqšr.*	a serpent that has sloughed its skin!
lnh.mlḫš ʾabd.	Let there be a charmer of the Destroyer for it,
lnh.ydy (33) *ḥmt.*	let there be an expeller of poison for it!

of the Deities', was the mountain of ʿAnatu. Its location is unknown, but it is described in KTU 1.13. Cf. Dietrich 2004, 21.

13 Yariḫu is the Moon god. The placename Larugatu is attested in the texts of Ebla. According to the Ugaritic *Legend of Aqhâtu* the city of Yariḫu was Abilūma, probably located north of the Sea of Tiberias. Deities could have several sanctuaries of course and cities could have different names.

14 Rašpu was the god of infectious diseases like pestilence. His city Bibite was possibly situated in Anatolia. Cf. Dietrich 2004, 21.

hlm.yṯq.nḥš.	Let him hit, let him bind the serpent,
yšlḥm.nḥš.ʿq(34)*š<r>.*	let him feed the serpent that has sloughed its skin,
yʿdb.ksʾa.wyṯb	let him place a chair and sit down!

<(34a) *tqrʾu.lšpš.ʾumh.*	She called to Šapšu, her mother,[15]
špš.ʾum.ql bl.	Šapšu, my mother, carry my voice
ʿm (34b) *ʿṯtrt.mrh*	to ʿAṯtartu in Mari.[16]
mnt.	My incantation is:
nṯk.nḥš.šmrr	A poisonous serpent has bitten,
(34c) *nḥš.ʿqšr.*	a serpent that has sloughed its skin!
lnh.mlḫš ʾabd.	Let there be a charmer of the Destroyer for it,
lnh.ydy (34d) *ḥmt.*	let there be an expeller of poison for it!
hlm.yṯq.nḥš.	Let him hit, let him bind the serpent,
yšlḥm.nḥš (34e) *ʿqšr.*	let him feed the serpent that has sloughed its skin,
yʿdb.ksʾa.wyṯb	let him place a chair and sit down!

---

(35) *tqrʾu.lšpš.ʾumh.*	She called to Šapšu, her mother,
špš.ʾum.ql bl.	Šapšu, my mother, carry my voice
ʿm (36) *ẓẓ.wkmṯ.ḥryth.*	to Ẓiẓẓu-and-Kamāṯu in Ḥariyātu.[17]
mnt.	My incantation is:
nṯk.nḥš.šm(37)*rr.*	A poisonous serpent has bitten,
nḥš.ʿqšr.	a serpent that has sloughed its skin!
lnh.mlḫš ʾabd.	Let there be a charmer of the Destroyer for it,
lnh (38) *ydy.ḥmt.*	let there be an expeller of poison for it!
hlm.yṯq.nḥš	Let him hit, let him bind the serpent,
yšlḥm.nḥš (39) *ʿqšr.*	let him feed the serpent that has sloughed its skin,

[15] Initially the scribe forgot the seventh strophe. In a marginal note he corrected his error. See lines 77-79.

[16] This line proves that Ištar of the North Mesopotamian city of Mari was equated with the Ugaritic goddess ʿAṯtartu (Astarte).

[17] Ẓiẓẓu, also written Ṭiṭṭu, means 'clay'. Kamāṯu is no doubt identical to the Moabite god Chemosh, but this god had more cult centers. Cf. Müller 1980, 10-11; 1999. For his city *Ḥryt* several proposals have been made (Müller 1999, 187b; Dietrich 2004, 21-22), but possibly we have here an example of the rare correspondence of *ḥ* and *q*, cf. Guillaume 1965, II, 9. If so, the toponym might be that of Moabite קְרִיּוֹת (Jer. 48:24, cf. 48:1).

y'db.ks'a.wyṯb>	let him place a chair and sit down!

---

(40) *tqr'u.lšpš.'umh.*	She called to Šapšu, her mother,
špš.'um ql.bl.	Šapšu, my mother, carry my voice
'm (41) *mlk.'ṯtrth.*	to Māliku in 'Aṯtarātu[18]
mnt.	My incantation is:
nṯk.nḥš.šmrr	A poisonous serpent has bitten,
(42) *nḥš.'qšr.*	a serpent that has sloughed its skin!
lnh.mlḫš 'abd.	Let there be a charmer of the Destroyer for it,
lnh.ydy (43) *ḥmt.*	let there be an expeller of poison for it!
hlm.yṯq.nḥš.	Let him hit, let him bind the serpent,
yšlḥm.nḥš (44) *'qšr.*	let him feed the serpent that has sloughed its skin,
y'db.ks'a.wyṯb>	let him place a chair and sit down!>

---

(45) *tqr'u lšpš.'umh.*	She called to Šapšu, her mother,
špš.'um.ql bl.	Šapšu, my mother, carry my voice
'm (46) *kṯr wḫss.kptrh.*	to Kôṯaru-and-Ḫasīsu in Kaphtor.[19]
mnt.	My incantation is:
nṯk.nḥš (47) *šmrr*	A poisonous serpent has bitten,
nḥš.'qšr.	a serpent that has sloughed its skin!
lnh.mlḫš 'abd.	Let there be a charmer of the Destroyer for it,
(48) *lnh.ydy.ḥmt.*	let there be an expeller of poison for it!
hlm yṯq.nḥš.	Let him hit, let him bind the serpent,
(49) *yšlḥm.nḥš.'qšr.*	let him feed the serpent that has sloughed its skin,
y'db.ks'a (50) *wyṯb*	let him place a chair and sit down!

---

(51) *tqr'u lšpš.'umh.*	She called to Šapšu, her mother,
špš.'um.ql.bl.	Šapšu, my mother, carry my voice

[18] Māliku is a Netherworld deity (Spronk 1986, 187) who was consulted on difficult matters of state in the city of 'Aṯtarātu, the biblical Ashtaroth Qarnaim in the Bashan area. Here the spirits of ancestors of the royal dynasties of Canaan, among them the dynasty of Ugarit, were questioned when they, possibly in the form of sulfuric gases at that time, were rising from fissures in the rocks.

[19] Kôṯaru and Ḫasīsu (Clever and Intelligent) was the technician among the gods of Ugarit. He was supposed to dwell in the two centers of excellent artisanship at that time, Egypt and Kaphtor (Crete).

ʿm (52) *šḫr.wšlm šmmh.*	to Šaḥaru-and-Šalimu in heaven.[20]
mnt.	My incantation is:
nṯk.nḥš (53) *šmrr*	A poisonous serpent has bitten,
nḥš ʿqšr.	a serpent that has sloughed its skin!
lnh.mlḫš (54) *ʾabd.*	Let there be a charmer of the Destroyer for it,
lnh.ydy ḥmt.	let there be an expeller of poison for it!
hlm.yṯq (55) *nḥš.*	Let him hit, let him bind the serpent,
yšlḥm.nḥš.ʿqšr.	let him feed the serpent that has sloughed its skin,
yʿdb (56) *ksʾa.wyṯb*	let him place a chair and sit down!

---

(57) *tqrʾu lšpš.ʾumh.*	She called to Šapšu, her mother,
špš.ʾum.ql.bl.	Šapšu, my mother, carry my voice
(58) *ʿm ḥrn.mṣdh.*	to Ḥôrānu in the Fortress[21]
mnt.	My incantation is:
nṯk nḥš (59) *šmrr.*	A poisonous serpent has bitten,
nḥš.ʿqšr.	a serpent that has sloughed its skin!
lnh.mlḫš (60) *ʾabd.*	Let there be a charmer of the Destroyer for it,
lnh.ydy ḥmt.	let there be an expeller of poison for it!

---

(61) *bḥrn.pnm.trġnw.*	Ḥôrānu's face turned pale,[22]
wtṯkl (62) *bnwth.*	because his posterity would remain childless.[23]
ykr.ʿr.dqdm	He left[24] the city of the east.[25]
(63) *ʾidk.pnm.lytn.*	Then he headed straight
tk ʾaršḫ.rbt	for Great Arašiḫ
(64) *wʾaršḫ.ṯrrt.*	and for Little Arašiḫ.[26]

[20] Red dawn and red sunset, giant sons engendered by Ilu with human females (KTU 1.23:52-64). These two demigods were instructed to build a sanctuary in the desert, possibly at the oasis Palmyra (De Moor 1987, 118, n. 9), close to where we think that Ḥôrānu had his earthly abode (Section 2.4).

[21] Cf. Section 2.2.

[22] Literally 'turned green'. Cf. Hebr. רַעֲנָן and *CAD* (A) 2, 232.

[23] If all the gods summoned would have turned against the snakes the serpentine offspring of Ḥôrānu would have been exterminated too. Therefore Ḥôrānu relents. Cf. Section 2.9.

[24] Cf. Hebr. נכר, Akkad. *nakāru*; elsewhere *tbʿ* is used in the same formula.

[25] See our comments in Section 5 above.

[26] Great Arašiḫ and Little Arašiḫ are the names of two major tributaries of the river Tigris. Cf. Section 2.4.

ydy.bʿṣm.ʿrʿr	He removed the juniper from the trees,
(65) *wbšḫt.ʿṣ.mt.*	yes, the Tree of Death from the shrubs.
ʿrʿrm.ynʿrn(!)h	The juniper — he shook it out,[27]
(66) *ssnm.ysynh.*	the date-cluster — he put it away,[28]
ʿdtm.yʿdynh.	the scab[29] — he took it off,
yb(67)*ltm.yblnh.*	the wart[30] — he carried it off.
mġy.ḥrn.lbth.	Ḥôrānu went to his house
w(68)*yštql.lḥẓrh.*	and proceeded to his residence.
tlʾu.dh<m>t.km.nḫl	The poison had become weak[31] like a wadi,[32]
(69)*tplg.km.plg*	it had flowed away like a ditch.[33]

(Ritual:)

(Groom:)

(70)*bʿdh.bhtm.mnt.*	‘‘Behind her the mansion’ is my incantation.’[34]

(Officiant:)

bʿdh.bhtm.sgrt	‘Behind her the mansion she closed,
(71)*bʿdh ʿdbt.ṯlṯ.*	behind her she let down the bronze (bolt).’[35]

(Groom:)

ptḥ.bt.mnt	‘‘Open up the house’ is my incantation.’

---

[27] In this as well as the following cola the original text has a play of words that cannot be reproduced in translation.

[28] Cf. Akkad. *nesû* (which should not be compared to W. Semitic *nśʾ*, cf. Akkad. *nasāḫu*).

[29] A metaphor, cf. Targumic Aram. עֲדִיתָא. Apparently the Tree of Life had become contorted by the poisonous spittle of the serpent. As a result, it was not as pleasant to the eyes as the Tree of Life anymore (cf. Gen. 2:9; 3:6; Song of Songs 7:8-9). The Tree of Death now resembled the knotty stem of a vine.

[30] Cf. Hebr. יַבֶּלֶת, in M. Hebr. also a metaphor for an outgrowth on a tree. Apparently the serpent's poison had distorted the tree.

[31] N-stem of *lʾy* ‘to be overpowered, become weak’, cf. Hebr. לאה. Apparently the uprooting of the root of all evil had had a beneficial effect.

[32] The water of which soon disappears, cf. Jer. 15:18; Mic. 1:14; Job 6:15-18.

[33] Cf. Ps. 58:5-8; *CAD* (Z), 9b; KTU 1.82:24.

[34] The groom quotes the first few words of the songs he wants the officiant to recite on his behalf.

[35] Hardly the complete song. Probably it was the beginning of a song about the well-known theme of the locked-out lover. See e.g. Kitchen 1999, 339; Sefati 1998, 291:11; Foster 2005, 945; Song of Songs 2:9b; 5:2-6.

(Officiant:)

(72) *pth̩.bt.wʾubʾa*(!).	‘Open up the house, that I may enter,[36]
hkl.wʾištql	the palace that I may come in.’

(Bride:)

(73) *tn.km.<mhry>.nh̩šm.*	‘Give a serpent as <my bridal gift.>,[37]
yh̩r.tn.km (74 *mhry.*	give a lizard as my bridal gift,[38]
wbn.bṯn.ʾitnny	yes, a son of the Dragon as a present for my love.’[39]

(Groom:)

(75) *ytt.nh̩šm.mhrk.*	‘I give a serpent as your bridal gift,
bn bṯn (76) *ʾitnnk*	a son of the Dragon as a present for your love.’

(Margin:)

(77) *ʾaṯr ršp.ʿṯtrt*	After Rašpu, ʿAṯtartu.
(78) *ʿm ʿṯtrt.mrh*	. . . to ʿAṯtartu in Mari.
(79) *mnt.*	My incantation is:
nṯk nh̩š	A serpent has bitten![40]

[36] The eroticism of the metaphor is evident.

[37] The connection between snake charming and the solemnization of marriage has a very interesting parallel in Egypt, cf. Drioton 1957, 60-61. In Babylonia pregnant women used to wear amulets of the demon Pazuzu to protect them against the child-robbing demon Lamaštu. The penis of Pazazu is a serpent. He is often depicted next to the sacred date palm. Cf. Heeßel 2004, Abb. 2, 21, 30. Of course the snake is understood as a phallic symbol in many other cultures, but in this particular context a Sumerian parallel furnishes conclusive evidence: ‘he lifted his penis, brought the bridal gift’, cf. Kramer 1969, 53; Vanstiphout 1997, 120-121.

[38] The solution proposed by Dietrich & Loretz 2009b, 80-82, involves one redundant word and two omissions which seems a bit too much. What clinches the matter is the circumstance that the Arabic cognate *wah̩r* or *wah̩rah* is a *venomous* reptile (Kazimirski 1860, 1499). Snakes and lizards were regarded as animals belonging to the same class, cf. Buchholz 2000, Abb. 18c; Pientka-Hinz 2009, 206-207.

[39] The Dragon is probably H̩ôrānu, the father of the serpents. For the love-present see Deut. 23:19; Mic. 1:7; Hos. 2:14.

[40] Apparently the scribe forgot this strophe and partially corrected his error by this marginal note. It proves once more that the written tablets served as mnemonics for the oral delivery of religious texts in Ugarit.

Bibliography

Abou-Assaf 1982 – A. Abou-Assaf *et al.*, *La statue de Tell Fekherye et son inscription bilingue assyro-araméenne* (Études Assyriologiques, 7), Paris.

Achenbach *et al.* 2007 – R. Achenbach *et al.* (eds), *Tora in der Hebräischen Bibel: Studien zur Redaktionsgeschichte und synchronen Logik diachroner Transformationen*, Wiesbaden.

Achilles 1986 – E. Achilles, 'Evil: πονηρὸς', NIDOTTE, vol. 1, 564-567.

Adamczewski 2012 – B. Adamczewski, *Retelling the Law: Genesis, Exodus–Numbers, and Samuel–Kings as Sequential Hypertextual Reworkings of Deuteronomy* (European Studies in Theology: Philosophy and History of Religions, 1), Frankfurt am Main.

Aḥituv 2008 – S. Aḥituv, *Echoes from the Paset: Hebrew and Cognate Inscriptions from the Biblical Period*, Jerusalem.

Ahn 2003 – G. Ahn, 'Dualismen im Kontext von Gegenweltvorstellungen: Die rituelle Abwehr der Dämonen im altiranischen Zoroastrismus', in: Lange 2003, 122-134.

Aitken 2011 – J.K. Aitken *et al.* (eds), *On Stone and Scroll: Essays in Honour of Graham Ivor Davies* (BZAW, 420), Berlin.

Albani 2004 – M. Albani, 'The Downfall of Helel, the Son of Dawn: Aspects of Royal Ideology in Isa. 14:12-13', in: Auffarth & Stuckenbruck 2004, 62-86.

Albright 1922 – W.F. Albright, 'The Location of the Garden of Eden', *AJSL* 39, 15-31.

Albright 1937 – W.F. Albright, 'The Canaanite God Ḥaurôn (Ḥôrôn)', *AJSL* 53, 1-12.

Alexander 1972 – P.S. Alexander, 'The Targumim and Early Exegesis of "Sons of God" in Genesis 6', *JJS* 23, 60-71.

Allen 1997 – J.P. Allen, '1. Cosmologies', in: Hallo *et al* 1997, 5-27.

Amiet 1992 – *Sceaux-cylindres en hématite et pierres diverses* (RSO, 9), Paris.

Amzallag & Avriel 2012 – N. Amzallag & M. Avriel, 'The Cryptic Meaning of the Isaiah 14 *Māšāl*', *JBL* 131, 643-662.

Andersen, F.I., 2009 – '2 (Slavonic Apocalypse of) ENOCH', in: Charlesworth 2009, vol. 1, 91-221.

Anderson 2000a – G. Anderson *et al.* (eds), *Literature on Adam and Eve: Collected Essays* (Studia in Veteris Testamenti Pseudepigrapha, 15), Leiden.

Anderson 2000b – G. Anderson, 'Ezekiel 28, the Fall of Satan, and the Adam Books', in: Anderson 2000a, 133-147.

Anderson 2009 – H. Anderson, '4 Maccabees', in: Charlesworth 2009, vol. 2, 531-564.

Anderson & Stone 1999 – G.A. Anderson & M.E. Stone, *A Synopsis of the Books of Adam and Eve* (SBL.EJL, 5), second edition, Atlanta.

Angel 2006 – A.R. Angel, *Chaos and the Son of Man: The Hebrew* Chaoskampf *Tradition in the Period 515* BCE *to 200* CE (Library of Second Temple Studies, 60), London.

Angerstorfer 1979 – A. Angerstorfer, *Der Schöpfergott des Alten Testaments: Herkunft und Bedeutungsentwicklung des hebräischen Terminus* בָּרָא *(bara) 'schaffen'*, Frankfurt a.M.

Anklesaria 1956 – B.T. Anklesaria, *Zand-Ākāsīh: Iranian or Greater Bundahišn*, Bombay.

Arneth 2007a – M. Arneth, *Durch Adams Fall ist ganz verderbt ... Studien zur Entstehung der alttestamentlichen Urgeschichte* (FRLANT, 217), Göttingen.

Arneth 2007b – M. Arneth, 'Die noachitischen Gebote (Genesis 9, 1-7): Die Priesterschrift und das Gesetz in der Urgeschichte', in: Achenbach *et al.* 2007, 7-25.

Arnold 2009 – B.T. Arnold, *Genesis* (New Cambridge Bible Commentary), Cambridge.

Arnold 2012 – B.T. Arnold, 'Genesis 1 as Holiness Preamble', in: I. Provan & M.J. Boda (eds), *Let us Go up to Zion: Essays in Honour of H.G.M. Williamson on the Occasion of his Sixty-Fifth Birthday*, Leiden, 331-343.

Assmann 1983 – J. Assmann, *Sonnenhymnen in thebanischen Gräbern*, Mainz am Rhein.

Astour 1987 – M.C. Astour, 'Semites and Hurrians in Northern Transtigris', in: M.A. Morrison & D.I. Owen (eds), *Nuzi and the Hurrians: Studies in Honor of Ernest R. Lacheman on his Seventy-fifth Birthday*, vol. 2: General Studies and Excavations at Nuzi 9/1, Winona Lake, 3-68.

Attridge & Oden, Jr 1981 – H.W. Attridge & R.A. Oden, Jr., *Philo of Byblos, The Phoenician History* (CBQ.MS,9), Washington.

Auffarth & Stuckenbruck 2004 – C. Auffarth & L.T. Stuckenbruck (eds), *The Fall of the Angels* (Themes in Biblical Narrative, 6), Leiden.

Aune 1997a – D.E. Aune, *Revelation 1–5* (WBC, 52A), Waco.

Aune 1997b – D.E. Aune, *Revelation 6–16* (WBC, 52B), Waco.

Baer & Gordon 2013 – D.A. Baer & R.P. Gordon (eds), *Leshon Limmudim: Essays on the Language and Literature of the Hebrew Bible in Honour of A.A. Macintish*, London.

Baly 1974 – D. Baly, *The Geography of the Bible*, rev. ed., Guilford.

Barker 2012 – M. Barker, 'Isaiah', in: J.D.G. Dunn & J.W. Rogerson (eds), *Eerdmans Commentary on the Bible*, Grand Rapids, 489-542.

Barnard 2010 – H. Barnard *et al.*, 'Chemical Evidence for Wine Production around 4000 BCE in the Late Chalcolithic Near Eastern Highlands', *Journal of Archaeological Science* 30, 1-8.

Barr 1992 – J. Barr, *The Garden of Eden and the Hope of Immortality: The Read-Tuckwell Lectures for 1990*, London.

Barr 2006a – D.L. Barr (ed.), *The Reality of Apocalypse: Rhetoric and Politics in the Book of Revelation*, Atlanta.

Barr 2006b – J. Barr, 'Is God a Liar? (Gen. 2–3) and Related Matters', *JThS* 57, 1-22.

Barrett & Caneday 2013 – M. Barrett & A.B. Caneday (eds), *The Historical Adam*, Grand Rapids.

Barron 1990 – B. Barron, 'Putting Women in Their Place: 1 Timothy 2 and Evangelical Views of Women in Church Leadership', *JETS* 33, 451-459.

Barthélemy 1965 – A. Barthélemy, *Dictionnaire Arabe – Français: Dialectes de Syrie: Alep, Damas, Liban, Jérusalem*, Paris.

Batto 2013 – B.F. Batto, *In the Beginning: Essays on Creation Motifs in the Bible and the Ancient Near East* (Siphrut, 9), Winona Lake.
Bauckham 2013 – R. Bauckham *et al.* (eds), *Old Testament Pseudepigrapha: More Noncanonical Scriptures*, Grand Rapids.
Bauer 1935 – J. Bauer, 'Die literarische Form des Heptemeron', *BZ* 1, 273-277.
Beasley-Murray 1999 – G.R. Beasley-Murray, *John* (WBC, 36), 2nd edition, Waco.
Beattie 2007 – G.A. Beattie, 'The Fall of Eve: 1 Timothy 2,14 as a Canonical Example of Biblical Interpretation', in: P.S. Alexander & J.-D. Kaestli (eds), *The Canon of Scripture in Jewish and Christian Tradition*, Lausanne, 207-216.
Beatty 2014 – D.R.G. Beattie, 'Genesis 3 Revisited', *ET* 125, 282-283.
Becking 2011 – B. Becking, 'Once in a Garden: Some Remarks on the Construction of the Identity of Woman and Man in Genesis 2–3', in: Becking & Hennecke 2011, 1-10.
Becking 2012 – B. Becking, 'Semitisch sprekende slangen: Over de betekenis voor de wetenschap van het Oude Testament van een bijzondere vondst in de piramideteksten', *NedThT* 66, 203-217.
Becking 2013 – B. Becking (ed.), *Reflections of the Silence of God: A Discussion with Marjo Korpel and Johannes de Moor* (OTS, 62), Leiden.
Becking & Hennecke 2011 – B. Becking & S. Hennecke (eds), *Out of Paradise: Eve and Adam and their Interpreters*, Sheffield.
Becking & Korpel 1999 – B. Becking & M.C.A. Korpel (eds), *The Crisis of Israelite Religion: Transformation of Religious Tradition in Exilic and Post-exilic Times* (OTS, 42).
Becking & Korpel 2010 – B. Becking & M.C.A. Korpel, 'To Create, to Separate or to Construct: An Alternative for a Recent Proposal as to the Interpretation of ברא in Gen 1:12:4a', *JHS* 10, Article 3.
Beckman 1983 – G.M. Beckman. *Hittite Birth Rituals* (Studien zu den Boğazköy-Texten, 29), Wiesbaden.
Beentjes 1997 – P.C. Beentjes, *The Book of Ben Sira in Hebrew: A Text Edition of All Extant Hebrew Manuscripts and a Synopsis of All Parallel Hebrew Ben Sira Texts* (VT.S, 68), Leiden.
Beentjes 2003 – P.C. Beentjes, 'Theodicy in the Wisdom of Ben Sira', in: Laato & De Moor 2003, 509-524.
Beinhauer-Köhler 2004 – B. Beinhauer-Köhler, 'Die Engelsturzmotive des *Umm al-Kitāb*: Untersuchungen zur Trägerschaft eines synkretistischen Werkes der härätischen Schia', In: Auffarth & Stuckenbruck 2004, 161-175.
Bembry 2011 – J. Bembry, *Yahweh's Coming of Age*, Winona Lake.
Berlejung 2012 – A. Berlejung *et al.* (eds), *Menschenbilder und Körperkonzepte im Alten Israel, in Ägypten und im Alten Orient* (ORA, 9), Tübingen.
Berner 2012 – C. Berner, 'Die eherne Schlange: Zum literarischen Ursprung eines "mosaischen" Artefakts', *ZAW* 124, 341-355.
Betz 1958 – O. Betz, 'Die Proselytentaufe der Qumransekte und die Taufe im Neuen Testament', *RdQ* 1, 213-234.
Beuken 2007 – W.A.M. Beuken, *Jesaja 13–27* (HThKAT), Freiburg i.B.
Black 1989 – M. Black, *Romans* (NCBC), 2nd ed., Grand Rapids.

Blair 2009 – J.M. Blair, *De-Demonising the Old Testament: An Investigation of Azazel, Lilith, Deber, Qeteb and Resheph in the Hebrew Bible*, Tübingen.

Blenkinsopp 2000 – J. Blenkinsopp, *Isaiah 1–39: A New Translation with Introduction and Commentary* (AncB, 19), New York.

Blenkinsopp 2011 – J. Blenkinsopp, *Creation, Un-Creation, Re-Creation: A Discursive Commentary on Genesis 1–11*, London.

Block 1998 – D.I. Block, *The Book of Ezekiel: Chapters 25–48* (NICOT), Grand Rapids.

Blumenthal & Van der Kaaden 1964 – M.M. Blumenthal & G. van der Kaaden, *Catalogue of the Active Volcanoes of the World Including Solfatara Fields*, 16: Turkey, Roma.

Boadt 1980 – L. Boadt, *Ezekiel's Oracles against Egypt: A Literary and Philological Study of Ezekiel 29–32* (Biblica et Orientalia. 37), Rome.

Bodi 1991 – D. Bodi, *The Book of Ezekiel and the Poem of Erra* (OBO, 104), Freiburg.

Böhlig & Labib 1963 – A. Böhlig & P. Labib, *Koptisch-gnostische Apokalypsen aus Codex V von Nag Hammadi im Koptischen Museum zu Alt-Kairo* (WZH, Sonderband), Halle-Wittenberg.

Böttrich 2012 – C. Böttrich, 'The "Book of the Secrets of Enoch" (2 En): Between Jewish Origin and Christian Transmission – An Overview', in: Orlov & Boccaccini 2012, 37-67.

Bohak 2008 – G. Bohak, *Ancient Jewish Magic: A History*, Cambridge.

Bolman 1938 – J. Bolman, *De edelstenen uit den Bijbel gezien in het licht der hedendaagse Edelsteenkunde*, Amsterdam.

Bonnet 1988 – C. Bonnet, *Melqart: Cultes et mythe de l'Héraclès tyrien en Méditerranée* (Studia Phoenicia, 7), Leuven.

Bordreuil 1985 – P. Bordreuil, 'Vénin de printemps, vénin foudroyant: À propos de RS 24.244 l.5', *UF* 15, 299-300.

Bordreuil 2007 – P. Bordreuil, 'L'antidote au vénin dans le mythe ougaritique de "Horon et les serpents" et le serpent d'airain de Nombres 21:4-9', in: W.G.E. Watson (ed.), *"He unfurrowed his brow and laughed": Essays in Honour of Professor Nicolas Wyatt* (AOAT, 299), 35-38.

Bordreuil 2012 – P. Bordreuil *et al.*, *Une bibliothèque au sud de la ville ***: Textes 1994-2002 en cunéiforme alphabétique de la maison d'Ourtenou* (RSO, 18), Lyon.

Bordreuil 2013 – P. Bordreuil, 'Peut-on parler de legs cananéen à propos de l'idée royale israélite?', in: D. Hamidović (ed.), *Aux origines des messianismes juifs: Actes du colloque international tenu en Sorbonne à Paris, les 8 et 9 juin 2010* (VT.S, 158), Leiden, 33-44.

Bordreuil 2014 – P. Bordreuil *et al.* (eds), *Les écritures mises au jour sur le site d'Ougarit (Syrie) et leur déchiffrement 1930-2010*, Paris.

Bordreuil & Pardee 1989 – P. Bordreuil & D.Pardee, *La trouvaille épigraphique de l'Ougarit*, t. 1, Concordance (RSO, 5), Paris.

Bordreuil & Pardee 2001 – P. Bordreuil & D.Pardee, '11. Une incantation (no 52)', in: M. Yon & D. Arnaud, *Études ougaritiques: I. Travaux 1985–1995* (RSO, 14), Paris, 387-391.

Bordreuil & Pardee 2004 – P. Bordreuil & D. Pardee, *Manuel d'Ougaritique*, vol. 2, Paris.

Borghouts 2007 – J.F. Borghouts, *Book of the Dead (39): From Shouting to Structure* (Studien zum Altaägyptischen Totenbuch, 10), Wiesbaden.

Bormann 2007 – L. Bormann, 'Sündigen und Sterben: Der Beitrag von Rom 5,12 zur Theodizeefrage,' in: N.C. Baumgart (ed.), *Philosophisch-Theologische Anstöße zur Urteilsbildung* (Lüneburgische Theologische Beiträge; Fs W. Brändle), Berlin 2007, 65-77.

Bornstein 2013 – M. Bornstein, 'The Jerusalem Ostracon אלקנארץ Reconsidered', *IEJ* 63, 26-38.

Bottéro & Kramer 2011– J. Bottéro & S.-N. Kramer, *L'érotisme sacré à Sumer et à Babylone*, Paris.

Bovon 1996 – F. Bovon, *Das Evangelium nach Lukas (Lk 9,51–14,35)* (EKK, 3/2), Zürich.

Boyce 1975 – M. Boyce, *A History of Zoroastrianism*, vol. 1 (HO, 1/2A), Leiden.

Boyce 1979 – M. Boyce, *Zoroastrians: Their Religious Beliefs and Practices* (Library of Religious Beliefs and Practices), London.

Bradshaw & Head 2012 – J.M. Bradshaw & R.J. Head, 'The Investiture Panel at Mari and Rituals of Divine Kingship in the Ancient Near East', *Studies in the Bible and Antiquity* 4, 1-42.

Brandenburger 1962 – E. Brandenburger, *Adam und Christus: Exegetisch-Religionsgeschichtliche Untersuchung zu Röm. 5:12-21 (1. Kor. 15)*, Neukirchen.

Bremmer 2000 – J.N. Bremmer, 'Pandora or the Creation of a Greek Eve', in: Luttikhuizen 2000a, 19-33.

Bremmer 2004 – J.N. Bremmer, 'Remember the Titans!', in: Auffarth & Stuckenbruck 2004, 35-61.

Bremmer 2012 – J.N. Bremmer, 'Titans', *Brill's New Pauly Online*, Leiden.

Bron *et al.* 2010 – F. Bron *et al.* (eds), *Dictionnaire des racines sémitiques*, vol. 2, fasc. 9, Leuven.

Brueggemann 1982 – W. Brueggemann, *Genesis: A Bible Commentary for Teaching and Preaching*, Atlanta.

Brunner 1988 – H. Brunner, *Altägyptische Weisheit: Lehren für das Leben*, Zürich.

Brunner-Traut 1975 – E. Brunner-Traut, 'Anonymität (der Götter)', *LÄ*, Bd. 1, Wiesbaden, 281-291.

Buchholz 2000 – H.-G. Buchholz, 'Furcht vor Schlangen und Umgang mit Schlangen in Altsyrien, Altkypros und dem Umfeld', *UF* 32, 36-168.

Bührer 2014 – W. Bührer, *Am Anfang ... Untersuchungen zur Textgenese und zur relativ-chronologischen Einordnung von Gen 1–3* (FRLANT 256), Göttingen.

Bunta 2007 – M. Bunta, 'Yhwh's Cultic Statue after 597/586 B.C.E.: A Linguistic and Theological Reinterpretation of Ezekiel 28:12', *CBQ* 69, 222-241.

Burdon *et al.* 1953 – D.J. Burdon, S. Mazloum, and C. Safadi, 'Groundwater in Syria', *UGGT Association Internationale d'Hydrologie Scientifique. Assemblée Générale Rome*, 377-388.

Burns 1989 – J.B. Burns, '*ḥôlēš ʿal* in Isaiah 14:12: A New Proposal', *ZAH* 2, 199-204.

Busch 1996 – P. Busch, *Der gefallene Drache: Mythenexegese am Beispiel von Apokalypse 12*, Tübingen.

Byron 2008 – J. Byron, 'Cain's Rejected Offering: Interpretative Approaches to a Theological Problem', *JSPE* 18, 3-22.

Canaan 1929 – T. Canaan, *Dämonenglaube im Lande der Bibel* (Morgenland, 21), Leipzig.

Calduch-Benages 2013 –N. Calduch-Benages, 'Gute und schlechte Ehefrauen im Buch Jesus Sirach – eine harmlose Unterscheidung?', in: Maier & Calduch-Benages 2013, 105-121.

Callender 2000a – D.E. Callender, Jr., 'The Primal Human in Ezekiel and the Image of God', in: M.S. Odell & J.T. Strong (eds), *The Book of Ezekiel: Theological and Anthropological Perspectives* (JBL Symposium Series, 9), Atlanta, 175-193.

Callender 2000b – D.E. Callender, Jr., *Adam in Myth and History: Ancient Israelite Perspectives on the Primal Human* (HSS, 48). Winona Lake.

Caplice 1974 – R.I. Caplice, *The Akkadian* namburbi-*Texts: An Introduction*, Los Angeles.

Caquot & Sznycer 1980 – A. Caquot & M. Sznycer, *Ugaritic Religion* (Iconography of Religions, 15/8), Leiden.

Carmichael 1992 – C.M. Carmichael, 'The Paradise Myth: Interpreting without Jewish and Christian Spectacles', in: P. Morris & D. Sawyer, *A Walk in the Garden: Biblical, Iconographical and Literary Images of Eden* (JOST.SS, 136), Sheffield, 47-63.

Carr 2003 – W.R. Carr, *In his Own Image and Likeness: Humanity, Divinity, and Monotheism* (CHANE, 15), Leiden.

Cassin 1973 – E. Cassin, 'La contestation dans le monde divin', in: A. Finet (ed.), *La voix de l'opposition en Mésopotamie: Colloque organisée par l'Institut des Hautes Études de Belgique 19 et 20 mars 1973*, Bruxelles, 89-110.

Cassuto 1961 – U. Cassuto, *A Commentary on the Book of Genesis*, tr. I. Abarahams, vol. 1, Jerusalem.

Cathcart 2011 – K.J. Cathcart, 'The Phoenician Inscriptions from Arslan Tash and Some Old Testament Texts (Exodus 12; Micah 5:4-5[5-6]; Psalm 91)', in: Aitken 2011, 87-99.

Charlesworth 2009 – J.H. Charlesworth, (ed.),*The Old Testament Pseudepigrapha*, 2 vols., Peabody [repr. of 1983 edition].

Charlesworth 2010 – J.H. Charlesworth, *The Good and Evil Serpent: How a Universal Symbol Became Christianized* (Anchor Yale Bible Reference Library), New Haven.

Chen 2013 – Y.S. Chen, *The Primeval Flood Catastrophe: Origins and Early Development in Mesopotamian Traditions* (Oxford Oriental Monographs), Oxford.

Childs 2001 – B.S. Childs, *Isaiah* (OTL), Louisville.

Cho 2007 – S.Y. Cho, *Lesser Deities in the Ugaritic Texts and the Hebrew Bible: A Comparative Study of Their Nature and Roles* (Deities and Angels of the Ancient World, 2), Piscataway.

Clemens 2001 – D.M. Clemens, *Sources for Ugaritic Ritual and Sacrifice*, vol. 1: Ugaritc and Ugarit Akkadian Texts (AOAT, 284/1), Münster.

Clemens 2007 – D.M. Clemens, [Review of Shipp 2002], *JNES* 66, 213-216.

Clifford 1994 – R.J. Clifford, *Creation Accounts in the Ancient Near East and in the Bible*, Washington.

Clines 1989 – D.J.A. Clines, *Job 1–20* (WBC, 17), Dallas.

Clines 1990 – D.J.A. Clines, 'What Does Eve to Help? And Other Irredeemably Androcentric Orientations in Genesis 1–3', in: D.J.A. Clines (ed.), *What Does Eve to Help? And Other Readerly Questions to the Old Testament* (JSOT, 94), Sheffield, 25-48.

Clines 2006 – D.J.A. Clines, *Job 21–37* (WBC, 18A), Nashville.

Cogan 2008 – M. Gogan, *The Raging Torrent: Historical Inscriptions from Assyria and Babylon Relating to Ancient Israel*, Jerusalem.

Cohn Eskenazi 2013 – T. Cohn Eskenazi, 'Das Leben von Frauen in der nachexilischen Zeit', in: Maier & Calduch-Benages 2013, 15-35.

Collins 2013 – C.J Collins, 'A Historical Adam: Old-Earth Creation View', in: Barrett & Caneday 2013, 143-175.

Collon 1975 – D. Collon, *The Seal Impressions from Tell Atchana/Alalakh* (AOAT, 27), Neukirchen-Vluyn.

Collon 1982 – D. Collon, *Catalogue of the Western Asiatic Seals in the British Museum: Cylinder Seals II: Akkadian, Post Akkadian, Ur III Periods, II*, London.

Collon 1987 – D. Collon, *First Impressions: Cylinder Seals in the Ancient Near East*, London.

Cooke 1964 – G. Cooke, 'The Sons of (the) God(s)', *ZAW* 76, 22-47.

Copeland Biella 2004 – J. Copeland Biella, *Dictionary of Old South Arabic: Sabaean Dialect* (HSS, 25). Winona Lake.

Cornelius 1994 – I. Cornelius, *The Iconography of the Canaanite Gods Reshef and Baʿal*: Late Bronze and Iron Age I Periods (*c* 1500–1000 BCE) (OBO, 140), Fribourg.

Cornelius & Niehr 2004 – I. Cornelius & H. Niehr, *Götter und Kulte in Ugarit: Kultur und Religion einer nordsyrischen Königsstadt in der Spätbronzezeit* (Zaberns Bildbände zur Archäologie), Mainz am Rhein.

Cross 1973 – F.M. Cross, *Canaanite Myth and Hebrew Epic: Essays in the History of the Religion of Israel*, Cambridge.

Crouch 2011a– C.L. Crouch, 'Ezekiel's Oracles Against the Nations in Light of a Royal Ideology of Warfare', *JBL* 130, 473-492.

Crouch 2011b– C.L. Crouch, 'חטאת as Interpolative Gloss: A Solution to Gen 4,7', *ZAW* 123, 250-258.

Cruz-Uribe 2009 – E. Cruz-Uribe, '*Stẖ ʿ3 pḥty* "Seth, God of Power and Might" ', *JARCE* 45, 201-226.

Curtis 2001 - R.I. Curtis, *Ancient Food Technology* (Technology and Change in History, 5), Leiden.

Curtis 2012 – A.H. Curtis, 'The God of the Father Re-revisited: The Relevance of Ugaritic ʾilʾib', in: Del Olmo Lete 2012, 121-129.

Dalley 1991 – S. Dalley, *Myths from Mesopotamia: Creation, The Flood, Gilgamesh, and Others*, Oxford.

Davidson 1988 – R.M. Davidson, 'The Theology of Sexuality in the Beginning: Genesis 3', *AUSS* 26, 121-131.

Davies 2006 – G. Davies, ' "God" in Old Testament Theology', in: A. Lemaire (ed.), *Congress Volume Leiden 2004* (VT.S, 109), Leiden, 175-194.

Day 1980 – J. Day, 'The Daniel of Ugarit and the Hero of the Book of Daniel', *VT* 30, 174-184.

Day 1985 – J. Day, *God's Conflict with the Dragon and the Sea: Echoes of a Canaanite Myth in the Old Testament* (UCOP, 35), Cambridge.

Day 1994 – J. Day, 'Ugarit and the Bible: Do They Presuppose the Same Canaanite Mythology and Religion?', in: G.J.Brooke *et al.* (eds), *Ugarit and the Bible: Proceedings of the International Symposium on Ugarit and the Bible Manchester, September 1992* (UBL, 11), Münster, 35-52.

Day 2000 – J. Day, *Yahweh and the Gods and Goddesses of Canaan* (JSOT.S, 265), Sheffield (repr. 2002).

Day 2011 – J. Day, 'The Flood and the Ten Antediluvian Figures in Berossus and in the Priestly Source in Genesis', in: Aitken 2011, 211-223.

Day 2013 J. Day, *From Creation to Babel: Studies in Genesis 1–11*, London.

Day 1998 – J.N. Day, 'God and Leviathan in Isaiah 27:1', *BS* 155, 423-436.

De Bondt 1947 – A. de Bondt, *De Satan*, Baarn.

De Hoop 1999 – R. de Hoop, *Genesis 49 in its Literary and Historical Context* (OTS, 39), Leiden.

De Hulster 2012 – I. de Hulster, 'Figurines from Persian Period Jerusalem?', *ZAW* 124, 73-88.

De Jonge 2000 – M. de Jonge, *Pseudepigrapha of the Old Testament as Part of Christian Literature: The Case of the Testaments of the Twelve Patriarchs and the Greek Life of Adam and Eve* (Studia in Veteris Testamenti Pseudepigrapha, 18), Leiden.

De Jonge & Tromp 1997 – M. de Jonge & J. Tromp, *The Life of Adam and Eve and Related Literature* (Guides to Apocrypha and Pseudepigrapha), Sheffield.

Del Monte & Tischler 1978 – G.F. Del Monte & J. Tischler *Die Orts- und Gewässernamen der hethitischen Texte*, Wiesbaden.

Del Olmo Lete 2008a – G. del Olmo Lete (ed.), *Mythologie et Religion des Sémites Occidentaux*, vol. 1: Ébla, Mari (OLA, 162), Leuven.

Del Olmo Lete 2008b – G. del Olmo Lete, *Questions of Semitic Linguistics: Root and Lexeme – The History of Research*, Bethesda.

Del Olmo Lete 2011 – G. del Olmo Lete, 'KTU 1.82: Another Miscellaneous Incantation/Anti-Witchcraft Text against Snakebite in Ugaritic', *Aula Orientalis* 29, 245-265.

Del Olmo Lete 2012a – G. del Olmo Lete *et al.* (eds), *The Perfumes of Seven Tamarisks: Studies in Honour of Wilfred G.E. Watson* (AOAT, 394), Münster.

Del Olmo Lete 2012b – G. del Olmo Lete, 'RS 92.2014: A New Interpretation', in: Del Olmo Lete 2012a, 143-157.

Del Olmo Lete 2013 – G. del Olmo Lete, 'KTU 1.107: A Miscellany of Incantations against Snakebite', in: O. Loretz *et al.* (eds), *Ritual, Religion and Reason: Studies in the Ancient World in Honour of Paolo Xella* (AOAT, 404), Münster., 193-204.

Del Olmo Lete 2014 – G. del Olmo Lete, *Incantations and Anti-Witchcraft Texts from Ugarit* (Studies in Ancient Near Eastern Records, 4), Berlin.

Del Olmo Lete & Sanmartín 2003 – *A Dictionary of the Ugaritic Language in the Alphabetic Tradition*, 2 vols, Leiden.

De Moor 1970a – J.C. de Moor, 'The Semitic Pantheon of Ugarit', *UF* 2,187-228.

De Moor 1970b – J.C. de Moor, 'Studies in the New Alphabetic Texts from Ras Shamra II', *UF* 2, 303-327.

De Moor 1971 – J.C. de Moor, *The Seasonal Pattern in the Ugaritic Myth of Baʿlu According to the Version of Ilimilku* (AOAT, 16), Neukirchen-Vluyn.

De Moor 1972 – J.C. de Moor, *New Year with Canaanites and Israelites* (Kamper Cahiers, 21-22), Kampen.

De Moor 1976 – J.C. de Moor, 'Rāpiʾūma – Rephaim', *ZAW* 88, 323-345.

De Moor 1977 – J.C. de Moor, 'Some Remarks on U 5 V, No. 7 and 8 (KTU 1.100 and 1.107)', *UF* 9, 366-367.

De Moor 1980 – J.C. de Moor, 'El, the Creator', in: G. Rendsburg *et al.* (eds.), *The Bible World: Essays in Honor of C.H. Gordon*, New York, 171-187.

De Moor 1986 – J.C. de Moor, 'Ugaritic Lexicographical Notes I', *UF* 18, 254-258.

De Moor 1987 – J.C. de Moor, *An Anthology of Religious Texts from Ugarit* (Nisaba,16), Leiden.

De Moor 1988a – J.C. de Moor, 'O Death, Where Is Thy Sting?', in: L. Eslinger & G. Taylor (eds), *Ascribe to the Lord: Biblical and Other Studies in Memory of P.C. Craigie*, Sheffield, 99-107.

De Moor 1988b – J.C. de Moor, 'East of Eden', *ZAW* 100, 105-112.

De Moor 1990 – J.C. de Moor, 'Loveable Death in the Ancient Near East', *UF* 22, 233-245.

De Moor 1997 – J.C. de Moor, *The Rise of Yahwism: The Roots of Israelite Monotheism*, 2nd ed. (BEThL, 91A), Leuven.

De Moor 1998a – J.C. de Moor, 'The Duality in God and Man: Gen. 1:26-27 as P's Interpretation of the Yahwistic Creation Account', in: J.C.de Moor (ed.), *Intertextuality in Ugarit and Israel* (OTS, 40), Leiden, 112-125.

De Moor 1998b – J.C. de Moor, 'Seventy!', in: Dietrich & Kottsieper 1998, 199-203.

De Moor 1999 – J.C. de Moor, 'The First Human Being a Male? A Respose to Professor Barr', in: A. Brenner & J.W. van Henten (eds), *Recycling Biblical Figures: Papers Read at a NOSTER Colloquium in Amsterdam, 12-13 May 1997* (STAR, 1), Leiden, 22-27.

De Moor 2003 – J.C. de Moor, 'Theodicy in the Texts of Ugarit', in: Laato & De Moor 2003, 108-150.

De Moor 2008 – J.C. de Moor, 'How Ilimilku Lost his Master (RS 92.2016)', *UF* 40, 179-189.

De Moor 2010 – J.C. de Moor, [Review], *Aula Orientalis* 23 (2005) [2010], 287-291.

De Moor 2012 – J.C. de Moor, 'The Order of the Tablets of the Baʿlu Myth', in: G. del Olmo Lete 2012a, 131-141.

De Moor 2014 – J.C. de Moor, 'Concepts of Afterlife in Canaan', *UF* 45, 373-388.
De Moor & Spronk 1984 – J.C. de Moor & K. Spronk, 'More on Demons in Ugarit (KTU 1.82)', *UF* 16, 237-250.
De Moor & Spronk 1987 – J.C. de Moor & K. Spronk, *A Cuneiform Anthology of Religious Texts from Ugarit* (SSS, 6), Leiden.
Denizeau 1960 – C. Denizeau, *Dictionnaire des parlers arabes de Syrie, Liban et Palestine* (Études Arabes et Islamiques, 3), Paris.
Dennis 2007 – J. Dennis, 'The "lifting up of the Son of Man" and the Dethroning of the "ruler of this world": Jesus' Death as the Defeat of the Devil in John 12,31-32,' in: G. Van Belle (ed.), *Death of Jesus* (BEThL, 200), 2007, 677-691.
Deutsch 2002 – R. Deutsch, 'Lasting Impressions: New Bullae Reveal Egyptian-Style Emblems on Judah's Royal Seals', *BARe* 28/4, 42-51.
De Villiers 2009 – G. de Villiers, 'Sin, Suffering, Sagacity: Genesis 2–3,' in: B. Becking & D. Human, *Exile and Suffering* (OTS, 50), Leiden, 3-17.
Dick 1999 – M.B. Dick (ed.), *Born in Heaven, Made on Earth: The Making of the Cult Image in the Ancient Near East*, Winona Lake.
Dietrich 2001 – M. Dietrich, 'Das biblische Paradies und der babylonische Tempelgarten: Überlegungen zur Lage des Gartens Eden', in: Janowski & Ego 2001, 281-323.
Dietrich 2004 – M. Dietrich, 'Der kult(ur)geographische und zeitliche Horizont ugaritischer und hurritischer Priester', *UF* 36, 11-39.
Dietrich & Kottsieper 1998 – M. Dietrich, & I. Kottsieper (eds), *"Und Mose schrieb dieses Lied auf": Studien zum Alten Testament und zum Alten Orient (Fs O. Loretz)* (AOAT, 250), Münster.
Dietrich & Loretz 2008 – M. Dietrich & O. Loretz, 'Ḥorōn, der Herr über die Schlangen: Das Verhältnis von Mythos und Beschwörung in KTU 1.100', in: M. Dietrich (ed.), *Orbis Ugariticus: Ausgewählte Beiträge von Manfried Dietrich und Oswald Loretz zu Fest- und Gedenkschriften* (AOAT, 343). Münster, 119-140.
Dietrich & Loretz 2009a – M. Dietrich & O. Loretz, 'Präventiv-Beschwörung gegen Schlangen, Skorpionen und Hexerei zum Schutz des präfekten Urtenu (KTU 1.178 = RS 92.2014)', *UF* 41, 65-73.
Dietrich & Loretz 2009b – M. Dietrich & O. Loretz, 'Urbild und Abbild in der Schlangenbeschwörung KTU 1.100: Epigraphie, Kolometrie, Redaktion und Ritual', *UF* 41, 75-108.
Dietrich & Mayer 1997 – M. Dietrich & W. Mayer, 'Ein hurritisches Totenritual für ʿAmmištamru III (KTU 1.125)', in: B. Pongratz-Leisten *et al.* (eds), *Ana šadî Labnāni lū allik: Beiträge zu altorientalischen und mittelmeerischen Kulturen*, (AOAT, 247), Neukirchen-Vluyn, 79-89.
Díez Macho 1988 – A. Díez Macho, *Biblia Polyglotta Matritensia*, Series IV: Targum Palaestinense in Pentateuchum, vol. 1, Matriti.
Díez Merino 1984 – L. Díez Merino, 'Los "vigilantes" en la literatura intertestamentaria', in: N. Fernandez Marcos *et al.* (eds), *Simposio biblico Español (Salamanca 1982)*, Madrid, 575-605.
Dijkstra 1989 – M. Dijkstra, *Ezechiël II: Een praktische bijbelverklaring* (Tekst en Toelichting), Kampen.

Dijkstra 1999 – M. Dijkstra, 'Mother', in: Van der Toorn 1999, 603-604.

Dijkstra 2006 – M.Dijkstra, 'Moses, the Man of God', in: R. Roukema *et al.* (eds), *The Interpretation of Exodus: Studies in Honour of Cornelis Houtman* (CBET, 44), Louvain, 17-36.

Dijkstra 2011 – M. Dijkstra, 'Ishtar Seduces the Sea-serpent', *UF* 43, 53-83.

Dijkstra 2013 – M. Dijkstra, 'Let Sleeping Gods Lie?', in: Becking 2013, 73-87.

Dijkstra & De Moor 1975 – M. Dijkstra & J.C. de Moor, 'Problematical Passages in the legend of Aqhâtu', *UF* 7, 171-215.

Dochhorn 2005 – J. Dochhorn, *Die Apokalypse des Mose: Text, Übersetzung, Kommentar* (TSHJA, 106), Tübingen.

Dochhorn 2005 – J. Dochhorn, *Schriftgelehrte Prophetie: Der Eschatologische Teufelsfall in Apc Joh 12 und seine Bedeutung für das Verständnis der Johannesoffenbarung* (WUNT, 268), Tübingen.

Doergens 1860 – R. Doergens, 'Consul Wetzstein's und R. Doergens' Reise in das Ost-Jordan-Land', *Zeitschrift für Allgemeine Erdkunde* 8-9 (1860), 402-420.

Dolansky 2007 – S. Dolansky, 'A Goddess in the Garden? The Fall of Eve', in: S. Malena & D. Miano (eds), *Milk and Honey: Essays on Ancient Israel and the Bible in Appreciation of the Judaic Studies Program at the University of California, San Diego*, Winona Lake, 3-21.

Dominicus 1994 – B. Dominicus, *Gesten und Gebärden in Darstellungen des Alten und Mittleren Reiches* (SAGA, 10), Heidelberg.

Draffkorn Kilmer 1987 – A. Draffkorn Kilmer, 'The Mesopotamian Counterparts of the Biblical Nĕpīlîm', in: E.W.Conrad & E.G. Newing (eds), *Perspectives on Language and Text: Essays and Poems in Honor of Francis I. Andersen's Sixtieth Birthday, July 28, 1985*, Winona Lake, 39-43.

Drioton 1957 – É. Drioton, *Pages d'Égyptologie*, Le Caire.

Dunn 1988a – J.D.G. Dunn, *Romans 1–8* (WBC, 38A), Waco.

Dunn 1988b – J.D.G. Dunn, *Romans 9-16* (WBC, 38B), Waco.

Dunn 2014 – J.E. Dunn, 'A God of Volcanoes: Did Yahwism Take Root in Volcanic Ashes?', *JSOT* 38.4, 387-424.

Durand, J.-M., 2008 – J.-M. Durand, 'La religion amorrite en Syrie à l'époque des archives de Mari', In: Del Olmo Lete 2008a, 161-172.

Dussaud 1936 – R. Dussaud, 'Le vrai nom de Baʿal', *Revue d'Histoire des Religions* 113, 5-20.

Edzard 1980 – D.O. Edzard, 'Köningslisten und Chroniken. A. Sumerisch', *RLA*, Bd. 6/1-2, 77-86.

Elior 2010 – R. Elior (ed.), *A Garden Eastward in Eden: Traditions of Paradise: Changing Jewish Perspectives and Comparative Dimension of Culture*, Jerusalem.

Emerton 1982 – J.A. Emerton, 'Leviathan and LTN: The Vocalization of the Ugaritic Word for the Dragon', *VT* 32, 328-331.

Epstein 1972-1973 – C. Epstein, 'Chronique archéologique: GOLAN: *dolmens*', *RB* 79, 404-407; 80, 560-563.

Fabry 1986 – H.-J. Fabry, 'נָחָשׁ', *ThWAT*, vol. 5, 384-397.

Fagnan 1923 – E. Fagnan, *Additions aux dictionnaires arabes*, Alger.

Fahd 1997 – T. Fahd, 'SHAYṬĀN, 1. In pre-Islamic Arabia', *The Encyclopaedia of Islam: New Edition*, vol. 9, Leiden, 406-408.
Fechter 1992 – F. Fechter, *Bewältigung der Katastrophe: Untersuchungen zu ausgewählte Fremdvölkersprüchen im Ezechielbuch* (BZAW, 208), Berlin.
Fernández Marcos 1998 – N. Fernández Marcos, *Introducción a las versiones griegas de la Biblia* (TECC, 64), second ed., Madrid.
Finkel 2014 – I. Finkel, *The Ark before Noah: Decoding the Story of the Flood*, London.
Finkel & Geller 1997 – I.L. Finkel & M.J. Geller (eds), *Sumerian Gods and their Representations* (Cuneiform Monographs, 7), Groningen.
Finkelstein 1966 – J.J. Finkelstein, 'The Genealogy of the Hammurapi Dynasty', *JCS* 20 (1966), 95-118.
Fockner 2008 – S. Fockner, 'Reopening the Discussion: Another Contextual Look at the Sons of God', *JSOT* 32, 435-456.
Foerster 1935 – W. Foerster, 'ἐχθρός', in: G. Kittel (ed.), *Theologisches Wörterbuch zum Neuen Testament*, Bd. 2, Stuttgart, 811-815.
Foster 2005 – B.R. Foster, *Before the Muses: An Anthology of Akkadian Literature*, third ed., Bethesda.
Fox 1967 – D.A. Fox, 'Darkness and Light: The Zoroastrian View', *JAAR* 35, 129-137.
Freilich & Pardee 1984 – D. Freilich & D. Pardee, '{ẓ} and {ṯ} in Ugaritic', *Syria* 61, 25-36;
Friedlander 1916 – G. Friedlander (ed.), *Pirḳê de Rabbi Eliezer, translated and annotated*, London 1916.
Frymer-Kensky 2006 – T. Frymer-Kensky, *Studies in Bible and Feminist Criticism*, Philadelphia.
Gadjimuradov & Schmoeckl 2007 – I. Gadjimuradov & R. Schmoeckl, *Der Garten Eden, die Sintflut und die Höhle: Die vulkanischen Geheimnisse des Anatolischen Meeres*, Bonn.
Gathercole 2003 – S. Gathercole, 'Jesus' Eschatological Vision of the Fall of Satan: Luke 10,18 Reconsidered', *ZNW* 94, 143-163.
Gathmann 2008 – S. Gathmann, *Im Fall gespiegelt: Der Abschluss der Tyrus-Sprüche in Ez 28,1-19* (ATSAT, 86), St. Ottilien.
Gaylord 2009 – H.E. Gaylord, '3 Greek Apocalypse of BARUCH, in: Charlesworth 2009, vol. 2, 653-679.
Gelston 2011 – A. Gelston, 'The Repentance of God', in: Aitken 2011, 453-462.
George 2003 – A.R. George, *The Babylonian Gilgamesh Epic: Introduction, Critical Edition and Cuneiform Texts*, 2 vols, Oxford.
Gertz 2004 – J.C. Gertz, 'Von Adam zu Enosch: Überlegungen zur Entstehungsgeschichte von Gen 2–4', in: M. Witte (ed.), *Gott und Mensch im Dialog* (Fs. O. Kaiser) (BZAW, 345/1), Berlin, 215-236.
Giesen 1990 – H. Giesen, 'Symbole und mythische Aussagen in der Johannesapokalypse und ihre theologische Bedeutung', in: K. Kartelge (ed.), *Metaphorik und Mythos im Neuen Testament* (QD, 126), Freiburg, 255-277.
Görg 1996 – M. Görg, 'Der "Satan" – der "Vollstrecker" Gottes?', *BN* 82, 9-12.

Gordis 1978 – R. Gordis, *The Book of Job: Commentary, New Translation and Special Studies*, New York City.

Gordon 2010 – R.P. Gordon, 'The Ethics of Eden: Truth-Telling in Genesis 2–3', in: K.J. Dell (ed.), *Ethical and Unethical in the Old Testament: God and Humans in Dialogue* (LHB, 528), London, 11-33.

Gordon 2011 – R.P. Gordon, ' "Couch" or "Crouch"? Genesis 4:7 and the Temptation of Cain', in: Aitken 2011, 195-209.

Gordon 2013 – R.P. Gordon, 'Evensong in Eden: As It Probably Was *Not* in the Beginning', in: Baer & Gordon 2013, 17-30.

Gosse 1988 – B. Gosse, *Isaïe 13,1–14,23 dans la tradition littéraire du livre d'Isaïe et dans la tradition des oracles contre les nations* (OBO, 78), Freiburg 1988.

Gräbner 2011 – S. Gräbner, 'Late Reception of Hauron Statue JE64735', *GM* 231, 35-40.

Grässer 1990 – E. Grässer, *An die Hebräer* (EKK, 17/1), Zürich.

Gray 1947 – J. Gray, 'The Canaanite God Horon', *JNES* 8, 27-34.

Grayson 1976 – A.K. Grayson, *Assyrian Royal Inscriptions* (Records of the Ancient Near East, 2), Part 2, Wiesbaden.

Grayson 1980 – A.K. Grayson, 'Königslisten und Chroniken. B. Akkadisch', *RLA*, Bd. 6/1-2, 86-135.

Greenberg 2005 – M. Greenberg, *Ezechiel 21– 37* (HThKAT), Freiburg.

Gregory 2012 – A. Gregory, *Ancient Greek Cosmogony*, London.

Gressmann 1927 – H. Gressmann, *Altorientalische Bilder zum Alten Testament*, 2.Auflage, Berlin.

Gröndahl 1967 – F. Gröndahl, *Die Personennamen der Texte aus Ugarit* (Studia Pohl, 1), Rom.

Grossfeld 1988 – B. Grossfeld, *The Targum Onqelos to Genesis* (The Aramaic Bible, 6), London.

Gruenwald 2014 – I. Gruenwald, *Apocalyptic and Merkavah Mysticism*, Second, Revised Edition (AJEC, 90), Leiden.

Guillaume 1965 – A. Guillaume, *Hebrew and Arabic Lexicography; A Comparative Study*, Leiden.

Gunkel 1895 – H. Gunkel, *Schöpfung und Chaos in Urzeit und Endzeit: Eine religionsgeschichtliche Untersuchung über Gen 1 und Ap Joh 12*, Göttingen.

Gurney 1977 – O.R. Gurney, *Some Aspects of Hittite Religion*, Oxford.

Gwynn 1897 – J. Gwynn, *The Apocalypse of St. John, in a Syriac Version Hitherto Unknown*, Dublin.

Haas 1982 – V. Haas.*Hethitische Berggötter und hurritische Steindämonen: Riten, Kulte und Mythen* (Kulturgeschichte der Antiken Welt, 10), Mainz a. R.

Haas 1994 – V. Haas, *Geschichte der hethitischen Religion* (HdO, 1.Abt., Bd. 15), Leiden.

Habel 1967 – N.C. Habel, 'Ezekiel 28 and the Fall of the First Man', *Concordia Theological Monthly* 38, 516-524.

Hagen 2012 – J.J. Hagen, 'No Longer "Slavonic" Only: A 2 Enoch Attested in Coptic', in: Orlov & Boccaccini 2012, 7-34.

Hagner 1993 – D.A. Hagner, *Matthew 1–13* (WBC, 33A), Waco.

Halton 2015 – C. Halton (ed.), *Genesis: History, Fiction, or Neither? The Bible's Earliest Chapters*, Grand Rapids.
Hallo *et al.* 1997 – W.W. Hallo *et al.* (eds), *The Context of Scripture*, vol. 1, Leiden.
Hamilton 1990 – V.P. Hamilton, *The Book of Genesis Chapters 1–17* (NICOT), Grand Rapids.
Ḫammade 1987 – Ḫ. Ḫammade, *Cylinder Seals from the Collections of the Aleppo Museum, Syrian Arab Republic*, vol. 1: Seals of Unknown Provenience (BAR International Series, 335), Oxford.
Ḫammade 1994 – Ḫ. Ḫammade, *Cylinder Seals from the Collections of the Aleppo Museum, Syrian Arab Republic*, vol. 2: Seals of Known Provenience (BAR International Series, 597), Oxford.
Handy 1994 – L.K. Handy, *Among the Host of Heaven: The Syro-Palestinian Pantheon as Bureaucracy*, Winona Lake.
Hartenstein 2009 – F. Hartenstein, 'Orte des Ursprungs und der Erneuerung: Altorientalische und biblische Paradiesvorstellungen', in: C. Karrer-Grube *et al.* (eds), *Sprachen – Bilder – Klänge: Dimensionen der Theologie im Alten Testament und seinem Umfeld* (Fs R. Bartelmus) (AOAT, 359), Münster, 35-48.
Hasitschka 2005 – M. Hasitschka, 'Joh 8,44 im Kontext des Gesprächsverlaufes von Joh 8,21-59', in: G. van Belle *et al.* (eds), *Theology and Christology in the Fourth Gospel: Essays by the Members of the SNTS Johannine Writings Seminar*, Leuven, 109-116.
Hawkins, J.D., 1981 – J.D. Hawkins, 'Kubaba. A. Philologisch', *RLA*, Bd.6/3-4, 257-261.
Hawley 2004 – R. Hawley, 'Hyssop in the Ugaritic Incantation RS 92.2014', *JANER* 4, 29-70.
Hays 2014 – C.B. Hays, *Hidden Riches: A Sourcebook for the Comparative Study of the Hebrew Bible and Ancient Near East*, Louisville.
Healey 1998 – J.F. Healey. 'The Kindly and Merciful God: On Some Semitic Divine Epithets', in: Dietrich & Kottsieper 1998, 349-356.
Heeßel 2002 – N.P. Heeßel, *Pazuzu: Archaeologische und philogische Studien zu einem altorientalischen Daemon*, Leiden.
Helck 1971 – W. Helck, *Die Beziehungen Ägyptens zu Vorderasien im 3. und 2. Jahrtausend v. Chr.* (Ägyptologische Abhandlungen, 5), 2.Auflage, Wiesbaden.
Hendel 1985 – R.S. Hendel, ' "The Flame of the Whirling Sword": A Note on Genesis 3:24', *JBL* 104, 671-674.
Hendel 1987 – R.S. Hendel, 'Of Demigods and the Deluge: Toward an Interpretation of Genesis 6:1-4', *JBL* 106, 13-26.
Hendel 2004 – R.S. Hendel, 'The Nephilim Were on the Earth: Genesis 6:1-4 and Its Ancient Near Eastern Context', in: Auffarth & Stuckenbruck 2004, 11-34.
Hendel 2013 – R.S. Hendel, *The Book of* Genesis: *A Biography* (Lives of Great Religious Books), Princeton.
Herdner – A. Herdner, *Corpus des tablettes en cunéiformes alphabétiques découvertes à Ras Shamra-Ugarit de 1929 à 1939* (MRS, 10), 2 tms, Paris.

Herrmann 1974 – W. Herrmann, 'Neue Belege für die Kuṯarāt', *ZÄS* 100, 104-108.
Hess 1990 – R.S. Hess, 'Splitting the Adam: The Usage of *'ādām* in Genesis I–V', in: J.A. Emerton (ed.), *Studies in the Pentateuch* (VT.S, 41), Leiden, 1-13.
Hess 1993 – R.S. Hess, *Studies in the Personal Names of Genesis 1–11* (AOAT, 234). Neukirchen-Vluyn.
Hess & Tsumura 1994 – R.S. Hess & D.T. Tsumura (eds), *"I Studied Inscriptions from before the Flood": Ancient Near Eastern, Literary, and Linguistic Approaches to Genesis 1–11*, Winona Lake.
Hiebert 1996 – T. Hiebert, *The Yahwist's Landscape: Nature and Religion in Early Israel*, Oxford.
Hoffner 1990 – H.A. Hoffner, *Hittite Myths* (SBL.WAW, 2), Atlanta.
Hoftijzer & Van der Kooij 1976 – J. Hoftijzer & G. van der Kooij, *Aramaic Texts from Deir ʿAlla* (DMOA, 19), Leiden
Holtz 1980 – G. Holtz, *Die Pastoralbriefe* (ThHK, 13), 5.Aufl., Berlin.
Hornung 1971 – E. Hornung, *Der Eine und die Vielen: Ägyptische Gottesvorstellungen*, Darmstadt.
Hornung 1982 – E. Hornung, *Der ägyptische Mythos von der Himmelskuh: Eine Ätiologie des Unvolkommenen* (OBO, 46), 3.Auflage, Freiburg.
Hosseini 2013 – Kh. Hosseini, *And the Mountains Echoed: A Novel*, New York.
Houtman 2000 – C. Houtman, *Exodus* (HCOT), vol. 3, Leuven.
Hultgård 2000 A. Hultgård, 'La chute de Satan: Larrière-plan iranien d'un logion de Jésus (*Luc* 10,18)', *RHPhR* 80, 69-77.
Hultgren 2003 – S. Hultgren, 'The Origin of Paul's Doctrine of the Two Adams in 1 Corinthians 15.45-49', *JSNT* 25, 343-370.
Humbach 1991 – H. Humbach *et al*, *The Gāthās of Zarathustra and the Other Old Avestan Texts*, 2 Parts, Heidelberg.
Humbert 1940 – P. Humbert, *Études sur le récit du paradis et de la chute dans la Génèse* (Mémoires de l'Université de Neuchâtel, 14), Neuchâtel.
Humphrey 2006 – E. M. Humphrey, 'To Rejoice or Not to Rejoice? Luke 10:17-24 and Revelation 12:1-17', in: Barr 2006a, 113-125.
Hurowitz 2009 – V.A. Hurowitz, 'The Divinity of Humankind in the Bible and the Ancient Near East: A New Mesopotamian Parallel', in: N. Sacher Fox *et al.* (eds), *Mishneh todah: Studies in Deuteronomy and Its Cultural Environment (Fs J.H. Tigay)*, Winona Lake, 263-274.
Hutter 1985 – M. Hutter, *Altorientalische Vorstellungen von der Unterwelt: Literar- und religionsgeschichtliche Überlegungen zu "Nergal und Ereškigal"* (OBO, 63), Freiburg.
Hutter 1999a – M. Hutter, 'Abaddon', in: Van der Toorn 1999, 1.
Hutter 1999b – M. Hutter, 'Lilith', in: Van der Toorn 1999, 520-521.
Insler 1975 – S. Insler, *The Gāthās of Zarathustra* (Acta Iranica: Troisième Série, Textes et Mémoires, 1), Leiden.
Isbell 1975 – C.D. Isbell, *Corpus of the Aramaic Incantation Bowls*, Missoula.
Isbell 1976 – C.D. Isbell, 'Two New Aramaic Incantation Bowls', *BASOR* 223, 15-23.

Izre'el 2001 – S. Izre'el, *Adapa and the South Wind: Language Has the Power of Life and Death* (Mesopotamian Civilzations, 10), Winona Lake.

Jacobsen 1939 – T.Jacobsen, *The Sumerian King List* (AS, 11), Chicago.

Jakubiak 2004 – K. Jakubiak, 'Some Remarks on Sargon II's Eighth Campaign of 714 BC', *Iranica Antiqua* 39, 191-202.

Janowski 1999 – B. Janowski, 'Azazel, עֲזָאזֵל', in: K. van der Toorn *et al.* (eds), *Distionary of 'Deities and Demons in the Bible*, Second Edition, Leiden, 128-131.

Janowski 2003 – B. Janowski, 'Jenseits von Eden: Gen 4,1-16 und die nicht-priesterliche Urgeschichte', in: Lange 2003, 137-159.

Janowksi & Ego 2001 – B. Janowski & B. Ego (eds), *Das biblische Weltbild und seine altorientalischen Kontexte*, Tübingen.

Jeremias 2002 – J. Jeremias, *Die Reue Gottes: Aspekte alttestamentlicher Gottesvorstellung* (BThSt, 31), 3.Aufl., Neukirchen.

Jeynes 2014 – C. Jeynes, (Review of Korpel & De Moor 2014). *Research Gate* (website), 1-17.

Jipp 2013 – J.W. Jipp, *Divine Visitations and Hospitality to Strangers in Luke-Acts: An Interpretation of the Malta Episode in Act 28:1-10* (NT.S, 153), Leiden.

Johnson 2009 – M.D. Johnson, 'Life of Adam and Eve', in: Charlesworth 2009, vol. 2, 249-295.

Joüon & Muraoka 2006 – P. Joüon & T. Muraoka, *A Grammar of Biblical Hebrew* (Subhsidia Biblica, 27), Roma.

Jüngling 1994 – H.-W. Jüngling, ' "Was anders ist Gott für den Menschen, wenn nicht sein Vater und seine Mutter?": Zu einer Doppelmetapher der religiösen Sprache', in: W. Dietrich & M.A. Klopfenstein (eds), *Ein Gott allein?* (OBO, 139), Freiburg, 365-386.

Kaiser 1962 – O. Kaiser, *Die mythische Bedeutung des Meeres in Ägypten, Ugarit und Israel* (BZAW, 78), Berlin.

Kaiser 1993-2003 – O. Kaiser, *Der Gott des Alten Testaments: Theologie des Alten Testaments*, 3 Bde (UTB, 1747, 2024, 2392), Göttingen.

Katz 2007 – D. Katz, 'Enki and Ninḫuršanĝa, Part One', *BiOr* 64, 568-589.

Katzenstein 1973 – H.J. Katzenstein, *A History of Tyre, from the Beginning of the Second Millennium B.C.E. until the Fall of the Neo-Babylonian Empire in 538 B.C.E.*, Jerusalem.

Kazimirski 1860 – A. de Biberstein Kazimirski, *Dictionnaire arabe-français*, 2 tms, Paris.

Kee 2009 – H.C. Kee, 'Testaments of the Twelve Patriarchs: A New Translation and Introduction', in: Charlesworth 2009, vol. 1, 775-828.

Keel 1972 – O. Keel, *Die Welt der altorientalischen Bildsymbolik und das Alte Testament: Am Beispiel der Psalmen*, Neukirchen-Vluyn.

Keel 1998 – O. Keel, *Goddesses and Trees, New Moon and Yahweh: Ancient Near Eastern Art and the Hebrew Bible* (JSOT.SS, 261), Sheffield.

Keel & Schroer 2002 –O. Keel & S. Schroer,*Schöpfung: Biblische Theologien im Kontext altorientalischer Religionen*, Freiburg.

Keel & Schroer 2010 –O. Keel & S. Schroer, *Eva – Mutter alles Lebendigen: Frauen- und Göttinnenidole aus dem Alten Orient*, 3.Aufl., Freiburg.

Keel & Uehlinger 1992 – O. Keel & C. Uehlinger, *Göttinnen, Götter und Gottessymbole: Neue Erkenntnisse zur Relgigionsgeschichte Kanaans und Israels aufgrund bislang unerschlossener ikonographischer Quellen* (QD, 134), Freiburg.

Keel-Leu & Teissier 2004 – H. Keel-Leu & B. Teissier, *Die vorderasiatischen Rollsiegel der Sammlungen "Bibel+Orient" de Universität Freiburg Schweiz* (OBO, 200), Fribourg.

Kellens 1994 – J. Kellens, *Le panthéon de l'Avesta ancien*, Wiesbaden.

Kenna 1971 – V.E.G. Kenna, *Corpus of Cypriote Antiquities, 3: Catalogue of the Cypriote Seals of the Bronze Age in the British Museum* (Studies in Mediterranean Archaeology, 20/3), Göteborg.

Kimberly 2010 – P. Kimberly *et al.*, *Volcanoes of the World*, 3rd Edition, Berkeley.

Kitchen 1999 – K.A. Kitchen, *Poetry of Ancient Egypt* (Documenta Mundi: Aegyptiaca, 1), Jonsered.

Kline 1991 – M.G. Kline, 'Gospel until the Law: Rom 5:13-14 and the Old Covenant', *JETS* 34, 433-446.

Klopper 2006 – F. Klopper, 'Springs and Wells in the Religious Conceptual World of Israel through Ancient Near Eastern Iconography', in: H.M. Niemann & M. Augustin (eds), *Stimulation from Leiden: Collected Communications to the XVIIIth Congress of the International Organization for the Study of the Old Testament, Leiden 2004* (BEAT, 54), 225-238.

Knibb 1978 – M.A. Knibb, *The Ethiopic Book of Enoch*, vol. 2, Oxford.

Knittel 2002 – T. Knittel, *Das griechische 'Leben Adams und Evas': Studien zu einer narrativen Anthropologie im frühen Judentum* (TSAJ, 88), Tübingen.

Koch 2004 – M. Koch, *Drachenkampf und Sonnenfrau* (WUNT, 184), Tübingen.

Kochavi 1989 – M. Kochavi, 'The Land of Geshur Project: Regional Archaeology of the Southern Golan (1987-1988 Seasons)', *IEJ* 39, 1-17.

Koester 2014 – C.R. Koester, *Revelation: A New Translation with Introduction and Commentary* (AncB, 38A), New Haven.

Kogan 2006 – L. Kogan, 'Animal Names in Biblical Hebrew: An Etymological Overview', in: L. Kogan *et al.* (eds), *Babel und Bibel 3*, Winona Lake, 257-306.

Korpel 1990 – M.C.A. Korpel, *A Rift in the Clouds: Ugaritic and Hebrew Descriptions of the Divine* (UBL, 8), Münster.

Korpel 1996a – M.C.A. Korpel, 'Avian Spirits in Ugarit and in Ezekiel 13,' in: N. Wyatt *et al.* (eds), *Ugarit, Religion and Culture: Essays Presented in Honour of Professor John C.L. Gibson* (UBL.12), Münster, 99-113.

Korpel 1996b – M.C.A. Korpel, 'Exegesis in the Work of Ilimilku of Ugarit', in: J.C. de Moor (ed.), *Intertextuality in Ugarit and Israel* (OTS, 40), 86-111.

Korpel 2003 – M.C.A. Korpel, 'Who Is Who? The Structure of Canticles 8:1-7', in: M.C.A. Korpel & J.M. Oesch (eds), *Unit Delimitation in Biblical Hebrew and Northwest Semitic Languages* (Pericope, 4), Assen, 89-120.

Korpel 2006 – M.C.A. Korpel, 'Queen Jezebel's Seal', *UF* 38, 379-398.

Korpel 2009 – M.C.A. Korpel, 'Kryptogramme in Ezechiel 19 und im 'Izbet-Ṣarṭa-Ostrakon', *ZAW* 121 (2009), 70-86.

Korpel 2010 – M.C.A. Korpel, 'חוֹתָם / חֹתֶמֶת – seal, signet ring', PDF downloaded from: http://www.otw-site.eu/KLY/kly.php.

Korpel 2012 – M.C.A. Korpel, 'Sterven goden?', *Schrift* 44 (259), 30-34.

Korpel & De Moor 2012 – M.C.A. Korpel & J.C. de Moor, *The Silent God*, paperback edition, Leiden.

Korpel & De Moor 2013 – M.C.A. Korpel & J.C. de Moor, 'Reaction to the Contributions of our Reviewers', in: Becking 2013, 169-179.

Korpel & De Moor 2014 – M.C.A. Korpel & J.C. de Moor, *Adam, Eve, and the Devil* (Hebrew Bible Monographs, 65), First Edition, Sheffield.

Kovacs 1995 – J.L. Kovacs, ' "Now Shall the Ruler of This World Be Driven Out": Jesus' Death as Cosmic Battle in John 12:20-36', *JBL* 114, 227-247.

Kreyenbroek 2013 – P.G. Kreyenbroek, 'Weltherr und Teufel in Schöpfungsmythen indo-iranischer Herkunft', in: Zgoll & Kratz 2013, 133-144.

Krings 1993 – V. Krings (ed.), *La civilisation phénicienne et punique: Manuel de recherche* (HO, 1/20), Leiden.

Kramer 1969 – S.-N. Kramer, *The Sacred Marriage Rite*, London.

Krüger 2008 – T. Krüger, 'Sündenfall? Überlegungen zur theologischen Bedeutung der Paradiesgeschichte', in: Schmid & Riedweg 2008, 95-109.

Kübel 2007 – P. Kübel, *Metamorphosen der Paradieserzählung* (OBO, 231), Fribourg.

Küchler 1986 – M. Küchler, *Schweigen, Schmuck und Schleier: Drei neutestamentliche Vorschriften zur Verdrängung der Frauen auf dem Hintergrund einer frauenfeindlichen Exegese des Alten Testaments im Antiken Judentum* (NTOA, 1), Freiburg.

Kulik 2004 – A. Kulik, *Retroverting Slavonic Pseudepigrapha: Toward the Original of the Apocalypse of Abraham* (Text-critical Studies, 3), Atlanta.

Kustár 2006 – Z. Kustár, 'Ez 28,11-19: Entstehung und Botschaft: Nachzeichnen eines komplexen traditionsgeschichtlichen Prozesses', in: R. Lux & E.-J. Waschke (eds), *Die unwiderstehliche Wahrheit: Studien zur alttestamentlichen Prophetie*, Leipzig, 199-227.

Kvanvig 1988 – H.S. Kvanvig, *Roots of Apocalyptic: The Mesopotamian Background of the Enoch Figure and the Son of Man* (WMANT, 61), Neukirchen-Vluyn.

Kvanvig 2011 – H.S. Kvanvig, *Primeval History: Babylonian, Biblical, and Enochic: An Intertextual Reading* (JSJ.S, 149), Leiden.

Laato 2015 – A. Laato, ' "The Children of Adam" in Deuteronomy 32:8-9', paper read at the SRB Conference Turku 2014 (forthcoming).

Laato & De Moor 2003 – A. Laato & J.C. de Moor (eds), *Theodicy in the World of the Bible: The Goodness of God and the Problem of Evil*, Leiden.

LaCocque 2006 – A. LaCocque, *The Trial of Innocence: Adam, Eve, and the Yahwist*, Eugene.

Lambert 1985a – W.G. Lambert, 'The Pair Laḫmu-Laḫamu in Cosmology', *Or.* 54, 189-202.

Lambert 1985b – W.G. Lambert, 'Trees, Snakes and Gods in Ancient Syria and Anatolia', *BSOAS* 48, 435-451.

Lambert 1986 – W.G. Lambert, 'Note brève: Niṣir or Nimuš?', *RA* 80, 185-186.

Lambert 1988 – W.G. Lambert, 'Old Testament Mythology in Its Ancient Near Eastern Context', in: J.A. Emerton (ed.), *Congress of the International Organization for the Study of the Old Testament (Jerusalem 24-08/29-08-1986)* (VT.S, 40), Leiden, 124-132.

Lambert 2013 – W.G. Lambert, *Babylonian Creation Myths* (Mesopotamian Civilizations, 16), Winona Lake.

Lambert id& Millard 1969 – W.G. Lambert &A.R. Millard, *Atra-Ḫasīs: The Babylonian Story of the Flood*, Oxford.

Lane 1991 – W.L. Lane, *Hebrews 1–8* (WBC, 47A), Waco.

Lanfer 2012 – P.T. Lanfer, *Remembering Eden: The Reception History of Genesis 3:22-22*, Oxford.

Lange 2003 – A. Lange *et al.* (eds), *Die Dämonen – Demons: Die Dämonologie der israelitisch-jüdischen und frühchristlichen Literatur im Kontext ihrer Umwelt*, Tübingen.

Lapinkivi 2004 – P. Lapinkivi, *The Sumerian Sacred Marriage in the Light of Comparative Evidence* (SAAS, 15), Helsinki.

Laroche 1968 – E. Laroche, 'Documents en langue hourrite provenant de Ras Shamra', in: J. Nougayrol *et al.*, *Ugaritica V* (MRS, 16), Paris.

Launderdale 2003 – D. Launderdale, 'Ezekiel's Cherub: A Promising Symbol or a Dangerous Idol?', *CBQ* 65, 165-183.

Lawson Younger 2007 – K. Lawson Younger Jr. (ed.), *Ugarit at Seventy-Five*, Winona Lake.

Lee 2012 – Y. Lee, *The Son of Man as the Last Adam: The Early Church as a Source of Pauls Adam Christology*, Eugene.

Legarreta Castillo 2014 – F. de Jesús Legareta Castillo, *The Figure of Adam in Romans 5 and 1 Corinthians 15: The New Creation and Its Ethical and Social Reconfiguration*, Minneapolis.

Leslau 1991 – W. Leslau, *Comparative Dictionary of Geʿez*, Wiesbaden.

Lessing 2009 – R.R. Lessing, *Amos* (Concordia Commentary), Saint Louis.

Levenson 1988 – J.D. Levenson, *Creation and the Persistence of Evil: The Jewish Drama of Divine Omnipotence*. Princeton.

Levin 2009 – C. Levin, 'Das verlorene Paradies (Genesis 2–3), in: S. Gehrig & S. Seiler (eds), *Gottes Wahrnehmungen* (Fs Helmut Utzschneider), Stuttgart, 85-101.

Levison 1988 – J.R. Levison, *Portraits of Adam in Early Judaism: From Sirach to 2 Baruch* (JSPSup, 1), Sheffield.

Levison 2000 – J.R. Levison, *Texts in Transition: The Greek Life of Adam and Eve* (SBL.EJL, 16). Atlanta.

L'Heureux 1979 – C.E. L'Heureux, *Rank among the Canaanite Gods El, Baʿal, and the Rephaʾim* (HSM, 21), Missoula.

Lichtheim 1980 – M. Lichtheim, *Ancient Egyptian Literature*, vol. 3: The Late Period, Berkeley.

Lichtheim 1997a – M. Lichtheim, 'The Destruction of Mankind (1.24)', in: Hallo *et al* 1997, 36-37.

Lichtheim 1997b – M. Lichtheim, 'The Shipwrecked Sailor (1.39)', in: Hallo *et al* 1997, 83-84.

Liddell & Scott 1968 – H.G. Liddell & R. Scott, *A Greek-English Lexicon*, rev. ed. H.S. Jones, Oxford.

Lindström 1983 – F. Lindström, *God and the Origin of Evil: A Contextual Analysis of Alleged Monistic Evidence in the Old Testament*, Lund.

Lipiński 1971 – E. Lipiński, 'El's Abode: Mythological Traditions Related to Mt. Hermon and the Mountains of Armenia', *OLP* 2, 13-69.

Lipiński 1981 – E. Lipiński, 'Allusions historiques dans la correspondence ougaritique de Ras Shamra: Lettre de Ewri-šarri à Pilsiya', *UF* 13, 123–126.

Lipiński 1995 – E. Lipiński, *Dieux et déesses de l'univers phénicien et punique* (OLA, 64). Leuven.

Lipiński 1996 – E. Lipiński, 'Egypto-Canaanite Iconography of Reshef, Baʿal, Ḥoron and Anat', *Chronique d' Égypte* 71, 254-262.

Lipiński 1997 – E. Lipiński, *Semitic Languages: Outline of a Comparative Grammar* (OLA, 80), Leuven.

Lipiński 2010 – E. Lipiński, *Resheph: A Syro-Canaanite Deity* (OLA, 181), Leuven.

Lisman 2013 – J.J.W. Lisman, *Cosmogony, Theogony and Anthropogony in Sumerian Texts* (AOAT, 409), Münster.

Loiseau 2013 – A.-F. Loiseau, 'Gen 4,7, une ancienne formule démonologique modifiée par les scribes?', *ZAW* 125, 479-482.

Loretz 1985 – O. Loretz, *Leberschau, Sündenbock, Asasel in Ugarit und Israel: Leberschau und Jahwestatue in Psalm 27, Leberschau in Psalm 74* (UBL, 3), Münster.

Loretz 1989 – O. Loretz, 'Der Wohnort Els nach ugaritischen Texten und Ez 28,1-2.6-10', *UF* 21, 259-267.

Loretz 1990 – O. Loretz, *Ugarit und die Bibel: Kanaanäische Götter und Religion im Alten Testament*, Darmstadt.

Loretz 2011 – O. Loretz, *Hippologia Ugaritica: Das Pferd in Kultur, Wirtschaft, Kriegsführung und Hippiatrie Ugarits – Pferd, Esel und Kamel in biblischen Texten* (AOAT, 386), Münster.

Lunt 2009 – H.G. Lunt, 'Ladder of Jacob', in: Charlesworth 2009, vol. 2, 401-411.

Luttikhuizen 2000a – G.P. Luttikhuizen (ed.), *The Creation of Man and Woman: Interpretations of the Biblical Narratives in Jewish and Christian Traditions* (Themes in Biblical Narrative), Leiden.

Luttikhuizen 2000b – G.P. Luttikhuizen, 'The Creation of Man and Woman in *The Secret Book of John*', in: Luttikhuizen 2000a, 140-155.

Luz 1990 – U. Luz, *Das Evangelium nach Matthäus* (EKK, 1/2), Zürich.

McAffee 2013 – M. McAffee, 'A Grammatical Analysis of Hittite ᵈ*El-ku-ni-ir-sa* in Light of West Semitic', *UF* 44, 201-216.

Macaskill 2012 – G. Macaskill, '2 Enoch: Manuscripts, Recensions, and Original Language', in: Orlov & Boccaccini 2012, 83-101.

McCord Adams – M. McCord Adams, 'Healing Judgment: Numbers 21:4-9 and John 3:14-21', *ET* 117, 196-197.

MacDonald 2013 – N. MacDonald, 'A Text in Search of Context: The *Imago Dei* in the First Chapters of Genesis', in: Baer & Gordon 2013, 3-16.

McGovern 2007 – P.E. McGovern, *Ancient Wine: The Search for the Origins of Viticulture*, Princeton.

Machinist 1983 – P. Machinist, 'Rest and Violence in the Poem of Erra', *JAOS* 103, 221-226.

Macintosh 1997 – A.A. Macintosh, *A Critical and Exegetical Commentary on Hosea* (ICC), Edinburgh.

McKinion 2004 – S.A. McKinion (ed), *Isaiah 1–39* (Ancient Christian Commentary on Scripture.OT, 10), Downers Grove.

McKenzie 1956 – J.L. McKenzie, 'Mythological Allusions in Ezek 28:12-18', *JBL* 75, 322-327.

MacRae 2000 – G.W. MacRae, 'The Apocalypse of Adam (V,5:64,1–85,32)', in: Robinson 2000, 151-195 (originally published as G.W. MacRae, 'The Apocalypse of Adam (V,5:64,1–85,32)', in: D.M. Parrott (ed.), *Nag Hammadi Codices V,2-5 and VI* , Leiden 1979).

MacRae 2009 – G.W. MacRae, 'The Apocalypse of Adam', in: Charlesworth 2009, 707-719.

Maher 1992 – M. Maher, *The Targum Pseudo-Jonathan: Genesis* (Aramaic Bible, 18), Edinburgh.

Maier 2013 – C.M. Maier, 'Gute und schlechte Frauen in Proverbien und Ijob: Die Entstehung kultureller Stereotype', in: Maier & Calduch-Benages 2013, 75-89.

Maier & Calduch-Benages 2013 – C. Maier & N. Calduch-Benages, *Schriften und spätere Weisheitsbücher* (Die Bibel und die Frauen - Altes Testament, 1.3), Stuttgart.

Mander 2008 – P. Mander, 'Les dieux et le culte à Ébla', in: G. del Olmo Lete 2008a, 1-160.

Marsman 2003 – H.J. Marsman, *Women in Ugarit and Israel: Their Social and Religious Position in the Context of the Ancient Near East* (OTS, 49), Leiden.

Martin 1986 – A.P. Martin, *2 Corinthians* (WBC, 40), Waco.

Martinek 1996 – M. Martinek, *Wie die Schlange zum Teufel wurde: Die Symbolik in der Paradiesgeschichte von der hebräischen Bibel bis zum Koran* (StOr, 37), Wiesbaden.

Marx 2000 – A. Marx, 'La chute de "Lucifer" (Esaïe 14,12-15; Luc 10,18): Préhistoire d'un mythe', *RHPhR* 80, 171-185.

Mathieu 2011 – B. Mathieu, 'Seth polymorphe: Le rival, le vaincu, l'auxiliaire', *Égypte Nilothique et Méditerranéenne* 4, 137-158.

Matoïan 2008 – V. Matoïan (ed.), *Le mobilier du Palais Royal d'Ougarit* (RSO, 17), Paris.

Marzouk 2015 – S. Marzouk, *Egypt as a Monster in the Book Ezekiel* (FAT, 2.Reihe, 76), Tübingen.

May 1962 – H.G. May, 'The King in the Garden of Eden: A Study of Ezekiel 28:12-19', in: B.W. Anderson & W. Harrelson (eds), *Israel's Prophetic Heritage – Essays in Honor of James Muilenburg*, New York, 166-176.

Mayer 1987 – W.R. Mayer, 'Ein Mythos von der Erschaffung des Menschen und des Königs', *Or.* 56, 55-68.

Mayer 2013 – W. Mayer, *Assyrien und Urarṭu I: Der Achte Feldzug Sargons II. im Jahr 714 v. Chr.* (AOAT, 395/1), Münster.

Mazzoni 1986 – S. Mazzoni, 'Continuity and Development in the Syrian and the Cypriote Common Glyptic Styles', in: M. Kelly *et al.* (eds), *Insight Through Images: Studies in Honor of Edith Porada* (Biblioteca Mesopotamica, 21), Malibu, 171-182, Pl. 31-35.

Meier 1980 – J.P. Meier, 'John the Baptist in Matthew's Gospel', *JBL* 99, 383-405.

Meier 1992 – S.A. Meier, *Speaking of Speaking: Marking Direct Discourse in the Hebrew Bible* (VT.S, 46), Leiden.

Meier 1999 – S.A. Meier, 'Destroyer', in: Van der Toorn 1999, 240-244.

Meinardus 1976 – O.F.A. Meinardus, 'St. Paul Shipwrecked in Dalmatia', *BA* 39/4, 145-147.

Merrill 1881 – S. Merrill, *East of the Jordan: A Record of Travel and Observation in the Countries of Moab, Gilead, and Bashan*, London.

Merrillees 2005 – P.H. Merrillees, *Catalogue of the Western Asiatic Seals in the British Museum, Cylinder Seals VI: Pre-Achaemenid and Achaemenid Periods*, London.

Mettinger 1976 – T.N.D. Mettinger, *King and Messiah: The Civil and Sacral Legitimation of the Isarelite Kings*(CB.OT, 8), Lund.

Mettinger 1987 – T.N.D. Mettinger, *In Search of God: The Meaning and Message of the Everlasting Names*, Philadelphia

Mettinger 2007 – T.N.D. Mettinger, *The Eden Narrative: A Literary and Religio-historical Study of Genesis 2–3*, Winona Lake.

Metzger 2009 – B.M. Metzger, 'The Fourth Book of Ezra', in: Charlesworth 2009, 517-559.

Meurer 2005 – G. Meurer, 'Die Verfehmung des Seth und seines Gefolges in den Pyramidentexten und in späterer Zeit', in: H. Felber (ed.), *Feinde und Aufrührer: Konzepte von Gegnerschaft in ägyptischen Texten besonders des Mittleren Reiches*, Leipzig, 173-188.

Meyers 1988. – C. Meyers, *Discovering Eve: Ancient Israelite Women in Context*, Oxford.

Middleton 2005 – J.R. Middleton, *The Liberating Image: The* Imago Dei *in Genesis 1*, Eugene.

Miglio 2013 – A.E. Miglio, 'A Study of the Serpent Incantation KTU^2 1.82:1-7 and its Contributions to Ugaritic Mythology and Religion', *JANER* 13, 30-48.

Milik 1972 – J.T.Milik, *Dédicaces faites par des dieux (Palmyre, Hatra, Tyr) et des thiases sémitiques à l'époque romaine* (BAH, 92), Paris.

Miller 2003 – P.D. Miller, [Review], *JNES* 62, 304-305.

Mittmann & Schmitt 2001 – S. Mittmann & G. Schmitt (eds), *Tübinger Bibelatlas*, Stuttgart.

Mizrahi 2013 – N. Mizrahi, 'The Textual History and Literary Background of Isa 14,4', *ZAW* 125, 433-447.

Moberly 2007 – R.W.L. Moberly,'The Mark of Cain–Revealed at Last?'. *HThR* 100, 11-28.

Moberly 2008 – R.W.L. Moberly, 'Did the Interpreters Get it Right? Genesis 2–3 Reconsidered,' *JThS* 59, 22-40.

Moberly 2009 – R.W.L. Moberly, *The Theology of the Book of Genesis*, Cambridge.

Montet 1935 – P. Montet, 'Les fouilles de Tanis en 1933 et 1934', *Kémi* 5, 11-14, Pl. X-XI.

Moo 1980 – D.J. Moo, '1 Timothy 2:11-15: Meaning and Significance', *Trinity Journal* 1, 62-83.

Mounce 2000 – W.D. Mounce, *Pastoral Epistles* (WBC, 46), Waco.

Müller 1969 – K.H. Müller, *Anstoß und Gericht: Eine Studie zum jüdischen Hintergrund des paulinischen Skandalon-Begriffs* (StANT, 19), München.

Müller 19980 – H.–P. Müller, 'Religionsgeschichtliche Beobachtungen zu den Texten von Ebla', *ZDPV* 96, 1–19.

Müller 1999 – H.–P. Müller, 'Chemosh', in: Van der Toorn 1999, 186-189.

Müller-Kessler 2005 – C. Müller-Kessler, *Die Zauberschalentexte in der Hilprecht-Sammlung*, Wiesbaden.

Münnich 2013 – M.M. Münnich, *The God Resheph in the Ancient Near East* (ORA, 11), Tübingen.

Muraoka 2009 – T. Muraoka, *A Greek-English Lexicon of the Septuagint*, Leiden.

Muscarella 1986 – O.W. Muscarella, 'The Location of Ulhu and Uiše in Sargon II's Eighth Campaign', *Journal of Field Archaeology* 13, 465-475.

Nanz 2001 – C. Nanz, ' "Hinabgeworfen wurde der Ankläger unserer Brüder (Offb 12,10) ...": Das Motiv vom Satanssturz in der Johannes-Offenbarung', in: K. Backhaus (ed.), *Theologie als Vision: Studien in de Johannes-Offenbarung* (Stuttgarter Bibelstudien, 19), 151-171.

Naveh & Shaked 1985 – J. Naveh & S. Shaked, *Amulets and Magic Bowls*, Jerusalem.

Nestle 1912 – E. Nestle, 'Generation of Vipers', *ET* 23, 185.

Neumann van Padang 1963 – M. Neumann van Padang, *Catalogue of the Active Volcanoes of the World Including Solfatara Fields*, 16: Arabia and the Indian Ocean, Roma.

Nickelsburg 2001 – G.W.E. Nickelsburg, *1 Enoch 1: A Commentary on the Book of 1 Enoch, Chapters 1–36; 81–108* (Hermeneia), Minneapolis.

Nickelsburg & VanderKam 2004 – G.W.E. Nickelsburg & J.C. VanderKam, *1 Enoch; A New Translation Based on the Hermeneia Commentary*, Minneapolis.

Niehr 2001 – H. Niehr, 'Die Wohnsitze des Gottes El nach den Mythen aus Ugarit: Ein Beitrag zu ihrer Lokalisierung', in: Janowksi & Ego 2001, 325-360.

Nielsen 1989 – K. Nielsen, *There Is Hope for a Tree: The Tree as Metaphor in Isaiah* (JSOT.S, 65), Sheffield.

Nolland 1989 – J. Nolland, *Luke 9:21–18:34* (WBC, 35B), Dallas.

Noort 1999 – E. Noort, 'Gan-Eden in the Context of the Mythology of the Hebrew Bible', in: G.P. Luttikhuizen (ed.), *Paradise Interpreted: Representations of Biblical Paradise in Judaism and Christianity*, Leiden, 21-36.

Noort 2000 – E. Noort, 'The Creation of Man and Woman in Biblical and Ancient Near Eastern Traditions', in: Luttikhuizen 2000a, 1-18.
Nougayrol 1970 – J. Nougayrol, *Le palais royal d'Ugarit*, t. 6 (MRS,12), Paris.
Nys 2013 – N. Nys, 'Een goedaardig monster in Mesopotamië: de schorpioen-hybride', *Phoenix* 59,2, 55-65.
O'Collins 2011 – G. O'Collins S.J., *Rethinking Fundamental Theology*, Oxford.
Oesch 1979 – J.M. Oesch, *Petucha und Setuma: Unterscuhungen zu einer überlieferten Gliederung im hebräischen Text des Alten Testaments* (OBO, 27), Freiburg.
Olson 2013 – D.C. Olson, *A New Reading of the* Animal Apocalypse *of 1 Enoch: "All Nations Shall Be Blessed"* (SVTP, 24), Leiden.
Onnis 2012 – F. Onnis, 'Une plaque en or à décor figuré du palais royal d'Ougarit', in: V. Matoïan *et al.* (eds). *Études ougaritiques II* (RSO, 20), Leuven, 185-220.
Orlov 2005 – A.A. Orlov, *The Enoch-Metatron Tradition* (TSAJ, 107), Tübingen.
Orlov 2011 – A.A. Orlov, *Dark Mirrors: Azazel and Satanael in Early Jewish Demonology*, Albany.
Orlov & Boccaccini 2012 – A.A. Orlov & G. Boccaccini (eds), *New Perspectives on 2 Enoch: No Longer Slavonic Only* (Studia Judaeoslavica, 4), Leiden.
Oshima 2012 – T. Oshima, 'When the Gods Made Us from Clay', in: A. Berlejung *et al.* (eds), *Menschenbilder und Körperkonzepte im Alten Israel, in Ägypten und im Alten Orient* (Orientalische Religionen in der Antike, 9), Berlin, 407-431.
Oswalt 1986 – J.N. Oswalt, *The Book of Isaiah: Chapters 1–39* (NICOT), Grand Rapids.
Oswalt 2003 – J.N. Oswalt, *Isaiah: The NIV Application Commentary*, Grand Rapids.
Otto 1996 – E. Otto, 'Die Paradieserzählung Genesis 2–3: Eine nachpriesterliche Lehrerzählung in ihrem religionhistorischen Kontext', in: A.A. Diesel *et al.*(eds), *"Jedes Ding hat seine Zeit ...": Studien zur israelitischen und altorientalischen Weisheit* (Fs D. Michel) (BZAW, 241), Berlin, 167-192.
Otto 2007 – E. Otto, 'Die Urmenschen im Paradies: Vom Ursprung des Bösen und der Freiheit des Menschen", in: Achenbach *et al.* 2007, 122-133.
Pardee 1980 – D. Pardee, 'The New Canaanite Myths and Legends', *BO* 37, 269-291.
Pardee 1987 – D. Pardee, 'As Strong as Death', in: J.H. Marks & R.M. Good (eds), *Love and Death in the Ancient Near East* (Fs M.H. Pope), Guilford, 65-69.
Pardee 1988 – D. Pardee, *Les textes para-mythologiques de la 24^e^ campagne (1961)* (RSO, 4), Paris.
Pardee 1997 – D. Pardee, 'Ugaritic Liturgy against Venomous Reptiles (1.94) (RS 24.244)', in: W.W. Hallo (ed.), T*he Context of Scripture*, vol. 1, 295-298.
Pardee 1999 – D. Pardee, 'Eloah אלה', in: Van der Toorn 1999, 285-288.
Pardee 2000 – D. Pardee, *Les textes rituels* (RSO, 12), 2 tomes. Paris.
Pardee 2007 – D. Pardee, [Review of Smith 2006], *Review of Biblical Literature* 03/2007.

Pardee 2011 – D. Pardee, 'Nouvelle étude épigraphique et littéraire des textes fragmentaires en langue ougaritique dits "Le Rephaïm" (*CTA* 20-22)', *Or* 80, 1-65.

Parpola 1997 – S. Parpola, *The Standard Babylonian Epic of Gilgamesh* (SAA. CT, 1), Helsinki.

Patmore 2012 – H.M. Patmore, *Adam, Satan, and the King of Tyre: The Interpretation of Ezekiel 28:11-19 in Late Antiquity* (Jewish and Christian Perspective Series, 20), Leiden.

Peels 2009 – E. (H.G.L.) Peels, 'The World's First Murder', In: H. Van Rooy *et al.* (eds), *Animosity, the Bible and Us*, Atlanta, 19-39.

Peels 2014 – E. (H.G.L.) Peels, (Review of Korpel & De Moor 2014), *Theologia Reformata* 57 (2014), 281-289.

Perriman 1993 – A.C. Perriman, 'What Eve Did, What Women Shouldn't Do: The Meaning of αὐθεντεῶ in 1 Timothy 2:12', *Tyndale Bulletin* 44, 129-142.

Pesch 1986 – R. Pesch, *Die Apostelgeschichte (Apg 13–28)* (EKK, 5/2), Zürich.

Peters 2008 – D.M. Peters, *Noah Traditions in the Dead Sea Scrolls: Conversations and Controversies of Antiquity*, Atlanta.

Pfeiffer 2000 – H. Pfeiffer, 'Der Baum in der Mitte des Gartens: Zum überlieferungsgeschichtlichen Ursprung der Paradieserzählung (Gen 2,4b - 3,24), Teil I: Analyse', *ZAW* 112 (2000), 487-500.

Phipps 1989 – W.E. Phipps, *Genesis and Gender: Biblical Myths of Sexuality and Their Cultural Impact*, New York.

Pientka-Hinz 2009 – R. Pientka-Hinz, 'Schlange. A', *RLA*, Bd. 12, Lief. 3/4, Berlin.

Pitard 1992 – W.T. Pitard, 'A New Edition of the "Rāpi'ūma" Texts: *KTU* 1.20–22', *BASOR* 285 (1992) 33-77.

Pitard 1998 – W.T. Pitard, 'The Binding of Yamm: A New Edition of the Ugaritic Text *KTU* 1.83', *JNES* 57. 261-280.

Pitard 2007 – 'Just How Many Monsters Did Anat Fight (*KTU* 1.3 III 38-47)?', in: L.K. Younger Jr. (ed.), *Ugarit at Seventy-Five*, Winona Lake, 75-88.

Pope 1955 – M.H.Pope, *El in the Ugaritic Texts* (VT.S, 2), Leiden.

Porter 1993 – S.E. Porter, 'What Does It Mean to Be "Saved by Childbirth" (1 Timothy 2.15)?', *JSNT* 49, 87-102.

Postell 2011– S.D. Postell, *Adam as Israel: Genesis 1–3 as the Introduction to the Torah and Tanakh*, Pickwick.

Premstaller 2005 – V. Premstaller, *Fremdvölkersprüche des Ezechielbuches* (FzB, 104), Würzburg.

Pritchard 1954 – J.B. Pritchard, *The Ancient Near East in Pictures Relating to the Old Testament*, Princeton.

Rapinchuk 1999 – M. Rapinchuk, 'Universal Sin and Salvation in Romans 5:12-21', *JETS* 42, 427-441.

Rasimus 2009 – T. Rasimus, *Paradise Reconsiderd in Gnostic Mythmaking: Rethinking Sethianism in Light of the Ophite Myth and Ritual* (NHMW, 68), Leiden.

Ravn 1960 – O.E. Ravn, *A Catalogue of Oriental Cylinder Seals and Impressions in the Danish National Museum* (Nationalmuseets Skrifter, Arkæologisk-Historisk Række, 8), København.

al-Rawi & Black 1989 – F.N.H. al–Rawi & J.A. Black, 'The Second Tablet of "Išum and Erra" ', *Iraq* 51, 111-122, plate XX.

Reed 2005 – A.Y. Reed, *Fallen Angels and the History of Judaism and Christianity: The Reception of Enochic Literature*, Cambridge.

Renz 1995 – J. Renz, *Die althebräischen Inschriften*, T. 1, Darmstadt.

Reyes 2001 – A.T. Reyes, *The Stamp-Seals of Ancient Cyprus*, Oxford.

Ridderbos 1963 – N.H. Ridderbos, *Beschouwingen over Genesis I*, tweede druk, Kampen.

Ridderbos 1987 – H.N. Ridderbos, *Het evangelie naar Johannes*, deel 1, Kampen.

Rigg 1942 – H.A. Rigg, 'Sargon's "Eighth Military Campaign" ', *JAOS* 62 (1942), 130-138.

Rippin 1997 – A. Rippin, 'S̲HAYṬĀN, 2. In the Ḳur'ān and Islamic Lore', *The Encyclopaedia of Islam: New Edition*, vol. 9, Leiden, 408-409.

Rippin 2001 – A. Rippin, 'Devil', *Encyclopaedia of the Qur'ān*, vol. 1, Leiden, 524-527.

Ritner 1997 – R.K. Ritner, 'The Repulsing of the Dragon (1.21) (Coffin Text 160)', in: Hallo 1997, 32.

Roberts 1971– J.J.M. Roberts, 'Erra–Scorched Earth', *JCS* 24, 11-16.

Roberts 1972 – J.J.M. Roberts, *The Earliest Semitic Pantheon: A Study of the Semitic Deities Attested in Mesopotamia before Ur III*, Baltimore.

Robinson 2000 – J.M. Robinson (ed.), *The Coptic Gnostic Libary: A Complete Edition of the Nag Hammadi Codices*, vol. 3, Leiden.

Röllig 1999 – W. Röllig, 'El-Creator-of-the-Earth', in: Van der Toorn 1999, 280-281.

Römer 2007 – W.H.Ph. Römer, 'Einiges zu den altmesopotamischen Beschwörungstexten in sumerischer Sprache, besonders zu einer ungewöhnlich formulierten Beschwörung gegen die Folgen von Schlangen- und Hundebiss, sowie Skorpionenstich', in: Th. R. Kämmerer (ed.), *Studien zu Ritual und Sozialgeschichte im Alten Orient* (BZAW, 374), Berlin, 303-314.

Ronning 1997 – J.L. Ronning, *The Curse on the Serpent (Genesis 3:15) in Biblical Theology and Hermeneutics*, PhD Diss., Glenside.

Rossell 1953 – W.H. Rossell, *A Handbook of Aramaic Magical Texts* (Shelton Semitic Series, 2), Ringwood Borough.

Rubinkiewicz 2009 – R, Rubinkiewicz, 'Apocalypse of Abraham', in: Charlesworth 2009, 681-705.

Runia 1986 – D.T. Runia, *Philo of Alexandria and the Timaeus of Plato*, Leiden.

Rüterswörden 1999 – U. Rüterswörden, 'Horon', in: Van der Toorn 1999, 425-426.

Ryckmans 1951 – G. Ryckmans, *Les religions arabes préislamiqiues* (Bibliothèque du Muséon, 26), Louvain.

Sadek 1987 – A.I. Sadek, *Popular Religion in Egypt During the New Kingdom* (Hildesheimer Ägyptologische Beiträge, 27), Hildesheim.

Sanders 1996 – P. Sanders, *The Provenance of Deuteronomy 32* (OTS, 37), Leiden.

Sasson 1980 – J.M. Sasson, '"The Tower of Babel" as Clue to the Redactional Structuring of the Primeval History [Gen. 1–11:9]', in: G.A. Rendsburg *et al.* (eds), *The Bible World*, New York, 211-219.

Saur 2008 – M. Saur, *Der Tyroszyklus des Ezechielbuches* (BZAW, 386), Berlin.

Scafi 2006 – A. Scafi, *Mapping Paradise: A History of Heaven on Earth*, London.

Scarlata 2012 – M.W. Scarlata, *Outside of Eden: Cain in the Ancient Versions of Genesis 4,3-16*(KHB, 573), London.

Schaeffer-Forrer 1983 – C.F.A. Schaeffer *et al.*, *Corpus des Cylindres-sceaux de Ras Shamra-Ugarit et d'Enkomi-Alasia*, t. 1, Paris.

Schellenberg 2009 – A. Schellenberg, 'Humankind as the "Image of God": On the Priestly Predication (Gen. 1:26-27; 5:1; 9:6) and Its Relationship to the Ancient Near Eastern Understanding of Images', *ThZ* 65, 97-115.

Schipper 2009 – B.U. Schipper, 'Die "eherne Schlange": Zur Religionsgeschichte und Theologie von Num 21,4-9', *ZAW* 121, 369-387.

Schlimm 2012 – M.R. Schlimm, 'At Sin's Entryway (Gen 4,7): A Reply to C.L. Crouch', *ZAW* 124, 409-415

Schmid 2008 – K. Schmid, 'Loss of Immortality? Hermeneutical Aspects of Genesis 2–3 and Its Early Reception', in: Schmid & Riedweg 2008, 58-78.

Schmid & Riedweg 2008 – K. Schmid & C. Riedweg (eds), *Beyond Eden: The Biblical Story of Paradise (Genesis 2–3) and Its Reception History* (FAT, 2.Reihe, 34), Tübingen.

Schmidt 1968 – W.H. Schmidt, *Alttestamentlicher Glaube*, Neukirchen-Vluyn (10th expanded edition, 2007).

Schneemann 2004 – M. Schneemann *et al.*, 'Life-threatening Envenoming by the Saharan Horned Viper (*Cerastes cerastes*) Causing Micro-angiopathic Haemolysis, Coagulopathy Acute Renal Failure: Clinical Cases and Review', *Quarterly Journal of Medicine* 97, 717-727.

Schöck 1993 – C. Schöck, *Adam in Islam: Ein Beitrag zur Ideengeschichte der Sunna* (Islamkundliche Untersuchungen, 168), Berlin.

Schöck 2001 – C. Schöck, 'Adam and Eve', *Encyclopaedia of the Qur'ān*, vol. 1, Leiden, 22-26.

Schoors 1972 – A. Schoors, 'Literary Phrases', in: L.R. Fisher (ed.), *Ras Shamra Parallels*, vol. 1 (AnOr, 49), Roma.

Schroer 1996 – S. Schroer, *Die Weisheit hat ihr Haus gebaut: Studien zur Gestalt der Sophia in den biblischen Schriften*, Mainz.

Schüle 2005 – A. Schüle, 'Made in the "Image of God": The Concepts of Divine Images in Gen 1–3', *ZAW* 117, 1-20.

Schüle 2006 – A. Schüle, *Der Prolog der hebräischen Bibel: Der literar- und theologiegeschichtliche Diskurs der Urgeschichte (Genesis 1–11)* (AThANT, 86), Zürich.

Schüle 2009– A. Schüle, 'The Divine-Human Marriages (Genesis 6:1-4) and the Greek Framing of the Primeval History', *ThZ* 65, 97-115.

Schwartz 2011 – L. Schwartz, *Milton and Maternal Mortality*, Cambridge.

Scurlock & Beal 2013 – J. Scurlock & R.H. Beal (eds), *Creation and Chaos: A Reconsideration of Hermann Gunkel's Chaoskampf Hypothesis*, Winona Lake.

Sedlmeier 2001 – F. Sedlmeier, 'Wider die Selbstvergottung: Der Fürst von Tyros und sein Selbstverständnis nach Ez 28,1-10', in: R. Brandscheidt & T. Mende (eds), *Schöpfungsplan und Heilsgeschichte* (Fs E. Haag), Trier, 271-297.
Sefati 1998 – Y. Sefati, *Love Songs in Sumerian Literature: Critical Edition of the Dumuzi-Inanna Songs*, Ramat Gan.
Segal 2007 – M. Segal, *The Book of Jubilees: Rewritten Bible, Redaction, Ideology and Theology* (JSJ.S, 117), Leiden.
Seow 1997 – C.L. Seow, *Ecclesiastes: A New Translation with Introduction and Commentary* (AncB, 18C), New York.
Shaked 2013 – S. Shaked *et al.* (eds), *Aramaic Bowl Spells: Jewish Babylonian Aramaic Bowls*, vol. 1 (Magical and Religious Literature of Late Antiquity, 1), Leiden.
Sharpe 1973 – J.L. Sharpe III, 'The Second Adam in the Apocalypse of Moses', *CBQ* 35, 35-46.
Shipp 2002 – R.M. Shipp, *Of Dead Kings and Dirges: Myth and Meaning in Isaiah 14: 4b-21* (Academia Biblica, 11), Atlanta.
Singer 1992 – I. Singer, 'Towards the Image of Dagon, the God of the Philistines', *Syria* 69, 431-450.
Singer 2007 – I. Singer, 'The Origins of the "Canaanite" Myth of Elkuniršа and Ašertu Reconsidered", in: D. Groddek & M. Zorman (eds), *Tabularia Hethaeorum: Hethitologische Beiträge. Silvin Košak zum 65. Geburtstag* (Dresdener Beiträge zur Hethitologie, 25), Wiesbaden, 631-642.
Ska 2008 – J.-L. Ska, 'Genesis 2–3: Some Fundamental Questions', in: Schmid & Riedweg 2008, 1-27.
Skehan & Di Lella 1987 – P.W. Skehan & A.A. Di Lella, *The Wisdom of Ben Sira* (AncB, 39), New York.
Smalley 1984 – S.S. Smalley, *1, 2, 3 John* (WBC, 51), Waco.
Smelik 2013 – W.F. Smelik, *Rabbis, Language and Translation in Late Antiquity*, Cambridge.
Smith 1898 – G.A. Smith, *The Historical Geography of the Holy Land*, 6th ed., London.
Smith 1988 – M.S. Smith, 'Divine Form and Size in Ugaritic and Pre-exilic Israelite Religion', *ZAW* 100, 424-427.
Smith 1994 – M.S. Smith, *The Ugaritic Baal Cycle*, vol. 1 (VT.S, 55), Leiden.
Smith 2004 – M.S. Smith, *The Rituals and Myths of the Feast of the Goodly Gods of KTU/KTU 1.23: Royal Constructions of Opposition, Intersection, Integration, and Domination* (SBL.RBS, 51), Atlanta.
Smith 2010 – M.S. Smith, *The Priestly Vision of Genesis 1*, Minneapolis.
Smith & Pitard 2009 – M.S. Smith & W.T. Pitard, *The Ugaritic Baal Cycle*, vol. 2: Introduction with Text, Translation and Commentary of KTU 1.3-1.4 (VT.S, 114), Leiden.
Sokoloff 2009 – M. Sokoloff, *A Syriac Lexicon*, Piscataway.
Speiser 1994 – E.A. Speiser, 'The Rivers of Paradise', in: Hess & Tsumura 1994, 175-182.
Spronk 1986 – K. Spronk, *Beatific Afterlife in Ancient Israel and in the Ancient Near East* (AOAT, 219), Neukirchen-Vluyn.

Spronk 1998 – K. Spronk, 'Down with Hêlēl! The Assumed Mythological Background of Isa. 14:12', in: Dietrich & Kottsieper 1998, 717-726.
Stadelmann 1967 – R. Stadelmann, *Syrisch-palästinensische Gottheiten in Ägypten* (Probleme der Ägyptologie, 5), Leiden.
Steenbrink 2011 – K. Steenbrink, 'Created Anew: Muslim Interpretations of the Myth of Adam and Eve', in: Becking & Hennecke 2011, 174-190.
Steiner 1991 – R.C. Steiner, 'The Mountains of Ararat, Mount Lubar and הר הקדם', *JJS* 42, 247-249.
Steiner 2001 – R.C. Steiner, *Early Northwest Semitic Serpent Spells in the Pyramid Texts* (HSS, 61), Winona Lake.
Stern 1982 – E. Stern, *Material Culture of the Land of the Bible in the Persian Period*, Warminster.
Stern 1999 – E. Stern,'Religion in Palestine in the Assyrian and Persian Periods', in: Becking & Korpel 1999, 245-255.
Stokes 2014 – R.E. Stokes, 'Satan, YHWH's Executioner', *JBL* 133 (2014), 251-270.
Stol 2000 – M. Stol, *Birth in Babylonia and the Bible: Its Mediterranean Setting* (Cuneiform Monographs, 14), Groningen.
Stolz 1972 – F. Stolz, 'Die Bäume des Gottesgartens auf dem Libanon', *ZAW* 84, 141-156.
Stone 1992 – M.E. Stone, *A History of the Literature of Adam and Eve* (SBL.EJL, 3), Atlanta.
Stone 2008a – M.E. Stone, 'Satan and the Serpent in the Armenian Tradition', in: Schmid & Riedweg 2008,141-186.
Stone 2008b N. Stone, 'The Four Rivers that Flowed from Eden', in: Schmid & Riedweg 2008, 227-250.
Stordalen 1992 – T. Stordalen, 'Genesis 2,4: Restudying a *locus classicus*', *ZAW* 104, 163-177.
Stordalen 2000 – T. Stordalen, *Echoes of Eden: Genesis 2–3 and Symbolism of the Eden Garden in Biblical Hebrew Literature*, Leuven: Peeters.
Strack & Billerbeck 1922-1961 – H.K. Strack & P. Billerbeck, *Kommentar zum Neuen Testament aus Talmud und Midrasch*, 5 Bde, München.
Stratton 1995 – B.J. Stratton, *Out of Eden: Reading, Rhetoric, and Ideology in Genesis 2–3* (JSOT.SS, 208), Sheffield.
Streck 1998-2001 – M.P. Streck, 'NIṢIR', *RLA*, Bd. 9, 589-590.
Stricker 1953 – B.H. Stricker, *De grote zeeslang*, Leiden.
Stuckenbruck 2004 – L.T. Stuckenbruck, 'The Origins of Evil in Jewish Apocalyptic Tradition: The Interpretation of Genesis 6:1-4 in the Second and Third Centuries B.C.E.', in: Auffarth & Stuckenbruck 2004, 87-118.
Stümpel & Joger 2009 – N. Stümpel & U. Joger, 'Recent Advances in Phylogeny and Taxonomy of Near and Middle Eastern Vipers – An Update', *ZooKeys* 31, 179-191.
Sulzbach 2004 – C. Sulzbach, 'Nebuchadnezzar in Eden? Daniel 4 and Ezekiel 28', in: M. Augustin & H.M. Niemann (eds), *Stimulation from Leiden: Collected Communications to the XVIIIth Congress of the International Organization for the Study of the Old Testament*, Leiden 2004, 125-136.

Tadmor 1958 – H. Tadmor, 'The Campaigns of Sargon II of Assur: A Chronological-Historical Study', *JCS* 12 , 22-40.
Talon 2005 – P. Talon, *Enūma Eliš: The Standard Babylonian Creation Myth* (SAACT, 4), Helsinki.
Taylor 1955 – V. Taylor, *The Gospel According to St. Mark: The Greek Text with Introduction, Notes and Indexes*, London.
Tazawa 2009 – K. Tazawa, *Syro-Palestinian Deities in New Kingdom Egypt: The Hermeneutics of Their Existence* (BAR International Series 1965), Oxford.
Teissier 1984 – B. Teissier, *Ancient Near Eastern Cylinder Seals from the Marcopoli Collection*, Berkeley.
Teugels 2000 – L. Teugels, 'The Creation of the Human in Rabbinic Interpretation', in: Luttikhuizen 2000, 107-117.
Te Velde 1977 – H. te Velde, *Seth: God of Confusion* (Probleme der Ägyptologie, 6), 2nd ed., Leiden.
Te Velde 1980 – H. te Velde, 'Horus und Seth', in: W. Helck & E. Otto (eds), *Lexikon der Ägyptologie*, Bd. 3, Wiesbaden, 25-27.
Te Velde 1984 – H. te Velde, 'Seth', in: W. Helck & E. Otto (eds), *Lexikon der Ägyptologie*, Bd. 3, Wiesbaden, 908-911.
Theobald 2005 – M. Theobald, ' "Ich sah den Satan aus dem Himmel stürzen ...": Überlieferungskritische Beobachtungen zu Lk 10,18-20,' *BZ* 49, 174-190.
Tigay 1982 – J. Tigay, *The Evolution of the Giglamesh Epic*, Phildelphia.
Tigchelaar 1996 – E.J.C. Tigchelaar, *Prophets of Old and the Day of the End: Zecharaiah, The Book of Watchers and Apocalyptic* (OTS, 35), Leiden.
Tigchelaar 1999 – E.J.C. Tigchelaar, 'Eden and Paradise: The Garden Motif in Some Early Jewish Texts (1 Enoch and Other Texts Found at Qumran)', in: G.P. Luttikhuizen (ed.), *Paradise Interpreted: Representations of Biblical Paradise in Judaism and Christianity*, Leiden, 37-57.
Trachtenberg 1961 – J. Trachtenberg, *Jewish Magic and Superstition*, repr. Philadelphia.
Tromp 2005 – J. Tromp, *The Life of Adam and Eve in Greek: A Critical Edition* (PVTG, 6), Leiden.
Tropper 1990– J. Tropper, *Der ugaritische Kausativstamm und die Kausativbildungen des Semitischen: Eine morphologisch-semantische Untersuchung zum Š-Stamm und zu den umstrittenen nichtsibilantischen Kausativstämmen des Ugaritischen* (ALASP, 2), Münster.
Tropper 2008 – J. Tropper, *Kleines Wörterbuch des Ugaritischen* (ELO, 4), Wiesbaden.
Tropper 2012 – J. Tropper, *Ugaritische Grammatik* (AOAT, 273), zweite Auflage, Münster.
Tsumura 1974 – D.T. Tsumura, 'A Ugaritic God *MT-W-ŠR*, and his Two Weapons (UT 52:8-11)', *UF* 6, 407-413.
Tsumura 2005 – D.T. Tsumura, *Creation and Destruction: A Reappraisal of the Chaoskampf Theory in the Old Testament*, Winona Lake.
Tur-Sinai 1957 – N.H. Tur-Sinai, *The Book of Job: A New Commnentary*, third ed., Jerusalem.

Uehlinger 1988 – C. Uehlinger, 'Eva als "lebendiges Kunstwerk": Traditionsgeschichtliches zu Gen 2,21-22(23.24) und 3,20', *BN* 43, 90-99.

Uehlinger 1992 – C. Uehlinger, 'Audienz in der Götterwelt: Anthropomorphismus und Soziomorphiusmus in de Ikonographie eines altsyrischen Zylindersiegels', *UF* 24, 339-359.

Unwin 1996 – P.T.H. Unwin, *Wine and the Vine*, London.

Urbach 1975 – E.E. Urbach, *The Sages: Their Concepts and Beliefs*, tr. I. Abrahams, Jerusalem.

Uvezian 1974 – S. Uvezian, *The Cuisine of Armenia*, London.

Van den Branden 1950 – A. van den Branden, *Les inscriptions thamoudéennes* (BBMus, 25), Louvain-Heverlé.

Van der Bergh 2013 – R.H. van der Bergh, 'The Missionary Character of Paul's Stay on Malta (Acts 28:1-10) According to the Early Church', *Journal of Early Christian History* 3/1, 83-97.

Van der Horst 1999 – P.W. van der Horst, 'Adam', in: Van der Toorn 1999, 5-6.

Van der Kooij 1981 – A. van der Kooij, *Die alten Textzeugen des Jesajabuches: Ein Beitrag zur Textgeschichte des Alten Testaments* (OBO, 35), Freiburg.

Van der Sluijs 2008 – M.A. van der Sluijs, 'On the Wings of Love', *JANER* 8, 219-251.

Van der Sluijs 2009 – M.A. van der Sluijs, 'The Ugaritic God *Hll*', *JNES* 68, 269-281.

Van der Toorn 1999 – K. van der Toorn *et al.* (eds), *Dictionary of Deities and Demons in the Bible*, Second Edition, Leiden.

Van Dijk 1964 – J.J.A. van Dijk, 'Le motif cosmique dans la pensée sumérienne', *AcOr* 28, 1-59.

Van Dijk 1989 – J. van Dijk, 'The Canaanite God Ḥauron and his Cult in Egypt', *GM* 107, 59-68.

Van Gessel 1998 – B.H.L. Van Gessel, *Onomasticon of the Hittite Pantheon*, Leiden.

Van Henten 2006 – J.W. van Henten, 'Dragon Myth and Imperial Ideology in Revelation 12–13', in: Barr 2006a, 181-203.

Van Keulen 2010 – P. van Keulen, in: M.N. van der Meer *et al.* (eds), *Isaiah in Context: Studies in Honour of Arie van der Kooij on the Occasion of his Sixty-Fifth Birthday*, Leiden, 109-123.

Van Ruiten 1999 – J.T.A.G.M. van Ruiten, 'Eden and the Temple: The Rewriting of Genesis 2:4–3:24 in *The Book of Jubilees*', in: Luttikhuizen 1999, 63-94.

Van Ruiten 2000a – J.T.A.G.M. van Ruiten, 'The Creation of Man and Woman in Early Jewish Literature', in: Luttikhuizen 2000a, 34-62.

Van Ruiten 2000b – J.T.A.G.M. van Ruiten, *Primaeval History Interpreted: The Rewriting of Genesis 1–11 in the Book of Jubilees* (JSJ.S, 66), Leiden.

Van Seters 1989 – J. Van Seters, 'The Creation of Man and the Creation of the King', *ZAW* 101, 333-342.

Van Seters 1992 – J. Van Seters, *Prologue to History: The Yahwist as Historian in Genesis*, Louisville.

Van Soldt 2010 – W. van Soldt, 'The Ugaritic Suffixes -*āyu* and -*ānu*', in: D. Shehata *et al.* (eds), *Von Göttern und Menschen: Beiträge zu Literatur und Geschichte des Alten Orients* (Fs B. Groneberg) (Cuneiform Monographs, 41), Leiden, 307-327.

Van Staalduine 1993 – E. van Staalduine-Sulman, 'The Aramaic Song of the Lamb', in: J.C. de Moor & W.G.E. Watson (eds), *Verse in Ancient Near Eastern Prose* (AOAT, 42), Neukirchen-Vluyn, 265-292.

Vanstiphout 1997 – H. L.J. Vanstiphout, 'The Disputation between Ewe and Wheat (1.180)', in: Hallo *et al* 1997, 575-578.

Van Wolde 1989 – E.J. van Wolde, *A Semiotic Analysis of Genesis 2–3: A Semiotic Theory and Method of Analysis Applied to the Story of the Garden of Eden* (Studia Semitica Neerlandica), Assen.

Van Wolde 2009a – E.J. van Wolde, *Reframing Biblical Studies: When Language and Text Meet Culture, Cognition and Context*, Winona Lake.

Van Wolde 2009b – E.(J.) van Wolde, 'Why the Verb ברא Does Not Mean "To Create" in Genesis 1.1–2.4a', *JSOT* 34.1, 1-21.

Van Wolde 2013 – E.(J.) van Wolde, 'One Bow or Another? A Study of the Bow in Genesis 9:8-17', *VT* 63, 124-149.

Van Wolde & Rezetko 2011 – E.(J.) van Wolde & R. Rezetko, 'Semantics and the Semantics of ברא: A Rejoinder to the Arguments Advanced by B. Becking and M. Korpel', *JHS* 11, Article 9.

Verbrugghe & Wickersham 1996 – G.P. Verbrugghe & J.M. Wickersham, *Berossos and Manetho Introduced and Translated: Native Traditions in Ancien Mesopotamia and Egypt*, Ann Arbor.

Vervenne 1995 – M. Vervenne, 'All They Need Is Love: Once More Genesis 6.1-4', in: J. Davies *et al.* (eds), *Words Remembered, Texts Renewed: Essays in Honour of John F.A. Sawyer*, Sheffield, 19-40.

Viberg 1992 – Å. Viberg, *Symbols of Law: A Contextual Analysis of Legal Symbolic Acts in the Old Testament* (CB.OT, 34), Stockholm.

Virolleaud 1941 – C. Virolleaud, 'Les Rephaïm: Fragments de poèmes de Ras Shamtra', *Syria* 22, 1-30.

Virolleaud 1968 – C. Virolleaud, 'Les nouveaux textes mythologiques et liturgiques de Ras Shamra (XXIVe campagne, 1961)', in: J. Nougayrol *et al.* (eds), *Ugaritica V* (Mission de Ras Shamra, 16), Paris, 545-606.

Vittmann 1995 – G. Vittmann, *'Riesen' und riesenhafte Wesen in der Vorstellung der Ägypter* (Veröffentlichungen der Institute für Afrikanistik und Ägyptollogie der Universität Wien, 71), Wien.

Vollenweider 1988 – S. Vollenweider, ' "Ich sah den Satan wie einen Blitz vom Himmel fallen" ', *ZNW* 79, 187-203.

Von Rad 1982 – G. von Rad, *Theologie des Alten Testaments*, Bd 1: Die Theologie der geschichtlichen Überlieferungen Israels, München.

Von Weiher 1971 – E. von Weiher, *Der babylonische Gott Nergal* (AOAT, 11), Neukirchen-Vluyn.

Vreugdenhil 2013 – G.C. Vreugdenhil, *Onheil dat voorbijgaat: Psalm 91 en de (oudoosterse) bedreiging door demonen*, Zoetermeer.

Wagenaar 2001 – J.A. Wagenaar, *Judgement and Salvation: The Composition and Redaction of Micah 2–5* (VT.S, 85), Leiden.

Wagner-Tsukamoto 2012 – S. Wagner-Tsukamoto, 'The Tree of Life: Banned or Not Banned? A Rational Choice Interpretation', *SJOT* 26, 102-122.

Wagner & Wilms 2010 – P. Wagner & T.M. Wilms, 'A Crowned Devil: New Species of *Cerastes* Laurenti, 1768 (Ophidia, Viperidae) from Tunisia, with Two Nomenclatural Comments', *Bonn Zoological Bulletin* 57, 297-306.

Wallace 1985 – H.N. Wallace, *The Eden Narrative* (HSM, 32), Atlanta.

Walters & Gooding 1973 – P. Walters & D.W. Gooding, *The Text of the Septuagint: Its Corruptions and Their Emendation*, Cambridge.

Waltke & O'Connor 1990 – B.K. Waltke & M. O'Connor, *An Introduction to Biblical Hebrew Syntax*, Winona Lake.

Walton 2011 – J.H. Walton, *Genesis 1 as Ancient Cosmology*, Winona Lake.

Ward Gasque 1992 – W. Ward Gasque, 'Malta', *ABD*, vol. 4, 489-490.

Wartke 1993 – R.-B. Wartke, *Urartu: Das Reich am Ararat* (Kulturgeschichte der Antiken Welt, 59), Mainz am Rhein.

Wasserstrom 1994 – S.M. Wasserstrom, 'Jewish Pseudepigrapha in Muslim Literature: A Bibliographical and Methodological Sketch', in: J.C. Reeves (ed.), *Tracing the Threads: Studies in the Vitality of Jewish Pseudeipgrapha* (SBL.EJL, 6), Atlanta, 87- 114.

Waters 2004 – K.L. Waters, 'Saved Through Childbearing: Virtues as Children in 1 Timothy 2:11-15', *JBL* 123, 704-735.

Watson 1999 – W.G.E. Watson, 'Helel', in: Van der Toorn 1999, 392-394.

Watson 2005 – R.S. Watson, *Chaos Uncreated: A Reassessment of the Theme of "Chaos" in the Hebrew Bible* (BZAW, 341), Berlin.

Watson 2007 – W.G.E. Watson, 'Syntax and the Meaning of Ugaritic *ṯmdl*', *UF* 39, 683- 687.

Watson & Wyatt 1999 – W.G.E. Watson & N. Wyatt, *Handbook of Ugaritic Studies* (HdO, 1/39), Leiden.

Wazana 2008 – N. Wazana, 'Anzu and Ziz: Great Mythical Birds in Ancient Near Eastern, Biblical, and Rabbinic Traditions', *JANES* 31 (2008), 111-135.

Weippert 2014 – M. Weippert, '^{d}Elkuniršа: Randbemerkungen zu UF 44 (2013), 201-216', *UF* 45, 537-541.

Wenham 1987 – G. Wenham, *Genesis 1–15* (WBC,1), Waco.

Westermann 1974 – C. Westermann, *Genesis*, Teilband 1: Genesis 1–11 (BKAT, 1/1), Neukirchen.

Westenholz 1997 – J.G. Westenholz, *Legends of the Kings of Akkade* (Mesopotamian Civilizations, 7), Winona Lake.

Wetzstein 1860: – J.G. Wetzstein, *Reisebericht über Hauran und die Trachonen*, Berlin.

Whitney 2006 – K.W. Whitney, *Two Strange Beasts: Leviathan and Behemoth in Second Temple and Early Rabbinic Judaism* (HSM, 63), Winona Lake.

Wiggermann 1994 – F.A.M. Wiggermann, *Mesopotamian Protective Spirits: The Ritiual Texts* (Cuneiform Monographs, 1), Groningen.

Wiggermann 1997 – F.A.M. Wiggermann, 'Transtigridian Snake Gods', in: Finkel & Geller 1997, 33-55.

Wiggermann 2000 – F.A.M. Wiggermann, 'Lamaštu, Daughter of Anu: A Profile', in: Stol 2000, 217-249.

Wiggermann 2001 – F.A.M. Wiggermann, 'Nergal. A. Philogisch', *RLA*, Bd. 8, Berlin. 215-223.

Wiggermann 2013 – F.A.M. Wiggermann, 'Sichtbare Mythologie: Die symbolische Landschaft Mesopotamiens', in: Zgoll & Kratz 2013, 109-132.

Wilckens 1987 – U. Wilckens, *Der Brief an die Römer (Röm 1–5)* (EKK, 6/1), 2.Aufl., Zürich.

Wildberger 1978 – H. Wildberger, *Jesaja* (BK.AT, 10/2), Neukirchen-Vluyn.

Winitzer 2013 – A. Winitzer, 'Etana in Eden: New Light on the Mesopotamian and Biblical Tales in Their Semitic Context', *JAOS* 133, 441-465.

Winitzer 2014 – A. Winitzer, 'Etana', *Encyclopedia of the Bible and Its Reception* 8, 57-59.

Winston 1979 – D. Winston, *The Wisdom of Solomon: A New Translation with Introduction and Commentary* (AncB, 43), Garden City.

Wintermute 2009 – O.S. Wintermute, 'Jubilees (Second Century B.C.: A New Translation and Introduction', in: Charlesworth 2009, 35-142.

Wirth 1971 – E. Wirth, *Syrien: Eine geographische Landeskunde* (Wissenschaftliche Länderkunden, 4/5), Darmstadt.

Wolfart 1966 – R. Wolfart, *Zur Geologie und Hydrogeologie von Syrien* (Beihefte zum Geologischen Jahrbuch, 68), Hannover.

Wright 2005 – A.T. Wright, *The Origin of Evil Spirits: The Reception of Genesis 6.1-4 in Early Jewish Literature* (WUNT, 2.Reihe, 198), Tübingen.

Wyatt 1981 – N. Wyatt, 'Interpreting the Creation and Fall Story in Genesis 2–3', *ZAW* 93, 10-21.

Wyatt 1996 – N. Wyatt, *Myths of Power: A Study of Royal Myth and Ideology in Ugaritic and Biblical Tradition* (UBL, 13). Münster.

Wyatt 1999 – N. Wyatt, 'Eve', in: Van der Toorn 1999, 316-317.

Yamada 2000 – S. Yamada, *The Construction of the Assyrian Empire: A Historical Study of the Inscriptions of Shalmanesar III (859-824 B.C.) Relating his Campaigns to the West* (CHANE, 3), Leiden.

Yarbro Collins 1976 – A. Yarbro Collins, *The Combat Myth in the Book of Revelation* (HDR, 9), Missoula, MA.

Yon 2006 – M. Yon, *The City of Ugarit at Tell Ras Shamra*, Winona Lake.

Young 1981 – G.D. Young (ed), *Ugarit in Retrospect: Fifty Years of Ugarit and Ugaritic*, Winona Lake.

Zevit 2013 – Z. Zevit, *What Really Happened in the Garden of Eden?*, New Haven.

Zgoll & Kratz 2013 – A. Zgoll & R.G. Kratz (eds), *Arbeit am Mythos: Leistung und Grenze des Mythos in Antike und Gegenwart*, Tübingen.

Zimansky 1990 – P. Zimansky, 'Urartian Geography and Sargon's Eighth Campaign', *JNES* 49, 1-21.

Zimmerli 1969 – W. Zimmerli, *Ezechiel*, 2. Teilband (BKAT, 13/2), Neukirchen-Vluyn.

Zwart 2000 – H. Zwart, 'What Is a Whale? Moby-Dick, Marine Science and the Sublime', In: D. Mieth & D. Pfaff (eds), *Erzählen und Moral. Narrativität im Spannungsfeld von Ethik und Ästhetik*, Tübingen, 185-214.

Index of Subjects

Abbadon 55, 241, 249
abdication 19, 93
Abel 126, 143, 225
Abiluma 277
Abraham 8, 136, 194, 199-203, 225, 263
abstraction 12, 235
Abū Ṣalābīḫ 93
abyss, see: Netherworld
actualization 151, 153, 243
Adam *passim*
– Second Adam 150, 198, 206, 231, 233-234, 251, 260, 310
Adam, see also: Adammu
Adamic Myth v, 5, 83, 88, 125, 158, 228, 234, 237, 239, 243, 248, 251-252, 256
Adammu v, 16, 24-28, 42, 48-49, 52-53, 57-59, 68-69, 71-75, 82, 84-85, 100, 119, 123-124, 126-128, 130, 136, 138, 141-144, 147, 150, 159, 174, 179, 186, 216, 219, 228, 234, 249, 251-252, 265-269, 271, 273
Adamtu 59
Adapa 99-100, 113, 297
adultery 140
adversary, see: enemy
Aegean, see: Greece; Greek
Aeon 71
Aether 109
afterlife 119, 188, 292, 332; see also: death; immortality; Netherworld; paradise
aggression, see: battle; combat; enemy
Agrĭ Dağı 29
Ahriman 107-108
Ahura Mazda 107-108
Akhenaten 117
Akkadian 5
– *ālu* 71
– *apkallu* 71, 100, 182
– *banû* 13, 267
– *bašmu* 63, 82, 143
– *erru* 103
– *erēru* 103
– *erṣetu* 6
– *kurību* 165
– *lullû* 27, 103, 268
– *maqātu* 266
– *māšu* 32, 40
– *mušḫuššu* 64
– *mušmaḫḫu* 64
– *muššuʾu* 155
– *nakāru* 280
– *naṣāru* 31
– *nesû* 281
– *niṣirtu* 31
– *pushālu* 46
– *siništum damiqtum* 269
– *šamû* 6
– *šaṭû* 55
– *šamāmu* 271
– *šimmatu* 271
– *šīru* 266
– *taknītu* 164
– *taknû* 164
– *ṭābūtu* 266
– *ṭūbtu* 266
– *ummu* 267
– *ušumgallu* 64
Alalaḫ 51, 288
Alalu 8
Alašia 74
Aldebaran 61-62, 96, 171-172, 253, 260, 269
Aleppo 18, 308; see also: *ḫlb*
Alexander 156
Allāh 209-211
allegory 190
ambiguity 77, 82, 86, 91, 104, 112, 119, 126, 135-136, 142, 145, 163, 179, 183, 210, 212, 237, 251, 258, 260, 262-263
Ambrose 148
Ammonite 151
Amorite 133, 146
amulet 45, 76-77, 81, 282, 305
Amun(-Re) 59, 90, 139

AN 93
Anat, see: ʿAnatu
Anatolia 17, 47, 53, 57, 84, 277, 300
ʿAnatu 6, 10, 14, 20-21, 31, 42, 46, 56, 71, 77, 79, 81-82, 123–140124, 139, 263, 270, 276-278, 302, 307
Anaximander 262
ancestors 6, 27, 57-58, 70-71, 93, 146, 279
androgyny 26, 57-58, 84, 89, 113, 122, 179, 186, 202, 208, 212, 258
angel, see: deity, – angel
Angra Maynu 107-108
animals vi, 46-48, 57, 61, 82, 98, 103, 106, 118, 121-122, 128, 136, 147, 149-150, 171-172, 189-190, 206, 244, 271, 275, 282, 299, 306
– hybrid 31, 105, 165, 306
animals, see also: horse; lion, etc.
annihilation, see: destruction
anonymity 79, 287
antediluvian 71, 100, 146, 148, 180, 182, 186, 191, 290
Anti-Lebanon 66-67
Antiochus IV 156
Anu 8, 95-97, 99-101
Anunna 94-107
Anzû 100, 315
Aphrodite 109
apocalyptic vi, 190,199-205, 207-208, 218, 225-226, 241-242, 259, 283-284, 294-295, 300, 303, 306, 308, 310, 312
Apollo 244
Apollyon 241, 244
Apophis 61, 90-92
apostasy, see: rebellion
apotropaic 173, 195, 223
apple 37, 59-60, 109
apple, see also: fruit; tree
apprehension, see: fear
Apsû 57, 102
Aqhâtu 13, 20-21, 77, 84, 124, 126, 139, 165, 267, 277, 293
Arabic words
– ʾ*Allāh* 209
– ʾ*āllih* 209
– ʾ*ilāh* 209
– *balasān* 59
– *ǧabbānah* 65
– *ǧinn* 210
– *ḥarūr* 54
– *ḥby* 31
– *ḥatf* 189
– *ḫiṯṯy* 50
– *ḫalīfa* 159, 210
– *darra* 265
– *raṣada* 69
– *sanām* 9
– *šarr* 55
– ʿ*aduww* 55, 84, 142
– *faḥl* 48
– *fāqa* 266
– *mārid* 71
– *hilāl* 49
– *waḥr* 45, 282
– *waḥrah* 46, 282
Aramaic 55, 65, 81, 122, 141, 181, 193, 208, 212, 221, 295, 297, 303, 308, 310, 314
Ararat 30-44, 83, 137, 150, 162, 170, 179-180, 246-247, 251, 255, 311, 315
Ararat Pilaf x, 37-39
Arašīḫ 29, 75, 280
Arasphes 21
Arasphes, see also: Rašpu
Arišu 81, 75
ark 30, 41, 43, 83, 105, 149-150, 193, 255, 294
arm 51, 53, 73
Armenia x, 30-32, 36-37, 41-43, 83, 105, 141-142, 204, 209, 227, 255-256, 302, 31, 311, 313
arousal, see: sexuality
ʾ*arṣ wšmm* 6-8
Aruru 89
Asael, see: Azazel
Asclepion 244
Asclepius 86, 223, 244
Ašertu, see: Aṯiratu
Asha 106
Asha-Vahista 108
Asherah 11, 157, 211, 213, 254

Ashur-naṣir-apli II 30, 42
asp, see: serpent; snake; viper
ass 46, 190
assassin, see: murderer
assembly, see: deity, – council
Assur (city) 29
Assur (god) 154
Assyria 32, 57, 68, 151, 289, 312
Assyrian 30-31, 32, 54, 151-154, 156-157, 171-172, 266, 289, 295, 312, 316
ʿAštarōt-Qarnayim 68, 279
Astarte 56, 67, 278
Astarte, see also: ʿAthtartu
Aṯiratu 7, 11-12, 26, 56, 58, 79, 82, 118, 144, 146, 168, 211, 213
Athiratu, see: Aṯiratu
Athiratu, see also: Asherah
ʿṯtpr 271
ʿAṯtapiru, see: *ʿṯtpr*
ʿAṯtarātu (city) 261, 279
ʿAṯtartu 19-21, 31, 46, 56, 79, 123, 270-271, 276, 278, 282
ʿAthtartu, see also: Astarte
ʿAthtaru 68, 148, 152, 271
Atlas 9, 109
atonement 200
Atraḫasis 27, 94, 96-97, 111-113, 125, 146-147, 149, 301
Athtaru, see: ʿAṯtaru
Atum 89-90
Augustine 51, 151, 230
author, see: scribe
awe, see: fear
Awēla 95-96
Ayyamur 18, 21
Azazel 191, 193, 200-202, 212, 286, 298, 306

Baal 14, 18, 21, 76, 83, 121, 152, 168, 218-219, 235-236, 252, 255, 263, 31
Baal, see also: Baʿlu
Baal Shamem 14
Babylon 104, 151, 158, 178, 191, 221
Babylonia(n) 5-6, 9-10, 23, 26, 30, 32, 40-41, 45, 51, 54, 57, 69, 71, 77, 84, 88, 94, 95-96, 98-103, 105, 111-113, 120, 125, 130, 136, 140, 142, 147, 149, 151-153, 156, 244, 255, 275-276, 282, 287, 289, 292, 294, 298-299, 300-301, 307, 309-312, 314-290
Bakhu 92
bad, see: evil
balsam 55
Baʿlu 6-7, 11, 12, 14, 18-19, 25, 28, 34, 43, 49, 53, 66, 71, 78-83, 93, 112-113, 121, 124, 140, 152-153, 155, 161, 168, 170, 173-174, 178, 216, 218-219, 252, 267, 270, 276, 291
Barisat 199
bark 82-83
barrenness, see: sterility
Baruch vi, 207, 294
basalt 9, 33, 75, 86-87
Bashan 65-67, 69, 78, 148, 218, 241, 247, 252, 279, 304
battle 14, 56, 77, 100-102, 109, 148, 153, 162, 170, 194, 219, 222, 226, 242, 300, 316
beard 96, 210
beauty 41, 77, 103, 109, 123, 131, 149, 164-166, 185, 207, 210, 213
beckoning 37, 39
beer 92, 94
bed 19, 48, 132, 148, 222
Be-elzebul 216, 219
beginning 5, 10, 45, 83, 107, 110, 120-121, 125, 127, 134, 137, 150, 189, 222-225, 234, 240-241, 250-251, 254, 261, 282, 285, 289, 295, 298
Behemoth 65, 191, 315
Bēlet-Ilī 42, 103, 149
Belial 55, 194
Beliar 192
Ben Sira vi, 125, 131, 187-189, 229, 258, 285, 288, 301, 310
Berossos 30, 105, 111, 314
Bibite 277
biblical theology 2, 308

binding 25, 44, 53, 66, 92, 174, 184, 187, 190-192, 218, 247, 252, 266, 275-280, 307
bird 11, 14, 18, 20-22, 49, 63, 100, 200, 315
bird, see also: black kite; eagle; falcon; swallow; vulture
Bit-enosh 193
bitterness 267-268
black kite 21
blasphemy 21, 79, 187
blessing 14, 34, 37, 83, 103, 121-122, 136, 188, 306
bliss, see: happiness
blood 27, 47, 57, 92, 94, 96, 101, 103, 109, 111, 271
boat 97-98
boat, see also: ark
boiling 61, 267
bowing 127, 209, 272
bowl 33, 39, 55, 81, 212, 297, 305, 310
boy 25, 72, 193, 209, 266
breast 51-52, 73, 96, 191
breastplate 165, 167
breath 98, 127-128, 147, 208, 241
breeding 10, 46, 48, 57, 59, 103, 150, 271, 275
bridal gift 45-47, 282
bride 45-48, 97, 123, 185, 189, 237, 271, 282
bronze 45, 73, 223, 281
brother 9, 11, 13, 19-20, 41, 103, 144, 150, 160, 225, 240
brow 25, 265
Buduḫdug 270
bulgur 37
bull 10-12, 14, 47, 59, 64, 92, 97, 105-106, 190
burghul 37
burial 69, 187, 218
burial grounds 69, 218
Byblos 6-9, 27, 31, 33, 41, 56-57, 71, 77, 85, 109, 254

Cain 126, 136, 142-145, 150, 179, 224-225, 240-241, 250, 288, 295
calamity, see: death; destruction; evil
camp 10, 20
Canaanite *passim*
Capernaum 220-221
captive 79
caravans 5
carob tree 41, 185, 210
castration 8, 109
cattle 10, 103, 172, 186, 190
cedar 72, 98, 270
Cehennem Tepe 32
celestials 17, 23, 27, 56, 153, 159, 201
celestials, see also: angel; deity; fall
Cerastes 61, 63-64, 174-175, 309, 315
chair 18, 276-280
champion 25, 27, 82, 219, 265
chaos 15, 81, 101, 104, 108-109, 259, 283, 295, 309, 312, 315
character 77, 86, 90, 104-105, 112, 130, 142, 144, 158, 166, 178, 212, 216, 237, 257, 269
chariot 42, 110, 113, 207
cheek 64
Chemosh 278, 305
cherub 31, 133, 165-166, 170-171, 184, 301
cherub, see also: angel; sphinx
child 6, 11, 15, 45-46, 48-49, 51, 71, 75, 105, 109, 127-128, 132, 134, 139-140, 144, 150, 159, 180, 187, 192-193, 195, 199, 210, 225-226, 238-242, 245, 249, 254, 257, 260, 272, 280, 282, 300, 307, 315
child, see also: boy; daughter; son; sterility
childbearing, see: childbirth
childbirth 46, 49, 51, 128, 139, 159, 180, 240, 245, 257, 272, 307
Christ 206, 223, 231, 235-236, 263, 287
Christ, see also: Jesus
circumcision 164, 167
city 1, 17, 29, 44, 75, 97, 102-103, 132-133, 145, 168, 221, 234, 247, 276-280, 316
civilization 2, 94, 98, 105

clay 12, 27, 66, 83, 94, 96, 98, 103, 111, 127, 149, 178, 209, 254, 278, 306
clean 121, 210
clean, see also: unclean
Clymene 110
cloud 43, 68, 71, 78-79, 100, 110, 152-153, 161, 196, 223, 255, 299
column, see: pillar
combat, see: battle
conception 49, 51, 127, 144, 159, 190, 257
conception, see also: fertility; sexuality
concubine 11, 50, 132, 159-160
conversion, see: repentance
copper 43, 257
copper, see also: bronze
Coptic 208, 295, 308
corpse 66, 79, 171
cosmogony, see: cosmology; creation
cosmology 1, 5-15, 57, 90, 171, 233, 283, 295, 300, 302, 315
cosmos 9-10, 16, 29, 35, 49, 59, 61, 78, 83, 94-95, 98, 101-102, 121, 123, 134, 226, 254, 262-263
counterpart 28, 138,140
covenant 39, 116, 149, 190, 263, 299
cow 14, 92, 113, 124, 130, 190
crater 29-30, 40, 77, 224, 237
creation v, ix, 1, 5-17, 20, 24-27, 32, 35, 44, 46-47, 57-59, 69, 72, 82-83, 85, 89-90, 92-94, 96, 98-99, 101-107, 110-113, 115-123, 125, 130-137,140-142, 144, 149-150, 156-157, 161, 165, 167-168, 176-179, 181-182, 185-186, 189-191, 195-199, 204, 207-213, 216-217, 222, 229, 231, 233-234, 243, 250-251, 254-255, 262
– by word alone 12-13, 82, 102, 111, 120, 178, 213, 254
– humans 1, 12, 26-27, 44, 46, 58, 94, 96, 99, 101, 111, 118, 119, 122, 130-131, 136, 141, 157, 165, 177, 189-190, 197, 199, 208, 210, 212-213, 287
creatio continua 12-13, 177, 254-255
creatio ex nihilo 12, 120,122, 178-178, 213, 233, 250-251, 253
creation, see also: deity, – creator; creatress
creationism 263
crescent 49-50, 160, 257
Crete 5, 279
crime, see: offenses
crocodile 171
crocodile, see also: dragon; Leviathan; monster; serpent
crucifixion 223, 226
cult, see also: offering; ritual
cup 33-34, 81
curse 1, 17, 21, 96, 129, 144, 150, 172, 183, 221, 223, 251, 308
Cyprus 1, 5, 48, 62-64, 70, 72-74, 85, 109, 154, 162, 180, 184, 222, 299, 304, 308

Dagan(u) 6, 12, 83, 270, 276
Dalmatia 227, 304
Daniel 163, 166, 170, 290, 311
Daniel, see also: Dani'ilu
Dani'ilu 13, 136
Darius I 151
darkness 40-41, 66, 69, 89, 100, 105, 107, 109, 121, 175, 185, 226, 241, 294
date palm 35, 44-45, 62, 73, 75, 78, 185, 210, 281-282
daughter 10, 49, 56, 79, 131-132, 150, 154, 183, 187, 190, 193, 219, 269, 271, 275, 315
dawn 24, 50, 107, 109, 153, 159-160, 280, 283
day 65, 99, 117, 119-120, 122, 133, 139, 165, 172, 175, 178, 182, 184-187, 191, 196-197, 200, 207, 213, 236, 271-272
death v, 1, 6-7, 11, 15, 17, 19, 24-26, 28-29, 40, 42-44, 48-49, 51-54, 66, 71, 75, 77, 79-82, 85, 90, 97-100, 106-109, 111, 113, 124, 126-127, 130-131, 134-135, 137-142, 144-146, 148, 150, 154, 157-160,

164, 170, 173-177, 179-180, 184, 189, 192, 194, 198, 213, 219, 224, 227-231, 235-236, 243, 251-252, 256-258, 260, 263, 265, 267-268, 272, 281, 291-292, 298, 300, 306
death, see also: Motu; Osiris
death, see also: deity, – death
Dedan 192
defeat 18, 26, 51, 53, 78-79, 81-82, 101-102, 113, 128, 139-140, 153, 195, 218, 228, 242, 251-252, 259-260, 272, 294
defeat, see also: victory
defloration 14, 271
Deir ʿAlla 161, 297
Deir el-Medina 76
deification 58, 145-146, 157-158, 160, 168-169, 187-188, 196, 206
deity *passim*
– accusation 20-21, 55, 194
– ambiguity 77, 82, 86, 91, 104, 112, 119, 126, 135-136, 142, 179, 183, 210, 212, 237, 251, 257, 260, 262, 264
– ancestral 6, 71, 93, 146, 279
– angel 55-56, 61, 71, 123, 147, 154, 167, 186, 183-187, 191, 196-197, 200-212, 220, 223, 233, 235, 241, 244, 247-248, 251, 259, 284, 308
– anger, see: wrath
– anthropomorphism 76, 122, 136, 178, 204, 313
– assembly 6, 9, 84, 96, 123, 153, 161
– benevolent, see: – goodness
– commandment, Law 114, 124-126, 128-130, 143, 177, 184, 198, 229, 229-231, 257-258, 262-263, 299, 314
– council – 84; see also: assembly
– creator 7-8, 10, 12-17, 20, 24-25, 32, 35, 47, 59, 82-83, 90, 93-94, 102, 107, 112-113, 117, 120-121, 134, 136-137, 157, 161, 168, 178-179, 209, 211, 222, 233, 254-255, 262, 291, 308
– creatress 11, 15-16, 25, 82, 118, 144, 149, 177, 254, 267
– death 27-28, 93, 97
– deceit 1, 107, 142, 201, 204-205, 224, 229, 236-238, 244, 248; see also: lying
– demon 11, 17, 24, 28, 45, 53, 55, 75, 77-78, 108, 143, 158, 163, 173-176, 180, 195, 209, 211-212, 216, 218-220, 222, 230, 235-237, 247, 250, 252, 259, 265-266, 268, 272, 282, 286, 292, 298, 301, 306, 314-315
– demonic, see: evilness
– drunken 9, 20-21, 31, 92, 150, 179
– dwelling 10-11, 17, 31-32, 43, 75, 79, 83, 96, 98, 125, 131, 145, 147, 163, 168-170, 173, 180, 182, 184, 187, 191, 201, 215, 233, 244, 249, 255, 259, 279, 269, 281
– evilness v, 24, 54-55, 61, 70-71, 74, 77-82, 84, 85, 97, 107-109, 112-113, 119, 138, 142, 159, 162-163, 174, 176-177, 179-180, 191-192, 194, 200, 203-206, 211-212, 216-219, 222, 226-227, 230, 234-235, 240, 243-245, 248-249, 251-252, 259, 263, 267
– father 6-7, 9-12, 15, 17-18, 32, 50, 53, 56, 59, 82-83, 85, 89-90, 102, 103, 109-110, 112-113, 117, 142, 144, 150, 159-160, 162, 174, 199, 216, 224, 243, 250, 257, 270, 282, 289
– fear 79, 82
– freedom 27, 40, 56, 139, 179
– gender 57, 130; see also: androgyny
– goodness 31, 54-55, 76-77, 108, 113, 119, 135-136, 138, 142, 149, 159, 184, 187, 202, 210, 216, 251, 263, 288, 300, 310
– helper 69, 75, 89, 100, 104, 135, 191, 259
– Holy Ones 193-194
– husband 11, 85, 109, 144, 168
– image 23, 48, 83, 104, 118,

122-123, 133, 138, 141, 150, 164, 171-172, 177-178, 194, 199, 201, 204, 206, 217, 220-221, 229, 231, 234, 244, 246-248, 272, 288-289, 292, 304, 309-310
– immortal, see: – living
– inspiration 242
– intervention 16, 28, 49, 82, 110
– jealousy 141, 199, 212, 215-216
– justice 106, 152, 198-199, 266
– law, see: – commandment
– lists 6-7, 53, 57-59, 105, 110, 134, 145-146, 161, 230, 234, 266, 270, 293, 295, 298
– living v, 1, 17, 27-28, 41, 44-53, 59, 71, 75, 77, 82, 85, 97-100, 107, 112-113, 122, 124, 134, 137, 139, 141-142, 149, 162, 177, 179, 188, 192, 195, 202, 208, 213, 199, 210, 223, 235, 249, 256, 259, 262, 284, 309
– love 23, 35, 46-47, 77, 81, 92, 109, 123, 148, 170, 276, 306, 310
– Lord 8, 10, 51, 76, 89-90, 107-108, 133, 140, 143-144, 150, 152, 160, 163-164, 172, 184, 186-187, 192, 195, 203, 207, 226, 240, 259
– malevolent, see: evilness
– mercy 39, 77, 85, 104, 142, 195, 195, 202, 205-206, 269,296
– monotheism, see: separate entry monotheism
– monotheism, see also: henotheism
– mortal 52, 71, 85, 99, 139, 148, 157, 179, 182, 194, 199, 209, 228, 233, 243, 251, 257, 309
– mother, see: mother
– name 7-9, 13-14, 18, 20, 24, 26, 29, 30, 31-33, 40, 43, 48-50, 53-56, 59-62, 66, 74, 77, 79, 83-85, 92, 96, 103, 107, 112-113, 118, 120-121, 126-127, 129-130, 142, 152, 155, 158-160, 167-168, 174-176, 178, 180, 183-184, 191, 194, 197, 200, 203, 208-209, 211-212, 216, 219, 221, 229, 235, 242, 248, 252, 254-255, 257, 260, 265-266, 270, 272, 275, 277, 304
– omnipotence 189, 301
– pair 6, 7-8, 21, 46, 48, 52-59, 77, 91, 93, 109-110, 121, 134, 141, 176, 196, 263, 270, 300
– personification 54, 143, 219, 230, 234-235, 249, 251-252
– potter 12, 83, 90,111, 135, 178, 254
– power 14-15, 17, 24, 27, 55, 58, 75, 77-78, 80-82, 101-102, 112-113, 126, 132,149, 153, 183, 196, 199, 208, 216, 219, 221-223, 230, 235, 237, 244, 248, 251-252, 256, 259, 268, 270, 289, 298, 316
– procreation v, 11, 46, 90, 112, 159
– providence 258
– seclusion 31
– sleep 32-33, 94, 96, 103, 133, 293
– soul 12
– Spirit/spirit 12-13, 27, 71, 94, 96, 107, 113, 119, 127-128, 148, 176, 178, 183, 185-186, 194, 196, 201, 210, 212, 215, 217-218, 232, 260, 279, 299, 315
– strength 54, 74, 76, 84
– theriomorphic 78, 91, 118, 129, 143
– voraciousness 11, 18, 25, 166, 174, 183, 265, 270-271
– wife 7, 11, 25, 28, 58, 79, 82, 105, 118, 146, 179, 254, 257
– wisdom 35, 95, 99, 107, 138,163-164, 166, 170, 197, 199
– wrath 82, 92, 144, 201, 203, 207-209, 218, 262
Deluge, see: Flood
demigod 98, 100, 111-113, 256, 280, 296
democratization 119, 258
demon, see: deity, – demon
demoniac 216, 218
demonization 158
Dendayn 192
deportation 153

descent 30, 36, 40, 164, 179, 184, 200, 210, 233, 269
descent, see also: fall
desert 44, 63, 65, 90, 92, 110, 113, 117, 153, 162, 171, 180, 191-192, 198, 200, 215, 218-219, 223, 237, 244-245, 247, 250, 256, 260, 280
destiny, fate 16, 56, 85, 109, 95, 97-98, 100, 102, 113, 170, 172, 183, 188, 237, 258
Destroyer 25, 162, 222, 241, 244, 249, 262, 266, 271, 275-280, 307
destruction 18, 97, 105, 198, 114, 203, 241, 261, 266, 270-271, 301, 312
Deuteronomistic 115, 125, 262
Devil ix, 2, 32, 52-53, 55, 77, 84-86, 107, 113, 141-143, 151-152, 154, 163, 177, 179-181, 194, 197-203, 209, 212, 215, 218, 222, 224-230, 235, 237, 240-241, 243-245, 248-252, 256-257, 259-260, 264, 266, 292, 300, 308
Devil, see also: demon; Satan
Devourer 18, 174, 270-271
Didānu, see: Ditānu
Dilmun 29
Dione 59
dirge, see: lamentation
disease, see: illness
disguise 20, 212, 221, 244
distinctiveness 2-3, 115, 127, 166, 177, 246
Ditānu 146
divine kingship, see: deification
dominion 18-19, 119, 123, 151, 186, 194, 216, 310
dragon 17, 46, 59, 61, 64-66, 68, 70, 74 92, 102-103, 131, 202-203, 218, 242-248, 250, 260, 282, 290, 293, 308, 313
dragon, see also: crocodile; monster; serpent; snake
dreaming 32-33, 190
drought 96
drunkenness 9, 20-21, 31, 92, 150, 179
dualism 89, 107-108, 113, 226, 232, 235, 283
duck 64
Dumuzi 47, 123, 310
dung 50
dyad, see: pair

Ea 35, 39, 100-103
eagle, see: bird
earth 6-12, 14, 17-18, 24-25, 31-32, 35-37, 40, 44, 48-49, 54, 56, 72, 75, 77, 82-85, 89, 93-96, 102, 104, 106, 108-110, 113, 118-121, 123, 130, 133-136, 140-141, 144, 148-151, 153, 159-160, 164, 166, 170, 182-184, 186-190, 196-204, 205, 208-209, 212, 216, 220, 231-234, 241, 243-246, 251, 255-257, 265, 270-271, 275, 280, 290, 292, 296, 308-309
Earth and Heaven 6-8, 89, 133-134
earthquake 203
east 5, 17, 29-32, 35, 40-41, 44, 54, 68, 75, 92, 145, 160, 177, 182, 185, 192, 280, 291, 293, 304
Ebla 57, 277, 305
Eden 1, 29-32, 43, 58, 70, 72, 83, 123-125, 127, 129, 133,-139, 141, 165, 167, 169,171-172, 179-180, 186-187, 192, 195, 202-204, 206, 225, 236, 247, 253, 255, 258, 262, 265, 283-284, 288, 291-295, 298, 301, 303-305, 309, 311-316
Eden, see also: paradise
Edom 35
Egypt(ian) v, 5-6, 9, 12-14, 18, 21-22, 45, 53-55, 57, 59, 61, 71, 75-78, 82, 84, 89-92, 101, 110, 112-113, 120, 124, 128, 130, 133, 136, 139, 142, 145, 165, 171-172, 178, 180, 226, 242, 269, 282, 286, 292, 299, 301-303, 308, 312-314
El 7-8, 10, 13, 16, 32, 34-35, 37, 56, 59, 83, 120, 126, 134, 139, 152,155-161, 163-164, 167-170, 178, 182-184, 191, 200-202, 211, 213, 215, 219, 246, 249, 252,

254-256, 258-259, 292, 301, 305, 307
El, see also: Eli; Ilu
elephant 190
Eli 202
Elijah 215
Elkunirsa 7, 33
Ellil, see: Enlil
Elos 6
Elymas 226
Elysean Fields 31
Elyon 7-8
enemy 24, 55, 81, 84, 102, 107, 142-143, 151, 162-163, 201, 203, 219, 221-222, 249, 225, 235
Enki 35, 47, 93-96, 298
Enkidu 64, 78, 97-98
Enlil 10, 34, 93-97, 100, 103
Enoch vi, 148, 156, 181-182, 184-185, 187, 190-191, 195-198, 220, 251, 283, 286, 295, 299-300, 302, 305-306, 308, 312
Enūma ēliš 10, 57, 70, 79, 98, 101-102, 191, 265, 268
Ephesus 238
eponym 58
Ereškigal 54, 297
Eridu 13, 99, 103, 111, 136
eroticism 45, 47, 92, 282, 287
Erra 26, 54, 77, 84, 88, 103-105, 112, 142, 205, 263, 286, 303, 308
Esagil 103
eschatology 65, 194, 204, 221, 223, 226, 242, 293-294
Etana 100
Etna 110
euphemism 14, 40, 188
Euphrates 7, 30, 34, 42-43, 47, 83, 96, 103, 137, 179, 211, 247, 249, 255, 258
Eve v, 2, 28, 31, 46, 48, 57-58, 62, 85, 124-125, 127-133, 136-144, 148, 172, 176-179, 181, 185-191, 195-198, 202-206, 208-213, 220, 225, 229, 231, 233, 236-238, 250-251, 257, 259, 262, 283-284, 287, 289, 293, 298, 300-301, 304, 307, 309, 311
evil v, 24, 54-55, 61, 70-71, 74, 77-82, 84-85, 95, 97, 107-109, 112-113, 119, 121, 126-136, 138, 142-143, 159, 162-163, 174, 176-177, 179-180, 185-186, 188, 191-192, 194-195, 201, 203, 205-206, 209, 211-212, 216-219, 222, 226-227, 229-230, 234-235, 240-241, 243-249, 251-252, 258-259, 262-264, 267, 281, 283, 288, 300-302, 311, 316
ewe 94, 314
execution 17-18, 20, 145, 154, 176, 257, 311
exile 56, 132, 154, 162, 180, 292
existence 12-13, 30, 90, 106-107, 109, 113, 119, 121, 138, 147, 188, 197-198, 213, 222, 233, 312
exorcism 216, 260
exorcism, see also: incantation; spell
eye 90, 92, 176, 195-196, 202, 281
Ezekiel vi, 163-172

faeces 50
falcon 20-23, 76, 203
falcon; see also: bird
fall of celestials 21, 23-24, 56, 72, 88, 147, 151-155, 158, 160-162, 167, 170, 182, 190, 197, 200, 204, 209, 216-217, 219-223, 225-226, 232, 237, 241-242, 245, 247, 249-250, 283-284, 288, 293-294, 308, 314
fall of Adam and Eve 49, 72, 124, 186, 205, 209-210, 222, 284-285, 293, 295, 316
family 11, 82, 97, 132, 149, 161, 193
fangs 21, 25, 173-174, 235, 265
fate, see: destiny
father 6-7, 9-12, 14, 18-19, 32, 50, 53, 56, 59, 82-83, 85, 89, 90, 93, 102-103, 109-110, 112-113, 132, 142, 144, 146, 150, 159-160, 162, 174, 199, 216, 224, 227-228, 242-243, 249, 257, 270, 282, 289
father, see also: deity

fear 81, 101, 265
Feast of Booths 52
female 9, 27-36, 28, 46-48, 57-58, 74, 89, 96, 109, 113, 128, 117, 130, 132-146, 179, 191, 133, 196, 203, 255, 271, 275
fertility 43, 49, 52, 246
fig 210
figurine, see: idolatry; image
finger 14, 37, 157
fire 37, 54, 61, 81, 98, 104, 106, 109, 166, 184-186, 191, 193, 196, 200-201, 209-211, 217, 241, 246, 250, 252, 296
firmament 9-10, 33, 40, 83, 121, 178, 255, 275
fish 11, 35, 42, 52, 63, 73-74, 101, 105
flame, see: fire
flee 61, 81, 154, 162, 218, 243
flesh 25, 72, 96, 128, 147, 186, 206, 266
Flood, cosmic 8-10, 13-19, 29, 31, 34, 48, 52, 57, 78, 83, 89, 110, 117, 120-121, 169, 178, 234, 268, 275, 288
Flood, deluge 30, 41, 71, 92, 96-98, 104-105, 111-112, 124, 146, 149-150, 180, 184, 193, 289, 290, 294, 296-297, 301
fog 16, 18, 54, 69, 81, 85, 110, 159, 241-242, 256, 270-271
folk etymology 30, 140
folk religion, see: popular religion
food 37-39, 43, 86, 94, 96, 99-100, 136, 173, 202, 267-268, 271-272, 275-280, 289
foot 35, 42, 62-63, 152, 162, 173, 202, 221, 230, 268
fortress 10, 17, 280
fortune, see: wealth
fossils 68
free will 143, 179, 189, 258, 263
free will, see also: ambiguity; deity, – freedom
friend 25, 77, 90-91, 98-99, 112, 157, 199, 210, 227, 238, 266
fruit 37, 41, 50, 75, 109, 113, 122, 124, 126, 130, 140, 172, 185, 189, 202, 204-206, 210, 212-213, 217, 246-247, 249, 256
fundamentalism 3
future 97, 139, 173, 190, 192, 206, 211, 221-222, 234, 242-243, 259

Gabriel 183-184
Gadre'el 191
garden 30-32, 41, 43, 58-59, 87, 113, 125, 127, 130, 133-137, 139, 150, 159, 165, 167, 169, 171-172, 177, 179, 180, 182, 185-186, 188, 192, 195, 202-203, 211-212, 225, 235-236, 243, 255-256, 258-259, 283-285, 288, 293, 303, 311, 312, 314, 316
gatekeeper 31, 136
Gathas 106-108
Gaṯru 146
Ge 8, 56
Geb 6, 89, 92
Ǧebel el-Drūz 44, 69
Gehenna 32, 201, 218, 246, 250
Gehenna, see also: Netherworld
gem, see: precious stone
Genea 71
genealogy 145, 216, 266, 294
generosity 19, 77, 85, 142, 200, 212, 216, 266
genitals 52
genitals, see also: penis; vulva
Genos 71
Gerasene 218-219, 252
gestures 39, 51-52, 73, 97, 149, 268
ghost, see: deity, – spirit; demon
giant 11, 32, 61, 67-71, 83, 86, 101, 109, 128, 143-144, 148, 162, 179, 182-183, 193, 105, 202, 241, 250, 280
– snake 69-70, 85, 101, 128, 143-144, 162, 241, 242
Gilgameš 17, 30, 40-42, 63, 97-99, 103, 111, 113, 140, 256, 294, 307
Gizeh 75
glass 65-69, 246, 252

glaze 139
glove 20
Gnosticism 208, 232-234, 238, 260, 286, 307-308
goat 47, 200
God/god/goddess, see: deity
Golan 69, 218, 293, 299
golem 72
Goliath 148
gold 34, 43, 46-47, 59, 109-110, 163, 165, 209, 255
good 13, 17, 28, 42, 44, 68, 76-77, 85, 97, 107-109, 113, 119, 121, 126-127, 130-132, 138, 142-143, 149, 156, 159, 163, 178-179, 184-187, 195, 205, 210, 216, 232, 251-252, 257-258, 260-264, 269, 287, 300, 310
good-natured 28, 85, 138, 249, 257, 269; see also: good
granary 43
grapes 41, 202-203
grave 162
Great Rift Valley 35
greatness, see: proportions
Greece/Greek v, 1, 33, 56, 59, 61, 66, 86-87, 89, 91,108-110, 112, 130, 133, 141, 146, 160, 192, 203, 207, 209, 217, 225, 227, 238, 241-243, 245, 257, 262, 287, 291, 294,-295, 301-302, 305, 309, 312
Greek words
– ἀνθρωποκτόνος 225, 240
– αρχή 240
– ἄρχων 226
– βασανίζω 218
– γυνή 239
– διάβολος 209, 215, 245
– δράκων 245
– ἐκβάλλω 216, 226
– ἔχιδνα 217, 227-228
– γέννημα 216-217
– γεννάω 216
– γίνομαι 216-217
– καλόν κακόν 131
– κρατήρ 33
– μνήμα 218
– ὄφις 228, 245
– πονηρὸς 240
– Σατανᾶς 245
– σκάνδαλον 219, 230
– σῴζω 239
– τεκνογονία 239-240
– τέκνον 241
–῞Ωραν 56
greeting 51, 230
groom 44-46, 48, 123, 271, 281
guilt, see: sin
Gulf of Aqaba 35
Gunkel, H. 15, 101, 258, 295, 309

Haddu 14, 53, 173
Hades 200
hail 191
hair 34, 52, 77, 97, 139
Ḫamanu 270
hand 14-15, 19-20, 25, 27, 34, 37, 39-41, 51-52, 73, 78-79, 83, 123, 150, 164, 176, 186, 202, 203, 227, 265, 268
happiness 137, 169, 172, 180, 182, 195, 259
Ḥariya 123
Ḥarra 26, 54, 103
Ḫasīsu 271
Hathor 92
Ḥaurān 54, 67-69, 86, 103, 218, 241, 247, 256, 269, 283, 295, 313, 315
Ḥaurān, see also: Ḥaurōn
Ḥaurōn 21-22, 50-51, 53, 75-77, 84, 112, 160, 202, 256
Ḥaurōn, see also: Ḥôrānu
Ḥawwāh, see: Eve
hawk, see: bird
head 6-7, 17-21, 52-53, 57, 59, 63-64, 68, 71, 73-74, 78, 81-82, 102, 109, 112-113, 141, 151-152, 155, 168, 172-173, 230, 242-245, 250, 267-268, 270-271
healing 12, 76, 86, 168, 216, 218-219, 223, 227-228, 244, 249, 251, 273, 302
heart 65, 90, 153, 208, 215, 269

heat 35, 37, 52-54, 61, 69, 109-110, 118, 227
heaven 6-9, 11, 14, 16-17, 20, 24-25, 31, 40, 42, 48-50, 56-57, 66, 68, 71, 76, 81, 83-84, 89, 92-95, 97-100, 104, 106-110, 113, 117-118, 120-121, 123-124, 130, 133-136, 140, 144-145, 151-155, 158-161, 167, 170, 178, 182-183, 190-191, 193, 196-197, 200-201, 204-205, 209-210, 220-223, 226, 231-234, 241-242, 244-245, 248, 250-251, 255-257, 260, 266-277, 275, 292, 296, 309
Ḫebat 58
Hebrew *passim*
Hebrew words
– *ʾ^{a}baddōn* 241
– *ʾādām* 118, 127
– *ʾēl* 6-9, 33-31, 59, 117, 120
– *ʾ^{e}lō^{a}h* 120, 209
– *ʾ^{e}lōhīm* 117, 120, 186
– *ʾiššāh* 140
– *ʾiššāh ṭōvāh* 269
– *ben ʾādām* 231
– *ben māwet* 268
– *bnh* 117, 140
– *brʾ* 117
– *brh* 272
– *brḥ* 61-62
– *gam* 134-135
– *gam* 265
– *dal* 271
– *dll* 271
– *dāmūt* 122
– *ha-ḥēmāh* 118
– *hēlēl* 50, 159
– *ha-l^{e}vānāh* 118
– *hāmōn* 61
– *ḥwtp* 189
– *ḥaṭṭāt* 140
– *ḥawwāh* 1
– *ḥlš* 153
– *ḥomer* 127
– *ḥph* 270
– *ḥpp* 270
– *ḥuppāh* 189
– *ṭwb* 138
– *yhwh ʾl* 126-127
– *yṣʾ* Hi. 121
– *yēṣer* 189
– *yārē^{a}ḥ* 118
– *kwn* L 12
– *klh* Pi. 119
– *kerem* 265
– *liwyāh* 61
– *lôyāh* 61
– *mdhbh* 152
– *mamšaḥ* 165
– *māmōt* 170
– *ma^{ʿa}śeh* 217
– *mśṭmh* 55, 194
– *mrhbh* 152
– *mōšāv* 98, 169
– *nkr* 280
– *nqb* 165
– *ʿbt* Pi. 266
– *ʿēzer* 28
– *ʿelyōn* 7-8, 161
– *ʿāfār* 127
– *ṣāfōn* 153
– *qnh* 144
– *q^{e}riyyōt* 278
– *r^{-}šīt* 120, 200
– *rōvēṣ* 143
– *rdh* 150
– *ra^{ʿa}nān* 280
– *rṣd* 69
– *rāqī^{aʿ}* 121
– *śāṭān* 55, 209
– *śar* 55, 194
– *šadday* 32, 142, 161, 255
– *šwṭ* 55
– *šwf* 128, 172
– *šemeš* 118
– *tôhū* 117
– *t^{e}hōm* 117
– *tannīn* 65-66, 144, 173
– *toknīt* 164
– *tōf* 165
heifer 190
heifer, see also: cow
Hekhalot 31

Hēlēl 24, 49, 84, 151-163, 217, 219-220, 223, 250, 257
Hēlēl, see also: Hilālu
Heliopolis 89
Helios 130, 132, 189, 212, 242
hell, see: Netherworld
Hellenism 89, 130-132, 189, 212, 242
henotheism 112, 128, 158, 209, 255, 258, 262
Hephaistos 109
Heracles 26
herb 31, 90-91
Hercules, see Heracles
Hermon 66-68, 137, 302
hero 6, 13-14, 20, 40-42, 71, 77, 98, 112, 124, 131, 139, 148-149, 157, 163, 166, 170, 258, 263, 290
heroine 131
Hesiod 56, 59, 108-111, 128, 130-131, 191
Hesperides 60, 121
Hilālu 24, 49-51, 84, 156, 158-160, 162, 180, 219, 221, 240, 244, 250, 257
Hilālu, see also: Hēlēl
Hinnom 32, 247
historiography 105, 116, 133,156, 242, 260-263, 284, 289-290, 302, 304, 306, 310, 312-313
Hittite 5. 7, 9-10, 32, 58, 89, 285, 295, 297, 302, 313
ḫlb 6
Ḥlš 6
hoe 93
homosexuality 90
Horaios, see: Ḥôrānu
Hôran 56, 100
Ḥorān(u), see: Ḥôrānu
Horeb 32, 186
horn 31, 63-64, 68, 70, 195, 244, 309
Ḥorrānites 219
Ḥôrōn, see: Ḥôrānu
Ḥoron(u), see: Ḥôrānu
Ḥôrānu 15, 17, 21, 26, 28-29, 44, 49-51, 53-56, 76-78, 84, 103-105, 110, 112-113, 128, 130, 136, 138, 142-145, 161-163, 167, 169-170, 175-177, 179-180, 183, 186, 194, 200-201, 203, 208, 211-212, 215, 219, 221, 223-224, 228, 237, 240-246, 248-252, 256-257, 259-260, 269-270, 280-281
Ḥôrānu, see also: Ḥaurōn
horse 42, 105, 110, 190, 241, 246
Horus 21, 76, 90-91, 209, 312
host 37, 102, 107, 248, 296
Ḥryt 278
hubris 156, 158, 179
hubris, see also: pride
human being 1-3, 11-12, 16, 22, 26-28, 39, 44, 46, 58-59, 70-73, 75, 77, 79, 81-82, 84-85, 89-90, 92, 94-105, 109-113, 115, 118-130, 134-142, 143, 146-148, 148-152, 156-157, 163-164, 168, 172-173, 177-181, 185-190, 193-195, 198-199, 202, 204, 211-212, 219, 222-225, 228-231, 233-234, 237-238, 240, 243, 249-251, 253, 256-257, 259-260, 262-263, 267, 269, 271, 280, 288, 291, 295, 297, 309, 312
humankind, see: human being
humanoid 26, 48, 51, 77, 95, 98, 103, 113, 122, 127, 143-144, 148, 179, 212, 258
humiliation 19-20, 152
Hurarṭ, see: Urarṭu
Hurrian 7-8, 10-11, 29, 53, 58, 89, 270, 276, 284, 292, 295
husband 11, 18, 60, 85, 109, 144, 168, 239, 269
Ḫuwawa 89
Ḥwt 58
Ḥwt, see also: Ḥawwāh
hymn 106, 117, 194, 202-203, 217, 284

Ialdabaoth 233
Iaoel 200, 202-203
Iapetus 121
Iblīs 55, 84, 210
ice 65, 77, 246

iconography iv-v, ix, 22-23, 30, 59-74, 76, 78, 80, 86-87, 91, 94, 135, 138, 162, 165, 200, 230, 242, 253, 257, 288-289, 299, 302
iconography, see also: image; seal; stele
idolatry 132-133, 204, 208, 236, 257, 298, 301; see also: image
Igigi 95-86
ʾil 6, *et passim*
Ilabrat 99
Ilāhūma, see: Ugar. *ʾilhm*
ʾilʾib 6-8, 53, 54, 59
ʾilh 6
ʾilhm 6
Ilimilku 13, 291, 299
illness 19, 86, 97, 175-176, 205-206, 218-219, 237, 277
Ilu *passim*
ʾil w ḥrn 54, 56
ʾil (w) šr 6, 54
image, see: deity, – image; idolatry HIER
immortality v, 17, 27-28, 44-53, 59, 71, 75, 77, 82, 85, 97-98, 100,112, 122, 124, 134, 137, 139, 141-142, 149, 177, 179, 198-199, 210, 259, 262, 284, 309
inanimate 57, 93, 135
Inanna 35, 47, 123, 310
Inbabe 42, 276
incantation 7, 11, 16, 24, 45, 49-50, 55, 65, 78, 81, 212, 28-219, 223, 260, 275-282, 286, 290-291, 296-297, 304
incest 11
injustice, see: justice
inscription 8, 35, 50, 54, 58, 159, 165, 177, 283, 288-209, 295, 297, 314, 315
intercourse, see: sexuality
Ipiq-Aya 95
Iran v, 41, 43, 107-108, 112-113, 233, 283-284, 297, 300
Irenaeus 233
iron 148, 289
irony 24, 152-153, 157, 167-168, 180, 236, 256-257
Isaac 194
Isaiah 151-163, 180, 191, 220, 259
Isis 89-90
Ištar 99, 276, 278
Islam vii, 24, 55, 72, 84, 58, 108, 142, 157, 163, 197, 209-210, 293-294, 308-309, 311, 315
ius talionis, see: *lex talionis*
Išum 104-105
Ittobaal III 167

Jabbok 211-212; see also: river
Jacob vi, 126, 183-184, 202-204, 211-212, 302
Jairus 219
Jared 187
Jebel, see: Ǧebel
Jerusalem 8, 32, 132, 137, 247, 250, 257, 261, 287, 290
Jesus 113, 152, 215-226, 228, 230, 234-235, 249-252, 263, 292, 294, 300
jewelry 42-43, 191
Jezebel 170, 299
Job 129, 163, 188, 215, 248, 263, 289, 295, 303, 312
John vii, 208, 216, 223-226, 229, 233, 240-241, 285, 295, 302, 304, 310
Jordan (river) 29, 137
Josephus 132
Judas 219
judgment 19, 79, 132, 185, 187, 192, 218, 222, 225, 246-247, 251-252, 302, 314
juniper 44, 75, 281
justice 106, 152, 198-199, 266

Kamāṯu 271, 278
Kaphtor 279; see also: Crete
Kara Su 30
Karatepe 7
kataduggû 27
kbb wʾadm 57
Khnum 90
KI 93
killing, see: death

king 6, 10, 12, 14, 19, 23, 37, 39, 52, 55, 71, 92, 95, 97, 102-103, 105, 122-123, 130, 133, 136, 146, 148, 151-154, 156-158, 162, 164-172, 175, 180, 197, 221, 241-242, 258, 261, 307, 310, 313, 315
king lists 145-146, 266, 298, 303, 304
kingship, see: royalty
Kirtu 18-19, 56, 93, 126, 136, 157
Kôṯarātu 49-51, 85-86, 127, 129, 142, 159, 180, 243, 257, 272
Kôṯaru 18, 79, 279
Kronos 6, 9, 31, 33, 56, 109, 112
Kubaba 28, 48, 52, 57-58, 85, 127, 139, 141, 179, 257, 296
Küçük Ağrı Dağı 32
Kumarbi 7-11
Kuntillet ʿAjrud 35
Kurdistan 43, 105
Kybele 85, 257
Kythera 109

Labbu 103
labor 1, 92, 96, 101, 140, 150, 194, 239
Ladon 60-61
Lagash 102
Laḫamu 9
Laḫmu 9
Lamaštu 45, 97, 282, 315
lamb 207, 314
Lamech 150, 193
lameness, see: paralysis
lamentation 52, 77, 85, 103, 151, 164, 167, 267, 310
lamentation, see also: mourning; noise; tears
Larugatu 277
Lebanon 66-68, 72, 75
legend 18-20, 65, 105, 139, 157, 163, 170, 236, 260-261, 277, 293, 306, 315
Legion 219, 252
Leviathan 61, 65, 67, 70-71, 74, 78, 81-82, 85, 100, 128, 138, 159, 177, 179, 191, 195-197, 200, 203, 218, 243-244, 246, 250, 256, 260, 267, 290, 293, 315
lex talionis 272
liar, see: lying
lie, see: lying
life *passim*
life, eternal, see: immortality
life, renewal of, see: procreation
lifetime 138, 146-147, 157, 162, 212
lifetime, see also: death
light 16, 36, 99-100, 118, 154, 160, 201, 207, 220, 226, 294
lightning 80, 110, 196, 220-221
likeness, see: image
Lilith 28, 286, 297
lion 75, 78, 131, 133, 171, 173
Lîtānu, see: Lôtānu
lizard 45, 46, 108, 282
Lôdānu 60-61
Lôdānu, see also: Leviathan; Lôtānu
longevity 137-138, 146, 212
Lôtānu 54-72, 82, 250, 267
love (human) 44-46, 112, 123, 139, 148, 238-240, 281-282, 310, 314
love, see also; marriage; sexuality
love song 44-46, 112, 123, 310
Lubar 193, 312
Lucifer 54, 151, 154, 160, 162, 220, 303
Ludānu, see: Lôdānu
Lugaldukuga 103
Lūli 154, 162, 180
luminary, see: light
lust, see: sexuality
lying 108, 124, 139, 200-201, 225, 229, 284

macrocosmic, see: proportions
maggot 66
magic 16, 18, 21, 53, 82, 108, 223, 226, 249, 252, 256, 260, 286, 305, 308, 310, 312
Maʾḫadu 5, 62
male 27, 36, 46-47, 52, 57, 59, 89, 96, 113, 118, 127, 130, 146, 191, 203, 238, 271, 275, 280, 291
Māliku 69, 271, 279

Malta 227-228, 298, 313, 315
Mamma 105
man 11, 19, 47, 48, 52, 62-63, 70-71, 73, 94, 106, 122, 128-130, 132, 140, 169, 186, 189, 202, 209, 213, 218, 228, 230, 231-232, 236, 239, 259, 285, 293, 301-302, 306, 313
Manātu 56
Marduk 10, 14, 35, 70, 79, 101-104, 139, 162
mare 45-46
Mari 57, 59, 135, 276, 278, 282, 287, 290, 293
marriage 45-46, 52, 77, 85, 93, 96, 111-112, 146, 237, 245, 282, 300-301, 309
masculine, see: male
Masis 32, 42
massacre, see: death
Māšu 32, 40-41
masturbation 89
matriarch 131
mediator 260
megalith 69, 218
Melqart 168, 286
melting 35, 110, 241
Memphis 90
menorah 206
merismus 54, 56
Mesopotamia(n) v, 5, 12-13, 27, 29-31, 35-36, 41, 71, 83, 93-105, 110-112, 123, 146, 149, 158, 182, 226, 255-256, 268, 276, 278, 288-289, 293, 297-298, 300, 306, 308, 314-316
metamorphosis 14, 17, 20-21, 44, 66, 76-78, 84-85, 91-92, 103, 104, 110, 118, 129, 142-144, 148, 159, 168, 197-198, 200, 202, 205, 212, 214, 221, 244, 248, 250, 256-257, 259, 300
metaphor 13, 19, 33, 45, 75, 107, 139-140, 142-143, 171, 177, 189, 234-235, 237, 239, 281-282, 309
metonomy 46
Michael 183,194,205-206
midwife 50, 85-86, 96, 142, 243, 257, 272
Minet el-Beida 5, 62
miracle, reversable 14
misogyny 132, 238
mockery, see irony; ridicule
modesty 238
monotheism 107-108,115, 118-119, 122, 126, 146, 158, 183, 209, 233, 255, 258, 262, 288, 291
moon 49-50, 84, 104, 109, 118, 121, 160, 182, 207, 257, 277, 298
monster 12, 61, 63-67, 70, 73-74, 79-81, 90, 92, 98, 101, 103, 105, 109, 111, 121-122, 133, 152, 159, 171-172, 174-175, 177, 180, 191, 218, 243-244, 246, 248, 252, 256, 303, 306-307
monster, see also: dragon
morning star 24, 50, 84, 152, 154, 160, 190, 220, 257
morning star, see also: star
mortality, see: death
Moses vi, 205-206, 223-224, 229, 293, 310
moth 131
mother 16, 46, 48, 56, 58, 82, 85, 90, 93-94, 96-98, 103, 105, 109-110, 121, 130, 140-141, 144, 170, 179, 187-189, 194, 198, 208, 223, 237, 254, 257, 259, 267, 271, 275-280, 293
mother, see also: deity, – mother
Môtu 11, 15, 28-29, 40, 43, 52-54, 80-82, 113, 170, 173-174, 176, 227, 235, 251
Môtu, see also: death
mountain 18, 29-37, 39-44, 65-67, 68-69, 78, 83, 92, 98, 100, 105, 137, 150, 153-154, 158, 161-162, 165-166, 169-171, 179-180, 182, 184-185, 193, 200-201, 211, 213, 215, 241, 246-247, 249, 251, 255-256, 259, 269-271, 276-277, 302, 311
mourning 25-26, 49, 267-268

mouth 11, 18, 25, 33, 61, 73, 79, 90-91, 98, 174-175, 206, 218, 236, 241-242, 265-266, 271-272
Murat Su 30, 32
murder, see: death
murderer 20, 143, 224-225, 227, 240
muzzle 66, 176
myth *passim*

Nabonidus 156
Naharu 19, 66, 79
Naharu, see also: river
Nahash 61
Nairi (lake) 41-42
nakedness 12, 64, 128, 139-140, 150, 169, 188, 258, 268
names v, 1, 7-9, 13-15, 18, 20, 24, 26, 29-33, 40, 42, 48-50, 53-55, 59-62, 65, 68, 74, 77, 79, 84-85, 91-92, 96, 103, 107, 112-113, 118-121, 126-127, 129-131, 135, 137, 140-142, 150, 152, 154, 156, 157-160, 165-168, 174-176, 178, 180, 183-184, 187, 191-194, 197, 200, 203, 208-212, 216, 219, 221, 228-229, 237, 244, 248-249, 252, 254-255, 257, 260-261, 265-266, 270, 272, 275, 277, 280, 290, 295, 297, 299, 304
naming 53-56, 103, 128, 140, 261, 266
Namma 93-94
navel 74
Nebuchadnezzar 151, 156-157, 311
necklace 149
Nephtys 81
Nergal 50, 96
Netherworld 17, 20, 31, 39-42, 44, 49, 54-56, 58, 66, 69, 71, 77, 90, 104, 109, 144-145, 154, 161, 170, 188, 190, 194-195, 217, 220, 241, 250, 268-269, 275, 279
New Testament 2, 88, 113, 117, 135, 141, 143, 162, 213, 215-252, 259, 260
New Year 52, 77, 213, 291
night 33, 36, 90, 92, 109, 118, 161, 175, 184-185, 204, 236, 257
Nimuš 30, 300
Ningirsu 102
Ninki 93
Ninlil 93
Ninmaḫ 94-95
Nintu 96, 149
Ninurta 100
Niṣir 30-31, 42, 300, 311
Noah 30, 43, 124, 150, 179, 193-194, 263, 294, 307
noise 96, 130
north 5, 43, 66, 153, 161-162, 182, 213, 284
Nubadig 58
nudity, see: nakedness
Nun 92
Nut 6, 89, 92

Oannes 105
occultation 50, 85, 160, 257
ocean, see: flood; sea
offense 18, 20, 124, 126, 258
offense, see also: sin
offering 6, 17, 32, 71, 97, 106, 132, 142-144, 200, 260 288
offspring 6, 52, 71, 74, 77-78, 82, 85, 94-95, 108, 121, 128, 148, 163, 172, 179-180, 183, 188, 190, 195, 210, 212, 215-219, 224, 226-228, 240-241, 243, 245, 249, 252, 256, 268, 280
Og 148
Okeanos 60
Ophite Myth 208, 233, 307
oppressor 111, 152-153, 158, 164
opulence, see: wealth
oral tradition 111, 117, 181, 196, 211, 282
oral tradition; see also: folk religion; popular tradition
orchard 43, 265
orchard; see also: garden; vineyard
Origen 151, 167, 208
Ornias 209
Ohrmazd 107-108

orphan 19
Osiris 55, 82, 89-90
Ottoman 32, 50, 257
Ouranos 6, 8, 56, 109
oxhide ingot 73-74

pair *passim*
palace 10-11, 43, 45, 79, 83, 255, 282
Palestine 5, 235, 311
Palmyra 7, 69, 280, 304
Pandora 130, 287
pantheon 5, 7, 17-18, 20-21, 33, 53-54, 56, 82, 84, 95, 112-113, 127-128, 155, 161, 168, 180, 234, 248, 255, 291, 296, 308, 313
parabiblical 143, 154, 179, 182-213, 215, 222, 224, 235, 252, 255, 259
parable 261-262
paradigmatic 178, 262-263
paradise 1, 3, 29-44, 72, 83-84, 137-138, 169, 184-185, 192, 195, 197-199, 205-206, 209-211, 213, 217, 221, 224, 229, 247, 249, 251-253, 256, 285, 288, 297, 305, 307, 309-310, 312
paralysis 18, 44, 271
patriarch 200
Paul 190, 223, 225-239, 251, 260, 297, 301, 304-305, 313
Pazuzu 45, 282
peace 95, 105, 186, 195
pendant 46-47
penis 11, 14, 45, 47, 148, 282
Penuel 184
Pergamon 234
Persia(n) 29, 133, 151, 242, 290, 311
pestilence 175-176, 236, 277
Peter 219, 235
petrifying, see: solidifying
Petuḥah 134, 147, 306
Phaeton 110-112
Phanuel 183-184
phallic symbol 45-46, 104, 282
Pharaoh 22-23, 75, 171-172
Pharisees 216-218, 224, 228, 240, 249
Philo Alexandrinus 130, 132, 189-190, 232, 308
Philo Byblius 6-9, 27-28, 31, 33, 41, 56-57, 71, 77, 85, 109, 254, 284
Philo Judaeus, see: Philo Alexandrinus
Phoenicia(n) 5, 7-8, 27, 50, 53, 84, 86, 141, 151-154, 157-160, 162, 165, 167, 170, 180, 194, 228, 254, 256, 284, 286, 288
Phoenicia(n); see also: Philo Byblius
piety 202, 239
pillar 9, 33, 184
Pirigallu 71
Pir Omar Gudrun 30
Pit 66, 154, 164, 166, 170, 180, 185, 194, 217, 241
Pit, see also: Netherworld
plague 17, 96, 176
planet 50, 154, 160
plant 17, 41-42, 90, 98-99, 106, 136, 150, 193, 256
Plato 190, 308
Pniel 184
poison 16-18, 21, 25-26, 28, 43-44, 46, 55, 59, 63, 69, 74-75, 85-86, 104, 107-108, 110, 126, 131, 142, 159, 173-176, 194, 198, 205-206, 212, 217-218, 221, 223, 228-229, 236, 240-243, 251, 256, 265-266, 268, 270-271, 275-282, 306, 309
polemics 198, 231-232, 243, 259
polemics; see also: ridicule
polygyny 11
polytheism 5, 102, 119, 126, 129, 134-135, 137, 146, 157, 262
Pontus 109
poorness, see: poverty
popular religion 71-72, 81, 101, 103, 116-117, 167, 190, 219-220, 234-235, 244, 248, 252, 259, 308
portrait 165
potash 139
potency 11, 14, 21, 59
poverty 19
prayer 46, 81, 106, 240
Prbḫt 50
precious stones 41, 165, 170-171, 184
pre-existence 90, 222

pregnancy 45-46, 81, 86, 105, 193-194, 217, 242, 245, 282
pregnancy; see also: childbirth
pride 151-152, 155, 163-171, 203
priest(ess) 52, 107, 115-123, 165, 167, 261, 267, 292
Priestly Writer 30, 115-122, 134, 136, 150, 167, 182, 290, 284, 290, 298, 306, 309-310
Prince 44, 52-55, 77, 84-85, 142, 154, 162, 176, 183, 194-195, 212, 216, 219, 222, 248, 252, 266
– of accusation 55, 194-195
prince, princess, see: royalty
procreation 11, 44-53, 75, 85-86, 90, 92-93, 104-105, 112-113, 122, 128, 134, 139, 142, 159, 162, 179, 194, 199, 213, 222, 240, 243, 245, 251, 257-259
procreation; see also: deity, – procreation
promiscuity 132
prophet 106-106, 132, 151-152, 156, 158, 166-172, 180, 191, 236, 259, 261, 293, 300, 303, 312
proportions 11, 22, 25, 34, 41, 43, 68, 71-72, 84, 98, 102, 138, 148, 171, 179, 202, 243, 251, 256, 259
prosecutor 222
prostitution 98, 132, 198
Protogonos 71
Pseudepigrapha 117, 162, 181-182, 203, 208-209, 211, 242, 247, 283, 285, 290, 300, 315
psychology 12
Ptah 90
Puġatu 20
punishment 21, 74, 109, 124, 129, 133, 147, 150, 152, 158-159, 180, 187-188, 218, 222, 239, 249-250, 256, 259, 272
purple 5
Pyramid Texts 48, 90, 304, 311
Python 242

Qadmu 162
Qarnīna 68
Qingu 101
quarreling, see: strife
queen, see: royalty
Qumran 173, 192-195, 217, 251, 312

Rabbah 148
Rahab 100, 152
rain 14, 29, 52, 78, 80, 100, 173, 218
rainbow 149
ram 11, 46, 59, 103
rank 5-6. 24, 27,48, 52, 95, 112, 161, 196, 204, 248, 301
Raphael 183, 185
Rāpiʾūma; see: Rephaim; Ugar. *rpʾum*
raptor 20-21, 100, 200
raptor; see also: bird
Rašpu 17, 270, 277, 282
Re 62, 90-92, 125
– see also: sun
rebel 18, 20, 39, 55, 71, 77, 84, 90, 96, 100, 110-112, 125, 130, 134, 136, 138, 144, 152, 161, 167, 170, 174, 183, 191, 215, 222, 249-251, 256-257, 259
rebellion 16-18, 24, 56, 82, 84-85, 89, 93, 95, 99-102, 104, 111-113, 147, 155, 160-161, 177, 182, 200-201, 205, 209, 211, 225-226, 237, 255-257
regret, see: repentance
rejuvenation 41-42
religion 1-3 5, 14, 24, 81, 89-90, 106-1-8, 112-113, 116, 120-121, 137, 149, 166, 178, 190, 209, 234-235, 243, 252, 254-255, 258-259, 262
– of Israel 2-3
remorse, see also: repentance
repentance 74, 245, 294
Rephaim 68, 148, 303
Resheph, see: Rašpu
responsibility 75, 77, 121, 123, 130, 176, 189, 194, 203, 209, 212, 257-258, 264

restoration 26, 113, 145, 183, 185, 192, 195, 198, 204, 211, 213, 223, 234, 249, 252, 257
resurrection 97, 206, 232, 235-236, 272-273
retribution 115, 125
Reuben 132
revenge 17, 82, 84-85, 110, 145, 159, 256
revivification 204, 219, 273
revivification, see also: resurrection
Rhea 56, 109
Rḥm(y) 11
rib 136, 186, 210; see also: scar; side
rich, see: wealth
ridicule 24, 151-171, 177, 180, 255, 257-259
righteousness 126, 163, 181-182, 185, 187-188, 192, 194, 197, 201, 205, 213, 222, 251, 258, 263
Rīr-Rīr 48
ritual 16, 44-53, 243, 281-282, 285, 287-288, 290, 292, 308, 310
river 7, 10, 29-30, 32, 47, 60, 66, 96, 98, 137, 169, 212, 247, 249, 275, 280, 310-311
roaring 66
robbery 19
rock 9, 35, 65-66, 68, 110, 185, 196, 241, 279
royalty 1, 5-7, 18-19, 27, 52, 55-56, 118-120, 123, 132, 141, 145-146, 151-171, 167-170, 175, 186, 197, 215, 258, 279, 283, 286-87, 289, 299
rule 17, 20, 27, 55, 76, 90, 100, 102, 104-105, 118-119, 141, 148, 150, 154, 157, 160-161, 163, 166, 170-171, 177, 180, 197-198, 200-201, 208-209, 216, 225-226, 249, 292, 300, 316
rule, see also: dominion; royalty

Sabaoth 202
Sabbath 117, 121
Sachmet 92
sacrifice, see: offering
Sadayēl 142
Šaḥar(u) 11, 159-160, 271, 280
Šaḥar(u), see also: dawn
Šalimu 11, 160, 271, 280
salt 57
salvation 1, 78-79, 190, 239, 242, 307, 314
Samael, see: Sammael
Šamaš 51, 275
Sammael 207, 221
sanctuary 18, 20-22, 43, 71, 103, 156, 168, 206, 261, 244, 280, 313
Ṣapānu 43, 84
Šapšu 16, 18, 25-26, 28, 44, 49, 51-52, 57, 77-78, 85, 118, 136, 266-268, 270-273, 275-277-280.
Šārā 55
Šar'el 183
Sariel 142, 154, 183-184, 203, 211-212, 220
Sargon II 42, 151, 153-154, 156, 162, 298, 312
Šarru 6, 55, 84-85, 154, 183
Šarru, see also: Prince
Šarruġāzizu 25, 72, 77, 85, 147, 216, 266-268
Satan 20-21, 24, 49, 54-55, 113, 132, 141-142, 144-145, 154, 162, 191, 194, 198, 203-207, 209-210, 215-230, 234-237, 240-245, 248-251, 283, 290, 294, 297, 305-307, 311-312, 314
Satan, see also: Satanael; Satanail; Sotona; Šayṭān
Satanael 207, 235, 306
Satanail 196-197
satire, see: ridicule
save, see: salvation
savior 71, 76, 78, 148, 218, 233-234, 251, 260
saw 35-36
Šayṭān 210
scab 75, 281
scar 74
scepter, see: staff
scholar, see: scribe
scolding 20, 79

scorpion 31, 48, 108, 131, 217, 221-222, 228, 230, 250, 252
scorpion-guard 20, 30-31, 78, 133, 169
scribe 5, 13-15, 41-42, 95, 152, 165, 188, 192, 250, 261, 278, 282
sea 17, 41-42, 61-68, 70, 79, 81-82, 84, 95, 100, 103, 105, 109, 127-128, 163-164, 168, 170-171, 177, 186, 188, 191, 194, 218-219, 244, 246, 252
– dragon/monster 63-67, 79, 90, 101, 152, 159, 243, 246, 248, 250
– serpent 61, 63-67, 70, 73, 79, 91, 101, 105, 121, 171, 159, 179, 192, 203, 244, 247-248, 250, 260, 267, 275–280
sea, see also: Flood; Yammu
seal 31, 35-36, 44, 48, 51-52, 62-65, 70, 72-74, 77-78, 85, 94-95, 101, 162, 164, 170, 222, 249, 289, 292, 296, 299-300, 304, 308, 312
Sea People 84, 103
secret 41, 163, 201
Šēdu 49, 77, 269
seduction 98, 147, 191, 198, 236-238, 251, 262, 293
semen 90
Šemiḫazah 174, 183
Senir 66
Sennacherib 154, 156, 180
sensation 57
seraph 184
Sergius Paulus 226
serpent *passim*
– biting, see: snakebite
– speaking 1, 59, 61, 93, 98, 109, 128-129, 212, 258
serpent, see also: snake
Seth (deity) 18, 21, 55, 76-78, 89-92, 112, 142, 242, 263, 289, 303-304, 312
Seth (human)) 205-206, 208, 212
seven day scheme 117, 120, 178
sexuality 1, 11, 28, 48, 57, 85, 90-91. 93, 96, 122-123, 128, 132, 140, 146-147, 179, 190, 193, 212-213, 236-237, 251, 255, 258, 271, 289, 307
– See also: homosexuality
Shadday, see: Hebrew words, – *šadday*
Shalmaneser III 42
Shalmaneser V 156
shame 66, 79, 128, 200-201, 258
Sharru, see: Šarru; Prince
Sheol, see: Netherworld
Shiryon 66
shortening 72, 251
shoulder 9, 13, 18, 35-36, 51, 83
shrieking 49, 100, 267, 272
Shu 9, 89, 92
Sibitti 104
sickness, see: illness
side 136, 140
sidewinder 63-65
Sidon 154, 162, 166, 168, 180, 221
sign 78, 145, 149
signet 164-165, 300
silver 163, 209
Simirria 42
sin 1, 28, 58, 84, 101, 109, 115, 124-126, 129-131, 138, 143, 147, 152, 155, 157, 163, 165-166, 176, 180-183, 189, 191, 195, 197, 199, 201, 203-205, 207, 211-212, 219, 225, 229-231, 235, 237-239, 241, 249-250, 257-259, 261-262, 292, 307, 309
Sinai 35, 116
Širk 157
skin 39, 68, 70, 136, 233
skin sloughing 41, 59, 140, 198, 275-281
sky, see: firmament; heaven
slaughter 14, 27, 94, 96
slaughter, see also: massacre; offering
šmm 6-8
šmm, see also: heaven
šmm, see also: Ugaritic: – *šmm*
šmm wthm 8, 48, 57, 110, 117-118
smoke 110, 210, 241, 250
snake 16-17, 25-26, 39, 41, 44-46, 48-49, 53, 59-60, 62-65, 69-72,

75-78, 85, 98, 102-103, 105, 108-109, 111, 113, 141, 143, 159, 218, 222, 224, 227-228, 236-237, 240, 249, 251, 266, 269, 280, 282, 300
snake, see also: serpent
snakebite 16, 71-72, 119, 124, 127-128, 173, 179, 198-199, 205-206, 212, 223-224, 227-229, 251, 271, 275-280, 282, 290
snake charming 16, 45, 48, 256, 275-280, 285
sneezing 89
snow 32-33, 41, 182, 191, 211
solidifying 65-68, 246
son 9-10, 146, 150, 187, 198, 237
– of God 146-147, 187, 190, 193, 218-219, 241, 269, 283, 289, 294
– of a (named) god 12, 24, 46, 56, 81-83, 90, 110, 146, 150, 153, 159-160, 170, 173-175, 235, 282-283
– of a human 12, 223, 225, 283, 292, 300-301
– of Ilu/El 56, 81-83, 150, 159, 170, 173, 211, 280
– of man, see: son of a human
– of the Devil 227, 249
– of the Dragon 46, 282
Sotona 197
soul 12, 144, 185, 271
soul, see also: spirit
source, see: spring
south 99, 298
speech 1, 3, 27, 52, 61, 93, 98, 198
speech, see also: serpent
speech, see also: *kataduggû*
spell 48, 92, 173, 310-311
spell, see also: incantation
sphinx 75, 165, 171
Spirit (Holy) 215, 260
spirit 13, 27, 71, 94, 96, 107, 113, 122, 127-128, 148, 176, 183, 216, 232
– evil 71, 107, 119, 176, 186, 194, 201, 210, 217-218, 316
– good113, 186, 196, 210, 212, 315
– healing 12
– of the dead 13, 185, 279, 299
spirit, see also: deity, – Spirit/spirit
spirit, see also: *kataduggû*
spittle 25, 37, 75, 212, 246, 265, 281
spring (season) 9, 29, 59, 275
spring (water 29, 42, 57, 69, 74, 137, 191, 196, 247, 249, 275
šr 6, 44, 52, 54-55, 142, 162, 175, 194
staff 22, 39, 49, 52, 78, 86, 223-224, 226
– of bereavement 52
– of widowhood 52
stallion 46, 271
star 24, 49-50, 52, 56, 84, 104, 109, 152-155, 158-160, 167, 184, 190, 207, 209, 220-223, 241, 248, 250, 257
star, see also: morning star
statuette, see: image
stele 18, 39, 51, 71, 78-80, 154
Sting 15, 25, 173-176, 217, 235-236, 265, 291
Sting, see also: Ugaritic – *qẓb*
sterility 56, 97
stone 9, 39, 40, 57, 80, 106-107, 165-166, 170-171, 184, 196, 275
stone, see also: precious –; rock
strife 269
Strymon 60
subduing 48, 76, 78, 269
substitution 25, 94, 99, 209-210
suffering 63, 219, 228, 292
Ṣūfism 210
sulfur 69, 241, 246-247, 250, 279
Sumerian 5, 10, 13, 16, 27, 29, 34, 45, 47-48, 63, 71, 93-95, 97, 112, 123, 282
sun 16, 31-32, 35-37, 39-42, 44, 74, 95, 99-100, 104, 106, 109-110, 113, 118, 121, 182, 196, 241
sun, see also: Šamaš; Šapšu
– god 35-36, 51, 62, 77-78, 89-90, 92, 110, 112-113
– goddess 15-16, 28, 44, 52, 77, 82, 85, 118, 138, 256-257, 266-267, 275

sunrise 11, 17, 29, 31-32, 35-36, 41, 44, 160
sunset 11, 31, 35-37, 40-42, 44, 83, 160, 184, 255, 270, 280
supplication, see: lamentation; prayer
Sutaean 104
swallow 49
sword 72, 164, 184, 203
sweat 265
synergism 173
Syria 1, 5, 44, 51, 69, 86-87, 218, 244, 256, 287

tablet 1, 8, 15-16, 21, 24, 28, 53, 55-56, 68, 81, 85, 95, 267, 272, 282
tail 31, 61-63, 66, 73
tallness 59-74, 98, 148, 171, 179, 183-184, 202, 256, 259
Talmud 55, 212; see also Index of Texts
Tannin, see: Tunnanu
Tāqiʿtu 127
Targum 125, 135, 183, 210, 212, 281, 283, 292, 295, 303
Tartarus 101
Taw 145
tears 25, 72, 92, 266-268
Tefnut 9, 89, 92
Tell Atchana 51, 289
Tell Qeni 44
Tell Qlēb 44
temple, see: sanctuary
Tendürük Daği 32
Tendürük Gölü 32
tent 7, 9-10, 83, 255
Terah 199
Teššub 58
technology 279
testicles 90, 109
Thalath 105
Thebes 90
theodicy 135
theogony 7, 108-110
theomorphousness 118, 122, 178
theophany 35, 65, 204
throne 18-19, 24, 37, 39, 66, 98, 152-153, 155, 160-161, 184-185. 196, 201, 203-204, 234, 246-247.249, 252
thumb 37
Tiâmat 61, 69, 79, 101-102, 105
Tiglath-Pileser III 156
Tigris 29-30, 34, 42-43, 47, 83, 96, 103, 137, 179, 211, 247, 249, 255, 258, 280
Titans 9, 146, 191, 287
Ṭiṭṭu 278
ṯkmn wšnm 9, 83
Tobijah 46
tomb 218, see also: burial
tongue 61- 63, 65, 175
Transcaucasia 43
transgression, see: rebellion; sin
transpiration 265
tree 17, 41-44, 60, 72-75, 78, 98, 108-109, 135, 138, 140, 142, 162, 171-172, 179, 185-186, 195, 198, 202-206, 210-213, 233, 249, 251, 256, 281, 298, 300, 305
– hybrid 43-44, 185, 198, 247
Tree of Death 17, 29, 43, 52, 75, 85, 113, 127, 134-135, 138, 144-145, 159, 179, 237, 251, 256, 281
Tree of Knowledge 127, 134-135, 138, 140, 179, 185-186, 192, 195, 205. 208, 233
Tree of Life 17, 24, 26, 29, 31, 43-44, 53, 59, 62, 75, 85, 113, 127, 133-135, 137-139, 142, 145, 159, 172, 179, 182, 185-186, 192, 195, 198, 205-206, 211-212, 223, 228, 237, 240, 247, 249, 251-252, 256-257, 259-260, 281, 315
tree, see also: carob tree; date palm; juniper; vine
Trinity 157
Trǵzz 40
Ṯrmg 40, 42
truth 106-108, 139, 224-225, 261, 295
Tubal-Cain 191
tuna, see: Tunnanu

Tunnanu 65-66, 81-82, 100, 144, 173, 177
Turkey 29, 31-33, 41, 50, 83, 255, 257
Tuttul 276
twin 32, 40, 44, 58, 89, 103, 107
 – mountains 32, 35-37, 41-44, 83
turnabout, see: repentance
Typhon 61, 109-110, 128, 244
Tyre 56, 133, 154, 163-164, 166-171, 180, 221

Uauš 42
Ugarit 1, 5-88, *et passim*
Ugaritic words
 – *ʾab* 6-10, 12, 59
 – *ʾab šnm* 9
 – *ʾabd* 18, 241, 266, 270-271, 275-280
 – *ʾabdy* 25, 162, 222, 241, 266
 – *ʾabn* 9, 57, 196, 275
 – *ʾadm* 12, 25, 57, 59, 265
 – *ʾadn* 10
 – *ʾal* 10, 59
 – *ʾapq* 29
 – *ʾark ḥnt* 77, 142
 – *ʾarṣ wšmm* 6-8, 121
 – *ʾil* 6-8, 10, 12-14, 20, 32, 54, 56, 59, 117
 – *ʾilʾib* 6-8, 53, 59, 117, 161, 289
 – *ʾilh* 6, 209
 – *ʾilhm* 6
 – *ʾum* 46, 271, 275
 – *ʾwl* 59
 – *bhtm* 6, 10, 45, 281
 – *bḥl* 271
 – *bly* 265
 – *bn ʾil* 6, 173
 – *bnwt* 13, 15, 17, 75, 216-217, 280
 – *bny* 13-15, 267
 – *bnt nš* 272
 – *brḥ* 61, 81, 197, 243
 – *bry* 272
 – *btl* 10, 14, 139
 – *btlt* 10, 14, 139
 – *bṯn* 46, 61, 65-66
 – *gml* 49, 160
 – *grš* 18, 219
 – *dl* 271
 – *dm* 47, 271
 – *dr bn ʾil* 6
 – *drr* 265
 – *gngn* 40
 – *hkl* 10, 45, 282
 – *hll* 24, 49-50, 159, 313
 – *hmlt* 66
 – *zbl bʿl* 216
 – *zwd* 271
 – *ḥby* 31
 – *ḥmr* 66
 – *ḥpn* 19-20
 – *ḥrḥrt* 54
 – *ḥrn* 53-54, 84
 – *ḥrr* 53-54, 103, 144
 – *ḫp* 270
 – *ḫršn* 44
 – *ḫṯ* 50
 – *ṭb* 266
 – *ṭbt npš* 28, 85, 138, 149, 269
 – *yḥr* 45, 282
 – *yṣr* 135
 – *yw* 127, 200, 255
 – *kbb wʾadm* 57
 – *ks* 33
 – *kwn* L 12-13
 – *lʾan* 270
 – *lwṯ* 12
 – *ll* 33, 161
 – *ltn* 54, 61-62, 81
 – *mbk* 10, 29, 275
 – *mdb* 268
 – *mlʾak* 248
 – *mmt* 19, 164, 170
 – *mpḥrt bn ʾil* 6
 – *nkr* 280
 – *nṣr* 267, 272
 – *mštʿlt* 11
 – *mṯb* 169
 – *ngʿ* 273
 – *nṭp* 20
 – *nky* 272
 – *npš* 12, 19, 28, 40, 149, 269, 271
 – *nšy* 268
 – *nšr* 22
 – *ʿbt* 266

– ʿd wšr 6, 44, 52, 54-55, 77, 142, 162, 175, 194
– ʿly N 25, 27, 265, 268
– ʿlyn 7-8, 161
– ʿn 9, 57, 196, 275
– ʾsr 269
– ʿqšr 140, 275-280
– ġzz 19, 25, 72, 77, 142, 200, 212, 266-267
– ġlm 77
– pg 219
– pwq 266
– pḥl 46-48, 57, 271, 275
– pr 50
– prbḫṯ 50
– qbl 271
– qblbl 271
– qdm 17, 75, 145, 160, 280
– qṭb 25, 174-177, 265
– qẓb 15, 174-177, 265
– qny 7-8, 10, 14, 20
– qnyt 11, 144
– rḫnt 269
– rpʾu 71, 168, 218
– rpʾum 148
– rʾišt 120
– ṯbš 272-273
– šdy 32
– šḥr 11, 159-160, 271, 280
– šlm 11, 160, 271, 280
– šmm 6-8, 25, 48, 57, 65, 81, 110, 117, 121, 266-267, 275, 280
– šnm 9-10, 32, 83
– šr 6, 44, 52, 54-55, 142, 162, 175, 194
– šrk 157
– tbʿ 18, 174, 280
– thm 8, 48, 57, 110, 117, 275
– thmt 10, 14, 29, 117, 275
– thw 117
– tʿrt 20
– ṯbṯ 272-273
– ṯkm 9, 13, 83
– ṯll 267-268
– ṯm 18, 271
– ṯr 10, 12
Ullikumi 9, 11, 33
unclean 121, 200
underworld, see: Netherworld
Upelluri 9, 32-33
Urarṭu 30-31, 42-43, 182, 193, 211, 259, 304, 315-316
Uraš 6, 102
Uriel 182-184
Uriel, see also: angel
'Urmensch' myth 232-233, 306
Urmia 41-42
Uruk 97
Ūta-napišti 41, 98

vegetation 103, 121, 183
venom, see: poison
Venus 50, 154, 161
viceroy see: substitution
victory 49, 64, 70, 78-80, 82, 92, 107, 109, 171-173, 219, 223, 226, 235, 246, 249, 252
victory, see also: defeat
vine 44, 52-53, 75, 185, 202-203, 210, 281, 313
vineyard 17, 25, 29-41, 43, 70, 83-84, 113, 127, 137, 150, 159, 179, 193, 211, 237, 246-247, 251, 258, 265
vineyard, see also: garden
violence 8, 95, 105, 193, 303
viper 55, 61, 63-65, 173, 194-195, 216-218, 224, 226-229, 240, 249, 305, 309, 311, 315
viper, see also: serpent; snake
virtue, see: righteousness
viticulture 43, 246, 303
void 89, 120
volcanism 9, 32-33, 35, 37, 44, 54, 66-69, 83, 103, 110, 170, 180, 182, 184-185, 191, 201, 203, 211, 218, 241, 246-247, 250, 255-256, 259
Vulgate 154, 160, 162, 220, 230
vulture 21
vulture, see also: bird

wadi 75, 281
waking 12, 33, 41, 94
war 35, 77, 96, 245, 276
warning 100, 131, 172, 240, 263
warning, see also: God, – patience

warrior 71, 95. 102, 174, 176
wart 75, 281
Watchers 181-185, 187, 190-191, 193, 203, 211, 213, 220, 222, 255
water 7, 29-30, 32-34, 57, 61, 66, 74, 83, 93, 100, 102, 106, 121, 137, 171, 179, 185, 188, 191, , 196, 211, 249, 252, 255, 258, 268, 281
Wē 96
wealth 163
wedding, see: marriage
weeping, see: tears
'Weltbaum' 72, 104, 135, 171, 180, 199, 256
west 29-32, 36-37, 40-41, 44, 182, 184-185,
whale 67, 316
wheat 72, 94, 210, 235, 314
whoring, see: prostitution
widow 19, 52
wife 7, 11, 25, 28, 48-49, 58, 75, 79, 82, 105, 118, 126, 129-131, 138, 140, 146, 150, 157, 177, 179, 193, 205, 209-210, 238-239, 254, 257-258, 269
wind 99-100, 177, 298; see also: spirit
wine 5, 20, 33, 39, 43, 52, 150, 179, 193, 229, 284, 303, 313
wing 12, 21, 35, 75, 99, 133, 160, 171, 202
wisdom 35, 95, 99, 107, 138, 141, 163-164, 166, 170, 185, 187, 197-199
wolf 76
woman 14, 28, 46-47, 52, 73, 85, 94, 96, 105, 122, 125, 128-132, 135, 138-139, 147, 149, 158, 169, 172, 177-178, 186, 188-189, 194, 202, 207, 209, 222, 230-231, 236, 238-239, 242, 244-245, 267, 269, 272
womb 96, 187-189
wordplay 13, 66, 96, 156
worm 66
worship 71, 90, 118, 167, 204, 209, 215-216, 255
wreath 61
writing 111, 187, 261; see also: scribe

Yagruš 18
Yammu 11, 17-19, 22, 25, 32, 65-66, 79-82, 113, 127, 170, 218, 246
Yammu, see also: sea
Yaṣṣibu 19, 93
Yaṭṭipānu 20-21
Yahwist 28, 35, 122, 135-136
Yariḫu 270, 277
Yariḫu, see also: moon
YHWH 8, 10, 69, 144, 247
YHWH-El 8, 126-127, 139, 200
young 14, 20, 22, 77, 93, 94, 112-113, 121, 124, 173, 178, 190
young, see also: boy; child
Yw (god), see: Ugaritic words

Zaphon 18, 34, 83, 153, 161, 255, 276
Zarathustra, see: Zoroaster
Zoroaster 106-108
Zeus 109-110, 112, 131
Ẓiẓẓu 271, 278

Index of Texts

Egyptian Texts

CoS 1, 32: 92
CoS 1, 32, 4: 61
Hymn of Akhenaten: 117
Instr. of Ankhsheshonq 25:14: 269
Cow of Heaven: 92, 113
Cow of Heaven, 3: 92
Cow of Heaven, 4-5: 92
Cow of Heaven, 8-28: 92
Cow of Heaven, 29-34: 92
Cow of Heaven, 35-47: 92
Cow of Heaven, 47-48: 92
Cow of Heaven, 49-60: 92
Cow of Heaven, 61-86: 92
Cow of Heaven, 87-91: 92
Cow of Heaven, 92-100: 92
Cow of Heaven, 104-106: 92
Cow of Heaven, 114-123: 92
Pap. Harris 501, I.7: 21
Pap. Insinger, 18:22: 269
Shipwrecked Sailor: 128
Tazawa 2009, 60, Doc. 1: 76
Tazawa 2009, 61, Doc. 3: 76
Tazawa 2009, 62-63, Doc. 4: 76
Tazawa 2009, 62-63, Doc. 5: 76
Tazawa 2009, 62-63, Doc. 6: 22
Tazawa 2009, 62-63, Doc. 7: 22
Tazawa 2009, 62-63, Doc. 8: 76
Tazawa 2009, 64, Doc. 11: 76
Tazawa 2009, 65, Doc. 12: 76
Tazawa 2009, 65, Doc. 13 76
Tazawa 2009, 67-68, Doc. 20: 22
Tazawa 2009, 68, Doc. 21: 76
Tazawa 2009, 68, Doc. 22: 77
Tazawa 2009, 70, Doc. 32: 75
Tazawa 2009, 119, B: 22
Tazawa 2009, 132-132: 76
Tazawa 2009, 160-163: 76

Mesopotamian Texts

Adapa: 99f.
Adapa: A/A':4: 99
Adapa: A/A':6: 99
Adapa: B:36-37: 99
Adapa: B:75-78: 99
Adapa: B:29'-31': 99
Adapa: B:61'-63': 99
Adapa: D:1-2: 99
Anzû: 100
Anzû ii.48-51: 100
Anzû ii.55: 100
Assyrian Kinglist, 2: 266
Atraḫasīs: 27, 94-97, 111ff., 125, 147
Atraḫasīs, I.1: 95
Atraḫasīs, III.v.46–vi.4: 149
CAD (A) 1, 375a: 59
CAD (A) 2, 232: 280
CAD (A) 3, 48a: 266
CAD (B), 87a-89a: 16
CAD (B), 141-142: 64
CAD (I/J), 140a: 266
CAD (K), 297b: 27
CAD (K), 413-415: 265
CAD (K), 559b: 165
CAD (M) 1, 245b: 266
CAD (M) 1, 401-403: 40
CAD (M) 2, 277b-278a: 64
CAD (P), 479b-480b: 46
CAD (P), 479-481: 271
CAD (P), 518a: 265
CAD (P), 548b: 265
CAD (Q), 137: 31
CAD (R), 12b: 144
CAD (S), 286b-287a: 269
CAD (Š) 1, 43: 32
CAD (Š) 1, 295: 271
CAD (Š) 2, 7-8: 271
CAD (Š) 3, 229a: 50
CAD (T), 84-85: 164
CAD (T), 156: 29
CAD (U), 128b-129b: 267
CAD (Z), 9b: 281
CAD (Z), 101a: 31
Cyprus Stele (Sargon II): 154
Disp. Ewe and Wheat: 94
En. Elish: 101f., 112
En. Elish i.1-5: 57
En. Elish i.67-74: 102
En. Elish i.99: 265

En. Elish I.134-144: 70, 101
En. Elish I.147-160: 101
En. Elish II.19-30: 70, 101
En. Elish II.23-34: 101
En. Elish III.27-34: 70
En. Elish III.81-92: 70, 101
En. Elish IV:19-28: 102
En. Elish IV:104: 79
En. Elish IV.119-120: 101, 191
En. Elish IV:135ff: 10
En. Elish IV.137-146: 101, 191
En. Elish VI.5-8: 268
En. Elish VI.29-34: 101
En. Elish X-XI: 98
Enki and Ninmaḫ: 94-95
Enki and Ninmaḫ, II,17-20: 95
Erra Ep.: 103ff., 112, 172
Erra Ep. I.7: 104
Erra Ep. I.33: 104
Erra Ep. I.38: 104
Erra Ep. I.113: 104
Erra Ep. I.116: 104
Erra Ep. I.120: 104
Erra Ep. I.181-184: 104
Erra Ep. II.14-15: 104
Erra Ep. III.15: 104
Erra Ep. II.6'-14': 104
Erra Ep. IV: 104
Erra Ep. IV.113: 104
Erra Ep. IV.127: 104
Erra Ep. IV.131: 84, 103
Erra Ep. IV.133: 95
Erra Ep. V.1-41: 104
Founding of Eridu: 13, 103, 111, 136
Founding of Eridu, Obv. 20-30: 136
Genealogy of Ḫammurapi, 1: 266
Gilg., Enkidu and the Underworld, 42: 63
Gilg., Enkidu and the Underworld, 85: 63
Gilg., Enkidu and the Underworld, 129: 63
Gilg., Enkidu and the Underworld, 140: 63
Gilg. Ep. OBV II.ii.53: 98
Gilg. Ep. OBV II.ii.73: 98
Gilg. Ep. OBV II.v.194: 98
Gilg. Ep. OBV III:iii.111: 98
Gilg. Ep. OBV III:iv.140-143: 99
Gilg. Ep. OBVA+BMI:i.7'-8': 99
Gilg. Ep. OBVA+BMI:ii.14'-iii.5': 99
Gilg. Ep.: 30, 40, 42, 97-100, 111, 113, 140
Gilg. Ep. I.29: 98
Gilg. Ep. I.37: 98
Gilg. Ep. I.48: 98
Gilg. Ep. I.56-58: 98
Gilg. Ep. I.99-106: 98
Gilg. Ep. I.207: 98
Gilg. Ep. II.292: 98
Gilg. Ep. V.6: 98
Gilg. Ep. V.294: 98
Gilg. Ep. VI: 99
Gilg. Ep. VII.88-89: 98
Gilg. Ep. VIII.39: 268
Gilg. Ep. VIII.63: 268
Gilg. Ep. IX.37-41: 40
Gilg. Ep. IX.42: 30
Gilg. Ep. IX.45: 31
Gilg. Ep. IX.170: 40
Gilg. Ep. IX.172-193: 40
Gilg. Ep. X.79-86: 40
Gilg. Ep. X-XI: 41
Gilg. Ep. XI.164-167: 149
Gilg. Ep. XI.207-241: 41
Gilg. Ep. XI.278-309: 41
KAR 4: 94
Lambert & Millard 1969: 95
Lambert & Millard 1969, 131-133 39
Lambert 1985b, 440: 42
Lambert 1985b, 447-448: 9
Lambert 2013, 87: 102
Lambert 2013, 147-277: 102
Lambert 2013, 169-171: 10
Lambert 2013, 202-204: 102
Lambert 2013, 209-217: 266
Lambert 2013, 232-236: 70
Lambert 2013, 237: 62
Lambert 2013, 238-240: 61
Lambert 2013, 279-526: 102
Lambert 2013, 301: 96
Lambert 2013, 303: 6
Lambert 2013, 311-315: 6, 102
Lambert 2013, 330-345: 94
Lambert 2013, 334-335: 6
Lambert 2013, 229: 95
Lambert 2013, 350-360: 94
Lambert 2013, 352-353: 6
Lambert 2013, 361-366: 103
Lambert 2013, 366-375: 13, 103

Lambert 2013, 372-373: 136
Lambert 2013, 384-386: 103
Lambert 2013, 407-408: 6
Lambert 2013, 417: 9
Lisman 2013, 23-25: 93
Lisman 2013, 25-27: 93
Lisman 2013, 28-39: 93
Lisman 2013, 31-35: 93
Lisman 2013, 40-44: 94
Lisman 2013, 48-53: 94
Lisman 2013, 57-59: 93
Lisman 2013, 60-64: 94
Lisman 2013, 63: 95
Lisman 2013, 77-81: 93
Lisman 2013, 122-125: 93
Lisman 2013, 159: 45
Lisman 2013, 159-160: 93
Lisman 2013, 163-164: 93
Lisman 2013, 164-165: 93
Lisman 2013, 170-172: 94
Lisman 2013, 173-174: 93
Lisman 2013, 176-177: 94
Lisman 2013, 177-181: 94
Lisman 2013, 186-195: 102
Lisman 2013, 218: 5
Lisman 2013, 196-200: 93
Lisman 2013, 256-281: 94
Lisman 2013, 262: 94
Lisman 2013, 293-309: 94
Lisman 2013, 324-329: 93
Lisman 2013, 330-346: 94
Sargon 8, 18-22: 42
Sargon 8, 96-102: 42
Sargon 8, 219: 43
Sargon 8, 220: 31
Sargon 8, 223: 43
Sargon 8, 225: 43
Sargon 8, 226: 43
Sargon 8, 227: 43
Sargon 8, 262: 43
Sargon 8, 265: 43
Sargon 8, 266-267: 43
Sargon 8, 274: 43
Sargon 8, 276: 43
Sargon 8, 295: 43
Sargon 8, 296: 43
Sargon 8, 303: 43
Sargon 8, 327: 43
Sargon 8, 329: 43
Sargon 8, 352: 43
Sargon 8, 356: 43
Sargon 8, 358: 43
Sargon 8, 369-378: 43
Sargon 8, 380-381: 43
Sargon 8, 386: 43
Sargon 8, 406: 43

Hittite Texts

Hoffner 1990, 12 275
Hoffner 1990, 40-43 8
Hoffner 1990, 52-61 10
Hoffner 1990, 52 9, 11
Hoffner 1990, 55-59 9
Hoffner 1990, 69-70 7
KBo 36.40: 53
KUB 12.61: 53

Iranian Texts

Gāthās of Zoroaster: 106ff.
Yasna 28:6: 107
Yasna 30:3-5: 107
Yasna 30:6: 107
Yasna 32:3-5: 107
Yasna 44: 107
Yasna 44:15: 107
Yasna 51:10: 107
Yasna 53:9: 107f.
Gr. Bundahishin I, 19-22: 108
Gr. Bundahishin Ia, 4: 108
Gr. Bundahishin Ia, 11: 108
Gr. Bundahishin Ia, 19: 108
Gr. Bundahishin IV, 15: 108
Gr. Bundahishin IV, 17: 108
Yašt 3:13: 108

Ugaritic Texts

KTU 1.1–1.6: 14f., 79, 81f., 124
KTU 1.1:II.23: 32
KTU 1.1:III.11-12: 32
KTU 1.1:III.12: 33, 169
KTU 1.1:IV: 25
KTU 1.1:IV:13-20: 127
KTU 1.1:IV:24-25: 18
KTU 1.2:I: 18
KTU 1.2:I:2: 18
KTU 1.2:I:3-9: 18f.
KTU 1.2:I:3: 18
KTU 1.2:I:14-16: 161
KTU 1.2:I.22-33: 81
KTU 1.2:I.36-38: 25
KTU 1.2:I.40: 79
KTU 1.2:III.11: 54
KTU 1.2:IV: 18
KTU 1.2:IV:1: 80
KTU 1.2:IV:5: 80
KTU 1.2:IV.11-12: 219
KTU 1.2:IV.12-13: 18
KTU 1.2:IV.18-26: 80
KTU 1.2:IV.19-22: 22
KTU 1.2:IV.25-26: 66
KTU 1.2:IV.27-31: 79
KTU 1.3:III.32–IV.4: 81
KTU 1.3:III.45: 81
KTU 1.3:IV.1-3: 18

KTU 1.3:V.5-11: 10
KTU 1.3:V.5-7: 169
KTU 1.3:V.11-12: 31
KTU 1.3:V.19-21: 10f.
KTU 1.3:V.22-25: 56
KTU 1.3:V.26-27: 10
KTU 1.3:V.30-31: 163
KTU 1.3:V.35-36: 12
KTU 1.4:I.12: 169
KTU 1.4:I.22: 144
KTU 1.4:III.1-6: 79
KTU 1.4:III.26: 144
KTU 1.4:III.30: 144
KTU 1.4:III.35: 144
KTU 1.4:IV.21-22: 29
KTU 1.4:IV.32: 144
KTU 1.4:VI.7-14: 79
KTU 1.4:VI.15: 267
KTU 1.4:VI.44-5: 173
KTU 1.4:VII.49: 39f.
KTU 1.4:VIII.1-9: 40
KTU 1.4:VIII.1-6: 269
KTU 1.4:VIII.7: 269
KTU 1.5:I: 173
KTU 1.5:I.1-5: 80f.
KTU 1.5:I.1-3: 61
KTU 1.5:I.3: 243
KTU 1.5:I.14-22: 66
KTU 1.5:I.15: 67
KTU 1.5:I.18: 265
KTU 1.5:I.21-22: 81
KTU 1.5:II.2-3: 11
KTU 1.5:II.5: 54
KTU 1.5:II.20-24: 173f.
KTU 1.5:IV: 37
KTU 1.5:V.13: 40
KTU 1.5:V.18-21: 14
KTU 1.5:V.19: 164
KTU 1.5:VI.11-26: 25
KTU 1.6:I.39ff: 11
KTU 1.6:I.53-65: 152
KTU 1.6:I.57-64: 152
KTU 1.6:II.30-37: 82
KTU 1.6:III: 33
KTU 1.6:V.7–VI.16: 82
KTU 1.6:VI.16-22: 82
KTU 1.6:VI.22-23: 49, 82
KTU 1.6:VI.22-29: 28
KTU 1.6:VI.49-50: 66
KTU 1.6:VI.51: 66, 171
KTU 1.6:VI.51-53: 81
KTU 1.10:III.4-11 14
KTU 1.11:3: 14
KTU 1.12:I.7-8 160
KTU 1.12:I.14-33 12, 122
KTU 1.12:I.14-16 151
KTU 1.13: 277
KTU 1.13:15: 265
KTU 1.14:I.14-15: 81
KTU 1.14:I.14: 18
KTU 1.14:IV.35-36: 168
KTU 1.14:VI.26-28: 123
KTU 1.15:II: 136
KTU 1.15:II.16-21: 34
KTU 1.15:V.16-17: 157
KTU 1.16:II.25-26: 267
KTU 1.16:II.27: 272
KTU 1.16:V:9-28: 18
KTU 1.16:V:26-30: 12
KTU 1.16:VI:40-58: 19f.
KTU 1.17–1.22: 20, 84, 139, 163, 277
KTU 1.17:I.26: 6
KTU 1.17:I.30-31: 9
KTU 1.17:II:9: 265
KTU 1.17:II.26-42: 49, 159
KTU 1.17:V.: 136
KTU 1.17:V.35: 165
KTU 1.17:VI.25-39: 124
KTU 1.17:VI.34-38: 139
KTU 1.17:VI.43-44: 124
KTU 1.17:VI–1.19:I: 77
KTU 1.18:IV.17-26: 20
KTU 1.18:IV.18: 20
KTU 1.18:IV.30-37: 21
KTU 1.19:I.7: 267
KTU 1.19:I.11-12: 267
KTU 1.19:I.12: 267
KTU 1.19:I.39-46: 82
KTU 1.19:I.45: 14
KTU 1.19:II.31-33: 268
KTU 1.19:II.38: 21
KTU 1.19:III.12: 14
KTU 1.19:III.26: 14
KTU 1.19:IV.45: 19
KTU 1.18:IV.57: 20
KTU 1.22:I.6: 272
KTU 1.22:I.4-7: 13f.
KTU 1.22:I.7: 255
KTU 1.22:II.18: 18
KTU 1.22:IV.8: 71
KTU 1.23: 11, 52
KTU 1.23:8-11: 44
KTU 1.23:8: 54
KTU 1.23:8-11: 44, 52f.
KTU 1.23:13: 11
KTU 1.23:16: 11
KTU 1.23:19: 169
KTU 1.23:24: 11
KTU 1.23:28: 11
KTU 1.23:40: 11
KTU 1.23:43: 11
KTU 1.23:46: 11
KTU 1.23:46-54: 160
KTU 1.23:52-64 280
KTU 1.23:61-63: 11
1.24 146
KTU 1.24:8: 271
KTU 1.24:40-42: 49
KTU 1.24:40-50: 159
KTU 1.24:42: 49
KTU 1.24:48-49: 272
KTU 1.39:2-4: 6
KTU 1.39:3: 9
KTU 1.39:5-8: 6
KTU 1.39:13: 32
KTU 1.40:34: 9
KTU 1.47:2-3: 6
KTU 1.41:11-13: 6
KTU 1.41:14-17: 6
KTU 1.41:30-32: 6

KTU 1.41:50: 71
KTU 1.46:6: 32
KTU 1.65:1-3: 7
KTU 1.65:1-11: 6
KTU 1.65:4: 9
KTU 1.82: 219
KTU 1.82:5: 149
KTU 1.82:6: 17, 49, 78
KTU 1.82:13: 17, 78
KTU 1.82:24: 281
KTU 1.82:26-27: 219
KTU 1.82:27: 17, 78, 268
KTU 1.82:32: 17, 78
KTU 1.82:35: 17, 78
KTU 1.82:41: 17, 78
KTU 1.83: 65f.
KTU 1.83:3-13 65f.
KTU 1.83:5-6 246
KTU 1.83:9 176
KTU 1.96:2: 165
KTU 1.100: 15-24, 43-49, 53, 57, 59, 86, 104, 123, 139f., 158, 223, 254, 269, 271, 275-282
KTU 1.100:1-2: 57
KTU 1.100:1: 8, 46, 48, 110, 196, 279
KTU 1.100:3-60: 53
KTU 1.100:11: 266
KTU 1.100:41: 68
KTU 1.100:58: 17
KTU 1.100:61-69: 74f.
KTU 1.100:61: 144, 200
KTU 1.100:62: 15, 17, 29, 44, 145, 216
KTU 1.100:63-64: 29
KTU 1.100:64-67: 44
KTU 1.100:65: 43
KTU 1.100:67-68: 17, 269
KTU 1.100:70-76: 45f., 85
KTU 1.100:74: 17
KTU 1.106:30: 17
KTU 1.107: 15-28, 43-47, 49, 53, 62, 84f., 98, 112, 123, 140, 158, 174, 234, 254f.
KTU 1.107:1-14 25
KTU 1.107:2-3: 27, 150
KTU 1.107:2: 43, 70, 150
KTU 1.107:3: 119
KTU 1.107:4-6: 174
KTU 1.107:6: 218
KTU 1.107:8-9: 72
KTU 1.107:8: 147
KTU 1.107:9: 272
KTU 1.107:10-12: 72
KTU 1.107:12: 272
KTU 1.107:13: 16
KTU 1.107:15-24: 52
KTU 1.107:15: 272
KTU 1.107:17: 61
KTU 1.107:19-23: 49
KTU 1.107:35: 174
KTU 1.107:45: 174
KTU 1.107:27': 28, 49, 85, 138, 149, 257
KTU 1.107:28'-31': 44, 49
KTU 1.107:28': 76
KTU 1.107:30': 77, 85
KTU 1.107:31': 269
KTU 1.107:32'-45': 63
KTU 1.107:32': 269
KTU 1.107:33': 270
KTU 1.107:36': 270
KTU 1.107:37'-44': 53
KTU 1.107:37': 6, 270
KTU 1.107:38'-39': 54
KTU 1.107:38': 269
KTU 1.107:39': 270
KTU 1.107:41': 270
KTU 1.107:43': 270
KTU 1.107:44'-45': 18, 242
KTU 1.107:44' 241, 270
KTU 1.107:45' 270
KTU 1.107:46'-47': 47
KTU 1.107:46': 128
KTU 1.107:52': 51
KTU 1.107:53': 50, 138
KTU 1.108:12: 32
KTU 1.108:24-25: 270
KTU 1.109:12-13: 6
KTU 1.109:15-18: 6
KTU 1.109:19-23: 6
KTU 1.109:24-28: 6
KTU 1.114: 150
KTU 1.114:10-11: 31
KTU 1.114:18: 9
KTU 1.114:20: 20, 31
KTU 1.114:21-22: 31
KTU 1.118:1-2: 6
KTU 1.119:25 120
KTU 1.123:1: 6, 270
KTU 1.123:3-4: 54
KTU 1.123:13: 55
KTU 1.141:31: 9
KTU 1.148:10: 6
KTU 1.148:23-25: 7
KTU 1.148:23-34: 6
KTU 1.162:6-7: 6
KTU 1.166:28: 61
KTU 1.169: 11
KTU 1.169:9-10: 75, 77
KTU 1.169:12-15 12, 219
KTU 1.178: 16f., 78
KTU 1.179: 49, 159, 269, 272
KTU 1.179:8'-12': 59
KTU 1.179:8'-9': 28, 234
KTU 1.179:8': 59
KTU 1.179:9': 8, 48, 57, 110
KTU 1.179:29: 17
KTU 1.179:33: 17
KTU 2.10:12-13: 82
KTU 7.163:4: 13
KTU 7.163: 272
KTU 7.163:1: 272
KTU 7.163:3: 272
KTU 7.163:4: 272
KTU 7.163:6: 273

RS 24.244: 15-28
RS 24.251+: 15-24
RS 92.2014: 17
U5N, No. 170:13-15: 7

Other North West

Semitic Inscriptions

KAI 26:A:III.18: 7
KAI 27:16-17: 51
KAI 27:22-27: 51
KAI 89:1: 58
KAI 129:1: 8
KAI 222:A:11: 7
KAI 244:3: 14
Renz 1995, 57: 35
Renz 1995, 62: 35
Renz 1995, 64: 35

Apocryphal and Parabiblical Texts

1 Baruch

3:26 216
3:31 198

3 Baruch (Greek)

9:7: 49, 198
9:1-7 207

3 Baruch (Slavonic)

9:1-7 207

4 Baruch

3:7: 125

4 Ezra

4:30: 130
6:49-52: 65, 192
7:116-119: 130

4 Maccabees

18:6-8 198, 237
18:8 237

Qumran

CD 173
CD 16:5 55
CD-A 3:20 195
CD-A 10:8-9 195, 212
1Q23 193
1Q24 193
1QapGen 2:1 193
1QapGen 2:6 193
1QapGen 2:9-18 193
1QapGen 5:3-4 193
1QapGen 5:13 193
1QapGen 6:1 194
1QapGen 10:12 193, 211
1QapGen 11:13-14 193
1QapGen 12.13-16 193
1QH[a] 194
1QH[a] 3:15 194
1QH[a] 3:16 194
1QH[a] 4:27 195
1QH[a] 11:8-18 245
1QH[a] 11:8-10 194
1QH[a] 11:8 194
1QH[a] 11:10 194
1QH[a] 11:12 194
1QH[a] 11:16 241, 245
1QH[a] 11:17-18 194, 217
1QH[a] 14:16-18 195, 211, 213
1QH[a] 16:5-26 195, 211, 213
1QIsa[a] 14:4 152
1QIsa[a] 14:12-15 153
1QM 13:4 55
1QM 13:11 55
1QM 17:5-6 194
1QS 3:23 55
1QS 4:23 195
3Q15 ix.7 257f.
4Q167, Fragm. 7 195
4Q167, Fragm. 8 195
4Q171, 2:1-2 195
4Q180, Fragm. 1.7 193
4Q203 193
4Q225, Fragm. 2, col. i:9 55
4Q225, Fragm. 2, col. ii:6 55
4Q225, Fragm. 2, col. ii:7 55
4Q225, Fragm. 2, col. ii:9-10 194
4Q225, Fragm. 2, col. ii:13-14 550
4Q252, col. i:2 147
4Q265, Fragm. 7, col. ii:14 195
4Q381, Fragm. 1 195
4Q381, Fragm. 10 195
4Q381, Fragm. 11 195
4Q381, Fragm. 11:3 195
4Q385c:3 192, 195, 213
4Q416, Fragm. 2, III.17 194
4Q418, Fragm. 9:18 194
4Q418, Fragm. 126, col. ii:11-12 195
4Q422, col. i:10 195
4Q433a, Fragm. 2, 3 137
4Q531, Fragm. 19:3-4 148
4Q532-533 193
11Q11 173, 195, 212
11Q11, col. ii:3-4 173, 195
11Q11, col. v.6 195
11Q11, col. v.7 195
11Q12, Fragm. 5:3 195

Wisdom of Ben Sira

– – 131, 187f., 213, 229, 258
15:14 189

25:15-16 131
25:24 125, 131, 189, 212
26:7 131
26:10 132
40:1 187, 189
40:11 188
40:12-16 188
40:17 188, 211, 213
40:27 188, 211, 213
40:18-27 188
42:13-14 132
43:20-25 65

TOBIT

1:9 216
8:6 46

WISDOM OF SOLOMON

– –198f.
1:12-15 198
2:23-24 141, 199, 211, 237
2:24 224, 243
4:1 199
5:15 199
7:1-6 199
8:17 199
10:1-2 199

PSALMS OF SOLOMON

14:2 195

1 ENOCH

1-36 182-185, 203, 211, 213, 220f., 255
6-11 182
6:3 183
6:7 183
7:12 183
8:1: 191
9 183
10 183
14:8-13: 191, 211
15:8-9 148
18:6-14 191
18:6-11 182
18:6-7 211
18:6 184
18:7 184
18:8-11 184
18:9-11 211
20–36 183
20:1-8 183
20:7 184
20:6 169
21:1-6 184
22 170
22:1-13 182
22:1-4 185
22:2-4 32, 211
22:3-4 211
23 185
24 185
24:2-3 185
24:3–25:6 185, 213
24:4 185
25:3 185
25:4-6 185
27:2-4 183
27:2 183
32:3-6 185
37-71: 191f.
40:9 183
54:6 183
60:7-8 191
60:7 74
60:8-9: 65
60:23: 192, 213
61:12: 192, 213
69:2 183
69:6: 191, 211
70:5-6 191, 211
70:8-9 183
70:13 183
72–82 181f., 213
72:2-37 182
72:4 182
72:35-36 182
73:1 182
77:3-4 211
77:3 182, 211, 213
77:4 172
83–90 190
85–90 190f., 213
85:3-8 190
85:4 190
86:1 190, 211
88:1-3 190

2 ENOCH

– – 195-198, 220
7 198
8 198, 211, 213
18 196
29:1-5 196
30:11-12 197, 212
31:3-6 197

JUBILEES

– – 186f.
2:2 186, 211
2:14 186, 212
3:3-4 186, 197
3:4-7 186
3:15-16 186
4:15 187
4:16-26 187
4:28-29 150
4:30 186
5:1 187
5:6-11 187, 191

APOCALYPSE OF ABRAHAM

– – 126, 199-203
1–3 199
5:6-12 199
6:14-15 199, 212
6:10-17 199
6:10-11 185
10:10-11 200
12 200
13:7-9 200
13:11-14 200f.
14:4 201
14:5 201
15:5-7 32, 201, 211
17:8-12 202
17:15 202
23:4-11 202, 211, 213
23:5 212

23:7-8 212
24:5 203, 225

APOCALYPSE OF ADAM
– – 204f., 208f., 232
1:2-5 208, 212
64:2-3 208
65:15-16 209
67:10-14 209

APOCALYPSE OF BARUCH
29:4 65

APOCALYPSE OF MOSES
– – 205f.
5–9 206
10:3 206, 212
12:2 206
13 206, 213

GREEK APOCALYPSE OF EZRA
2:11 192

LADDER OF JACOB
– – 126, 203f.
2:7 202f., 211
2:18 202f.
3:2 203, 211f.
4:1-3 184
6:11-13 203
7:20-22 203

LIFE ADAM AND EVE
– – 204ff., 220
12–16 204
19:2-3 205, 212
25 205, 211, 213
32 205
36 205
39:3 205
40-43 205
44:1 205

TESTAMENT OF ABRAHAM
19 194

TESTAMENT OF ADAM
– – 206
3:3 206

TESTAMENT OF LEVI
5:10-12 192
18:10-14 192, 211

TESTAMENT OF REUBEN
3–6 131
5:1 131

TESTAMENT OF SOLOMON
1:10-12 209
20:14-17 209
20:16-17 204

ODES OF SOLOMON
Ode 43: 212

Rabbinic Texts

MISHNA
Abot 2:10: 217
Ber. R. 20:11 208

BABYLONIAN TALMUD
ʿAbod. Zar. 22b 236
Ḥag. 12a 72
Sanh. 38a 197
Sanh. 38b 72
Sanh. 100a 72
Sanh. 100b 269
Shab. 146a 236
Yeb. 63a-b 269
Yeb. 103b 236

JERUSALEM TALMUD
Sanh. VII.9 [25d] 55, 212

MIDRASH
Gen. R. 1:26 72, 212
Gen. R. 8:1 72, 212
Gen. R. 8:10 71
Gen. R. 9:5 137
Gen. R. 12:6 72
Gen. R. 15:7 72
Lev. R. 14:1 72, 212
Lev. R. 20:2 72, 212
Mek. Exod. 5:8 246
Pes.K. 23:1, M. 334213
Midr. Ps. 59b 269

TARGUM ONKELOS
Gen. 2:15: 125

TARG. PS.-JONATHAN
Gen. 2:21 210

PESIQTA DE-R. KAHANA
23:1, M.334 213

PIRQE DE-R. ELIEZER
14 221

Greek, Latin and Coptic Texts

AESCHYLUS
Prom. Bound, 365-366 110

AMBROSE
Explan. Ps., Ps. 118.3.34 152

APOCRYPHON OF JOHN
II, 20:35–21:14 233

AUGUSTINE OF HIPPO
Doctr. chr., 3.37 151

BEROSSOS
Verbrugghe & Wickersham 1996
105, 111f.

PSEUDO-APOLLODORUS OF ALEXANDRIA
Library, 1.1.1 110
Library, 1.1.3 56
Library, 1.6.3 110
Library, 2.5 59

HESIOD
Theog. 108ff
Theog., 116-133 109
Theog., 134-138 109
Theog., 147-206 109
Theog., 211-225 109
Theog., 333 109
Theog., 371-382 109
Theog., 453-506 109
Theog., 453-491 56
Theog., 558-589 109
Theog., 585 131
Theog., 590-612 131
Theog., 713-721 191
Theog., 820-868 59
Theog., 984-992 111

HOMER
Odys., IV.561-569: 31

IRENAEUS
Adv. Haer., 1.30 233

ORIGEN
Princ., 1.5.4 167
Princ., 4.3.9 151

OVID
Met. 110
Met., 2, 1-366 110

PHILO OF BYBLOS
(pagenumbers of:)
Attridge & Oden 1981
Phoen. Hist. 33 28
Phoen. Hist. 36-37 57
Phoen. Hist. 40-41 71
Phoen. Hist. 46-49 6, 9
Phoen. Hist. 46-55 8
Phoen. Hist. 50-51 7, 31, 56
Phoen. Hist. 52-53 56
Phoen. Hist. 54-55 56
Phoen. Hist. 58-59 33
Gilg. Ep. IX.170: 40Phoen. Hist. 64-65 41
Phoen. Hist. 64-69 77

PHILO OF ALEXANDRIA
Opif., 151b-c: 189

PLATO
Tim. 190

XENOPHON
Econonomics, III.14-15: 131

Arabic Texts

QUR'ĀN
Sura 2:30: 209f., 212
Sura 2:34: 209, 211
Sura 2:37-38: 211, 213
Sura 4:1: 210
Sura 7:11-24: 209, 211
Sura 7:12: 209
Sura 7:20-22: 210
Sura 7:23: 211, 213
Sura 15:28-44: 209, 211
Sura 17:61-63: 209, 211
Sura 17:66: 209
Sura 18:50: 209ff.
Sura 20:116-123: 209, 212
Sura 20:120-123: 210
Sura 20:122: 211, 213
Sura 55:15: 210

Index of Biblical Texts

Hebrew Bible

Genesis

1–11 115, 261
1–4 115
1–3 88, 231
1 101, 116-123, 125, 136, 140, 150, 167, 182, 186
1:1–2:4 117, 126
1:1–2:3 116, 119
1:1-2 120f.
1:1 199
1:2-8 121
1:2 196
1:6-7 10
1:8-10 121
1:11 225
1:12 121
1:14-18 118
1:16 118
1:18 150
1:20-22 121
1:22 122, 150
1:24 121
1:26-28 26f., 58
1:26-27 118, 122, 138
1:26 27, 122, 149f., 197, 204, 232
1:27 119, 231
1:28-30 119, 123
1:28 27, 49, 119, 122, 150
1:31 119
2–6 119
2–4 115, 123-145
2–3 28, 83f., 115f., 123ff., 129, 137, 140, 142, 158, 167, 169, 188f., 238, 259
2 111, 167, 230f.
2:1-3 117
2:1-2 119
2:4–3:24 125f.
2:4–3:22 130f.
2:4 121, 133f.
2:7 12, 26, 58, 127, 136, 187, 232
2:8 125, 136
2:9 75, 125, 134f., 138, 186, 281
2:10-14 125, 137, 169
2:9-14 249
2:15 125, 136, 150
2:16-17 125, 186
2:16 125, 230
2:17 43, 125, 138
2:18 28, 135, 138, 178, 186
2:19-20 128
2:19 58, 136
2:20 127
2:21-25 186
2:21-23 136
2:21 74, 210
2:22 131, 140
2:25 128, 139
3 128, 141, 143, 151, 198, 217, 224, 230, 236-239, 243f., 248, 257f.
3:1-6 237
3:1 135, 139f.
3:3-5 186
3:3-4 43
3:3 134, 138
3:4 138f., 155, 221
3:5-7 127
3:5 24, 26, 135f., 143
3:6 75, 281
3:7 128, 139f., 150, 258
3:8-11 140
3:10-11 150
3:10 128, 139
3:11 230
3:12 135, 189, 258
3:14-19 129
3:14-15 172f.
3:14 221
3:15-16 128
3:15 49, 72, 128, 222f., 230, 245
3:16 139f., 239
3:17 127, 230
3:19 43, 127, 187, 189
3:20 48, 130, 140f., 187f.
3:21 127, 136, 233
3:22 133, 135, 186
3:24 133, 186
4 123, 137, 143, 224, 250
4:3-4 125f.
4:1 140
4:3 143
4:5 144
4:7 128, 143
4:8-19 136
4:8-11 150
4:8-10 143
4:8 144, 225
4:9 225
4:12 144
4:14-15 145
4:14 144
4:15 145
4:16 144f.
4:17–5:32 140
4:17 145

4:18	216
4:22	191
4:23-25	145
4:23-24	150
4:25	127
5–9	145-150
5	145
5:1-2	26
5:5	146
5:8	146
5:11	146
5:14	146
5:17	146
5:20	146
5:21-24	182
5:27	146
5:31	146
5:32	146
6	148, 179, 190
6:1-6	183
6:1-4	146f., 182
6:1	146f.
6:2	149, 187, 193, 269
6:3	147
6:4	148, 187, 190, 195
6:5-7	147
6:5	147
6:7-13	187
6:9-19	146
6:17	147
6:22	124
7:5	124
7:9	124
7:15	147
7:16	124
7:22	147
8:4	30, 150
8:17	122, 150
9	150
9:1-7	145
9:1	122
9:2	119, 123, 150, 265
9:4-5	271
9:6	26, 150
9:7	150
9:12-17	149
9:20-21	43
9:20	150
9:21-27	150
9:21-23	9
13:10	265
13:17	265
14	8
14:5	68
14:18	8
14:19	8
14:20	8
14:22	8
15:11	200
16:2	140
18	136
22:13-14	59
24:13	272
24:16	269
25:3	216
25:32	267
26:7	269
30:3	140
32	136, 184
32:22	35
32:25	183, 212
47:15	267
47:19	267
49:4	132
49:17	63
49:24	59

Exodus

14:21	177
15:7	176
15:8	65, 246
17:13	153
22:2	35
22:28-29	143
23:7	126
25:18-22	165
28:17-20	165
34:6	269
34:19-20	143
39:10-13	165

Leviticus

3:16	143
11:10	121
11:46	121
16	200
20:25	121
24:11	79

Numbers

11:4	135
21:4-9	223
21:6	223
21:9	223

Deuteronomy

3:11	148
5:25	267
8:15	222
23:19	46, 282
28:43	19
28:54	148
32:6	12f.
32:8	146
32:23-24	176
32:24	174, 265
32:38	143
33:2	35

Joshua

12:4	148
13:12	148
18:8	265
24:2	199
24:3	265

Judges

1:2	265
9:33	35

1 Samuel

20:31	160, 268
25:3	269
26:16	160, 268

2 Samuel

11:2	269
12:5	160, 268
22:5-6	40
22:16	10

1 Kings

6:23-28 165
6:32 165
6:35 165
19 215
19:5-8 200

2 Kings

6:22 79
15:5 40
23:10 250

Isaiah

3:16-24 191
4:5 270
5:7 265
6:8 265
9:5 216
10:33-34 172
11:8 217
13:1-14:32 151
14 84, 110, 151-163, 166, 170, 177, 180, 190, 197, 219ff., 223, 226, 242, 250, 252, 258
14:1-8 152
14:1-3 151
14:4-21 151
14:4 152
14:5 226
14:9-21 23f.
14:9-11 153
14:9 151
14:12-15 84, 153ff., 157f., 162
14:12-14 151, 161
14:12-13 154, 220
14:12 24, 49, 151, 154, 160ff., 220, 226
14:13-15 24
14:13 160ff., 221
14:14 155, 161
14:15 161, 220f., 226
14:16-27 152
14:16-17 153
14:19-20 162
14:19 156, 162, 226
14:20 163, 216
14:21 163
14:29 217
14:31 161
17:12 66
17:14 175
22:4 268
22:11 225
23:1 159
23:3 153
23:6 159
23:12 154
23:14 159
24:22-23 192
24:23 118
25:6 37
27 246
27:1-5 246
27:1 61, 171, 173, 218, 243, 247, 259
27:2-6 247
27:2-3 265
27:11 12
27:12 247
30:6 194, 217
30:26 118
40:22 9
42:9 225
43:1 12
43:13 225
43:27 130
44:2 12
44:24 12
45:9 12
45:11 12
45:21 225
51:9 173
51:15 66
53 263
55:1-3 37
57:20 219
59:5 217
64:7 12

Jeremiah

5:8 48
6:23 66
10:16 12
15:18 281
17:5-6 54
22:24 164
27:13 267
31:35 66
44:15-30 132
44:15 132
48:1 278
48:6 44
48:24 278
50:42 66
51:19 12
51:42 66

Ezekiel

13 132
13:17-23 132
16 132
17:22-24 172
19 167
21:17 159
23 132
23:20 48, 190
26:36 175
27:3-9 153
27:36 175
28–32 177, 258
28 24, 83f., 154, 157f., 163-171, 180, 197, 221, 226, 243, 252
28:1-19 163-171
28:1-10 166
28:2 155, 168f.
28:3-7 170
28:3-5 166
28:3 166
28:6 24, 155, 166
28:7-10 166
28:8-10 169
28:8 166, 168, 170

28:9 24
28:10 167
28:11-19 166
28:12 164f., 170
28:13 155, 167, 169, 265
28:14 133, 169f.
28:15 167
28:16-19 169
28:16 24, 153, 165, 170, 196
28:17 155, 169f.
28:18 153, 167, 170
28:19 175
28:20-26 166
29–32 167, 171f., 180
29:3 144, 171
29:5 65, 162, 171, 215, 244
31 84, 171
31:5-6 171
31:8-9 265
31:8 171
31:10-18 172
31:18 172
32:1-15 172
32:2 171
32:3-6 65, 171, 244
32:17-32 151
33:11 267
38:6 161
38:15 161
39:2 161
39:11 66
47:1-12 169, 247
47:16 54
47:18 54

Hosea

2:14 46, 282
6:7 130, 181, 195
8:6 59
13:14 174, 176f.

Joel

1:9 267
4:18 169

Amos

4 132
4:1 132
9:3 128, 179
9:6 140

Micah

1:3–4 35
1:7 46, 282
1:8 268
1:14 281
2:6 20
5:6-7 55

Nahum

2:12-13 171

Habakkuk

3:8 35

Haggai

2:23 164

Zechariah

1:10-11 265
3:2 234
11:2 159
14:6 65
14:8 169

Psalms

8 27
8:5-9 26
19:4 9
23:5 37
36:7 10
42:7-8 29, 169
46:5 169
49:15 265
58:5-8 281
58:5 229
65:7 66
68:6-7 144, 218
68:8-9 35
68:16-17 69
68:23 176
74:13 171
74:14 61, 65, 162, 173, 215, 244, 259
82 84, 177
82:7 154
88:5 40
88:6 40
91 173, 180, 195, 259
91:5-6 175
91:6 173f.
91:13 65, 173
95:5 236
104 117
104:26 61
115:15 8
116:3 40
116:9 265
121:2 8
124:8 8
134:3 8
137:5 268
139:9 160
139:13 189
139:15 189
140:4 29, 270
146:5-6 8
147:14 143

Job

1–2 234
1:6-12 222
1:7 144, 265
1:12 129, 144
1:21 129, 188
2:2 265
3:8 61
5:7 129, 188
6:15-18 281
7:12 171
7:20 129
9:24 265
10:9 12, 127
10:21 40
12:19 267
14:1 129, 188
15 177
15:7-16 84

15:7 129, 188
16:22 40
18:11 175
18:13 15, 174
18:14 175
20:4 129, 188
24:17 175
26:10 61
26:13 61, 173, 243, 259
27:16 127
27:20 175
30:15 175
31:26 50
31:33 129f., 181, 188
32:13 170
33:22 19, 164
37:9 10
38:16 10
40:25 61, 173
41:11-13 61, 242
41:23 61

PROVERBS
3:19-20 10
15:24 19
16:14-15 55
18:22 149
19:12 55
20:2 55
21:9 269
21:19 269
23:32 229
25:24 269
27:15 269
31:10-31 131

SONG OF SONGS
1:9 48
2:9 45, 281
5:2-6 45, 281
7:8-9 75, 185, 281
7:11 119

QOHELET
4:9 138
7:17 267

ESTHER
1:11 269
2:3 269
2:7 269

DANIEL
4:4-18 177
7:2-8 244

1 CHRONICLES
21:1 234

New Testament

MATTHEW
3:7 163, 216ff., 224, 228
3:19 240
4:1-11 215
4:1-10 235
4:8-9 215
4:11 216
5:22 246f.
5:29-20 247
6:13 240
10:28 247
11:23 220
12:20-35 216
12:24 216
12:26 216
12:34 216ff., 224, 240
13:19 240
13:38 240
16:23 219, 230, 235
18:9 247
19:4 225
23:33 216, 218, 224, 247
24:21 225
24:29 222

MARK
1:12-13 215, 235
3:7 192
3:22 216, 219
3:23 216
3:29 183
4:15 219, 240
4:35-31 218
5:1-20 218
5:3 218
5:5 218
5:7 218f.
5:9 202f.
5:21-43 219
5:25-34 219
6:45-52 218
6:56 219
8:33 219, 230, 235
9:34 55
9:43 247
9:45 247
9:47 247
13:19 225
13:25 222
16:18 222

LUKE
3:7 224
4:1-13 235
4:1 215
4:13 216
3:12 227
8:12 240
10 222
10:13-14 221
10:15-20 220
10:15-19 28, 234
10:15 220f.
10:18-19 221
10:18 154, 220-223, 225, 242

10:19 173, 222, 228, 230
10:20 222
11:11 228
11:14-22 192
11:15 216
11:17-18 216
12:5 247
13:16 219
22:3 219
22:31 219

JOHN

1:1-2 225
3:14-15 223
3:14 223
8:1-20 224
8:21 224
8:44 224f., 227, 240
12:31 223, 225f.
13:27 219
14:30 226
16:11 226
17:15 240
23:43 213

ACTS

5:3 219
10:38 219
13:10 226f.
26:18 219
28 228
28:1-10 227f.
28:1-6 228
28:6 227

ROMANS

3:13 228f.
5 238
5:12-14 229f.
5:12 130, 229ff., 237
5:14 230
7:9 235
7:13 235
16:17-18 230
16:20 230

1 CORINTHIANS

5:5 234
7:5 234
10:9 223
11:7-9 230f.
11:11-12 231
15 176, 235f.
15:4 236
15:22 130, 231
15:25 230
15:27 230
15:42-44 235
15:45-47 231-234
15:46 232ff.
15:47 234
15:55 235f.
15:56 235

2 CORINTHIANS

2:11 234
11:2 237
11:3 229, 236, 238
11:14 234
12:4 213
12:7 234

EPHESIANS

3:12 227
6:12 240

PHILIPPIANS

2:6 155

1 THESSALONIANS

2:18 234
5:21 261

2 THESSALONIANS

2:9 234
3:3 240

1 TIMOTHY

1:20 234
2 238
2:13-15 238ff.
2:13-14 132, 229
2:14 239
2:15 239
3:6-7 219
5:5 234

2 TIMOTHY

2:26 219

HEBREWS

2:14 237

JAMES

3:6 247

1 JOHN

2:13-14 240
3:8 225, 241
3:10 241
3:11-12 224, 240f.
3:12 227
3:15 240
5:18-19 240

REVELATION

2:7 213, 247
2:8-9 234
2:11 249
2:13 234, 244
2:17 249
2:21-22
2:24 234
3:9 234
4:6 65, 246
6:13 223
8:10 223, 244
9:1 241, 244
9:3-10 241
9:11 55, 241, 244
9:14 247
9:16-17 241
9:17-18 246
12 242-245, 247f., 260
12:1 245
12:3-4 244
12:3 243ff.
12:4 245
12:5 245
12:6 244f.
12:7 173

12:9 141, 173, 223, 243-246, 248, 250
12:10 244
12:12 244
12:13 244f.
12:14 244f.
12:14-16 245
12:15-16 61
12:15 245
12:16 245
12:17 245
13:1 243
13:2 245
13:4 245
13:11 245
14:10 246
14:18-19 246
15:2 65, 246
16:13 245
17:1 243
17:3 243f.
17:7 243
17:9 243
19:20 246
20:2 243, 245, 249f.
20:7 234
20:10 237, 246
20:13 237
21:8 246
22 249
22:1-2 247, 249
22:1 247
22:2 249

www.ingramcontent.com/pod-product-compliance
Lightning Source LLC
Chambersburg PA
CBHW061422300426
44114CB00014B/1505
* 9 7 8 1 9 0 9 6 9 7 8 9 8 *